MW01709514

ART & ILLUSTRATION FOR THE CLASSROOM

A GUIDE FOR TEACHERS & PARENTS

Rhian Brynjolson

PEGUIS PUBLISHERS
WINNIPEG • MANITOBA • CANADA

Printed and bound in Canada by Hignell Printing Limited

98 99 00 01 02 5 4 3 2 1

Canadian Cataloguing in Publication Data

Brynjolson, Rhian.

Art & illustration for the classroom

Includes bibliographical references and index.
ISBN 1-895411-90-4

1. Art—Study and teaching (Elementary). I. Title.

N362.B79 1998 372.5'044 C98-920203-8

Book and cover design: David Ashcroft
Cover illustration: *Cardinal* by Teresa Whiteway, Matheson Island School
Back cover illustration: Simon Wiwsionski, South Oaks School

Peguis Publishers
100-318 McDermot Avenue
Winnipeg, Manitoba
Canada R3A 0A2
Toll free: 1-800-667-9673
Email: books@peguis.com

For young artists like Noni and Iain

Contents

Acknowledgments

I would like to thank all of the very talented teachers and visual artists who I have had the privilege of working with, and who have been colleagues sharing teaching strategies and project ideas. Thanks to all of the friends and neighbors who have taught me—by their good example—how to work with children.

I would also like to thank the school staff and students who have worked on the art for this book, the Manitoba Arts Council's Artists in the Schools Program, and Frontier School Division in Manitoba. Thanks, especially, to Noni and Iain Brynjolson, and to Luxton School and Wellington School in the Winnipeg School Division.

Thank you to editor Leigh Hambly for providing strong direction (and painless criticism). And last, but not least, thanks to my family for their help and encouragement.

Introduction

Who This Book Is For

Art and Illustration for the Classroom is written for teachers, childcare workers, parents, and school administrators. It is intended to provide a framework for teaching art in a way that is integrated with regular classroom activity. The book focuses on art for elementary students from nursery to grade eight. Parents may use this book to evaluate and augment the art program offered by their child's school, and as a guideline to offer supplemental materials and encouragement at home.

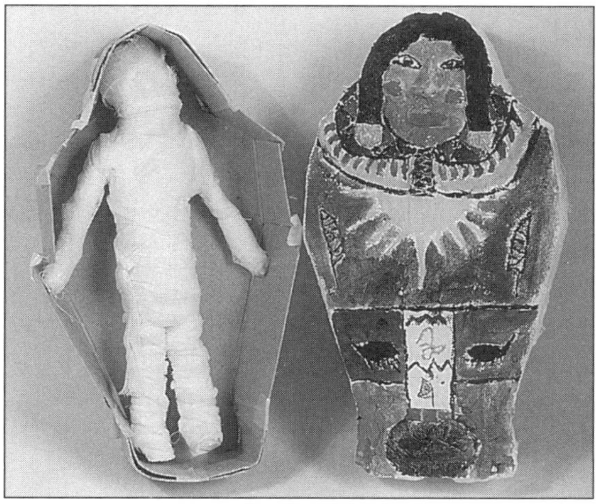

Mummy and Sarcophogus, plaster wrap, gauze, cardboard, paint, Noni Brynjolson, grade 6, Luxton School

Fig. I.1. Ideas for art projects should be relevant to topics of study. When Noni made this, she and her classmates were studying ancient Egypt. **See color plate.**

How to Use This Book

Chapter 2 examines why it is important to teach art. It also discusses children's developmental progress in art and provides a theoretical framework for the art exercises. Chapters 3–15 provide information on basic techniques, materials needed to do the exercises, and reference books to have handy. (In most cases these are children's picture books. At the time of publication, they were all in print and readily available.)

Enrichment exercises provide ways for you to adapt the activity to your curriculum and to the needs of your students. In some cases, the exercises are designed to provide challenge and variation for advanced students. In other cases, they provide tips for adapting the exercise for younger students. The enrichment section also provides methods for using the exercises to illustrate student writing (or as a starting point for developing stories).

At the back of the book, you will find a chapter on looking at art and a glossary of technical terms and art materials. Helpful tips are scattered throughout the book.

The book is laid out as a step-by-step art program. The exercises follow one another in a progressive sequence that develops skill and ability. However, there is no rule that says you can't paint with students or begin book illustrations on the first day of school. The book provides a framework for an art program that you can adapt to your curriculum, your schedule, and the needs and interests of your students.

Have fun!

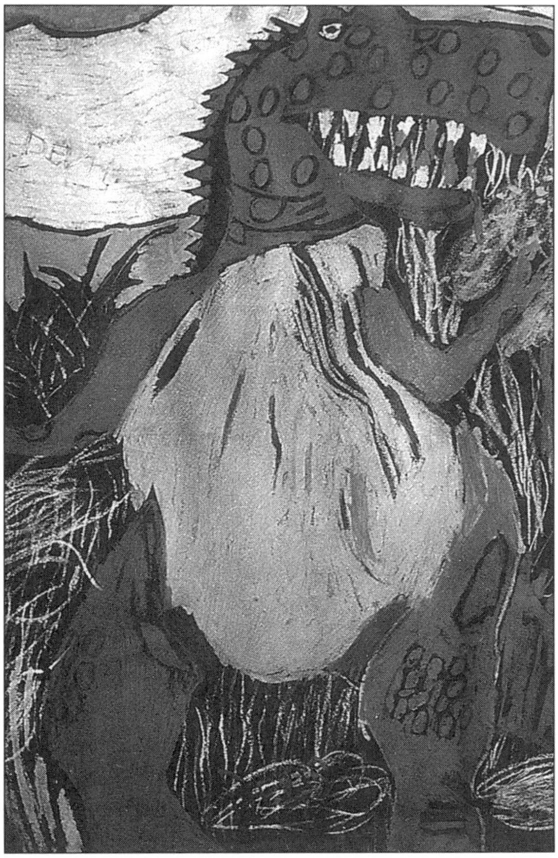

oil pastel and ink on paper, Devin Scott, age 9, Matheson Island School

Fig. I.2. Devin worked hard on his large drawing of a T-Rex. **See color plate.**

Part 1
Art Education

Part 1 introduces basic approaches to art education and suggests ways to establish a classroom art program. Practical suggestions are offered for teaching successful art lessons—including tips for evaluation and self-evaluation.

Part 1 also explores the theory behind teaching visual art and why art education is important. It discusses visual literacy, and summarizes children's developmental progression in art; teachers can use this information to help them plan appropriate exercises for their students. There is also a brief discussion of using visual art to teach "reluctant" learners, and tips for teaching "gifted" students.

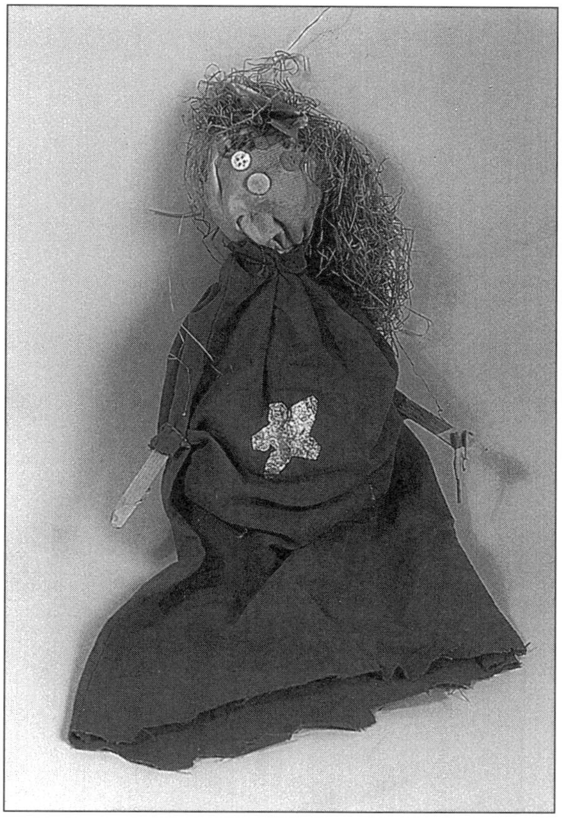

Alice, cloth and miscellaneous materials, Noni Brynjolson, age 8

Fig. Pt. 1.1. Playing with puppets of all kinds is useful for developing story lines for creative writing.

1
Art and Illustration for the Classroom

Everyone Can Learn to Draw

How students feel toward their art is important. Often students in a class will point to one classmate and say, "She's the artist." This implies that the other students in the classroom do not see themselves as artists. They believe they can't draw and never will be able to.

Interestingly, students don't, as a rule, point to one classmate and say, "She's the author." Writing, whether fun or functional, is an ordinary part of the school day. Although we recognize some students as excelling, we encourage all students to view themselves as writers. We should be using the same kind of approach with art.

The ability to draw is not an inborn talent. In many other cultures, proficiency in drawing is more widespread. "(W)here drawing is a prescribed part of the curriculum, or…where drawing constitutes an important vein of cultural life, nearly every child manages to obtain and retain a certain minimal level of competence" (Gardner 1980, 160). Adult students with no art experience or ability who are enrolled in beginning level drawing courses can make significant progress. This kind of progress is documented by Betty Edwards (1989) who asked her students to make portrait drawings before and after some practice and instruction in look-drawing.

Some people may have more or less experience or ability. However, everyone can learn to draw.

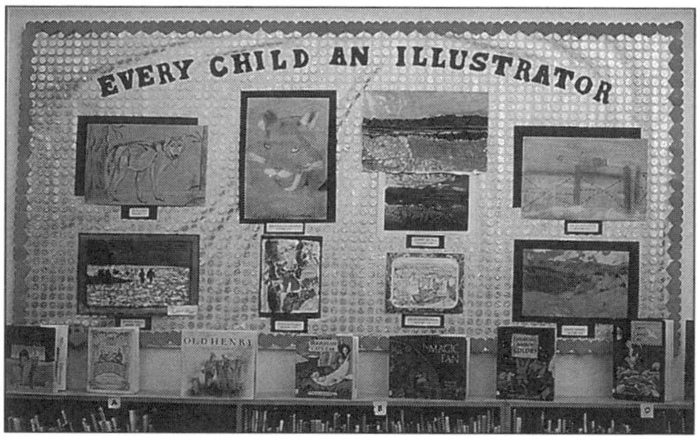

Jean Rennie (teacher), Wellington School Library

Fig. 1.1. Display of students' work

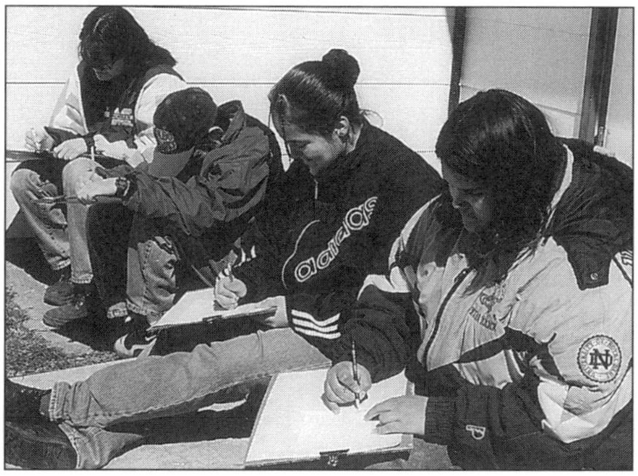

Fig. 1.2. Students drawing outdoors at Pine Dock School

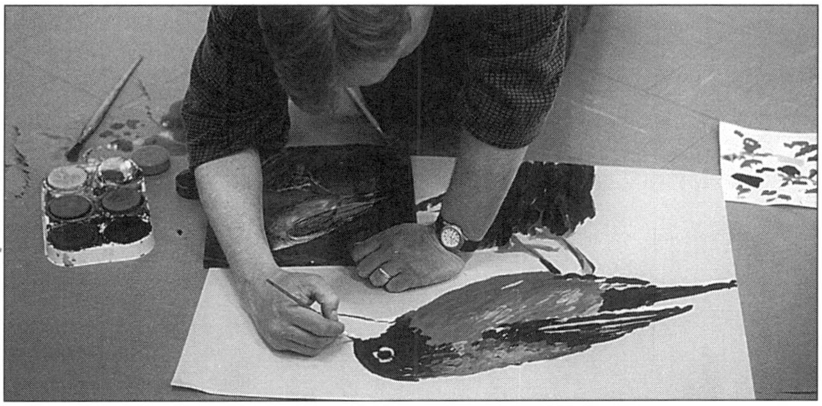

Fig. 1.3. Even school principals can learn to draw. Here, Craig gets into the picture at Matheson Island School.

What Art Education Is—and What It Isn't

Art activity in the classroom needs to have certain characteristics in order to be successful. Art activities should allow students to:

- explore art media
- learn specific techniques
- become familiar with the elements of design
- become critical viewers of visual information
- express ideas and solve problems through graphic media

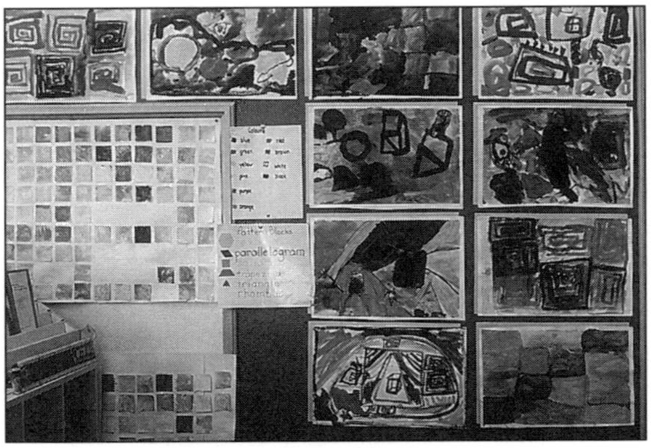

Donna Massey-Cudmore and Andrea Stuart (teachers), grade 1–3, Wolseley School

Fig. 1.4. The students in this classroom are learning about color and shape.

Some researchers at Cornell University (Brittain 1979, 154–155) went through the interesting exercise of constructing an "anti-creativity program." They thought about what kind of classroom would *discourage* creative thinking, innovative visual art, and individual expression. They concluded the class would have the following characteristics:

- materials stored safely out of student's reach
- prescribed times for drawing and painting
- complete demonstration for every lesson
- a teacher's model for the end product
- step-by-step procedures for cutting, pasting, and folding
- rewards for conformity and similarity
- photocopied sheets for coloring activities
- an emphasis on neatness
- extra practice time to students who are developmentally unready
- stereotyped designs for holiday projects

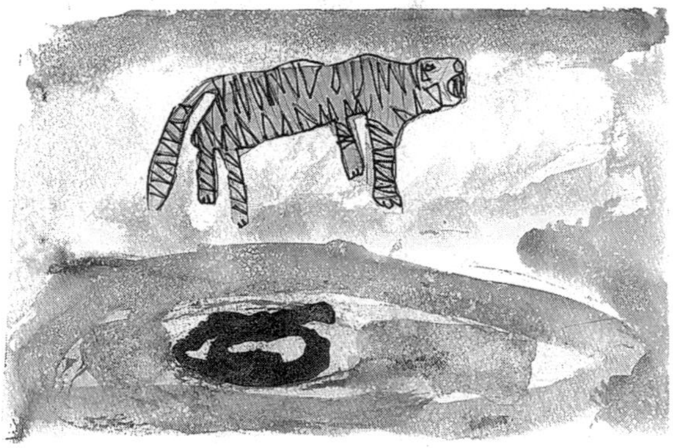

Tiger and Quicksand, Michael Hill, age 8, St. John's Ravenscourt School

Fig. 1.5. Innovation and creative thinking are important elements of children's art.

Brittain (1979, 156) continues, "It was thought that this program would be fairly effective in eliminating genuine spontaneity and creativity from the Kindergarten."

Although I have worked in many classrooms that are frighteningly close to the negative model just described, I don't believe that teachers are intentionally stifling creativity. Rather, they are passing on a familiar method of teaching. One kindergarten teacher I know told me that when she was in elementary school she was once put in a corner for not coloring in the "correct" color. She clearly remembers the humiliation she felt. For years, she said, she was afraid to try art activities with her students for fear of not knowing how to teach them properly. To her credit, her sensitivity to this issue has made her an outstanding teacher—of art and of other subjects. Professional development and collaboration between classroom teachers, art teachers, artists, administration, and museum and art gallery staff have been found to be effective in interdisciplinary art education (Roucher & Lovano-Kerr 1995, 22).

Art activities should be more than a "filler" between other subjects. They should not be prescribed, patterned activities or merely exercises in following directions. Coloring sheets are alive and well in elementary schools although they serve no useful purpose. This applies as well to the use of computer graphics. Students don't learn from using "clip art." But there are valuable aspects to computer drawing programs; varying line widths, patterns, value, colors, combining images with text, as well as advanced spatial applications such as CAD (computer assisted drafting) programs. Computers can be used to scan student artwork for Internet or animation projects combined with student voice-overs or text.

Art activities should provide challenges, choices, and opportunities for problem solving. They should:

- relate to the topic of study and to students' interests
- provide opportunities for expression
- reward originality and innovation
- teach skills and allow students to gain knowledge about the world and their place in it

The exercises in this book are conceived—and will hopefully be implemented—in this spirit.

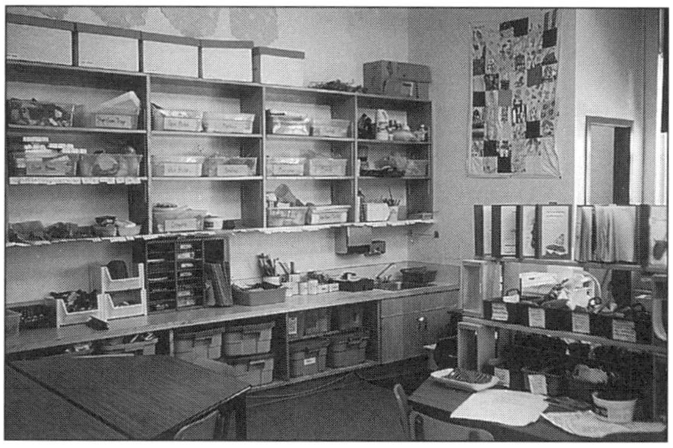

Donna Massey-Cudmore and Andrea Stuart (teachers), Wolseley School

Fig. 1.6. An art-friendly classroom has a sink, large windows for natural light, labeled storage containers, table space, and an activity center.

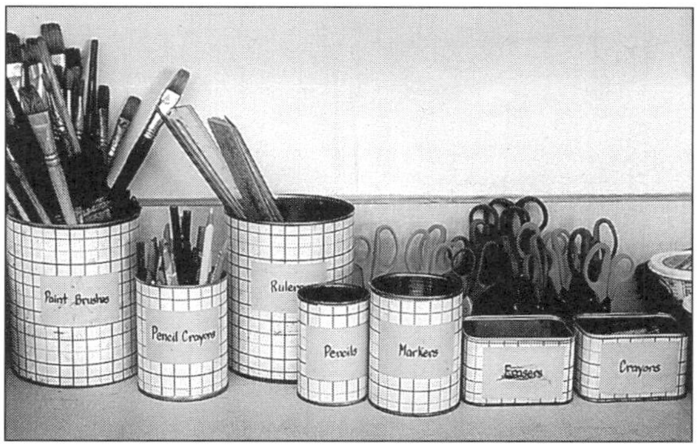

Donna Massey-Cudmore and Andrea Stuart (teachers), Wolseley School

Fig. 1.7. Labeled storage containers make for easy clean up.

The Art-Friendly Classroom

- Visual awareness is an important part of an art program.
- Much of the information we receive in advertising, via the Internet, in newspapers, on television and video is a combination of writing and visual images. It is important that students become critical viewers of visual information.
- You can assist by having rich visuals available to your students: children's picture books, calendars, posters and art cards, natural objects (including such things as leaves and stones with a variety of shapes, colors, and textures), and so on. You may also want to invite artists to the classroom and visit museums and art galleries (see Afterword).
- Art activities should be a regular part of classroom activity.

An art-friendly classroom:

- has a variety of art materials available to students
- sets time aside for look-drawing
- uses student sketchbooks (or journals that combine drawing and writing)
- incorporates art activities into the regular curriculum

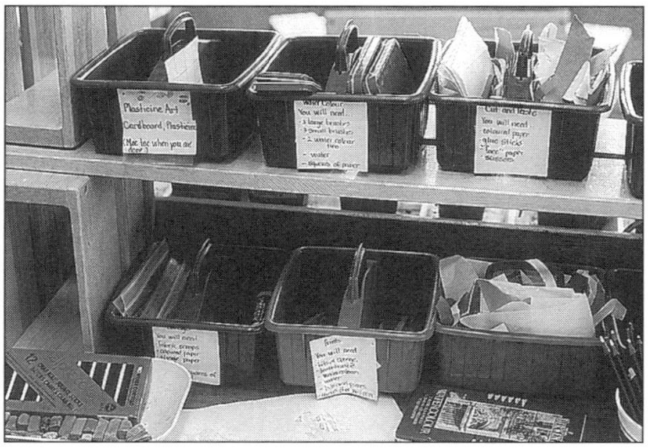

Donna Massey-Cudmore and Andrea Stuart (teachers), Wolseley School

Fig. 1.8. Art materials—organized and ready to use!

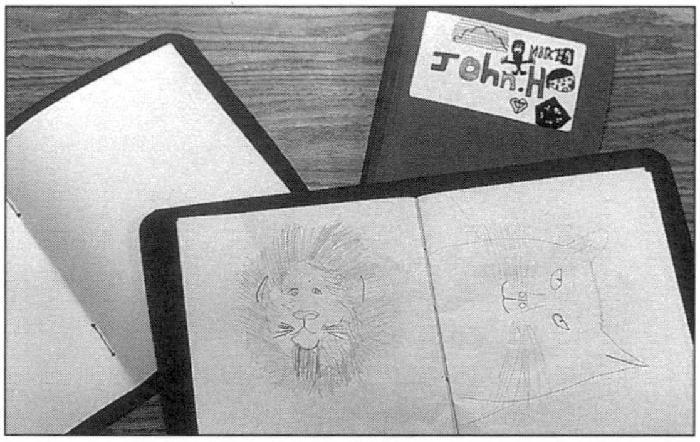

sketchbooks, grade N–4, Ministik School

Fig. 1.9. These students are using their sketchbooks to practice look-drawing.

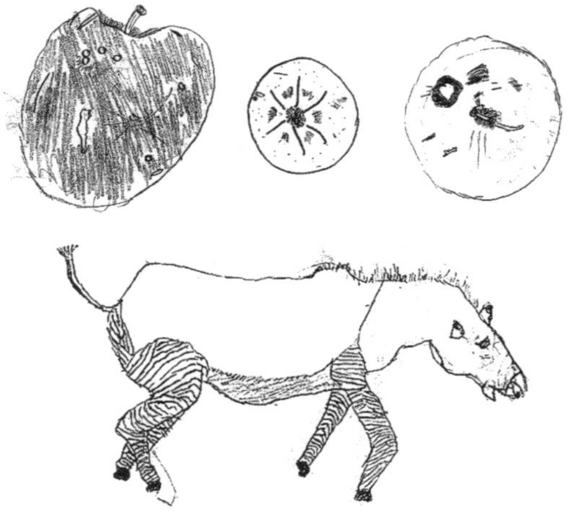

Apple and ***Zebra,*** pencil on paper, Faye Millen, age 10, San Antonio School

Fig. 1.10. Two illustrations from Faye's sketchbook. She picked simple subjects to draw that related to topics she and her classmates were studying.

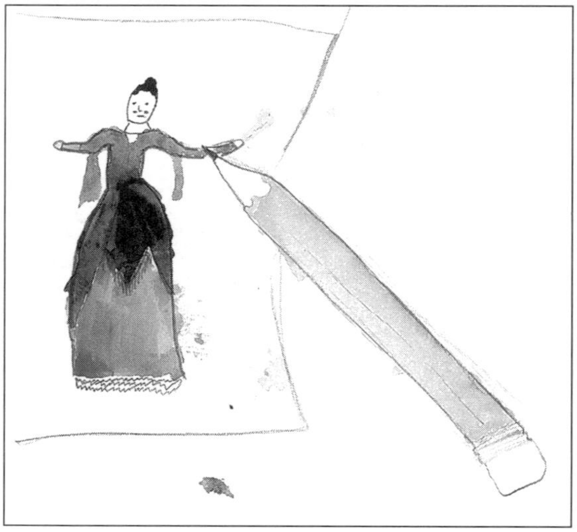

pencil and paint on paper, Noni Brynjolson, age 8, Luxton School

Fig. 1.11. Sketchbooks should allow students to exercise their imagination.

- has rich visuals or objects available that relate to a current topic of study
- includes an ongoing display of student artwork

In terms of the physical space, an art-friendly classroom has:

- a sink (or pails of water) for paint water and clean up
- a large window for natural light
- a tiled, not carpeted, floor area (spills are easier to clean up)
- large bulletin boards for displaying artwork
- lots of accessible shelf space for storing art materials and supplies
- a closed or locking cupboard (or storage boxes) for storing more occasional, expensive, or fragile materials
- labeled storage containers for organizing commonly used items (this makes clean up easier)

A paint easel and low tables are useful for young students. For older students, table space provides more flexibility than individual desks. An "art center" in a corner of the classroom provides a quiet working space where students may choose to spend extra time. Have a variety of materials—including supplies for drawing, painting, printmaking, illustration, collage, and sculpture—available to students on a rotating basis.

I have visited classrooms where loud music was playing or students were practicing Ninja moves on their classmates during art classes. Art, like other subjects, requires concentration. Students should feel safe, relaxed, and free from excessive distraction—or very little will be accomplished. Students are often at their best when they are absorbed in hands-on activities that they enjoy. When you use art to teach the regular curriculum, you can interest even the most reluctant learners and create a more settled classroom.

Student Sketchbooks

Sketchbooks may be used exclusively for drawing, or as "idea journals," incorporating writing and sketching. The sketchbooks of Leonardo da Vinci, for example, contain careful studies of hands, faces, and draped cloth as studies for his paintings and sculptures; imaginative, fanciful caricatures and designs for flying machines; and careful representations of plants and anatomy about which he had developed some scientific theories. However they are used, sketchbooks can serve several functions:

- Your students can use sketchbooks to practice look-drawing and to develop drawing skills. Keep your students interested in art by giving them simple objects to draw, in ten- to fifteen-minute sessions, several times a week. Ideally, these objects will relate to topics being studied, or be of special interest to your students.
- Even a simple object, such as an apple, can be made interesting to draw. Challenge your students to draw from a new point of view (from the top, cross section, the core of the apple, and so on). Alternatively, have them vary the drawing media: give them colored pencils with a piece of window screen placed underneath the page, or a twig dipped in ink. Work up to more difficult subjects (bicycles, for example) gradually. See chapter 3 for ideas.
- Encourage your students to exercise their imagination when using their sketchbooks. This is an important first step in problem solving and generating new ideas. It is also fun. Begin the drawing session with a statement such as, "Pretend you have won the prize for the book of the year. Draw the front cover of the book." Or, "Leonardo da Vinci designed a flying machine almost five hundred years ago. It was to be built out of wood and metal. What do you think it looked like?" If your students' eyes light up and they produce wacky, elaborate drawings, you know you've given them an interesting problem.
- Drawing exercises should relate to topics being studied in class. Some sketches might become the starting point for a journal entry or a story. The Anti-Coloring Book series is a good resource of imaginative problems, especially for those days when you run out of ideas.
- Students may also use their sketchbooks for keeping research notes. Students can take their sketchbooks with them to the library or on field trips to record information, both visually and in writing. A student who has drawn and labeled an insect is likely to remember the three body parts, six legs, and strange mouth parts. A student studying ancient Egypt may sketch visual information and add in short, written descriptions. The popular Eyewitness series is a model for what this kind of research can look like, and an example of how visual images can spark a student's interest in a subject and provide valuable information. Another benefit to this approach is that the finished research project is more likely to contain the student's own description of the visual information than it is to be a parroting of the original text.

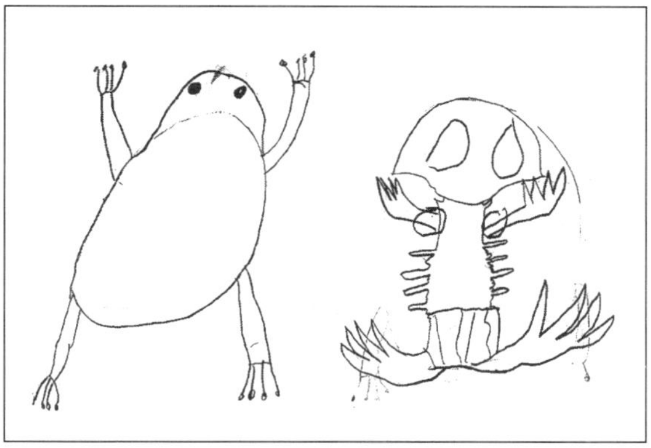

Frog and X-Ray View of Frog, Jeffrey Gagnon, age 10, San Antonio School

Fig. 1.12. Jeffrey was challenged to think about what an x-ray view of his subject might look like.

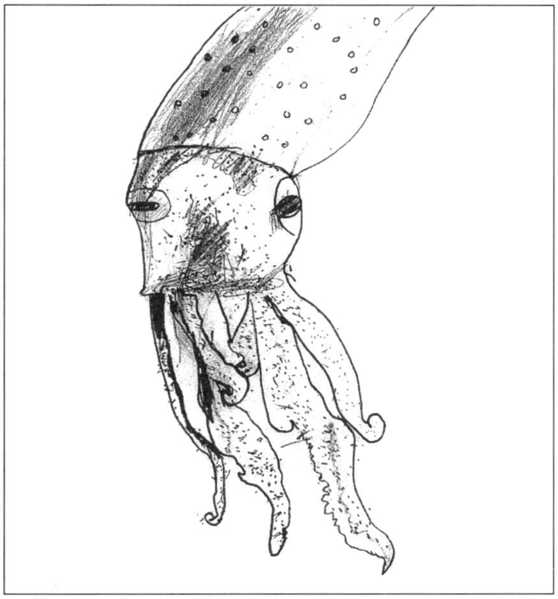

Squid, pencil on paper, Jeffrey Gagnon, age 10, San Antonio School

Fig. 1.13. Jeffrey used his sketchbook when he was studying underwater creatures.

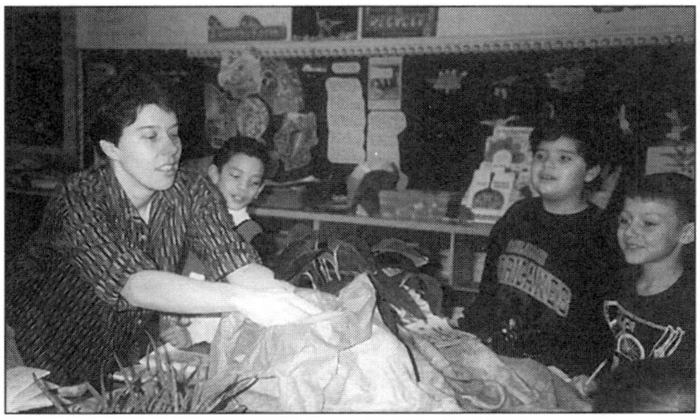

Fig. 1.14. The author builds a volcano with grade 2 students. Students then hid toy dinosaurs in a surrounding "forest" of houseplants. This kind of still life provides an interesting study for young children to draw.

The "How To" of Teaching Art Lessons

Interesting Subjects

The theme or subject of an art lesson should have some relevance to the curriculum and be of interest to your students. Although bottles, bones, and flowers are common still-life subjects in famous paintings, they won't necessarily grab your students' attention. Model dinosaurs hidden in a "forest" of houseplants (with burlap draped over a coffee can and orange tissue paper stuffed in the top for a "volcano") is an example of a far more interesting study for young students.

Preparation

Preparation is key to successful art lessons. Having art materials readily available in your classroom makes set up much easier. Lay out all the necessary supplies ahead of time, along with supplies for clean up (make sure you involve your students in the routine clean up of art materials). You might want to try a new art technique yourself before attempting it in front of your students. As in a new science experiment, you may need to adapt the materials and process to ensure that the technique works!

Demonstration

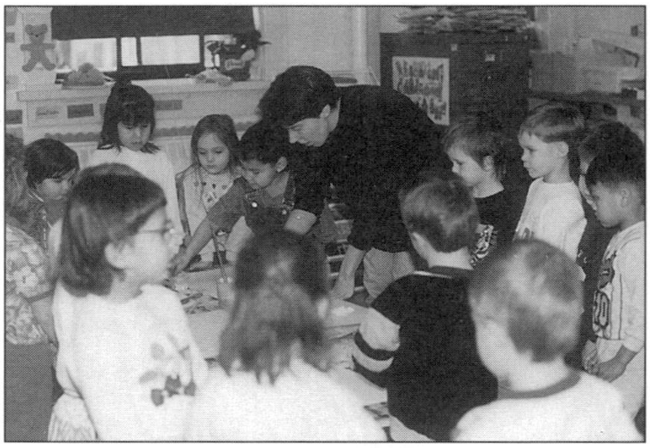

Fig. 1.15. Demonstration is important for visual learners. Here, the author is painting with nursery students at Luxton School.

It is important that you demonstrate the technique being taught. Visual learners may not be able to follow oral or written instructions (ideally, you would demonstrate the technique, explain the process aloud, and leave written instructions on the chalkboard). You can do your demonstration at the beginning of the class, or step-by-step throughout the lesson. The problem is that students may want to copy your model exactly. Somehow you have to demonstrate a technique and still encourage student innovation. Try demonstrating only a piece at a time. For example, for the lesson on shadow puppets cut out a dog's head, a turtle's body, and an elephant's leg. Punch a hole in a piece of paper and attach movable pieces without making a whole shadow puppet. For a painting class, show students how to mix a variety of green paint without painting a whole landscape. Help those students who are insecure by brainstorming with the class for a list of ideas for drawing subjects or solutions to problems.

Start Small

When you are trying a new technique, subject, or approach with your students, try a very small sample, or short drawing session first. You may have to adapt the lesson for your students and it is better to discover this on a postcard-size painting than on a wall mural. A teacher that I admire used to send her students into the hallway, two at a time, to try a new art technique with a parent volunteer. Their samples were gathered up from September to November and used to decorate calendars (which became Christmas presents for parents). When students had mastered a new technique, they could apply it to the book illustrations that they had been planning in their sketchbooks.

Suggestions or Criticisms

When you offer suggestions or criticism to students, be tactful. Remember that many students are terrified to put a mark on paper. Always offer a positive comment before making a suggestion to the student about how to improve the drawing. Make only one suggestion at a time and offer it in the form of a problem to solve: "You drew the ears exactly the right shape! Oh, but the dog looks smooth. How could you make it look furry?"

If students are working together at a table, point out the individual strengths in each student's work: "I like the way the tree branches overlap the sun in this picture, Danna. The texture marks you used really make your dog look furry, Laura. Jessica, you have the rectangular shape of that cow's head exactly." In these ways, students can learn from one another's strengths. They also discover that they each have something to offer their classmates.

Process

In math lessons, we normally ask students to show their work. This is doubly important for visual art. The process of developing an image from the rough-sketch stage through to the finished picture hanging on the wall allows students to literally see the steps they used in problem solving and completing a project. This gives you opportunities to teach approaches to creative thinking and problem solving, and to assess the process that students used in carrying out their projects.

Evaluating Projects

There is a balance to be struck between the teacher's requirements for a project and student innovation. On the one hand, if students' art projects all look the same, then the lesson was generally a failure.

Innovation and creative thinking are the defining elements of young students' artwork. These elements have been much admired and imitated by artists throughout history.

On the other hand, the basic requirements of the project should be met. If you asked students to represent texture in their drawing and one student omitted, or refused to include, any suggestion of texture in a drawing of a hedgehog, this is a problem. Was the lesson clear? Did it fit the student's developmental stage? Does the student lack the confidence to try a new approach? Are your students so stuck on one approach to drawing that they are reluctant to stretch? Would they be willing to try the new approach in a rough copy in their sketchbooks? (If they tell you that they've invented an alien hedgehog that has no prickles, hand them a pencil and tell them they have the beginnings of a great story!)

Evaluating students' work serves two purposes: (1) it allows you to measure the effectiveness of your teaching methods, and (2) it lets you track the development of individual students. Keep in mind that evaluation of progress requires that you keep a *portfolio* of each student's work throughout the year. If you can't keep all of the students' original work, make photocopies for their portfolio. Use the following questions to help you evaluate your students' work:

- Was there time and effort invested in the project?
- Does the student's rough work (practice sketches, notes, problem-solving process, response journals, and so on) indicate that the concept has been mastered?
- Are the project requirements met or exceeded?
- Does the student arrive at a creative or innovative solution to the problem?
- Does the student's work show progress over the course of the project, or throughout the year?
- Is the student able to transfer skills; that is, were techniques or concepts that were learned in previous lessons applied to other projects or subjects?

Students' Self-Evaluation

Having students evaluate their own work is an important learning tool for them. For students who tend to be critical of their work, it will be helpful for them to narrow their dissatisfaction down to those particular parts of their picture they are unhappy with. Once identified, those pieces might be changed, or drawn differently the next time. If students are pleased with their efforts, it may be helpful to them—and to the students near them—to understand which particular aspects of drawing or design caused the image to be successful. This information will allow students to repeat their success.

Students can analyze their own work by using the guidelines for looking at art and applying the guidelines to their own work (see Afterword).

2
A Theoretical Perspective of Teaching Art

Why Teach Art?

Why teach art? This question is especially relevant today. In most elementary classrooms, art programs are nonexistent, underfunded, misapplied, and/or taught in isolation from other curriculum. This situation indicates a profound misunderstanding of the pedagogy of art education and of the creative and cognitive processes involved in visual art.

To be fair, most teachers, childcare workers, and school administrators have received very little training in visual arts. Added to this limitation is a cultural myth about the "genius" of artists and artistic personalities that supposes art is inaccessible to the average person and is best left to "experts." There is also confusion about what constitutes "good" art, and a barrage of media images—kitschy, masterful, commercial, abstract, and photographic—that seem to defy classification. Furthermore, an influential and recurring "back to the basics" movement has narrowly defined education as reading, writing, and arithmetic, separate from and excluding other areas of study.

There are, however, several compelling reasons why art should be taught in elementary schools.

- *Drawing is an important pre-writing activity.* There is a strong relationship between drawing and writing. Evidence suggests that creative art activities provide a good foundation for a reading program. Graphic symbol systems are an early means to organize, express, and communicate ideas (Wilson and Wilson 1982, 23). Young children draw pictures long before they are able to write. Learning to draw is considered to be an important developmental stage. Through this process, children develop motor skills and learn that putting marks on paper is a way to communicate ideas.

- *Student's intellectual development can be observed and tracked through their drawings.* Brittain (1979, 203) believes developmental readiness for reading and writing can be diagnosed through a child's development in drawing. Progress in the ability to draw closed forms and organize those forms on paper can indicate readiness for shaping letters and learning to read and write.

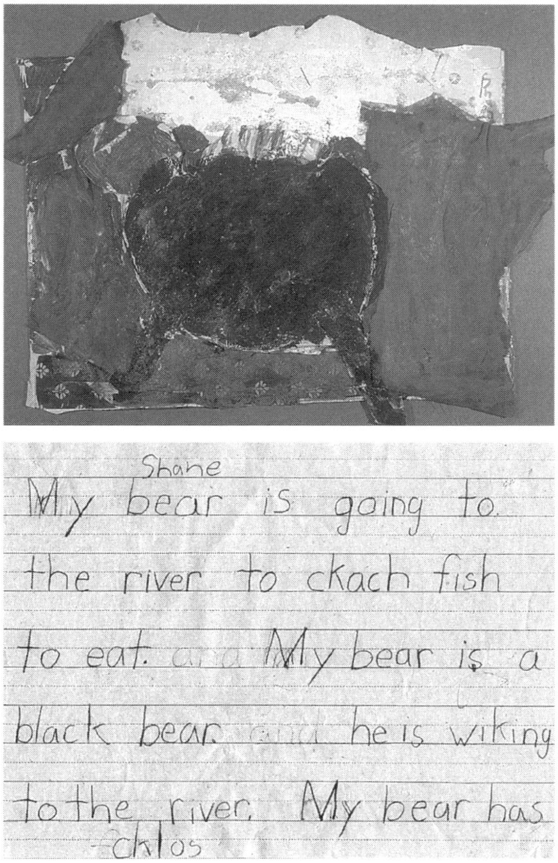

My Bear, mixed-media collage, Shane, grade 2, Wellington School

Fig. 2.1. Beginning with an illustration can help to motivate beginning writers. The enthusiasm for using art materials and producing an image carries over into the written exploration of the picture.

- *Visual art provides opportunities for experiential learning.* As students handle materials, they gain sensory knowledge and vocabulary about shapes, lines, textures, patterns, values, spatial relations, and colors (Brittain 1979, 171). They learn to hold and manipulate a variety of tools—pencils, scissors, paintbrushes, markers, hammers, glue, and so on.

- *Art involves cognitive processes.* As children draw, paint, cut, and paste, they learn how to make choices and solve problems. On another level, they are learning models for cognitive processes—that is, how to think. What children perceive—about themselves, their family, their environment—are symbolized graphically and re-ordered on paper. Like young scientists, they are constructing visual models of their experience that they can re-arrange and re-construct (Arnheim 1969, 257).

- *Art is a learned activity that requires instruction.* Unfortunately, art activities are often used as fillers between subjects and as exercises in following directions. As a result, a majority of students don't receive any training in basic art skills. Research shows that at about the age of eight or nine students may stop drawing if they are not properly instructed and encouraged (Gardner 1980). This age represents a critical period in the development of students' drawing. Many become very dissatisfied with their own work and easily frustrated if they can't accurately represent the surface appearance of their subject.

- *Art contributes to understanding and development in other subject areas.* Visual and linguistic information are combined in every subject area (Johnson 1993, 23). Musical notation, geography, scientific models, engine diagrams, graphs, and computer circuit board design all require graphic communication. Training students to "read" and communicate visual information is important for their comprehension and communication of ideas generally.

  Added to this is evidence of the importance of visual imagery to learning. Research indicates that learning is enhanced when both brain hemispheres are actively engaged. "The visual imagery a person remembers due to pictorial input is recalled more rapidly, more holistically than the words the person uses to describe the images he or she is remembering" (Sinatra and Stahl-Gemake 1983, 203).

- *More and more information is transferred visually.* Visual literacy and basic competency in visual art are becoming increasingly important for daily living and in preparing students for a variety of careers. Engineering, computer technology, television, architecture, video, cartography, navigation, graphic design, advertising, fashion, and physics all rely on visual models.

- *Art is fun.* Mixing colors with goopy paints or building a model city out of wooden crates is engaging and challenging work in which students willingly participate. Using challenging art projects and illustration to teach core curriculum turns bored students into enthusiastic learners. Discipline issues often decline during art activities. Using more visual art as part of the regular program can help to create a happier classroom.

Visual Literacy

Students need to be "visually literate." This is not the same as what has been passively called "art appreciation." Visual art is a means of communication; as with literature, we don't merely "appreciate" it, we read it, digest it, grapple with ideas, struggle with its meaning, are influenced by it. Likewise, we "read" images. This requires knowledge of visual forms in art and our environment, and an understanding of the influences of design and the meaning of graphic symbols. Visual information is present in art masterpieces and in modern media.

> Even though we are not always conscious of doing so, we are constantly responding to visual forms in our environment. People who are totally unaware of the manner in which they are affected by visual forms are vulnerable to control by perceptual forces they cannot understand, judge, or change. Such people are, in effect, perceptually illiterate (Chapman 1978, 121).

Although most children are able to interpret visual information in a literal way, they require education in order to use abstract cognitive skills. They need to learn skills for "analyzing, synthesizing, and interpreting the visual image" (Goldstone 1989, 592).

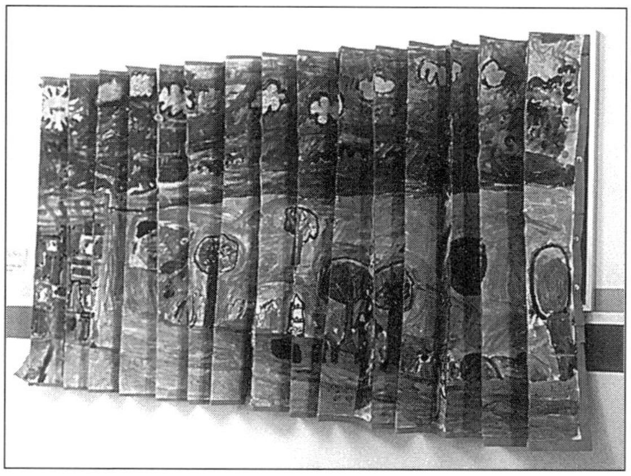

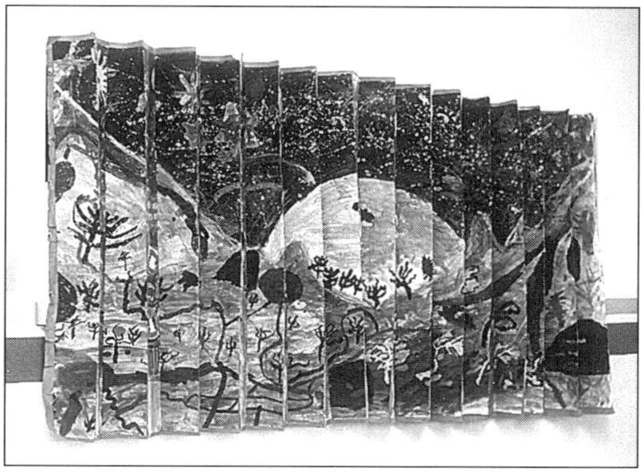

grade 1–3 class, Wolseley School

Fig. 2.2. A study in contrasts or "opposites" was the starting point for this mural. (top) Viewed from one side, it is a summer day. (bottom) Viewed from the other side, it is a winter night. Teachers: Donna Massey-Cudmore and Andrea Stuart

Developmental Stages in Art— An Age-Appropriate Program

Children pass through a sequence of predictable stages in their drawing, parallel to their development in other areas. Each of these developmental phases requires a slightly different approach in art education.

Pre-School and Nursery

Children begin by scribbling. They learn to get a grip on a pencil, develop motor skills, and discover that the pencil leaves marks behind on the paper. They progress to closed forms that are roughly oval or circular. These forms typically evolve into "tadpole" people, with enclosed forms for the center, lines for appendages (legs and arms, and later, toes and fingers) and dots and lines for the eyes and mouth. At this stage, children's drawings are very symbolic—they draw what they know or perceive about a person; they are not at all concerned that their drawing does not correspond to a person's actual appearance. In fact, children seem unconcerned about their end product altogether, although they may be vulnerable to an adult's response, whether critical or supportive.

There are several important issues for early-years educators and parents to be aware of when working with this age group:

- Children take their art seriously. The determination displayed by young children who are learning to master a variety of tools should be respected. Adults should provide opportunities and respect students' attempts to handle pencils, hole punches, markers, crayons, paintbrushes, glue, modeling clay, and other basic materials. Adult "help" can interfere with this struggle to master the task, and remove the satisfaction that comes from succeeding (Brittain 1979, 196).
- Very young children are much more interested in the process than they are in the product of their art activity. Craft activities and teacher-directed activities may produce items that are "acceptable" to adults, but they are of little value to very young children. In fact, directed activities with standard outcomes might actively discourage children, as their own efforts don't match the teacher's model.
- Complicated or pre-planned art projects at this level require a great deal of "housekeeping" by adults. Time spent preparing, replenishing, and cleaning up is time taken away from interaction with students.
- When children draw or paint, they begin to talk to observers. This, however, does not take away from art activities. On the contrary, researchers have found that nursery students spend longer at an art activity if an adult is present to offer dialogue, encouragement, and choices about materials and methods (Brittain 1979, 142).
- Children often change their ideas about what the marks on the paper represent, but they are starting to understand that these marks can be a subject of dialogue. The child is beginning to realize the use of drawing as a graphic symbol system, and is beginning to understand it as a means for communication. This is an important parallel to—or early phase of—the writing process.
- Very young children require very basic materials and the opportunity to master tools and basic skills. They need freedom from pre-planned or prescribed patterns in art activities. And they need quiet, supportive attention from adults so that they can verbalize about their art.

Early Years

Sometime between kindergarten and grade two, a student's development in drawing can be used to diagnose reading-readiness. A child's use of closed forms and intentional lines of a variety of lengths and directions are indications that he or she is ready to begin printing—and reading. Any attempts to introduce reading or letters of the alphabet to children who are still at the scribbling stage may be unproductive or damaging.

During the early years, students begin to master more complex symbols. They can eventually organize houses, people, and trees onto a baseline at the bottom of the page, with a strip of blue and a sun representing the sky at the top. This is not what the sky actually "looks" like—but the child has spatially organized the sky to be "above" the rest of the picture.

Children at this stage remain relatively unconcerned about the actual appearances of the subjects they draw. They are still recording what their experiences of their subjects are, rather than what they see. This leads to inventive solutions—x-ray vision, simultaneous views of all sides of an object, and cross sections. Complex parts of a subject are represented schematically—a triangle for a nose, an oval for a finger. Children seem unaware, or unconcerned, that their drawings do not match the reality. This requires tact from the adult who must respond to the child's efforts (see Afterword).

Children's efforts should be respected. Their awkward attempts to represent and re-order their subjects are important learning processes for them. Their ability to spontaneously create, and their innovations with form and color can produce expressive and beautiful images.

The organization of subjects in the picture emerges parallel to narrative sequence. As forms are organized on paper, so too is a comprehensible narrative about the picture. Left to themselves, children will create "spontaneous story drawings" (Wilson and Wilson 1982, 102).

One result of story drawings is that children at this stage may become preoccupied with violent themes in their drawings. Cartoon violence and imaginary characters, and graphic media provide a safe means for children to explore "all of the power, passion, fears, and hopes that can populate the mind of a young child..." (Gardner 1980, 113–114). An adult perspective can be provided by responding sensitively to and discussing the role-playing and stories present in children's drawings.

This suggests that children require some time apart from directed art activities to explore their own themes and concerns, or to respond to their environment.

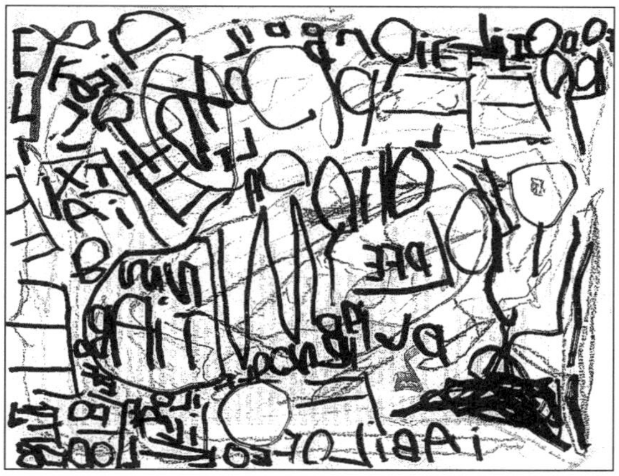

marker and crayon on paper, age 5 student, Luxton School

Fig. 2.3. Drawing and letters decorate the page. At this age, drawing is a way to learn the coordination, spatial orientation, and graphic communication necessary for learning to write.

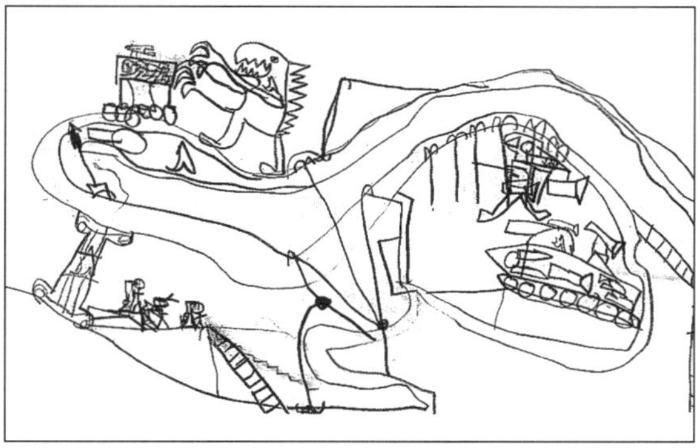

Monster, Ninjas, and Tank, pencil on paper, age 7 student, Luxton School

Fig. 2.4. Children create intricate worlds as they struggle to make sense of their feelings and experiences.

As organization and storytelling emerge in children's drawings, children can use these developing skills in illustration. At this age, students are able to plan their work. Storyboards can be used to develop a pictorial sequence with accompanying text (see chapter 6). This is a good tool for teaching students how to write. It is also a good way to develop a child's interest in drawing and writing, and to show the child how to achieve a sense of competence as a young illustrator and author. Writing and illustrating stories can become an important classroom activity at this stage.

In addition to illustration projects, there are a few other strategies that can be added at this stage.

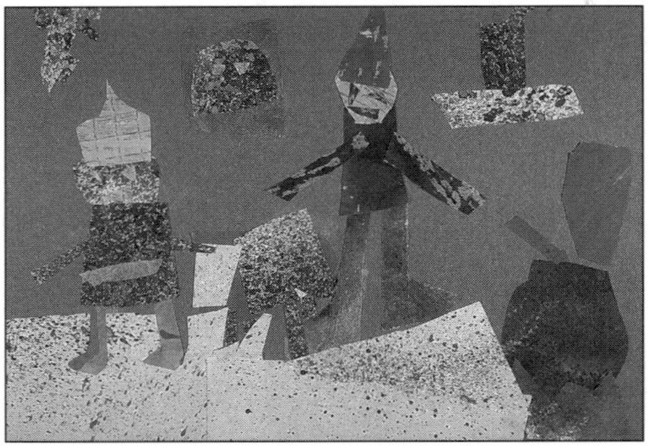

Simon Wiwsionski, age 7, South Oaks School

Fig. 2.5. Young students need the opportunity to explore a variety of art materials and approaches. To make this picture, Simon used sponge painting, splatter painting, and crayon rubbings. He then used scissors and glue to build his illustration.

- *Cut and paste.* The beginning ability to organize the picture may be aided by the use of a cut-and-paste approach (see chapters 4 and 10). Cutting and pasting gives students more choices and control over where parts of the picture will be placed, and how the parts will relate.
- *Art materials.* Students can be introduced to a variety of art materials to build experience and vocabulary, and to help maintain their interest in visual art. Art materials should be readily accessible in the classroom.
- *Look-drawing.* Some look-drawing might be (gently) introduced at this stage (see chapter 3). When students observe and draw a variety of subjects, they often find new solutions to representing forms on paper. The resulting visual awareness, experience with form, and technique will be helpful to them as they begin to want to draw more "realistically" and communicate more sophisticated ideas.

Middle Years

Very young children tend to approach art spontaneously and expressively. But sometime between grades two and six, this approach is replaced by "dogged realism" and "literal" images. This is when students show "a single-minded determination to achieve photographic realism in drawing—to show everything just the way it appears to the lens of the camera" (Gardner 1980, 11).

The expressive content of students' work may decline as students become more interested in the accurate representation of their subject. It is during this stage that students need to be taught how to draw. Otherwise, they may become discouraged with their efforts and stop drawing.

During this period of mastering accurate representation in drawing, students may discard the schemes and symbols they have used up to this point. The resulting "transitional" drawings, as they reach toward drawing what they see, will appear awkward, even ugly. These "awkward" drawings, however, should be recognized as indications that students are grappling with new solutions (Arnheim 1969, 266).

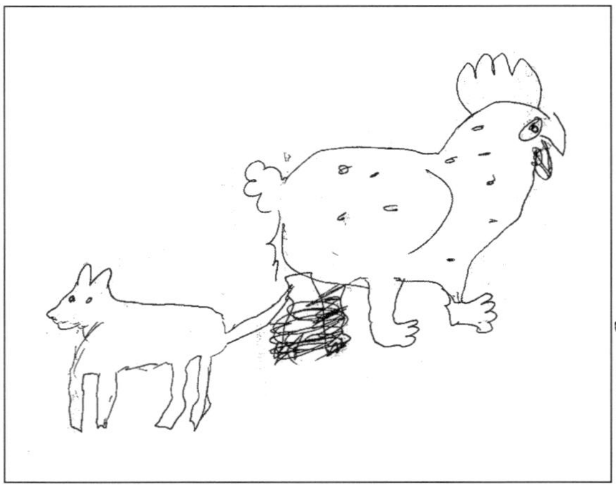

Dog and (4-Legged) Chicken, pen on paper, adult drawing

Fig. 2.6. If students reach the critical ages of 9 through teens without receiving instruction in drawing, they may not progress, or they may give up drawing entirely.

Students might be cautious about trying these new solutions, since the results will not be immediately satisfactory. For students with low self-esteem or for those who lack confidence, going from the familiar to the unfamiliar as they reach for new solutions is a scary process.

To sum up, students in "middle years" require training in how to draw. They require respectful and supportive response to their efforts. They can continue with illustration projects as they improve their ability to organize concepts and ideas and can be introduced to simple design issues (see chapter 6). They still require some non-directed drawing time, perhaps in a sketchbook or journal (see chapter 1). They also need continued access to a variety of art materials and forms.

It is helpful at this stage if adults model a positive and self-forgiving attitude toward their own efforts to draw. As students struggle with making "accurate" drawings, they may become very self-critical or aware of how they "measure up" to their peers. Channel this growing self-awareness into constructive self-evaluation and introduce basic language and concepts for looking at and under-standing visual images (see Afterword).

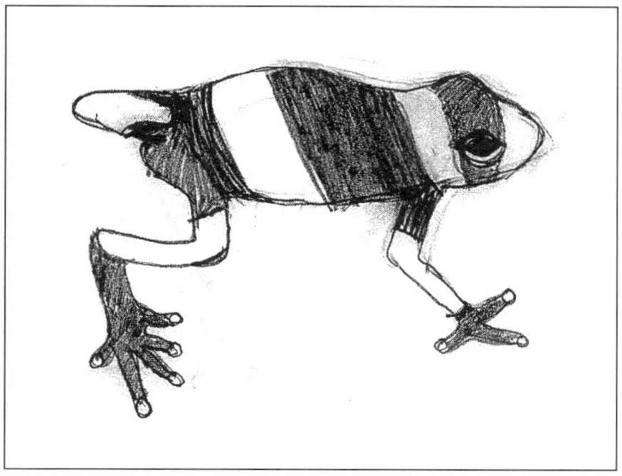

Poison Dart Frog, pencil on paper, Tessa Millen, age 10, San Antonio

Fig. 2.7. Sometime between grades 2 and 6, students begin to strive for and value accuracy in their drawings.

Preteens and Adolescents

Between grades six and eight, young people begin to shake off the grip of literal thinking and become interested once again in self-expression. Social interaction, identity, and powerful emotions become important concerns—and subjects—for drawing. If students have been given a good training in how to draw, they will have a good foundation for expressing themselves graphically (that is, through drawing). Students at this age are also able to use design concepts in their compositions, to express more sophisticated ideas.

Adolescent students can work through a variety of issues and formats graphically. The problems presented to them should be intellectually challenging, and should be responsive to their interests and concerns.

Several subject areas are often drawn during this stage. Favorite subjects are portraits and people. This is natural since relations with other people become of foremost importance at this age. This interest also includes cartooning and caricature, which offer some protection from the pressures of realistic representation. Cartoons are a "safe" style of drawing, because they are not intended to "look real." They can be expressive, but it is more difficult for peers to judge them as inadequate drawings.

Cartooning and caricature also allow students to channel their energy and imagination elsewhere. Some students will construct whole "worlds" of fantastic characters—an activity that might be a good starting point for creative writing projects. Many students gain "solace and strength" from graphic activity (Gardner 1980, 206), and so a balance must be struck between (potentially intrusive) instruction in art and free drawing time.

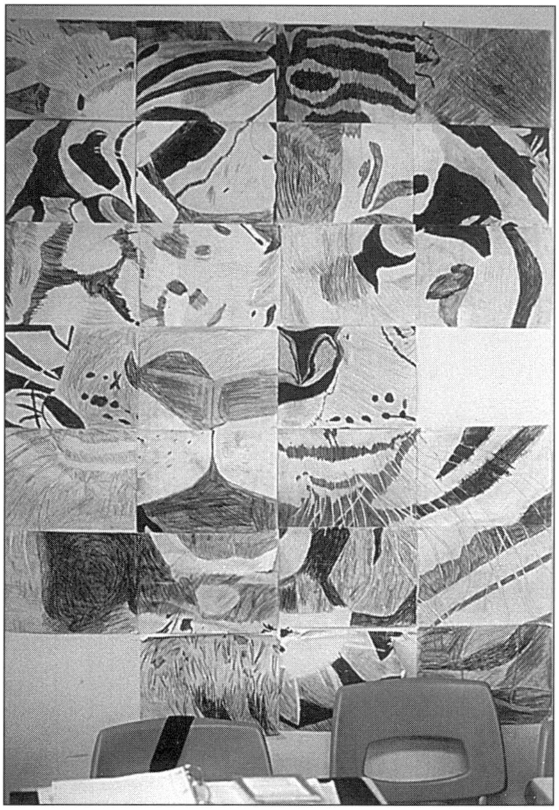

Tiger, cooperative project, grade 6, Niakwa Place School

Fig. 2.8. Older students can build confidence in visual arts with projects that are cooperative or media-based.

The kind of doodling often resorted to by students of this age indicates that they are prepared for experimentation with more abstract concepts and forms. Introduce them to design concepts (see chapter 6), and have them apply the concepts of design to issues and topics of interest to them. Emphasis on design problems can offer another "safe" format for drawing. It can provide a "formula" for expressing ideas and a means for organizing and re-ordering images.

To sum up, preteen and adolescent students need a balance between drawing instruction and self-expression. Offering problems or projects related to design can provide a "safe" challenge and can assist students in finding new frameworks for ordering their visual ideas. A sketchbook will be an important tool for self-expression, problem solving, and as an observation tool for research.

Motivating Reluctant Learners

In most subject areas, illustration can be an important "bridge" from images to text for many students. There are several circumstances where illustrations can be of use in the classroom.

Special Needs Students

Multiple aspects of intelligence have been recognized and studied. When Gardner (1980) introduced his theory of multiple intelligence, he identified several distinct categories of intelligence. Spatial intelligence includes orientation, recognition, depiction, and symbolization, and is distinguishable from linguistic, mathematical, and musical intelligences (Gardner 1983, 176). For students who demonstrate predominately—or exclusively—spatial intelligence, visual art makes school comprehensible and bearable. Many students who are "academically delayed," "learning disabled," or who have "behavior problems," have predominant use of the right brain hemisphere, where spatial intelligence resides (Gardner 1980, 151). These students will not understand oral or written instruction, but may respond to a visual-kinesthetic approach. They may excel if projects are introduced through demonstration, or if they can solve graphic problems and use art materials.

There is also some evidence that developments in drawing ability—exercising the right brain hemisphere, gaining confidence in self-expression through drawing, and developing coordination and concentration—transfer to other endeavors. We are "supple symbol users because of our ability to mobilize these operations that prove peculiar to one symbolic domain as well as certain versatile operations which lend themselves to deployment across a range of symbolic domains" (Gardner 1983, 308).

There are many students I have worked with whom teachers have described to me as "slow," "difficult," "a behavior problem," "rude," "hard to motivate," "disruptive," "learning disadvantaged," "FAS," "FAE," "ADD," "short attention span," or (more diplomatically, and with more respect for the student's privacy and dignity), "bouncy." Not all of these students respond positively to all visual arts activities. However, sometimes to the surprise of the classroom teacher (who, it is hoped, will begin to incorporate more visual approaches to teaching to these students), a large proportion do.

Some of these revelations are dramatic. One little boy in a nursery class (who had already been held back a year) was completely nonverbal. He had been diagnosed with fetal alcohol syndrome (FAS).* This little person watched very carefully as I demonstrated how to spread Plasticine on a cardboard backing and made basic fish-like shapes. He not only (mutely) accomplished these tasks, which were challenging enough for his classmates, but he was innovative. His fish's fins stuck out from the picture. He impressed texture onto the fish with a pencil, overlapped weeds in front of his fish, and added bubbles. This demonstrated sophisticated visual reception and thinking skills that had been previously unrecognized by his teacher (who, in all fairness, had never received any training in visual arts).

Another student was extremely disruptive, frequently leaving his seat and talking loudly off topic and out of turn. He seemed unable to focus on written work, and had trouble sitting through my initial (and mainly verbal) presentation. He seemed distracted while I demonstrated the technique, but when the time came to apply the painting technique, he went right to work and became very involved in studying the landscape photograph and in mixing colors. The resulting painting showed that he had paid attention to the instructions—or the examples—of color mixing and light and dark values, as well as to which materials he would need and how to use them. He sat through the remaining seventy-minute period without moving from his seat or speaking, and had the patience to complete his painting and even to repaint an area of the sky that he was dissatisfied with. The teacher was surprised that the student had not been "a problem" during the class.

I have encountered many such students over the five years I have worked in schools as a visiting artist. There is increasing evidence of and interest in theories of multiple intelligences that might explain the situations I have experienced and give clues as to how these "special needs" students might be teachable.

> Children with learning difficulties—and especially those with reading problems—tend to have late-occurring or "mixed" dominance; significantly, these same children are often tapped by observers as having an especially deep and abiding involvement with graphic expression. It certainly makes sense to suggest that drawing will continue to hold special attraction for those

---

* Alcohol can cause pre-natal damage that can range from severe FAS to difficult-to-diagnose trace fetal alcohol effect.

youngsters who, for one or another reason, evince trouble in expressing themselves in what has become the chief symbol system of the culture (Gardner 1980, 151).

According to Gardner (1980), most school-age children have developed dominance of the left brain hemisphere—that is, dominance of linguistic capabilities. But not all children develop the same way. Students who have difficulty reading, writing, or speaking may express themselves—that is, may understand and process information—visually, and may respond to visual approaches in teaching.

Tucker (1995, 27), a teacher/researcher, writes of his experiences with the "visualizers" in his class: "I concluded that it was not mere laziness or stubbornness, but a cognitive mismatch between them and a class where most of the thinking was done by writing or talking about writing."

For these students, the more oral instruction they are given, the more confused they may become. Presenting information or instruction with few words, with more demonstration and graphic displays combined with tactile information—opportunities to handle materials—is most effective. For students who may otherwise see themselves as failures at school, the opportunity to draw, and to improve and excel and be recognized for their competence and expression of their ideas in visual art, makes a world of difference. Illustration may be the only "bridge" they can use to comprehend text.*

Gifted Students

The term "gifted" tends to set students apart. Gardner (1980, 221) uses the term "advanced," which seems more appropriate, since even artists like Picasso and Klee progressed along developmental stages similar to other children.

Students gifted in visual art tend to pass through the same developmental stages as other students. They just pass through them more rapidly and can easily transmit an image graphically—they draw really well for their age.

Advanced students present a special challenge to art educators. They tend to be more interested in personal exploration and expression than in art instruction. In fact, it may be very difficult to question aspects of their drawing, as advice is seen as an intrusion. They have a system that works, and they want to stick to it.

* The larger question remains—if the education system is set up to recognize only students with linguistic and mathematical intelligence, does it not exclude students who have predominately (or exclusively) visual-spatial (artistic) intelligence? Can we afford to do this in a culture in which visual imagery and graphic display are becoming primary means of communication?

They must be coached with enormous tact and forgiveness. Artistic ability may be the one area that they believe (or are told) is "special" about them, and they will guard this jealously. Students who believe that they "already know how to draw" may simply ignore suggestions, or may feel uncomfortable with the awkward results of trying a new technique or medium. Painting or collage may seem very imprecise compared with what they can accomplish in a pencil drawing. However, it is important for advanced students to experience a range of possibilities for their work. Try having them experiment on photocopies or traced copies of their work, so they don't "ruin" their original drawings. Introduce design problems to challenge advanced students to solve problems graphically, in drawing and in composition.

Advanced students need to be "visually literate" (see page 15) in order to progress in their work—to look critically at their own work and other visual images, to make judgments, and to respond to visual information. To do this, they need to know the elements and principles of design and color theory. In short, they require a mix of sensitivity and informed teaching.

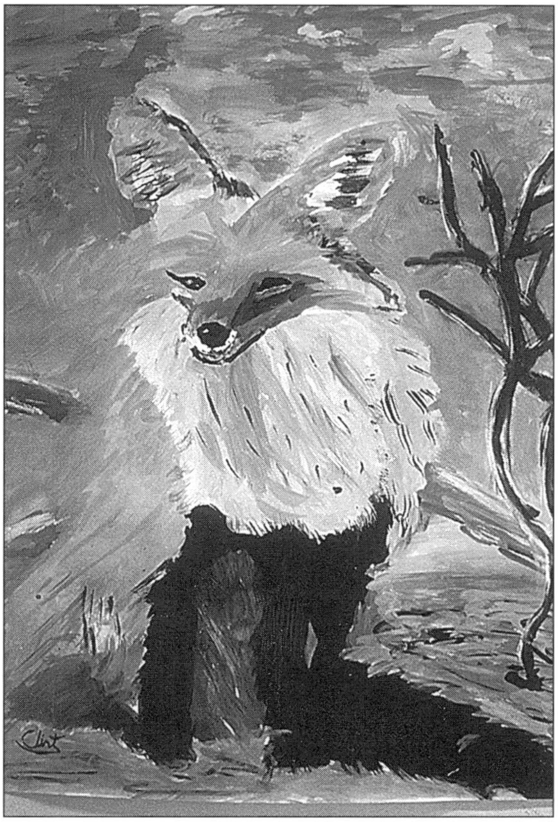

tempera paint on Bristol board, Clinton Whiteway, grade 4–8 class, Matheson Island School

Fig. 2.9. Clinton paid careful attention to light and dark values, accurate color, and interesting brush marks in this painting of a fox. **See color plate.**

Part 2
Learning to Draw

For students to feel successful with visual art, it is important for them to learn some basic drawing skills. Around the age of nine, they often become very critical of their own drawing. They begin to see the world through the conventions of realistic representation and photography, and they want their own drawings to "look real." Unless they are given some instruction, they may become discouraged at their inability to draw and give up altogether.

Teachers and parents who see themselves as "bad" at art will be relieved to know that age is no barrier for learning to draw. Anyone can learn, if taught some very basic skills. Drawing classes should be free of comparisons and ridicule, including self-ridicule. Drawing is not a contest. It is a pleasurable and worthwhile activity.

The drawing exercises in Part I focus on look-drawing. Look-drawing is drawing what is seen, rather than what is assumed, about a subject. To supplement look-drawing in the classroom, you may want to incorporate other kinds of drawing into your students' program:

- *Free drawing time:* During free drawing time, students draw subjects of their choice. This is a good outlet for those students who would otherwise decorate their math books with superheroes or geometric patterns. If students seem "stuck" for ideas of what to draw, have some resources handy—"how-to-draw" books, The Anti-Coloring Book series, calendar photos, simple objects (small toys or natural items), children's picture books, postcards, and so on. You may wish to set some parameters; for example, you will not accept hurtful or derogatory drawings. Free drawing time may be evaluated based solely on the time a student invests in drawing.
- *Response journals:* Ask students to record their activities and reflections in a combination of writing and pictures. Response journals may be used to remember and reflect on a field trip, a "choice time" activity, or a presentation to the class by a visitor; to observe change or progress of plant growth or weather; and so on. Journals allow you to evaluate how much information, including visual information, your students have remembered, absorbed, and found interesting.
- *Reading response, or "guided imagery":* Students read, or are read to, and then sketch their interpretation or favorite part of the story or poem. Reading response may also be used as a directed activity where students are asked to draw how the main character may have felt in a particular situation, what the most exciting part of the story was, and so on. If the students have had basic instruction

in drawing, you can use reading response to evaluate how much of the text students absorbed or understood, or which facets caught their imagination.

- *Invention and problem solving:* Students can use drawing to solve a math problem, or to design a simple machine or a computer circuit board. These sketches are often symbolic or schematic rather than realistic and may include some written notation. They can provide a bridge between manipulatives and written work in most subject areas. These sketches are an important aid for visual thinkers and allow teachers to see the processes that each student used to solve the problem.

- *Projected images:* Students use an "accidental" image as the starting point for a picture. They make a small, quick scribble on their page and then look closely to see if they can turn this haphazard collection of lines and shapes into a picture, by emphasizing some lines and adding details.

  This can be turned into a game: have students take turns making scribbles for one another. Students might look at cloud shapes, paint blots (dab a bit of paint on the paper, fold in half, and open the paper to see an interesting shape), or look at a series of cracks in a ceiling (see *It Looked Like Spilt Milk*).

  Projected images allow students to use their imagination to transform images, and to produce fanciful, rather than realistic, images. Students may also learn to enjoy drawing. This exercise is successful if students become more spontaneous with their drawings and begin to allow themselves to experiment with new approaches.

3
The Basic Elements of Drawing

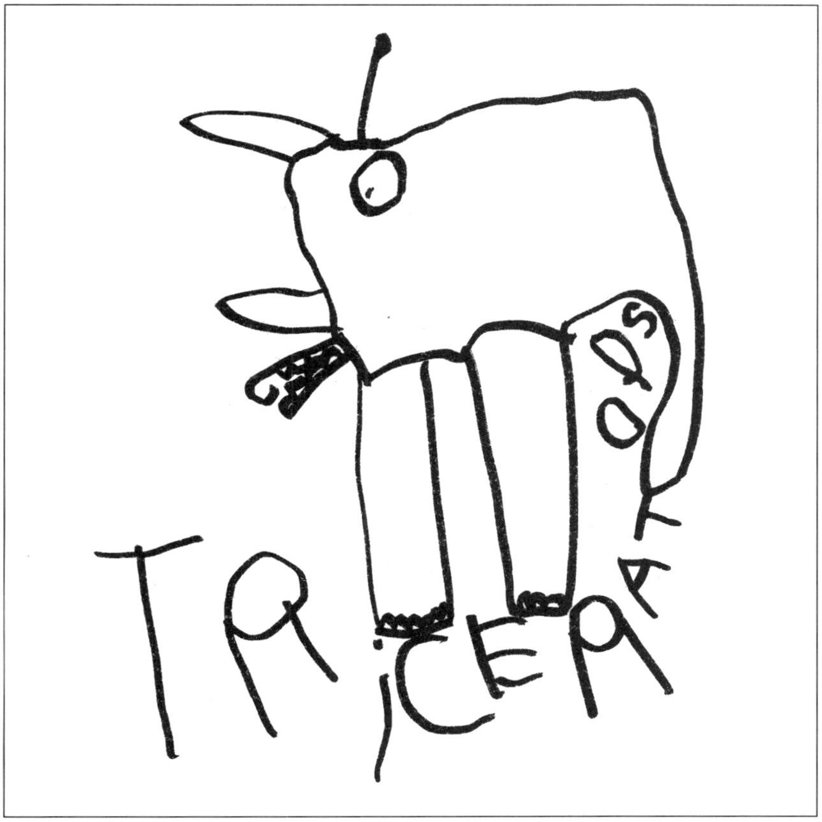

Triceratops, marker on paper, 5-year-old student, Luxton School

Fig. 3.1. Children begin drawing with a playful, symbolic approach to their subject.

Introduction

In this chapter, the basic elements of drawing—shape, line, texture, pattern, value, and space—are treated as approaches to drawing. (Color, another basic element, is discussed in chapter 8.)

An interesting outcome of the drawing exercises that follow is that your students may begin to look at things, and see things, differently. If they have been working on a lot of negative space drawings, and then they look at trees on their way home from school, they may begin to *see* the spaces between the branches and focus on these interesting, irregular areas of blue (sky) rather than on the branches. If they have been spending several sessions on blind contour and line drawings, they may stop and trace the paths of crooked tree trunks, branches, and twigs. You may notice that your students are becoming visually aware.

Materials

- sketchbooks (or white photocopy paper, 8½" x 11" or 21.5 cm x 28 cm)
- pencils (HB graphite is fine; an arrangement of hard—H, 2H, 3H—and soft—B, 2B, 3B, 6B—pencils might be fun to experiment with)
- erasers
- rulers
- scissors
- glue or gluesticks
- optional: see materials in Enrichment exercises

Students will require visual references—something to look at while they draw—for these exercises. They are not "copying." They are gathering and recording visual information while observing and learning about a subject. Learning to draw an accurate representation should not deter students from expressing their own vision or style of drawing, or prevent a teacher from valuing unorthodox, quirky, or imaginative solutions. Students can be actively encouraged to add imaginative elements later—to take their "literal" drawings and transform them into something symbolic, whimsical, or irrational.

Tips for Successful Drawing Classes

Before your students start look-drawing, here are some suggestions for successful drawing classes:

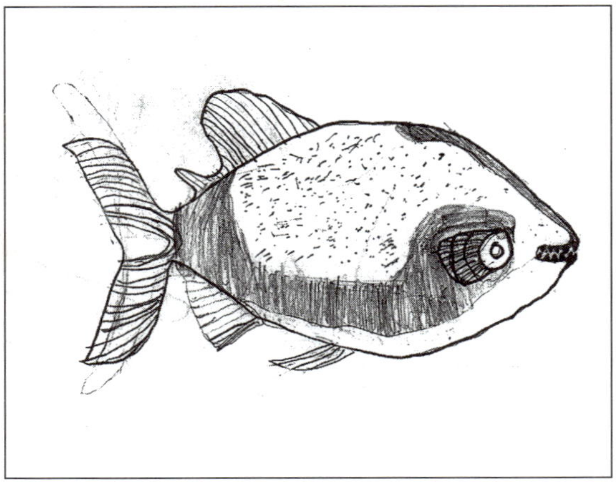

pencil on paper, Scott McPherson, grade K–3, San Antonio School

Fig. 3.2. Start drawing lessons with simple subjects that relate to the students' topic of study. Scott did this pencil drawing while he was researching fish.

- *Collect materials and subjects for drawing.* Begin with simple subjects that relate to your topic of study and that are of interest to your students (fig. 3.2). You might start with fruits and vegetables, beetles, or leaves. Later you can move on to more difficult subjects or groups of subjects such as spiders, buildings, a stack of toys, or a bicycle. These might be presented as actual objects, photographs, magazine or calendar photos, posters, another artist's drawing of the subject (as in an art postcard or calendar), or a toy or model of the subject.
- *Try the exercise yourself first.* You'll want to know if the subject is appropriate for the exercise, where students might experience difficulty, and how much time the exercise might require. You'll also get a sense of how the exercise "feels." Is it difficult, relaxing, fun, or challenging?
- *Make sure your students have sketchbooks or portfolios for storing loose drawings.* These are ideal for organizing students' work and for keeping a record of their progress in drawing.
- *Decide which vocabulary or concept* you want to select to highlight and integrate with the drawing exercise. For example, you might select a pumpkin as the subject for a drawing. When you ask students what they notice about the pumpkin, they might respond with words such as *bumpy, huge, smooth, hard, grooves, orange, speckled,* and *warty*. A grade-seven student might notice the curvature of lines of longitude on the pumpkin. If you sliced the pumpkin open, it might make a more interesting drawing subject. As well, you could use the sliced pumpkin to demonstrate the concepts of "inside" and "outside" to a kindergarten class, or to teach fractions (such as one-half or one-quarter) to students in grade three.

spinoff re-read

- *Think of questions* you could ask your students that will help them become interested in the subject. You might begin by simply asking them what they see or notice.

- *Discuss parts of the subject that students might find difficult to draw.* If they were drawing leaves, this might include: intricate parts (the veins on a leaf), overlapping parts ("one leaf is on top of another—I can only see part of the oak leaf"), or unusual views ("one leaf is curled over, so we can see the underside").

- *Give a quick demonstration of the exercise.* This will make the exercise more accessible to students who are visual/kinesthetic learners, and you can model a good attitude toward drawing. A sense of humor helps! There is a danger that the students will simply copy the teacher's product. Since the idea is to encourage individual and innovative work, demonstrate only the necessary steps; leave your example unfinished, and discuss or brainstorm alternative solutions.

- *Begin with short drawing sessions* (ten minutes). Work up to longer sessions as students learn how to observe and concentrate.

Tip: The patience required for look-drawing is a hard lesson in itself. Concentration can be affected by a student's level of confidence, prior drawing experience, developmental readiness, and external factors (the noise level in the room, whether the student has had lunch, and so on). Begin with short sessions, simple subjects, lots of encouragement, and offer advice gently!

Shape

A shape can be defined as an enclosed area, having two dimensions when represented on paper. Shape is also a schematic device for analyzing a subject for a drawing. Some shapes are "organic" (for example, jellybean, amoeba, teardrop) and some are "geometric" (circle, square, triangle).

Exercises for teaching about shape—scribble drawing or "gesture" drawing, negative space drawing, and geometric shape drawing—show students how to:

- see their subjects as a whole entity
- become more aware of their subject's size and placement on the page
- begin to judge proportion (sizes and placement of the parts of the subject relative to each other)
- see the shapes contained within the subject

Drawing shapes is fundamental to the drawing process. Scribbling and drawing simple enclosures and shapes that symbolically represent the subject are early phases in a child's development in drawing. Scribbling the gesture of a subject and building the form of the subject out of geometric shapes are the two most common means for a visual artist to begin a representational drawing. Just as a drawing of an orange would begin with a circle, a drawing of a horse would begin with an arrangement of circles, ovals, and rectangles. The structure of the subject has to be established before lines, texture, pattern, and value can be added.

Books to Have Handy

Picture Books
Strega Nona
The Lazy Bear
Zoom Upstream

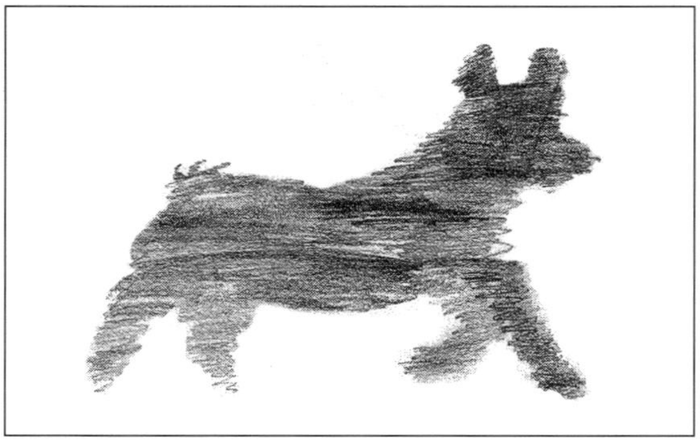

pencil on paper, Noni Brynjolson, age 11

Fig. 3.3. A finished scribble-drawing looks like a shadow.

Tip: Encourage your students to hold their pencil loosely, near the eraser end. That way, they'll get a more relaxed scribble and a lighter mark on their paper. It may help them to imagine that their pencil is a feather, and that if they squeeze too hard they may break it.

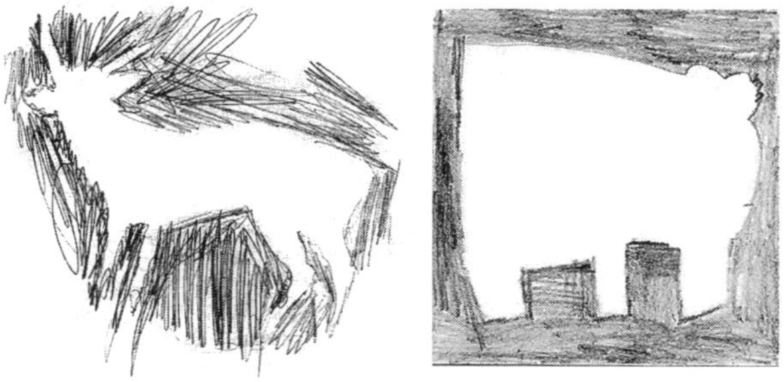

pencil on paper, grade 4–6 students, Luxton School

Fig. 3.4. Looking at the negative spaces that surround a subject gives clues about (a) how the parts of the subject fit together, and (b) how the subject relates to the background and to the edges of the page.

Fig. 3.5. Simplifying a subject into geometric shapes is the most basic and important lesson in learning how to draw. A horse is difficult to draw, but ovals, rectangles, and triangles are easy! Learning to see the geometric shapes contained in a subject will solve problems with proportion and placement later on.

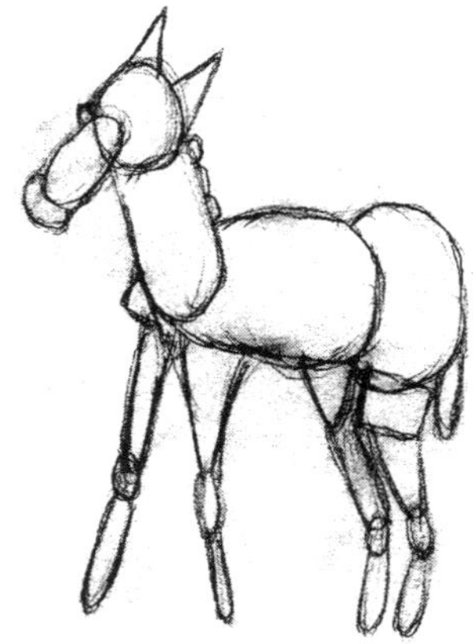

pencil on paper, Noni Brynjolson, age 11

Appropriate Subjects

Have your students look at objects that have obvious geometric shapes or that have fairly simple forms, without excessive details. Almost any subject can be simplified into basic geometric shapes. Fruits and vegetables have fairly obvious shapes. Trucks, simple machines, and small buildings (houses rather than cathedrals) also have straightforward shapes. Animals contain basic shapes (a bird, for example, may have an oval body, round head, and triangular beak).

Scribble-Drawing

Before your students begin their own drawings, have them look carefully at the drawings in *Zoom Upstream*. Note how each drawing is made almost entirely of scribbled pencil marks. Now, let your students select an object they want to draw. In their sketchbooks, have them use scribble-drawing to reproduce the shape of their object. The result will be a scribbled silhouette or "shadow" of their subject (fig. 3.3).

Negative Space

Students in about grades two and up may be ready to try negative space drawing. Explain to them that negative space is the area between and around parts of an object. Negative space drawings will help them to see the shapes of spaces between parts of their subjects (fig. 3.4). Have your students use scribbling to fill in all the shapes around their subject, leaving the subject itself blank. For negative space exercises, look at how the subject "contains" some space. Some examples are a bagel (the hole in the center), a bicycle wheel (the spaces between the spokes), and a daisy (the spaces between petals).

Geometric Shapes

Another approach you can use to teach students about shape is to have them look for the geometric shapes contained within their subject (circles, ovals, squares, triangles, and so on). Look at *Strega Nona* with your students. Ask them what geometric shapes they can see in the houses. Look at *The Lazy Bear*. What shape is the bear's head? What shape is the body, the legs, the ears?

Now ask your students what shapes they see in their own subjects. Have them draw a geometric, simplified version of their subject in their sketchbooks (fig. 3.5).

Learning to use geometric shapes to construct a subject is an important step in learning how to draw. Students should be encouraged to practice and gain confidence with this approach.

Other Exercises

Have your students try some of the following exercises to build their awareness of shape:

- Play with pattern blocks and tanagrams. In the course of play, students will discover how pieces interlock and combine to make a picture; for example, a house, a sunflower, a dog (fig. 3.6).
- Cut cardboard or mat board into geometric shapes. Glue these onto a cardboard backing to build pictures, and then paint them. (See Part 4 for more on paint and painting techniques.)
- Take a walking tour of the neighborhood and look-draw, or simply point out geometric shapes seen along the way. Some examples are square windows, rectangular fence posts, circular wheels.
- Use tear-and-paste to build up the shapes of a subject (fig. 3.7). Tear small pieces of construction paper and glue the pieces onto a colored paper background. Pieces can be easily added or deleted to obtain an image. This exercise works well for very young students who have trouble using scissors.
- Look at quilts and quilt patterns. The pieces in each block are made from geometric shapes. Design quilt squares of oil pastel and paint, cut them out, and glue onto construction paper, cut colored paper, or fabric.
- Borrow some "how-to-draw" books from the library. Most of these books start off drawings with simple, geometric shapes. These will reinforce the drawing process you are teaching and give students experience drawing a range of subjects.
- Draw on paper that has been cut into a geometric shape that approximates the shape of the subject (for example, a semicircle for drawing a Japanese paper fan; a long rectangle for drawing a side view of a car).
- Advanced students can try structural drawings using volumes (three-dimensional forms) instead of flat shapes. (See page 39 for how to draw volumes.)

Tip: If students are working from a laminated photograph (or an expendable photocopy), they can use a marker to draw the geometric shapes directly onto the photo.

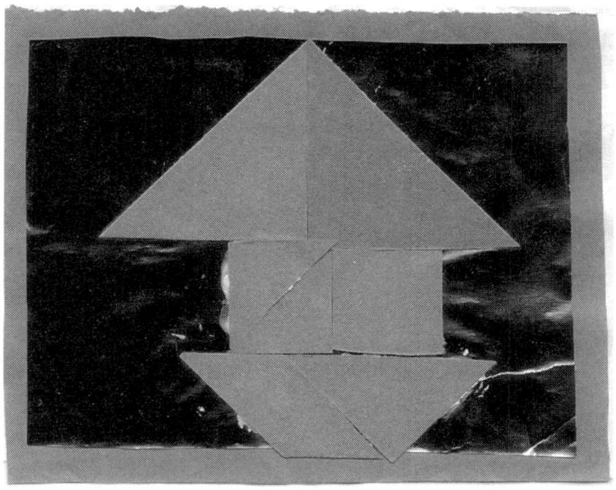

cut paper collage, Noni Brynjolson, age 8, Luxton School

Fig. 3.6. This simple picture is built out of tanagrams—geometric shapes cut from construction paper and glued onto foil.

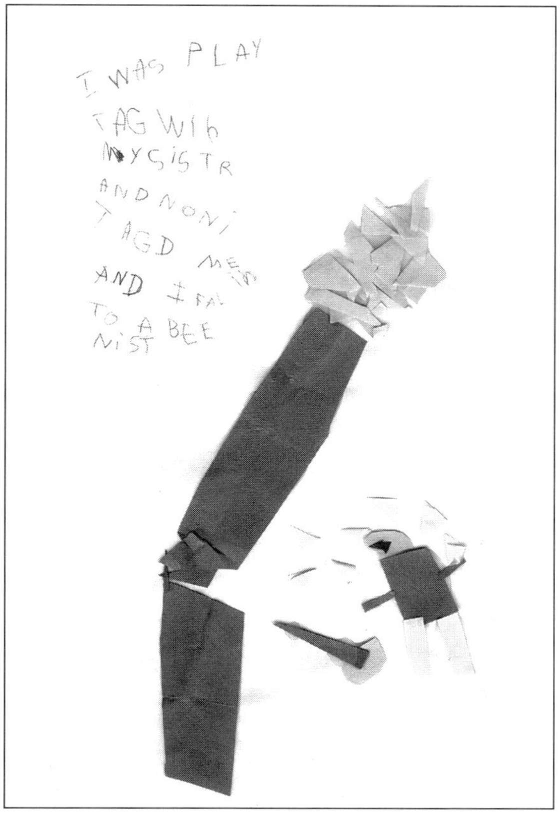

I Fell Into a Bee's Nest, colored paper collage, 6-year-old student, Luxton School

Fig. 3.7. The shapes in this picture were built from cut-and-torn paper pieces.

Books to Have Handy

Picture Books
Would They Love a Lion?

Teacher References
Draw!
Drawing on the Right Side of the Brain

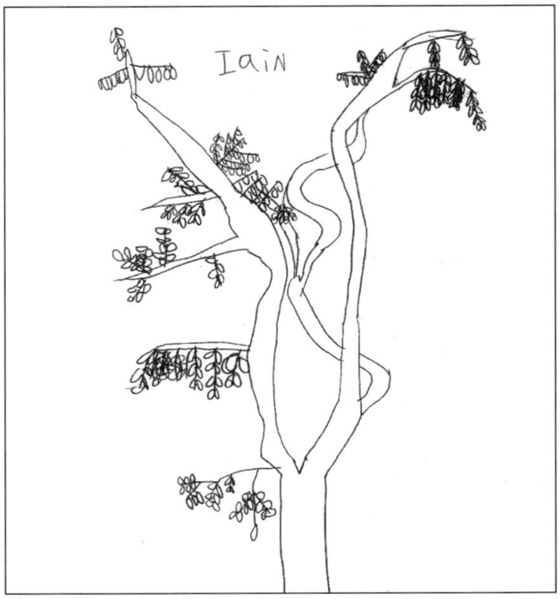

pencil on paper, Iain Brynjolson, age 7, Luxton School

Fig. 3.8. In this drawing, Iain has looked carefully at the contours of the main branches, where the lines bend, wobble, and overlap.

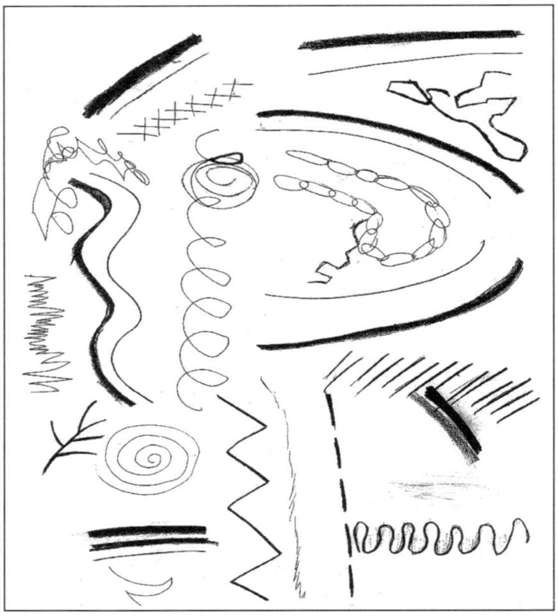

pencil on paper, Danna Slessor-Cobb, age 10

Fig. 3.9. Varieties of lines

Line

A line is created when a pencil is pulled across a piece of paper. The line may be very light, very black, even engraved into the paper. Its weight or darkness depends on the grip on the pencil, how sharp the pencil is, and the hardness or softness of the lead. Line exercises require careful looking and recording, and help students develop observation skills, hand-eye coordination, and patience with detail.

When representing a subject on paper, a line is used to describe the *contour* of the subject. The contours are the outside and interior edges. It is easy to perceive the edges on a two-dimensional subject —for example, magazine photo of an apple, poster of a model dinosaur, or postcard picture of a cat—because the image is flat and edges are definite. On a three-dimensional subject—a "real" cat, an apple, or toy dinosaur, for example—the edges are less obvious.

When drawing an accurate contour, it is important to draw what is seen rather than what is assumed about a subject (fig. 3.8). The contour of an apple is probably not a perfect circle, but has bumps and dips in its curvature.

Appropriate Subjects

Begin contour drawings with simple subjects such as leaves, fruits, and vegetables, and build toward more intricate forms such as hands, plants, faces, animals, machinery, and bicycles. Students will require a visual reference—a photo, object, or model—to look at while they draw.

Method

Show *Would They Love a Lion?* to your students. Discuss with them the interesting line qualities—straight or wobbly, thick or fine, broken or smooth. Students may wish to quickly try these kinds of lines in their sketchbooks. They can do this by "doodling" a variety of lines. Encourage them to experiment with more or less pressure on the pencil, drawing lines quickly or slowly, until a page is filled (fig. 3.9).

Blind Contour Drawing

Have students select a subject to draw. Then let them do a blind contour drawing. The idea is to not look at the paper while drawing, but to look closely at the contours of the subject.* This exercise helps students of about grades two and up see the detail in the subject in

* There is a good section on blind contour drawing in ***Drawing on the Right Side of the Brain*** by Betty Edwards.

front of them, learn hand-eye coordination, and develop a feel for an interesting line. Blind contour drawing rarely looks like an accurate drawing of the subject (fig. 3.10); rather, it is a technique used to get a feeling for contour drawing. The results are often intricate, quirky, and funny.

Before students start their blind contour drawings, have them look carefully at their subject. Ask them to note the outside edges and interior details, jagged edges or bumps, where pencil lines will need to change direction or become wobbly, smooth edges where lines can curve gently or become straight, and so on.

Have students hold the photo of their subject in front of their drawing papers, then turn sideways in their chairs, or put a piece of loose paper over their drawing hands. This way, they cannot look at the paper while they are drawing.

Tip: Have students trace lightly with a pencil over a photograph of their subject (or in the air between their eyes and their subject) to help them feel the way their hands will move when they are drawing.

Tip: When doing blind contour drawings, remind students to not peek at their drawings. Also remind them that the more slowly they move their pencils, the more detail they will have time to see. Be prepared for giggling when students finally peek at their work! Blind contour drawing is especially fun for drawing faces—from magazine photos, friends, or mirrors. The results, if they are recognizable, are caricatures (or aliens!).

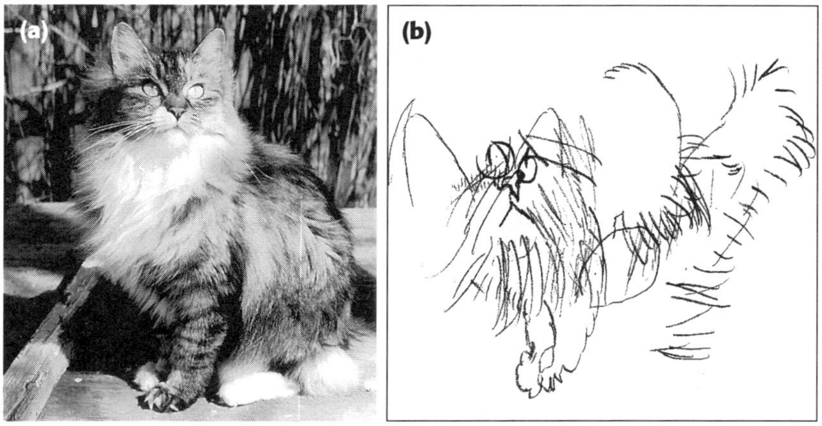

Cat, pencil on paper, Danna Slessor-Cobb, age 10

Fig. 3.10. (a) A close-up photograph of an animal makes a good drawing subject. Danna looked carefully at this photo when she did her blind contour drawing. **(b)** Blind contour drawings produce quirky, expressive drawings, with no form to hold the details together. It is an important exercise for teaching observation skills and hand-eye coordination. The results are always fun!

Contour Drawing

When they are finished their blind contour drawings, students can try drawing the contours of their subjects again. This time they are allowed to "sneak" glances at their papers. The emphasis should still be on looking at the edges of the subject rather than at the paper.

Encourage students to use multiple outlines. As they draw the contours of their subjects on paper, urge them to draw around the edges three or four times, with one line more or less on top of the other. Every time they draw the contour of the subject, they may notice a slightly different aspect of the subject. Then they can choose which line they think is the most accurate or interesting, and erase the rest. Alternatively, students can leave the extra lines in to show an object in motion, or to decorate the space around the object. When students use multiple outlines, they become less cautious and less easily frustrated with their drawings (fig. 3.11).

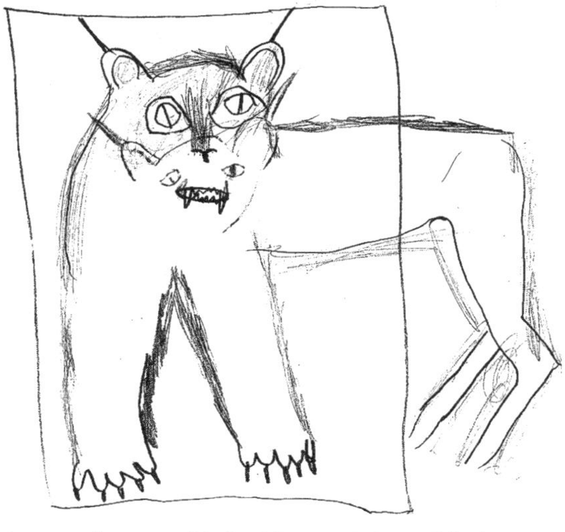

Lynx, pencil on paper, Iain Brynjolson, age 7, Luxton School

Fig. 3.11. The partially erased pencil marks and detail in this drawing show that the student was reassessing his original marks and observing new things about his subject. He also selected and outlined what he felt to be the most successful part of his drawing. Using multiple outlines gave him the confidence to continue and not erase the whole drawing.

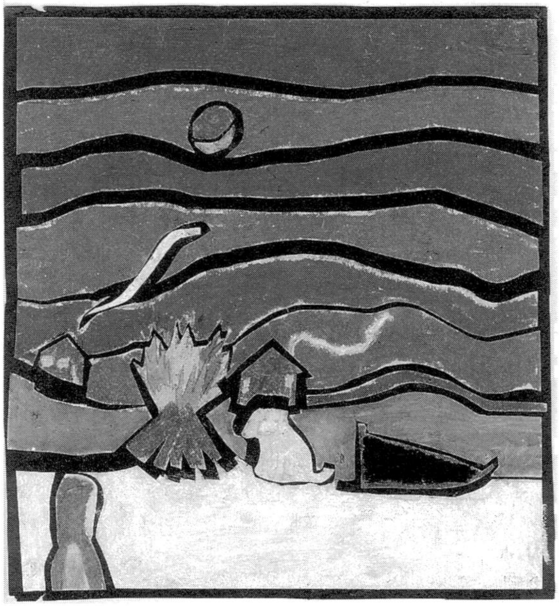

Camping Out, oil pastel cutouts on paper, Noni Brynjolson, age 8, Luxton School

Fig. 3.12. After this student looked at illustrations by Ted Harrison, she drew with oil pastels, then cut out pieces of the drawing and spaced them on black paper to create interesting, flowing lines.

Other Exercises

Here are some more exercises your students can do to build confidence and experience with line:

- Try line drawing with different media (for example, a sharpened twig or pointy paintbrush dipped in ink; three colored pencils taped together; a fat marker; a squeeze bottle full of paint; a squeeze bottle of glue followed by a line of string) to get different qualities of line (fig. 3.12). See *Draw!* (pages 8–22) for other ideas.
- When the leaves are off the trees, in late autumn or early spring, go outside and look at tree branches—they are crooked, straight, curved, droopy, and so on. Sketch or simply describe them. What other lines can you see? Look for lines formed by telephone wires, cracks in the sidewalk, fence boards, and so on.
- With chalk, draw long lines (wavy, zigzag, curved, dotted, and so on) on cement and walk them. (This exercise is for younger students.)
- Take time for sketching and doodling in sketchbooks. Sketchbooks may become rich sources of ideas for stories and more elaborate drawings later.

Books to Have Handy

Picture Books
The Lazy Bear

Texture and Pattern

Although texture and pattern are different concepts, they are lumped together here because they are commonly added into a drawing at the same stage—after the shapes and lines have been established. They are also compatible in terms of technique—they require careful observation and recording of detail, often with repeated pencil marks. Often only one or the other is important in a subject, although very challenging subjects may combine both texture and pattern.

Texture

Texture can be defined as "how something feels when you touch it." Textures are furry, smooth, bumpy, rough, soft, feathery, scaly, and so on. The challenge is to represent these textures on a smooth piece of drawing paper.

For very young students, it may be useful to start by passing around objects or scraps, such as feathers, shells, and sandpaper, that have interesting textures. Ask students to describe the textures of the objects, aloud or in journals, and then cut and glue the scraps onto cardboard to produce a textured picture.

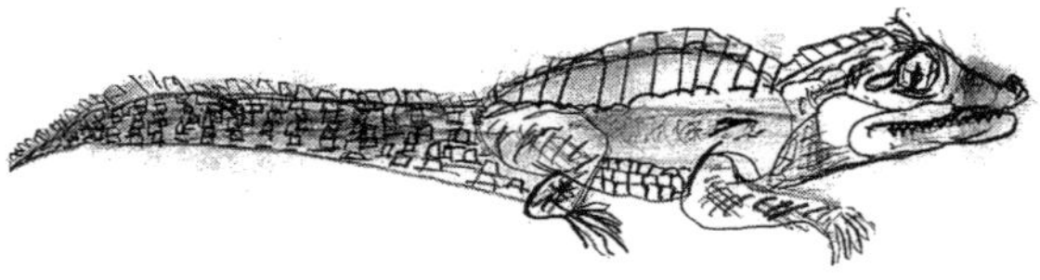

Young Crocodile, pencil on paper, Noni Brynjolson, age 8, Luxton School

Fig. 3.13. Adding texture provides some of the detail that helps to make a drawing look "real." A bumpy, scaly crocodile makes an interesting subject.

To draw textures that represent tactile information on a two-dimensional plane, students need to experiment with a variety of ways to make marks on paper.

Tip: If a subject is furry, the length and direction that the fur grows will determine the length and direction of pencil marks. A rough, furry, or bumpy surface will also affect the contours (edges) in the drawing. Fur may also cause the pattern on an animal to have jagged edges (for example, the stripes on a tiger are jagged rather than smooth).

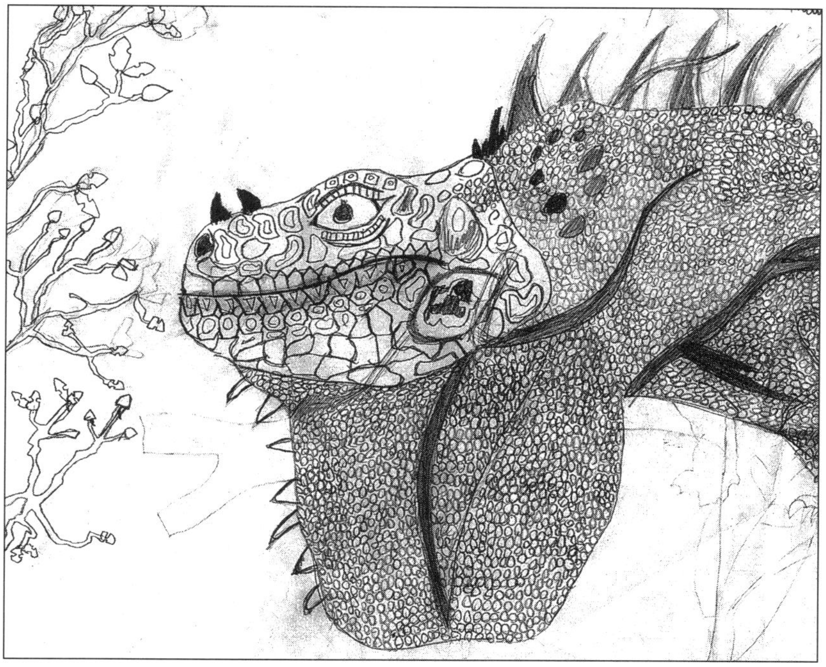

Iguana, pencil on paper, Matthew Banman, age 11, Elm Creek School

Fig. 3.14. Matthew had the patience required to faithfully reproduce the texture of this iguana. The pencil marks form an intricate pattern on the paper.

Appropriate Subjects

Appropriate subjects for drawing texture have an interesting surface. Some examples include a photograph or accurate model of an alligator, a scaly fish, a furry fox, a prickly cactus, and a wrinkled face (figs. 3.13 and 3.14).

Pattern

Pattern, in drawing, refers to repeated shapes or repeated areas of color. The spots on a leopard, colors on a butterfly, and stripes on a tiger are all examples of patterns. Often the challenge for students is to see the *variety* in the pattern. Leopards' spots aren't circular, but are shaped like irregular paw prints. The black triangles on the butterfly's wing may vary in size. The stripes on a tiger are not composed of regular, vertical lines, but of irregular, curved shapes with "fuzzy" edges (fig. 3.15). Students are apt to see the pattern, but not the differences within it.

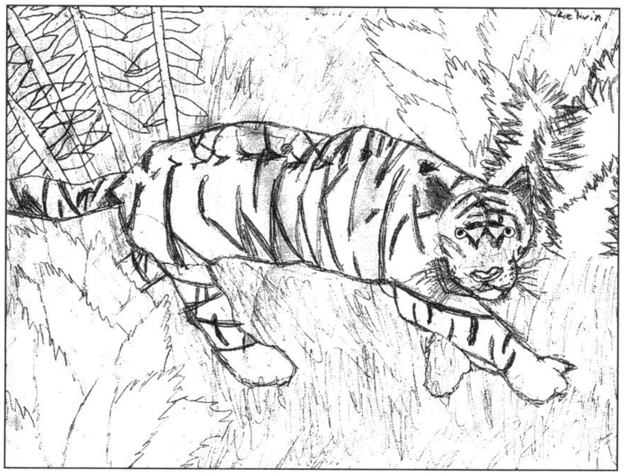

Tiger, pencil on paper, Kelvin Thielman, age 10, Elm Creek School

Fig. 3.15. Kelvin has accurately drawn in the contours and patterns of the tiger.

Appropriate Subjects

Interesting subjects for drawing patterns—besides leopards, butterflies, and tigers—include buildings (the windows form a geometric pattern), some kinds of tropical fish, insects, and tropical plants.

Method for Texture and Pattern

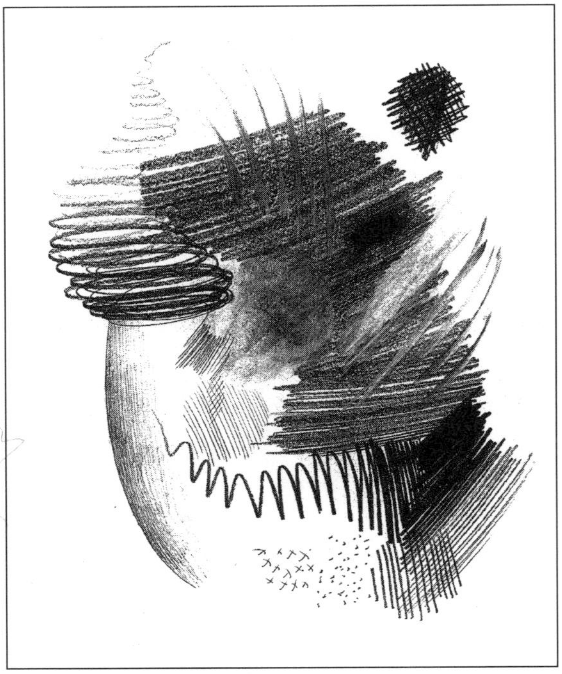

pencil marks, Noni Brynjolson, age 12, Luxton School

Fig. 3.16. Noni has experimented with a variety of pencil and eraser marks.

Look at *The Lazy Bear* with your students. Ask them: "The paper that the bear is printed on is smooth to touch, so how does the artist let us know that the bear is furry?" Also point out the areas of colorful geometric patterns that decorate parts of Wildsmith's illustrations.

Ask students to describe the textures and patterns of the subjects they are going to draw, and to think about what kinds of marks they might make with their pencils to show those textures and patterns in their drawings. Have them try out different kinds of marks in their sketchbooks. For texture, students can try dots, parallel lines ("hatching"), intersecting lines ("crosshatching"), small *x*s, shading with the sides of their pencils, and making light marks by running the edge of an eraser through areas that have been shaded (fig. 3.16). Drawing patterns may require drawing the outlines of repeated shapes.

Other Exercises

Here are additional exercises your students can do to build their awareness of texture and pattern:

- Try crayon rubbings. Place white photocopy paper over a hard, bumpy surface and rub with the side of a crayon. Lego, window screens, Pegboard, corrugated cardboard, and tree bark are good examples of objects that have bumpy surfaces. Rubbing over the textured surface will leave a pattern on the paper. Rubbings can be done in the classroom or outdoors.
- Impress textures (burlap, mesh bags, buttons, plastic forks, and so on) into clay or Plasticine.
- Have someone place an assortment of objects in a blind "touch box." Reach into the box and describe the objects by feel.
- Place an assortment of objects in a pail and have students arrange them into patterns on a table or glue the objects to paper. Long strips of paper work well for patterns. The strips can be tacked along the edge of bulletin boards for border designs.
- Sort objects or photographs by texture category (for example, rough, furry, smooth) and describe the textures.
- Sketch, sample, and describe the textures of various foods.

More exercises for teaching an understanding of pattern can be found in most elementary math curricula.

Value

Value refers to the light and dark colors on a subject, as well as to the areas of reflected light and shadow. Adding shading and highlights will make a subject appear three-dimensional—as if it has *volume*. Discerning areas of light and dark values is a necessary skill to have before tackling the extra challenge of working in color.

Appropriate Subjects

For value drawings, black-and-white photos (from magazines, calendars, and so on) are the easiest subjects. Many have bright lights and dark shadows. Most young students and those inexperienced in art can draw light and dark patterns (like stripes on a zebra), but may find areas of reflected lights and shadows difficult to discern. Advanced students can work from color photographs that have obvious light and dark values.

Method

Have your students look at *Jumanji* and notice where parts of the drawing are white, gray, or black. Ask them to guess what the light source is (sunlight, a lamp, candlelight, and so on).

Shadows can become an important part of a picture's content. Find interesting shadows in picture books such as *The Night Rebecca Stayed Too Late* and *The Magic Paintbrush*. How do these shadows affect the mood of the picture?

Begin by having students make a value chart (or "gray scale"). They can do this by drawing a long rectangle divided into boxes, and shading each successive box darker than the one before it—from very light pressure on the pencil to very firm, black marks (fig. 3.17).

Next, ask students to notice the light and dark values on their subject. Have them draw a portion of their subject in their sketchbook and practice shading in the darker values. If the drawing becomes too dark, students can "draw" highlights with their erasers; that is, use an edge of the eraser to lighten areas of the picture.

Other Exercises

Have students do some of the following exercises to build their awareness of light and dark values:

- Look at picture books that show night scenes. Notice how changing the light source changes the atmosphere or mood of the picture. Describe or draw how the atmosphere or mood changes.

Books to Have Handy

Picture Books
Jumanji
The Magic Paintbrush
The Night Rebecca Stayed Too Late

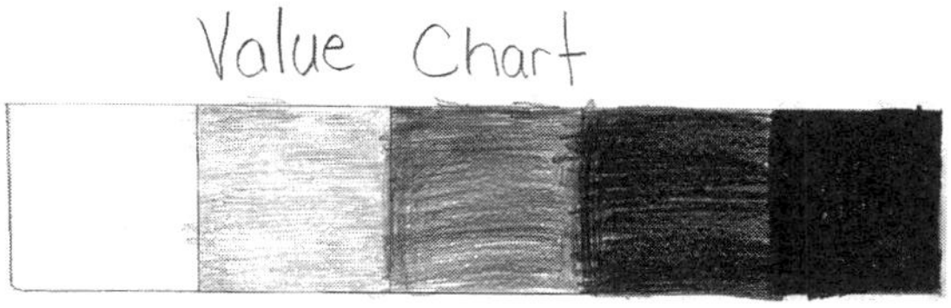

pencil on paper, grade 6 student, Luxton School

Fig. 3.17. A value chart ("gray scale") is a good warm-up exercise for drawing with a variety of light and dark colors.

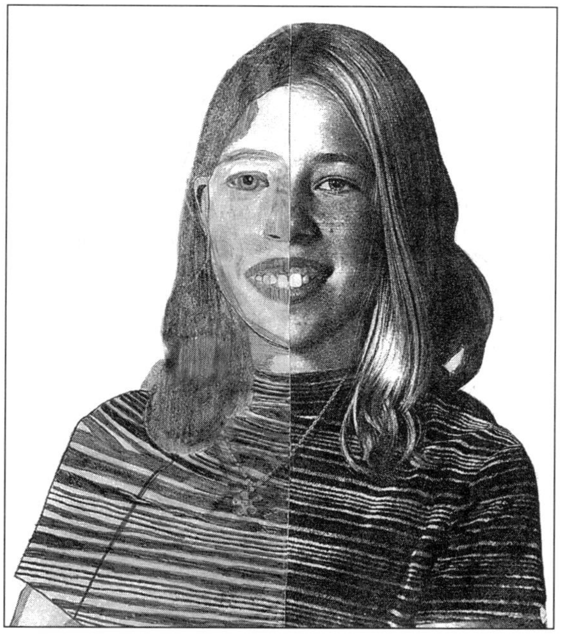

Self-portrait, photocopy and pencil on paper, Pamela Greenwood, grade 6, Treherne Elementary School

Fig. 3.18. Half of Pamela's picture is a photocopy of her school photograph; the other half is a pencil drawing. She has done a careful job of matching the values in her photocopy.

Tip: If students are drawing "from life" (for example, an actual object on their desk, a hard-boiled egg, or a stack of white geometric volumes such as cubes, spheres, cones) values will be difficult to see in diffused light. Set the objects on a white piece of paper. Then turn off the overhead lights and use sunlight, or aim a desk lamp at the object, to provide more obvious light and shadow.

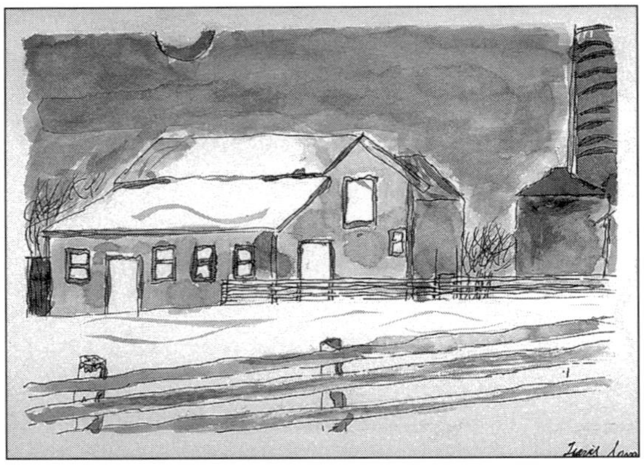

ink and wash drawing, Travis Spence, age 14, San Antonio School

Fig. 3.19. This black, white, and gray study of a landscape was done as a preliminary to a watercolor painting. Travis, an advanced student, picked out the light and dark values from a color photograph.

- Try a value drawing with white chalk on black paper, with charcoal and chalk on gray paper, with white and black paint on gray paper, or with black paint and varying amounts of water (for a "wash" drawing) on white paper (fig. 3.19).
- Make hand shadows (for example, hold up two fingers for rabbit ears) with the overhead projector and trace the resulting shadows onto paper. Fill in with paint or decorate the silhouette of the subject.
- Make shadow puppets (see chapter 7).
- Shine a flashlight on simple geometric volumes such as a sphere, cube, and pyramid, or small toys or models. Predict where the edges of shadow will fall. Sketch the results.

Combining Basic Elements

Students are now ready to combine shape, line, texture, pattern, and value into a single drawing (fig. 3.20). Explain that an artist normally begins a drawing with simple geometric shapes (the rough "blueprint" for the drawing), carefully adds a line drawing over the shapes, then adds texture marks or pattern, and, finally, light and dark values. All together, this is "how to draw." A challenging subject will display all the elements. Students might try a complete drawing of a variety of subjects. These drawings take time. You may want to allow several short sessions for combined drawings.

You may also want to introduce your students to works by a variety of visual artists and illustrators. Ask the students which elements of drawing are used or emphasized in the works. (The picture books listed in this chapter are a good beginning.)

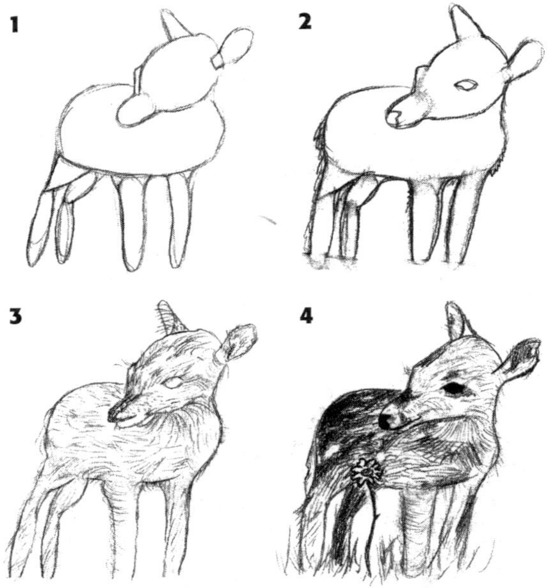

Fawn, pencil on paper, Noni Brynjolson, age 11

Fig. 3.20. These successive drawings show how **(1)** shape, **(2)** line, **(3)** texture and pattern, and **(4)** value are added in the progression of a finished drawing.

Enrichment

- Draw a picture with mystery or humor. Look at *The Mysteries of Harris Burdick* or *Changes* with your students. Discuss how the illustrator made the pictures interesting by combining unrelated subjects, like turning a bicycle wheel into an apple, into one drawing. Have students use magazine photos or a combination of landscape photos and real objects to find two unrelated subjects to draw. When the subjects are combined, they should be mysterious or funny. Students may want to do a small, quick pencil drawing in their sketchbooks first to see how the separate elements look together. This may be used as a starting point for creative writing.

Books to Have Handy

Picture Books
Changes
The Mysteries of Harris Burdick

Space

Space does not fit sequentially with the other elements of drawing. Shape, line, texture, pattern, and value deal more typically with drawing particular subjects or pieces of the background. The considerations of space have more to do with drawing the environment or background of the picture, and with where and how the subjects or parts of subjects will be placed in the picture. For example, an illustrator will design a character first—building the image with shape, line, texture, pattern, and value—and then begin designing the whole scene, including considerations of space, into which the character and other main items may be traced or redrawn. The image is then "finished" in the medium of the illustrator's choice—for example, paint, pencil crayon, or ink.

Books to Have Handy

Picture Books

How the Animals Got Their Colors
If You're Not From the Prairie
Zoom Away

Ways to Achieve an Illusion of Depth

In a drawing, space refers to the area surrounding the subject(s) in the picture, the relation of nearer and farther parts of the subject, and to the illusion of depth. On a flat, two-dimensional piece of paper, an illusion of depth is created in the following ways:

- *Size and Placement:* To show the distance between subjects, one object may be drawn larger and placed near the bottom of the page, while another in the distance may be a mere dot placed higher on the page.
- *Overlapping:* Some parts of the picture may overlap others—for example, one building may be in front of (and partly obscuring) the building behind it (fig. 3.21).
- *Volume:* Volume can be defined as the amount of space that an object occupies. Shading and highlighting in lighter and darker values add a sense of volume to a subject and background pieces. Objects appear three-dimensional, rather than flat on the paper (fig. 3.22).
- *Foreshortening:* A foreshortened view of an elephant's trunk, for example, will give a sense of its length. The trunk is wide at the tip where it is closest to the viewer, and it "recedes" into the faraway distance of the elephant's head—just like the road in the single-point perspective drawing on page 40.
- *Color:* The parts of the landscape that are in the far distance tend to take on a bluish tinge and have paler, less intense color. A color may be reduced (mixed with its complement), paled (tinted), or cooled (mixed with blue) to make it appear to have faded into the distance (see chapter 8).
- *Flat or Shallow Spaces:* Sometimes, a decision is made by the artist to create a flat or shallow space by reversing the above choices; that is, by using bright colors throughout, placing objects

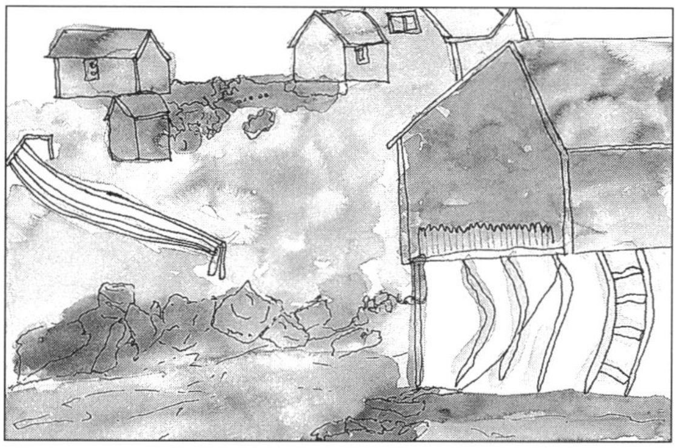

Landscape, watercolor and ink on paper, John Madina, age 10, Wellington School

Fig. 3.21. In this drawing, John used overlapping to achieve an illusion of depth. The building that is close-up is larger. It is placed lower down on the page and overlaps one of the buildings in the background.

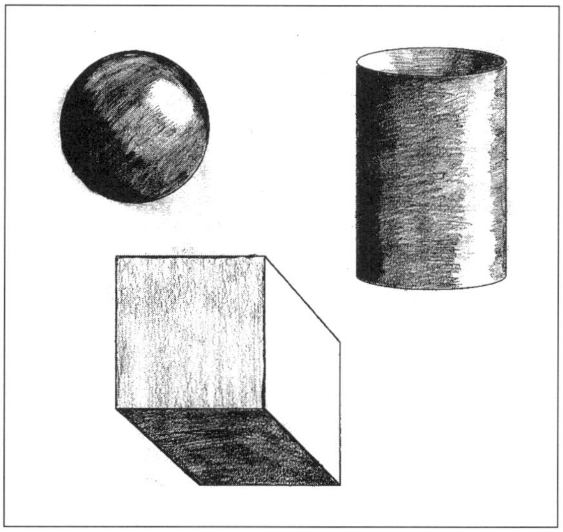

pencil on paper, Katie MacSwain, age 15, Wanipigow School

Fig. 3.22. Katie shaded these volumes with pencil to produce the light and dark values that make them appear three-dimensional.

side by side instead of overlapping, and so on. In many other cultures, pictorial space is conventionally shallow or flat. This causes the images to appear as an overall pattern rather than to "stand out" from the background. See *How The Animals Got Their Colors*.

- *Perspective:* Perspective simply means a point of view. European Renaissance art developed a view from a single point in space —a trick used to indicate depth and distance. This technique is used especially in architectural drawings.

Perspective

Tip: Encourage students to use dotted lines instead of solid lines to connect to the vanishing point. These will make the end product look less confusing.

Drawing perspective involves teaching some "tricks" and conventions. It is, therefore, worth going through them step by step. These may be too difficult for very young students. Try single-point perspective beginning in about grade three. You can teach two-point perspective beginning in grade five.

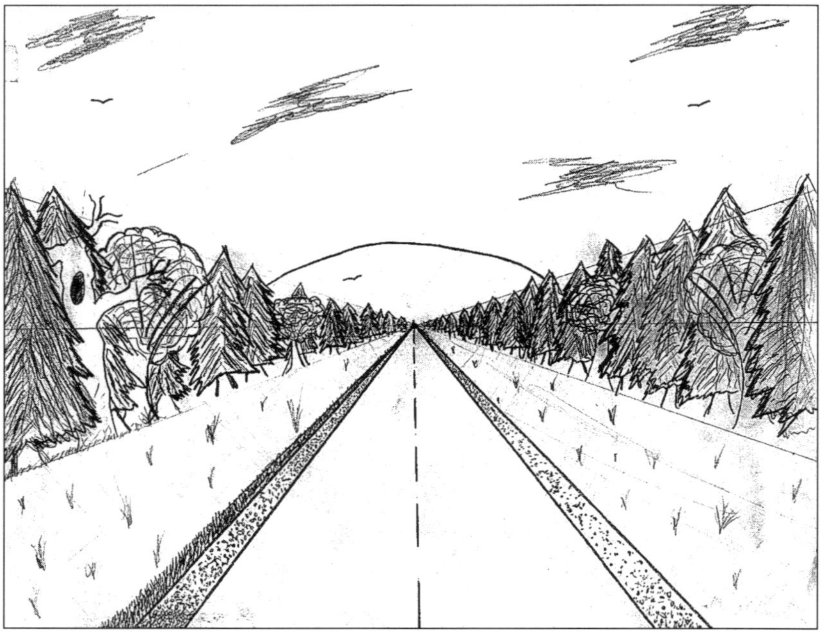

Road to Hollow Water, pencil on paper, Steven Bird, age 15, Wanipigow School

Fig. 3.23. This drawing makes use of single-point perspective. The height and width of all the elements of the picture (road, verge, and trees) are determined by lines radiating from one point on the horizon.

Single-Point Perspective

Tip: For extreme perspective, place vanishing points close together. For more gradual (normal) views, place the vanishing points as far apart as possible. Students may want to place the vanishing points off the page, on the far edges of their desk, and tape their paper to the desktop.

Start by looking at *If You're Not From the Prairie*, or taking your students outside. Point out that roads, sidewalks, telephone poles, and fence posts appear to be different heights or widths, depending on how close or far away they are from you. Ask students to look at the people or large objects close to them (in the picture book or along the street) and to notice how they must look down to see the bottoms of these people and objects, and that the people and objects appear to be quite large. Now, have your students look for the horizon line (the place where the earth and the sky meet) and notice that faraway objects (near the horizon line) appear smaller and higher up in their field of vision than objects that are near.

The simplest way for your students to start a single-point perspective drawing is to have them draw a road that is going to disappear into the distance. Have them do the following.

1. Draw a straight line (also referred to as a horizon line) horizontally across the center of a piece of paper.
2. Make a dot, called a "vanishing point," along this line near the middle of the page.
3. Make two dots, at least 3" (8 cm) apart, along the bottom edge of the page. (These dots determine how wide the road will be.)
4. Take a ruler and connect each of the two dots to the vanishing point on the horizon. (That's a road, vanishing into the distance).
5. Near the bottom of the page, off to one side, draw a large fence post.
6. Use a ruler to draw lines connecting the top and bottom of the post to the vanishing point. (Tell your students they are going to draw a fence and that the lines they just drew will determine the height and placement of all the poles in the fence.)
7. Draw a fence. Posts appear to be closer together as they recede into the distance, so that is how they should be drawn in the picture (figs. 3.23 and 3.24).

Tip: Before having your students do their own two-point perspective drawing, show them how on the chalkboard. Have them follow you step by step. Initially, this will merely be an exercise in following directions. Once they catch on, they can begin to transform the cubes into buildings, or attempt architectural drawings from photographs or field trips.

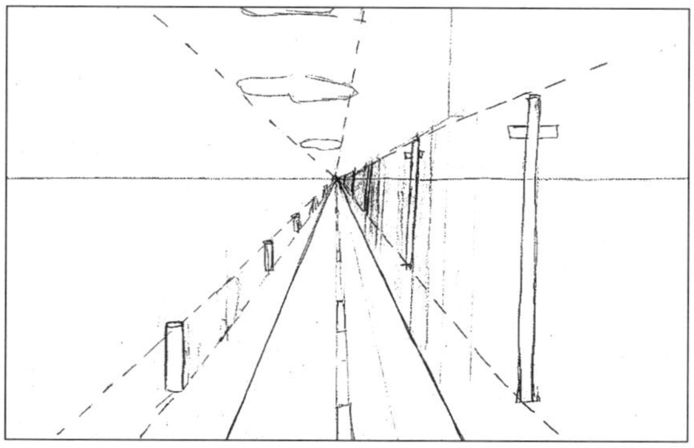

Noni Brynjolson, age 11

Fig. 3.24. Single-point perspective

Two-Point Perspective

Single-point perspective is adequate for many scenes, and is helpful in deciding where to place subjects that are closer to or farther from the viewer. But for architectural drawing—exterior faces and interior details—two-point perspective is required to represent the angles as we see them.

For two-point perspective drawings, begin by having students look at a three-dimensional cube (some math manipulative sets contain large cubes). Point out that although each side is a square with parallel edges and right angles, when the cube is turned slightly some of the edges appear to change direction (they no longer appear horizontal). Look at *Zoom Away* with your students. Notice the lines where the walls meet the ceiling or floor. Ask: "Are the lines horizontal on the page, or do they appear tilted?" Remind students that how something looks depends on where they stand, and how they look at it. Now, on a new piece of paper, have your students do the following:

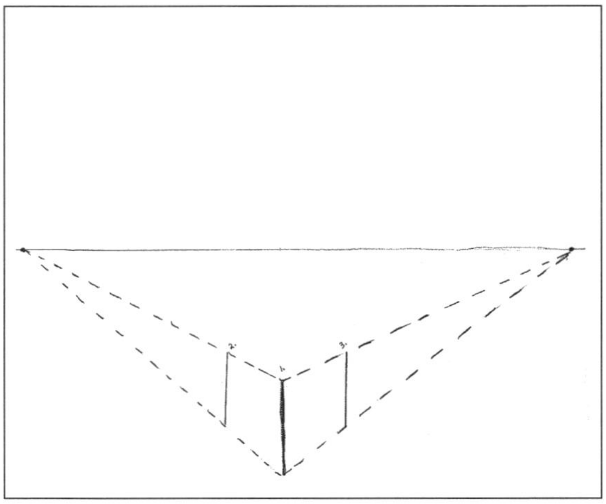

Noni Brynjolson, age 11

Fig. 3.25. Two-point perspective, step one

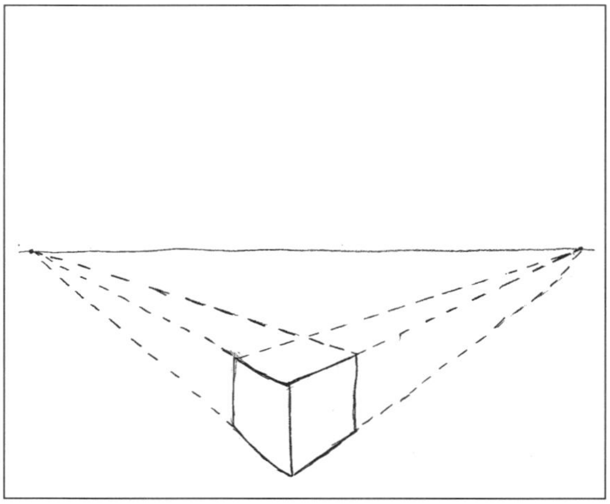

Noni Brynjolson, age 11

Fig. 3.26. Two-point perspective, step two

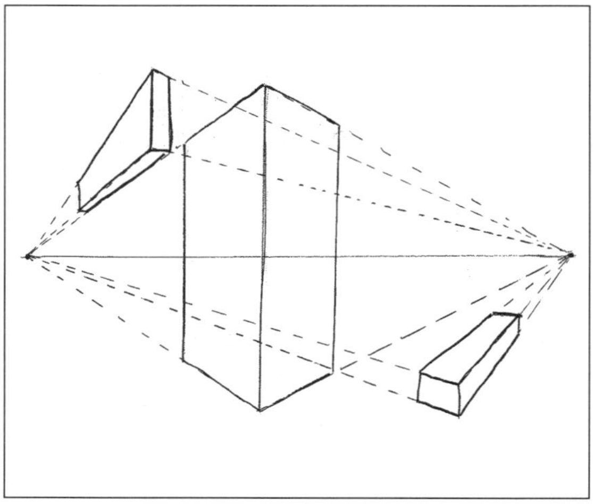

Noni Brynjolson, age 11

Fig. 3.27. The placement of the vanishing points on the horizon, and the height and placement of the first vertical line, will affect the shapes and views of the blocks.

1. Draw a horizon line across the center of the page.
2. Place one dot on the far left, along the horizon line, and another on the far right (these are the vanishing points).
3. Draw a 3" (8 cm) vertical line somewhere near the center of the page, below the horizon line.
4. Connect the top and bottom of this line to each vanishing point.
5. Draw two vertical lines—one to the left and one to the right of the 3" (8 cm) vertical line. The heights of these lines will be determined by where they are placed within the connecting lines (fig. 3.25).
6. Draw a line from the top of the vertical line on the left over to the vanishing point on the right. Draw a line from the top of the vertical line on the right over to the vanishing point on the left. These lines will form the back edges of the cube (fig. 3.26).

Note: The placement of the vertical lines and the distance between the two vanishing points will affect the shape that you end up with (fig. 3.27). If the two lines are equal distance from the vanishing points, you will have a cube. Otherwise, you will have a rectangular prism (a long box).

Students may not want to go through this lengthy process every time they draw a picture. Now that they have experienced how linear perspective works, they may prefer to carefully look-draw their subject and then check and adjust their angles afterwards using the above methods.

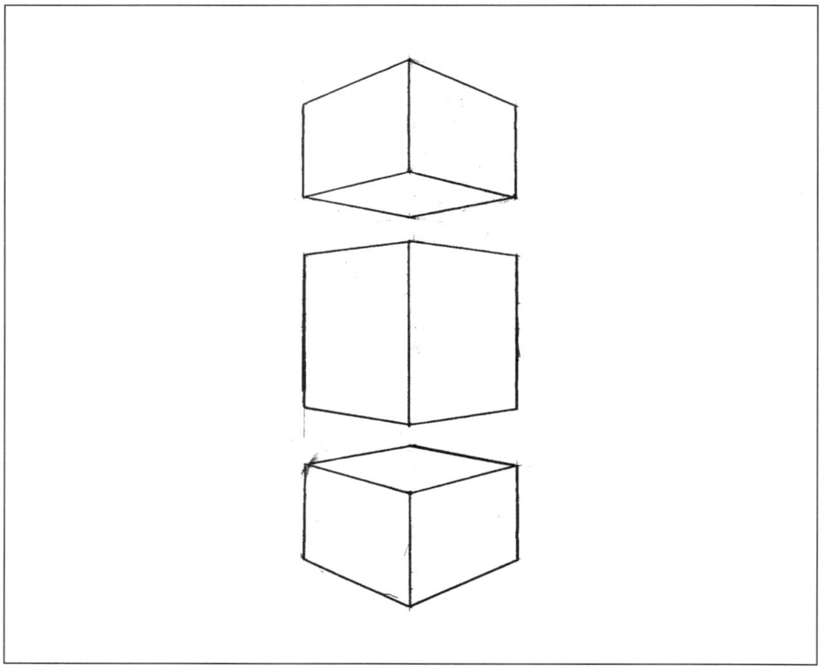

pencil on paper, Rachel Bushie, age 14, Wanipigow School

Fig. 3.28. Blocks drawn with two-point perspective

Using Cutouts

Another useful way to teach perspective, combined with other basic considerations of space, is to have students work with cutout subjects. They can do this by placing the cutouts on the background or landscape that may have been drawn with single- or two-point perspective.

To start, have students draw animals, people, or objects on a piece of paper. Photocopy these several times, reducing or enlarging each time, then cut out each shape. Prepare an envelope for each student and put the cutout pieces in the envelopes for safekeeping (see chapter 4, pages 53–57).

Remind your students about perspective and have them draw a background for the pieces.

Students may then take the cutout drawings from their envelopes and place them according to the same principles as above; that is, place large pieces near the bottom of the page, and place smaller pieces closer to the horizon line so they look farther away (fig. 3.29).

Now, just for fun, have students place the pieces to create an "impossible" picture (fig. 3.30) or a picture with shallow space.

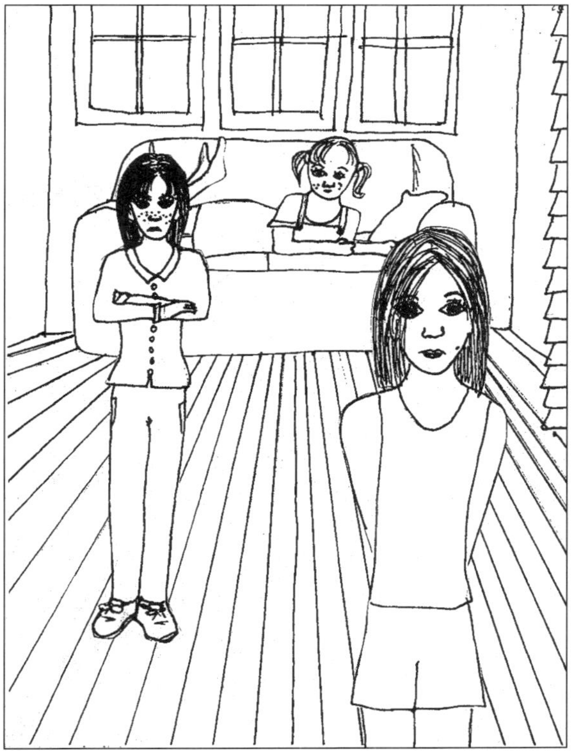

photocopies/cut and paste, Noni Brynjolson, age 11

Fig. 3.29. These cutouts were placed on the background drawing with the objective of creating as much depth as possible. The large figure is placed lowest on the page. The medium-size figure overlaps the small figure reclining in the background.

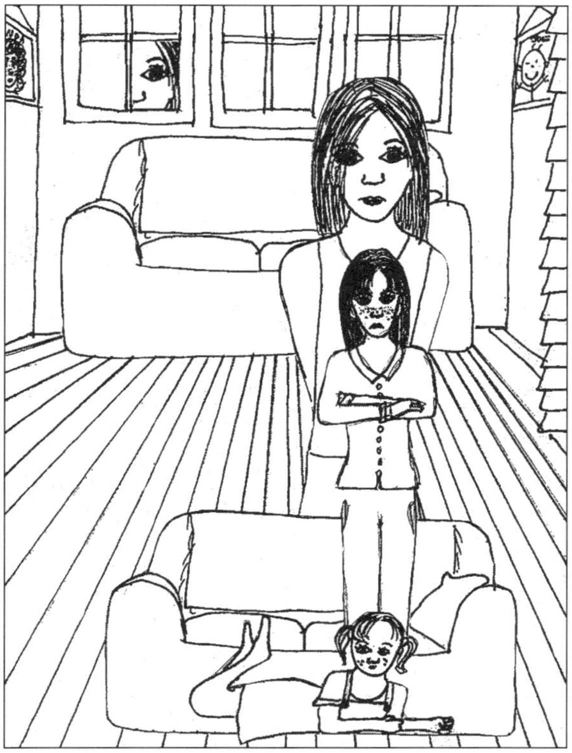

photocopies/cut and paste, Noni Brynjolson, age 11

Fig. 3.30. These figures were arranged to make an "impossible" picture. The distortion of space makes the viewer's eye linger on the picture, trying to make sense of the space.

Enrichment

- Try architectural drawings of buildings in your neighborhood (fig. 3.31).

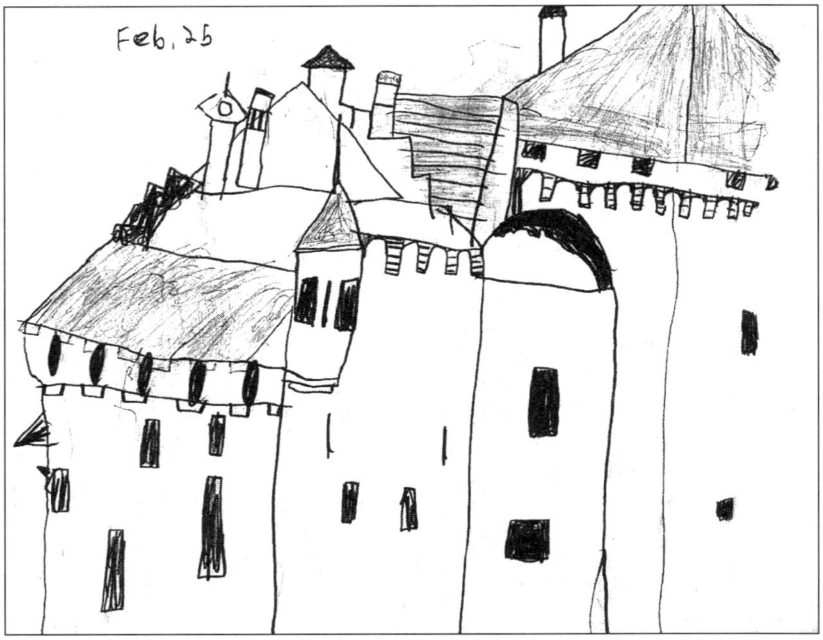

Castle, pencil on paper, Iain Brynjolson, grade 3 student, Luxton School

Fig. 3.31. This young artist looked carefully at a photograph of a castle to do this architectural drawing.

Vocabulary (see appendixes for definitions)

blind contour
contour
crosshatching
depth
field of vision
foreshorten
form
geometric shapes
hatching
highlights
horizon line
horizontal
line
line qualities
look-drawing
negative space
overlap
pattern
perspective
scale
scribble-drawing
shading
shape
solid
space
still life
tanagrams
texture
value
value chart
vanishing point
vertical
volume
wash drawing

4
Drawing Media

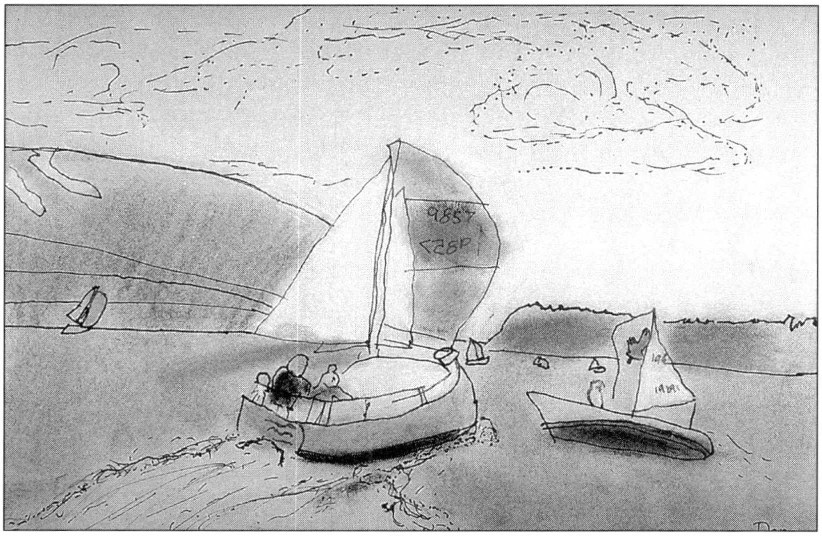

Sailing, ink and soft pastel, Dana Patrick, grade 4, Wellington School

Fig. 4.1. Using a very fine-tipped marker, Dana created an interesting variety of lines. He later used soft (chalk) pastels to add light and dark values.

Introduction

In this chapter, students will learn how to draw with media other than pencil on paper. Whether they are using ink, charcoal, or chalk, the techniques are really just extensions of the drawing techniques they learned in chapter 3. Students will also use multiple images, and add cut-and-paste and retracing techniques in the drawing process. These techniques give them more choices about the placement and overlapping of pieces in their drawings.

The ability to use different media offers students a variety of possibilities and challenges. These include:

- opportunities to revisit, in depth, some of the basic elements of drawing
- ways to produce more dramatic and "finished" end products that are not possible with a pencil drawing (see Part 4 for information on color media for drawing and painting)
- new tools to experiment with and fresh ways to draw familiar subjects, which help to maintain students' interest in drawing

Books to Have Handy

Picture Books

Alexander, Who Used to be Rich Last Tuesday
Chicken Little (and other books illustrated by Steven Kellogg)
The House at Pooh Corner
Where the Wild Things Are
Would They Love a Lion?

Materials

- sketchbooks
- paper (white photocopy paper, 8½" x 11" or 11" x 17"; 21.5 cm x 28 cm or 28 cm x 43 cm)
- pencils
- erasers
- pens ("ultra-fine"-tipped, black markers labeled "nontoxic"; some markers for overhead projectors fit this description)
- drawing nibs ("crow quill")
- small containers of nontoxic ink (these produce a scratchier, drippy line)
- paint smocks (ink may stain clothing)
- optional: penholders; white Mayfair paper, or neutral colors of construction paper; soft (chalk) pastels

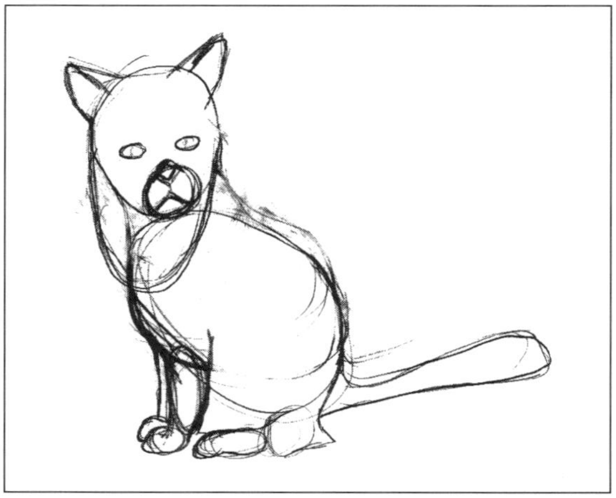

pencil sketch, Noni Brynjolson, age 11

Fig. 4.2. When students do quick practice sketches in their notebooks, they find drawing is easier when they are ready to start their good copies.

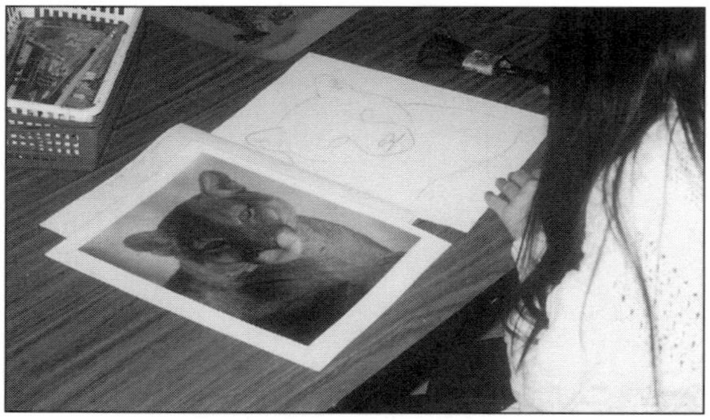

grade 4 student, Luxton School

Fig. 4.3. Students should begin their good copy with a careful look-drawing of their subject on a large piece of paper. They should pay attention to the geometric shapes and contours of the subject.

Drawing with Ink

In an ink drawing, the marks are much blacker and more obvious—and much less erasable—than those used in a pencil drawing. For some students, this may be a problem. They may become overcautious and fearful of mistakes when they work with a permanent medium. You can, however, turn this into an advantage. Students learn that mistakes can be drawn over or incorporated into the drawing. The inkblot on the page might become a rabbit; the "wrong" line around the subject might be emphasized or turned into a shadow.

Drawing in ink helps students become more aware of and interested in individual marks and line qualities. The black marks and lines produced by ink can emphasize the texture and pattern in a drawing. This often compensates for other weaknesses in a student's ability to produce an aesthetically pleasing piece of work. The student is likely to be satisifed with and gain confidence by the result.

Preparation

Before starting this exercise, collect visual references—magazine photos, calendar photos, books, and objects. Students can use these for their main subjects and settings.

It may be helpful to plan to do this exercise over several drawing sessions on different days. Have students practice drawing their subjects on the first day. The next day, they can draw the "good copy," experiment with pens, and add ink to the good copy. This approach may be especially helpful for students with shorter attention spans.

Appropriate Subjects

Appropriate subjects for texture drawings have interesting surfaces. Some suggestions are alligator skin, fish scales, fox fur, sweaters, and cactus. Visual references should be close-up photos, with a clear picture of surface detail (see page 34).

Method

Using pencils, have students try some practice sketches of their subject in their sketchbooks. Practice drawings should be small (maximum 4" x 4"/10 cm x 10 cm). Students can begin with scribble-drawing, or they can try drawing the geometric shapes they see in their subjects.

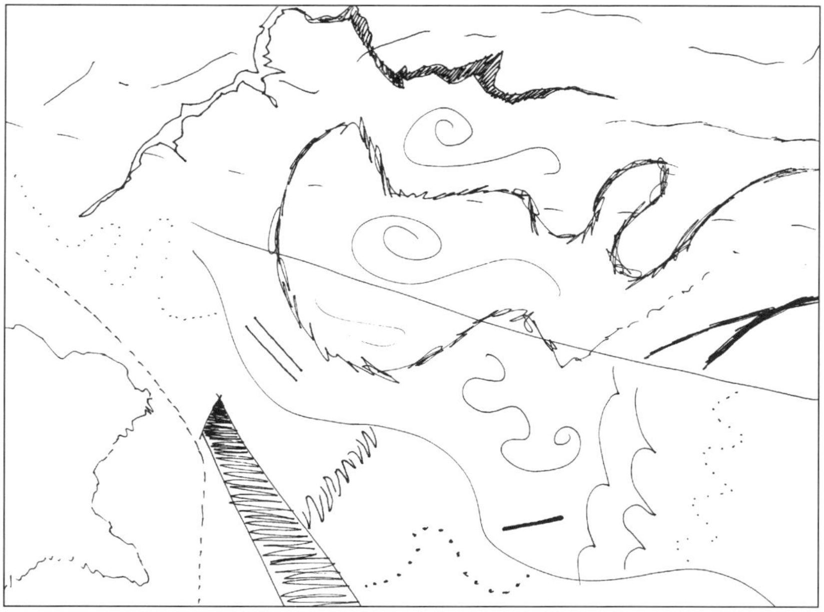

grade 6 student, Luxton School

Fig. 4.4. Trying a variety of lines

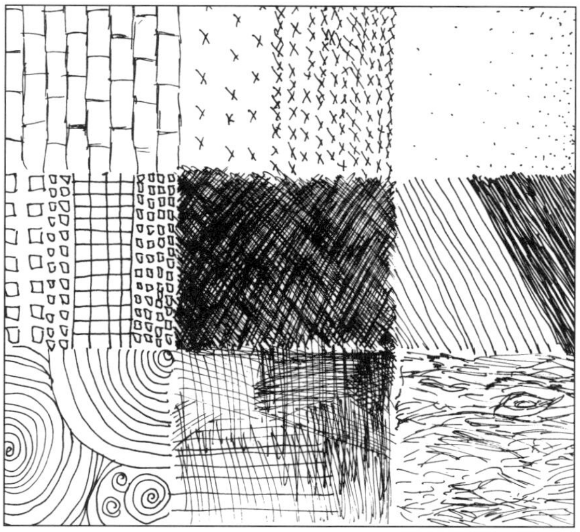

grade 6 student, Luxton School

Fig. 4.5. Filling a page with a variety of lines and patterns

Tip: Caution students to work slowly with the pens. The ink marks are not erasable.

For an intensive drawing class, or if students are having difficulty with their drawings, review chapter 3.

When students are comfortable with their practice sketches (fig. 4.2), have them use pencil to sketch their subject and background onto large sheets of paper. Remind them to draw their subject large enough to fill the page. While they are doing these pencil drawings, they should pay attention to the shape and contours of their subject (fig. 4.3). However, they should avoid "shading in" areas with pencil. Have them set aside their drawings when they are done.

Students are now ready to begin experimenting with ink. Like pencil drawing, ink drawing uses line, pattern, and texture. Small, close marks are used to produce areas of dark value.

Show *Chicken Little* to your students. Have them note the interesting qualities of the lines—straight or wobbly, thick or fine, broken or smooth. With their pens, students may wish to quickly try drawing these kinds of lines in their sketchbooks (fig. 4.4).

Review with students the kinds of marks they might make with their drawing pens to show the textures of their subject (see page 36). Look at the pen marks, including the overlaid parallel lines called "crosshatching," in *Where the Wild Things Are*, *Chicken Little*, *The House at Pooh Corner*, and *Alexander, Who Used to Be Rich Last Tuesday*. Have students try out different kinds of marks—dots, *x*s, repeated lines, hatching, and crosshatching—in their sketchbooks (fig. 4.5).

Now, have students add texture marks to their larger drawings (fig. 4.6). Explain to them that the closer the marks, the darker the value. When their subject is a light color, they should make texture marks farther apart.

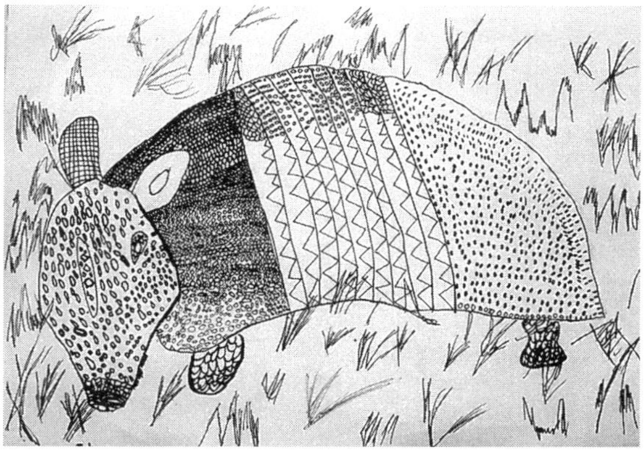

Armadillo, fine-tipped marker on paper, grade 4 student, Luxton School

Fig. 4.6. This student used a variety of marks and patterns to represent the animal's texture. The initial drawing must be large enough to allow for adding interior detail.

Tip: Pen nibs that have been dipped in ink produce a scratchy, often blotchy, line. If students touch the tip of the pen to scrap paper after dipping it in ink, they may be able to reduce blobs and drips.

Tip: Too much chalk pastel will make the ink lines fade or disappear; over-rubbing with the Kleenex will cause chalk to disappear and ink lines to fade.

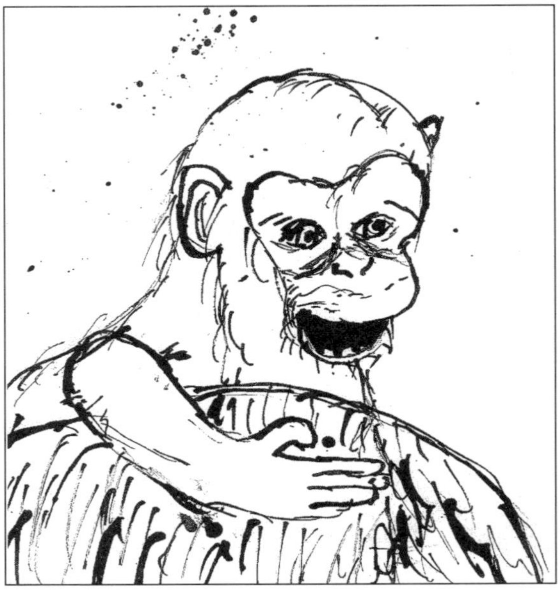

Chimp, ink drawing, Noni Brynjolson, age 11

Fig. 4.7. Drawing with a twig dipped in ink resulted in interesting, irregular, blobby lines in this piece.

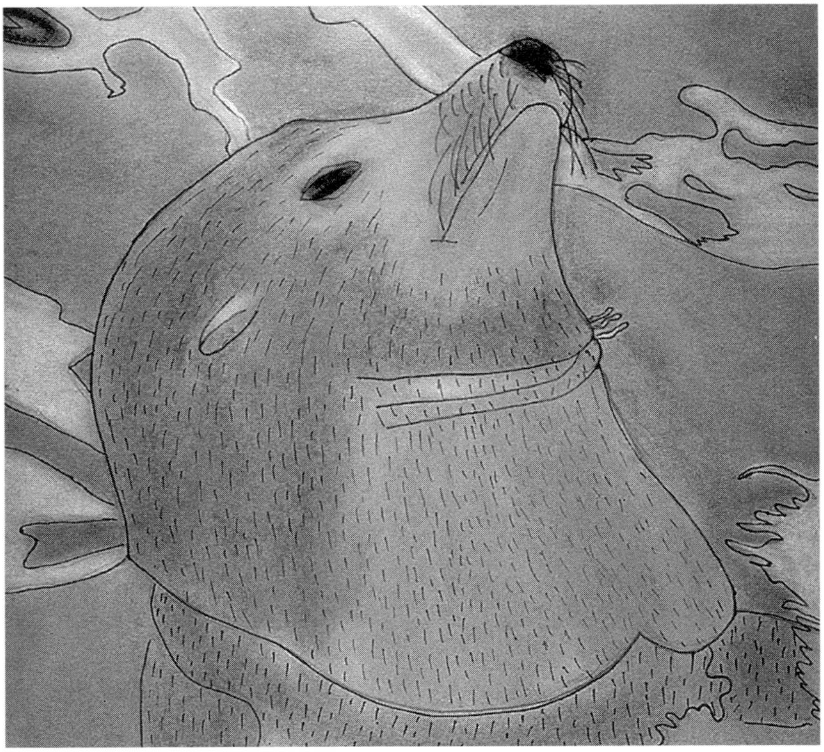

Sea Lion, fine-tipped marker with soft pastel, Alexis-Lee Tahimic, grade 5, Wellington School

Fig. 4.8. Color can be added to a drawing with soft (chalk) pastels.

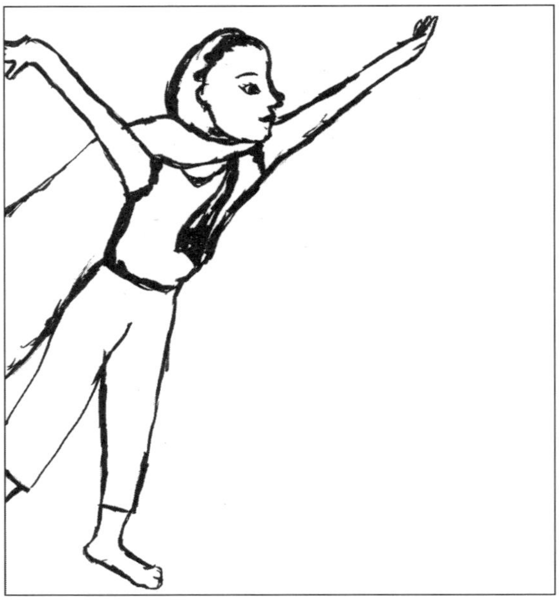

Dancer, ink drawing, Noni Brynjolson, age 11

Fig. 4.9. Drawing with a paintbrush dipped in ink allowed for more variation in the width of lines.

Tip: For easy clean-up, use "washable" drawing ink or watery black tempera paint. Wash pen nibs thoroughly after use, to avoid clogging.

Enrichment

- On Mayfair or construction paper, try chalk (or soft) pastels on top of an ink drawing (fig. 4.8). Work with a small amount of chalk at a time, wiping and blending colors with a Kleenex. Encourage students to mix colors (for example, yellow-green, brown-green), rather than to use colors straight from the box. (See chapter 8.) If students need a darker shade of a color, suggest they mix brown or dark blue with the color, rather than black (too much black will make all the colors appear gray). To prevent a lot of smudging, draw in the lightest colors first, then the medium values, and the dark colors last. Spray with fixative after students have left for the day, or laminate, photograph, or place in plastic sleeves to preserve drawings and prevent smudging.
- For an interesting, wobbly line quality, use a penholder and a variety of nibs dipped in ink, or sharpened twigs of different diameters dipped in ink (figs. 4.7 and 4.9). Use these techniques on a drawing that isn't too precious (students may not admire the ink drips and blotches on a drawing that took them hours to complete).
- Use ink drawings in a series of illustrations. Work small (4" x 4" or 10 cm x 10 cm) pieces of paper, or photocopy elements of the drawing and cut and paste them together. For example, make multiple copies of the main character, cut and paste onto new paper, and draw in a new scene on each piece of paper.

Students could also photocopy the setting and redraw the character in a different pose (see page 53).

- If students have used permanent ink in their drawings and Dessin or Mayfair paper, they can use a wash of watercolor paint on top (fig. 4.10). (See chapter 11.) A premixed solution of watery tempera paint can also be used (fig. 4.11) to wash over areas of the drawing (test the ink first to ensure that it really is permanent). Look at *Would They Love a Lion?*. Discuss how the color doesn't always follow carefully inside the lines.

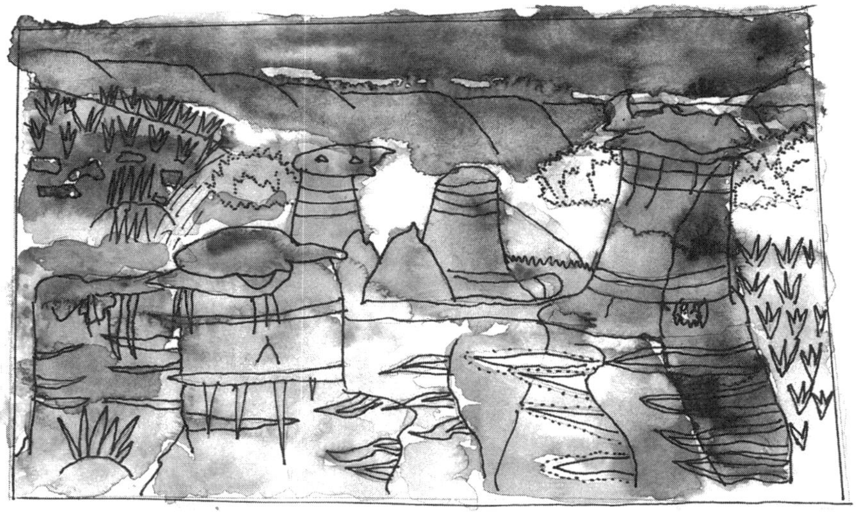

Landscape, watercolor and ink, Marc, grade 4, Wellington School

Fig. 4.10. A variety of zigzag, wobbly, and dotted lines define this watercolor painting of rock formations.

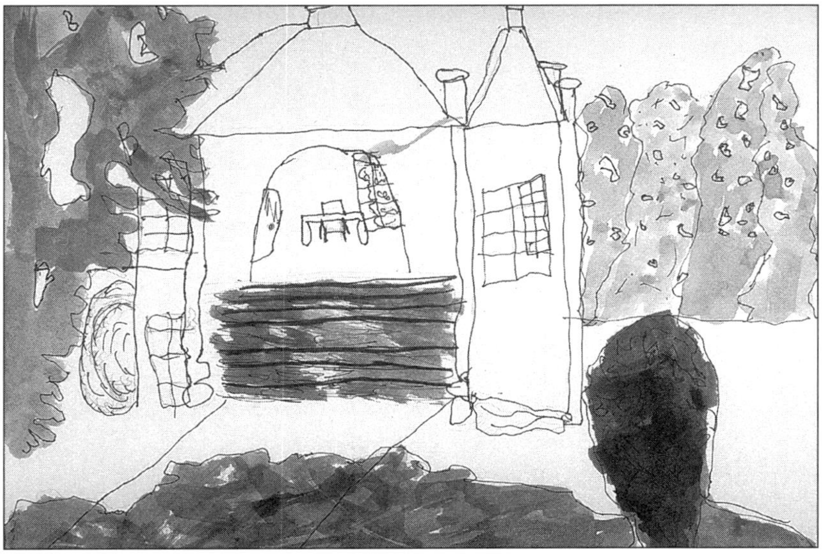

ink and wash drawing, Nicole Hammerstedt, age 12, San Antonio School

Fig. 4.11. A wobbly line drawing with a wash of diluted black paint makes for an interesting—and commonly used—illustration technique.

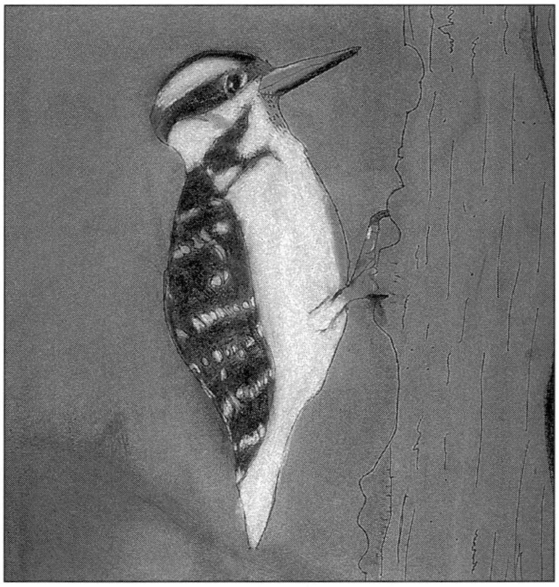

Woodpecker, ink and chalk, Dalene, grade 5, Wellington School

Fig. 4.12. Although Dalene used a black pen for her initial lines, the strength of the drawing is in the contrast between light and dark values that were added with chalk and charcoal.

Materials

- "vine" charcoal (good for initial sketches and finer lines)
- "compressed" charcoal (produces a true black line)
- white chalk
- gray "sugar" paper, construction paper, or brown butcher's paper (or paper designated for use with charcoal; make sure it has a soft or textured surface and is a neutral color)
- Kleenex
- "kneaded" erasers
- spray fixative (keep in locked cupboard; do not use when students are present; use in well-ventilated area) (See appendix D.)

Books to Have Handy

Picture Books
Jumanji
The Magic Paintbrush

Tip: Young students and those inexperienced in art may be able to draw light and dark colors (like stripes on a zebra), but may find reflected light and shadow difficult. Start them with subjects that have very obvious shadows.

Tip: Even a "black" bear may have sunlight reflecting on its back to make it appear white; a zebra has a dark and light pattern, and may also have a shadow on its belly.

Charcoal and Chalk

Charcoal and chalk are excellent media for studying value because of the dramatic light and dark effects they can produce. The resulting drawings are soft-edged; shape and value rather than line and detail are emphasized.

Charcoal and chalk smudge and rub out easily. This may frustrate careful students who strive for perfection in their work. On the other hand, it may help to coax them into a more relaxed drawing style, with soft edges that are drawn and redrawn. You might find it helps to call these drawings "studies." Explain that a study is different from a finished drawing. It is usually a piece of a subject rather than a whole scene, has unfinished edges, and may have multiple outlines or even multiple sketches of the same subject on the page where the artist has tried several different versions. A study, then, is a learning exercise rather than an accomplished end product.

Preparation

Working with charcoal and chalk can be messy. Classroom desks or tables will need to be washed off afterwards. Students will have to wash their hands. Working in an art room or outdoors is ideal. Clean up will require much less fuss. Wherever you work, provide an opportunity for students to clean their hands when the lesson is over.

To minimize smudging, decide whether finished drawings will be sprayed with fixative (see appendix D), laminated, placed in a plastic sleeve, or displayed out of the reach of passersby. Read through chapter 3 on drawing shape and value.

Find visual references such as magazine photos and calendar photos for students to use as guides for their main subjects. Place photos in a plastic sleeve if you are concerned about charcoal or chalk fingerprints.

Appropriate Subjects

Black-and-white magazine photos are the easiest and most appropriate subject (fig. 4.13). Color photos with obvious reflected light areas and dark shadows will also work. If students are drawing from "life" (for example, an actual object, a friend, their own face in a mirror), they will have difficulty seeing values in a diffused light. Turn off the overhead lights and use a desk lamp instead.

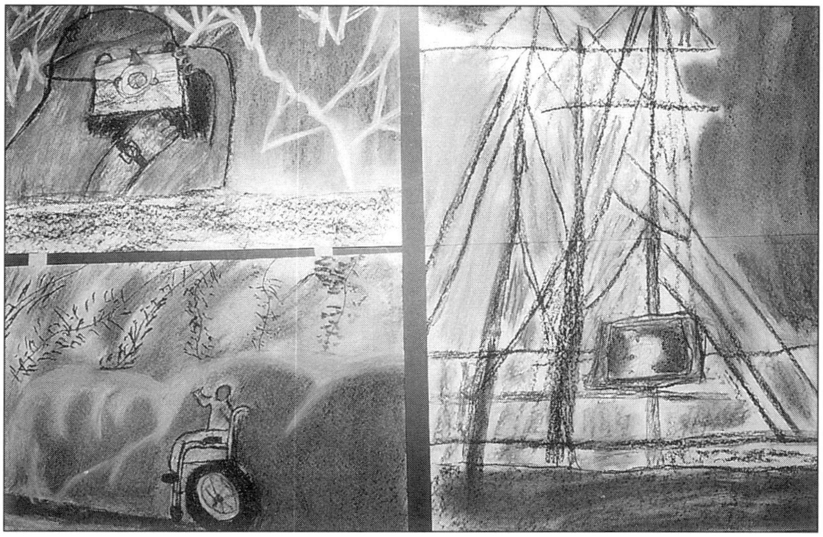

charcoal and chalk, grade 5 students, Luxton School

Fig. 4.13. Working from two black-and-white magazine photos, students combined the images into one drawing. They used very jagged lines and strong contrast to convey action and drama.

Tip: Chalk drawings smudge easily. There are several ways to cut down on smudging: (1) Start with white chalk and save black (compressed charcoal) until the last. (2) Blend gray tones with a rolled-up piece of Kleenex. (3) Instead of blowing charcoal dust off of the paper, lift the paper by one corner and shake gently over the floor. (4) Place scrap pieces of paper under hands to avoid fingerprints.

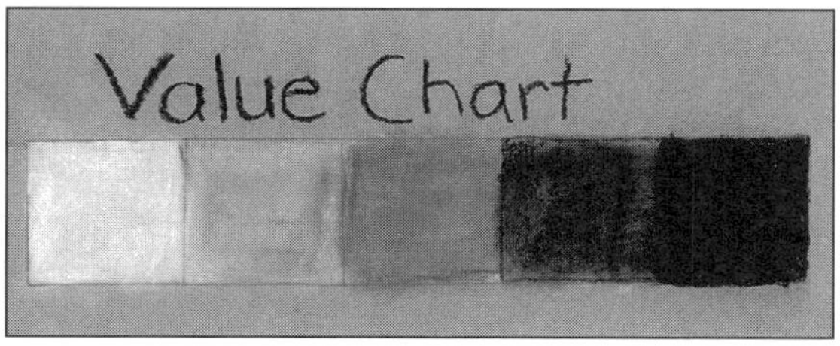

charcoal and chalk, grade 6 student, Luxton School

Fig. 4.14. Having students make a value chart is a useful introduction to drawing with charcoal and chalk. They become familiar with the media and are able to recognize the range of values they can produce.

Method

Look at *Jumanji* with the class. Notice the strong contrast between the light and dark areas of the illustrations. In other books, such as *The Magic Paintbrush*, shadows are an important part of the image. Begin by making a value chart ("gray scale") with white chalk on one end (lightest value), a mix of chalk and charcoal in the center, and charcoal at the other end (darkest value) (fig. 4.14). Ask students to notice the light and dark values on their subjects. (You may want to review values in chapter 3.)

Before your students continue, quickly demonstrate the following to them:

- Draw the shape of an animal.
- Shade in areas, starting with the lightest (white, light gray), then the medium and dark grays.
- Shade in the black areas last to avoid smudging (fig. 4.15).
- For subjects with a pattern, such as a spotted leopard, shade in the overall gray tones, then add the spots last. This is easier than drawing around each spot.

Some students may find it difficult to switch from drawing "lines" to drawing areas of value. For students having difficulties drawing the shape of their subject, see chapter 3.

After your students have left for the day, spray their drawings with a thin coating of fixative (some brands of aerosol hairspray also will work). Test the fixative first to make sure it is clear, not yellow. Make sure you work in a well-ventilated area. You can also preserve chalk drawings by photographing or laminating them, or by protecting them in plastic sleeves.

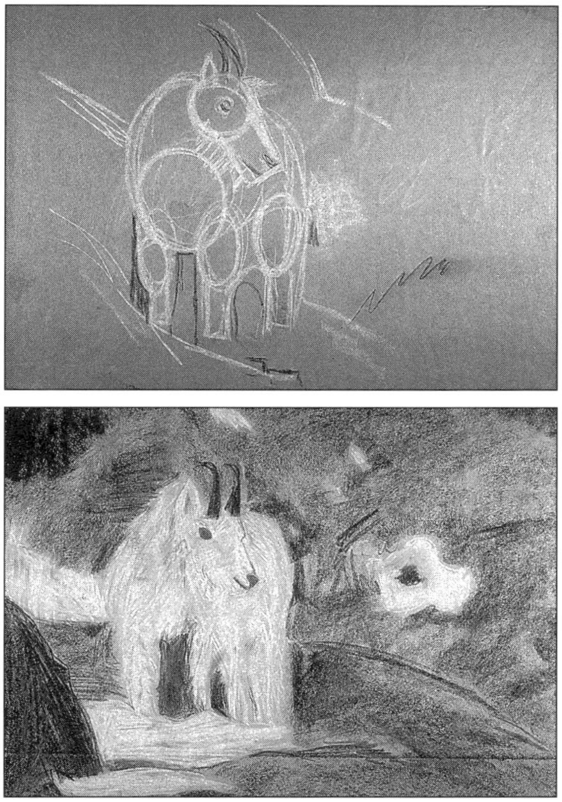

Mountain Goat, white chalk and vine charcoal on brown paper, Noni Brynjolson, age 11

Fig. 4.15. Noni started by sketching the geometric shapes of her subject. Next, she added the light values with chalk, then the gray tones with a mixture of chalk and charcoal. She added the dark values last, to cut down on smudging.

Enrichment

- Try working on white paper, covering the entire sheet with vine charcoal, and "drawing" the light values with an eraser.
- Have students make value drawings with white chalk on black paper. This exercise causes students to look very carefully at the highlights, rather than the shadows, in their image.
- Have students draw on black construction paper with a squeeze bottle of white glue. When the glue dries, it leaves a black line. Students can color between the lines of glue with chalk pastel. The dried glue will leave an irregular glossy line (fig. 4.16).
- Make value drawings using a range of pencils (2H, HB, 2B, and 4B) and a soft "gum" eraser on white Mayfair paper.
- For oversize drawings, try working with "compressed" charcoal and white chalk on an oversized piece of brown butcher paper (32" x 48" or 81 cm x 122 cm per student). Good subjects might be "giant" insects (magnified from magazine photos), dinosaurs, heavy machinery, and so on (fig. 4.17). If you have access to a camera, photograph students with their giant creations and encourage them to write a story, or display the giant drawings to add atmosphere to the classroom!
- Students can use soft (chalk) pastels to add color to a value study (see page 116). Have students look carefully at a reference photograph and try to mix and match their colors and values (fig. 4.18).

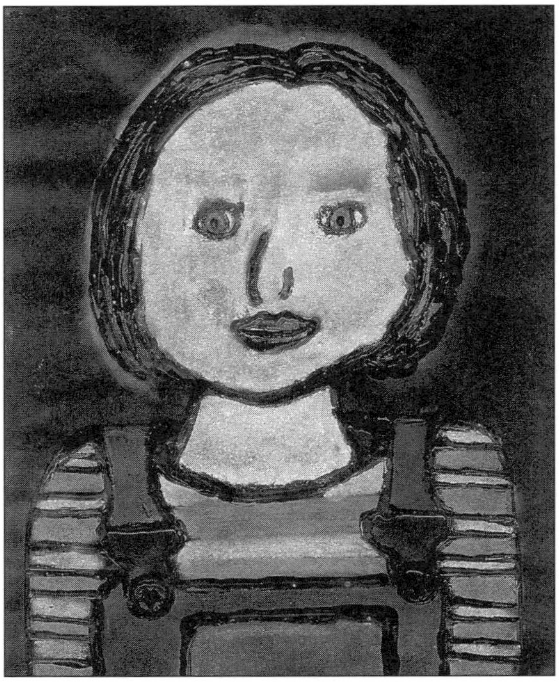

glue and chalk pastel on black paper, Danna Slessor-Cobb, grade 6, Luxton School

Fig. 4.16. Danna began by drawing the contours of a self-portrait on black paper. She then "drew" over the pencil lines with a squeeze-bottle of white glue. The glue, which is clear when it dries, left an interesting, wobbly black line. Danna then colored between the glue lines with chalk pastels.

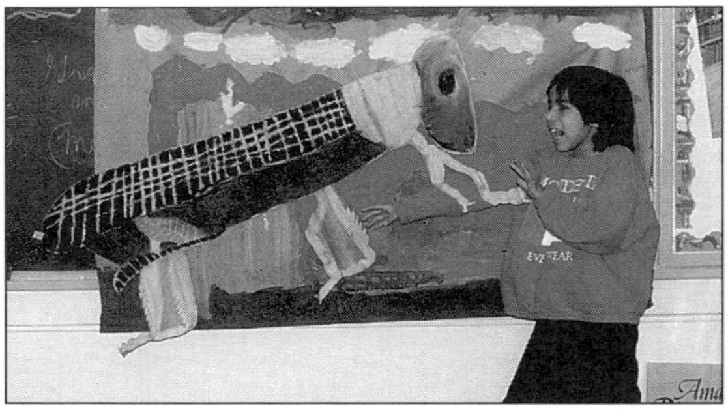

chalk and charcoal on brown paper, Derek, age 9, Luxton School

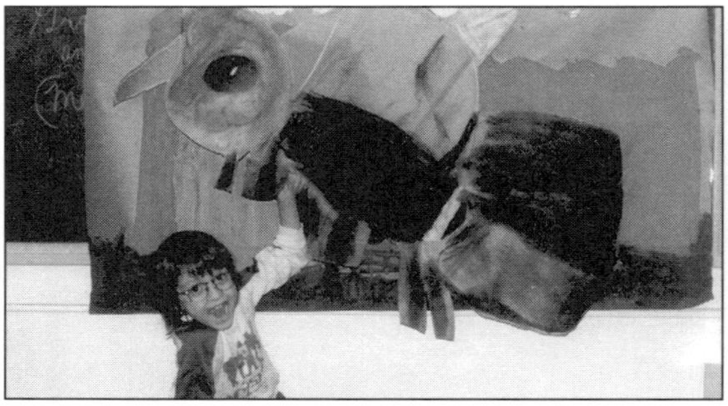

chalk and charcoal on brown paper, Daniel, age 10, Luxton School

Fig. 4.17. These giant bugs were drawn on brown butcher paper. The students in this classroom painted two backdrops to use for these photographs.

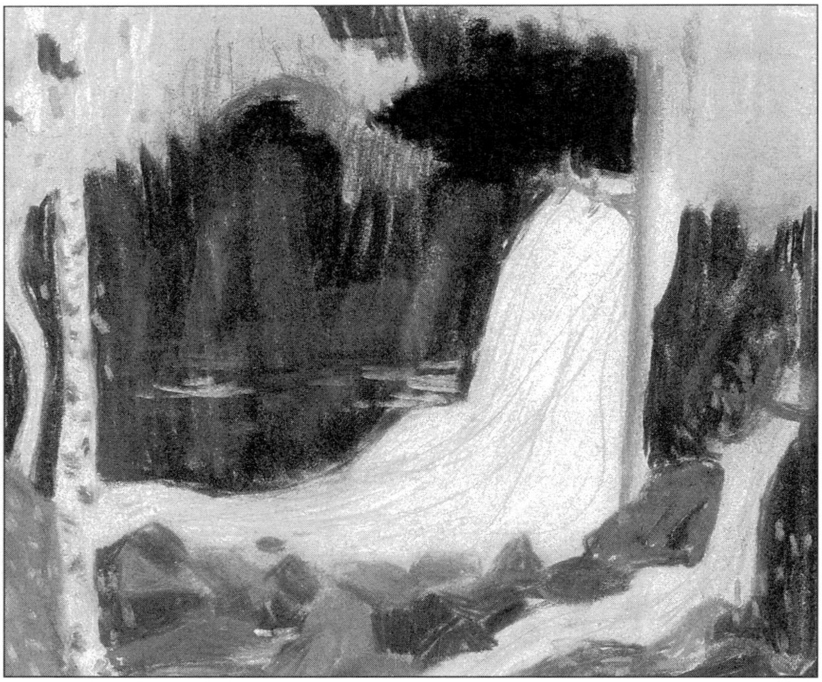

chalk pastel on construction paper, Noni Brynjolson, age 11

Fig. 4.18. In this drawing, Noni did a careful study of color and value from an art postcard. She began with light colors and added the dark colors last. This work is a study of Tom Thompson's *Woodland Waterfall.*

Multiple Images

Layered drawings can be produced by cutting and pasting multiple images. This approach to drawing requires several stages. First, students develop a drawing of a subject and several drawings of background pieces. Then all these pieces are multiplied, either using a photocopier or retracing them on an overhead projector, and combined into a single image. This image can be considered as the finished product, or may be reworked in a variety of media (fig. 4.19).

The approach to layered drawings is similar to an approach used by many artists. They draw studies of various subjects in their sketchbooks and then combine the subjects into a single painting. For an example, see the sketchbooks of Leonardo da Vinci. Students have an advantage—they have access to a photocopier and/or overhead projector to help them redraw their subjects!

Both young and advanced students will find there are several advantages to using multiple images and a cut-and-paste technique:

- Students have more control of and choice over the placement of parts of the image (see chapter 6 for information on how to compose a drawing). The pieces are separate, and they can be moved around like a puzzle to test different combinations.
- Students will produce a different kind of image—crowded, richer, with overlapping pieces. This is helpful to students who have trouble figuring out how to treat the space around their subject, or who are still coloring a strip of blue across the top of the page and a strip of green across the bottom.
- Layered drawings work well for young students who often do not have the attention span needed for sustained work in a single project. They can draw different subjects on different days. The drawings can be photocopied for them, and they can cut out and assemble the pieces later on. (See Enrichment, page 56, for ideas on how to use these pieces with young students.)

Materials (for drawing)

- sketchbooks
- pencils
- erasers
- paper ($8\frac{1}{2}$" x 11" or 22 cm x 28 cm; Dessin is preferred)
- felt markers (black, permanent, nontoxic, fine-tipped)

Books to Have Handy

Picture Books

Changes
8 O'Cluck
If You're Not From the Prairie
The New Baby Calf
Who Is the Beast?

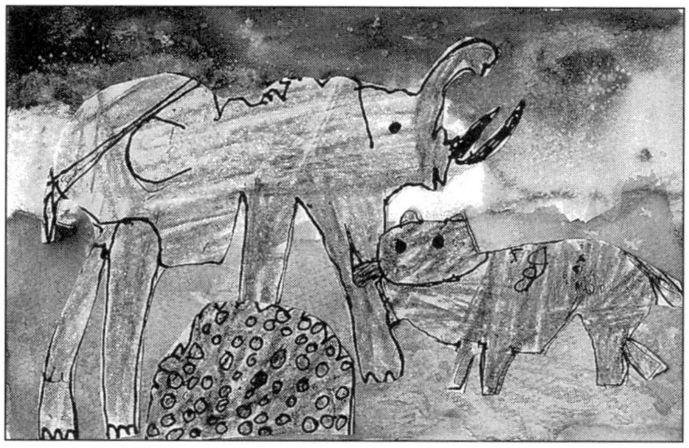

from ***Rhino and Elephant Go Swimming,*** photocopy cutouts on watercolor background, Mark Savage, age 6, Elm Creek School

Fig. 4.19. Mark did careful look-drawings of an elephant and a rhinoceros. He also drew this bush to indicate the habitat of his animals. The drawings were then photocopied to provide characters to illustrate every page of Mark's story. **See color plate.**

Appropriate Subjects

Students will require a visual reference; an object (for example, a model dinosaur), book, or magazine photo of their subject. Appropriate subjects include any single, easily recognizable subject. Calendar photos of animals in a setting work well; crowded landscapes are more difficult. In the case of subjects that are strictly imaginary (for example, dragons), it may help to find photos of related subjects (see chapter 5).

Preparation

You may want to read chapter 3 on drawing (shape, line, texture, and pattern) for tips on how to approach drawing the subject.

Find a volunteer to help with photocopying or arrange to have a couple of overhead projectors in the classroom (a sunny window works as well) for tracing students' drawings.

Method (for initial drawing)

Tell your students it is worth spending time on their initial drawing! They will be re-using this image with a variety of media and techniques. Begin by having them do practice drawings in their sketchbooks. Encourage them to try scribble-drawing, drawing geometric shapes, and blind contour drawing as "warm-up" exercises (see chapter 3).

When your students are ready, have them draw their subjects on white paper. Remind them to pay special attention to the contours and surface textures (fig. 4.20), and to avoid shading in the dark values.

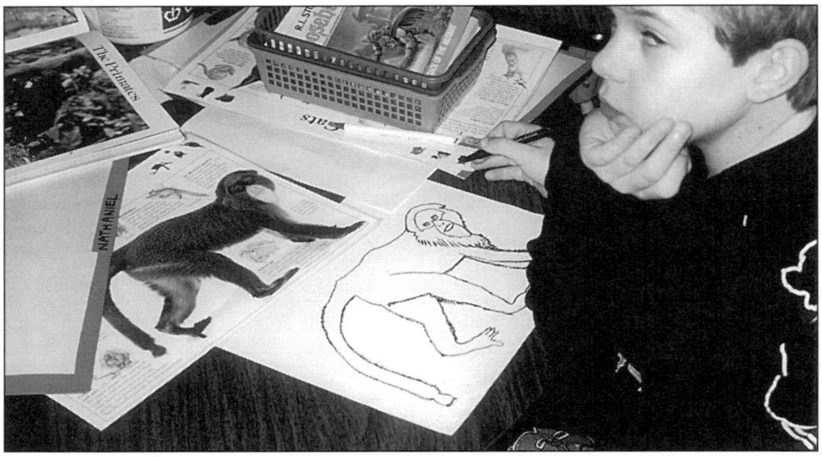

Ben Gammon, grade 6, Luxton School

Fig. 4.20. Ben drew a jagged line to show the furry edges of his subject.

Students should focus on one subject in their drawing. For example, have them draw only the owl and the branch it is sitting on, not the forest. Background elements will be drawn separately.

On another piece of paper (and perhaps after more practice in their sketchbooks), students can draw parts of their backgrounds. Use visual references. For example, look at *Who Is the Beast?* with your students. Notice how the different leaves and flowers are shaped and contain interesting patterns and how leaves are attached to branches. Students may draw fewer "lollipop" trees after viewing these illustrations. Remind students to pay attention to edges, pattern, and texture, and to avoid shading in. If they are drawing an outdoor scene, they will draw particular pieces of the background—individual leaves or trees—rather than the whole forest.

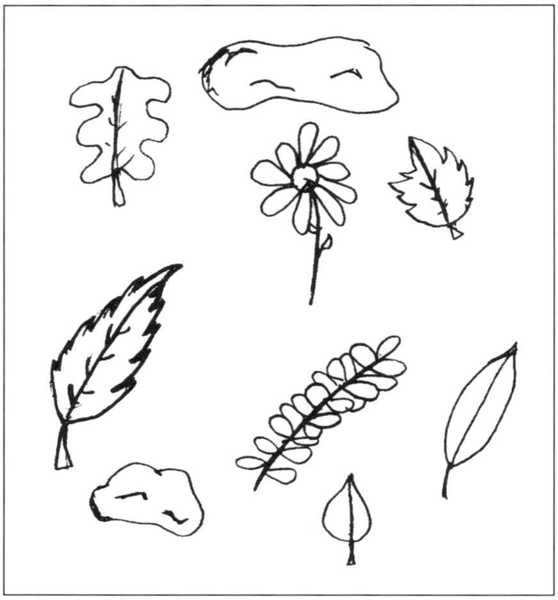

pencil on paper, grade 3 student, Luxton School

Fig. 4.21. Drawing pieces of the background

Method (for copying)

Make multiple photocopies of each of the finished drawings (fig. 4.22), including some that are larger and smaller than the initial drawing. Ask for volunteers to run the photocopier.

Look at *If You're Not From the Prairie* or *The New Baby Calf.* Notice how:

- those elements of the pictures that are close-up are larger and are positioned near the bottom of the page
- those elements in the middle distance are slightly smaller and higher on the page
- those elements that appear to be in the distance are much smaller and nearer the horizon line, where the sky meets the ground

Ask students what this suggests to them about where they should place their large, medium, and small cutouts on the page in order to create an illusion of depth in their picture.

Look at *Who Is the Beast?* with your students. Notice how the tiger is hidden by the leaves (the foreground elements) and how some of the flowers and leaves are hidden behind the tiger (these are in the background). Encourage your students to overlap their cutout drawings.

Students can begin cutting out their various photocopies. Remind them to save the original drawing and a photocopy or two for other projects! Encourage them to experiment with different arrangements of these pieces on an 8½" x 11" (21.5 cm x 28 cm) piece of paper. This size of paper will seem crowded, but will encourage overlapping, and a much richer image will result.

Photocopy this image for use with other media (see Enrichment, page 56) (fig. 4.23). Add color with pencil crayons.

Materials (for copying)

- access to photocopier, windows, or overhead projectors
- paper (white photocopy, 8½" x 11" or 21.5 cm x 28 cm)
- scissors
- pencils
- glue or gluesticks
- black markers
- pencil crayons

Tip: Don't hand out glue until students have arranged all pieces. This will encourage them to overlap and give thought to the placement of pieces.

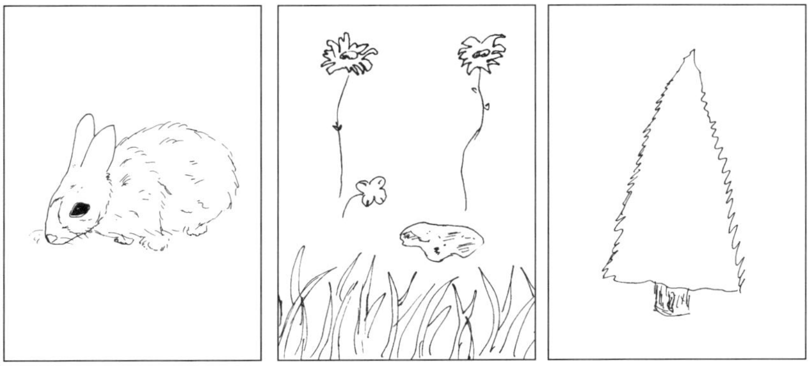

photocopies, Noni Brynjolson, age 11

Fig. 4.22. Multiple copies can be made on a photocopier. The advantage of using a photocopier is that images can be enlarged or reduced to fit the size of the drawing. Multiple copies can also be made by tracing the image several times onto white paper or directly onto the good copy. For tracing, hold the paper against a bright window or on the glass of an overhead projector. By tracing the backside of an image, the subject can face in the opposite direction.

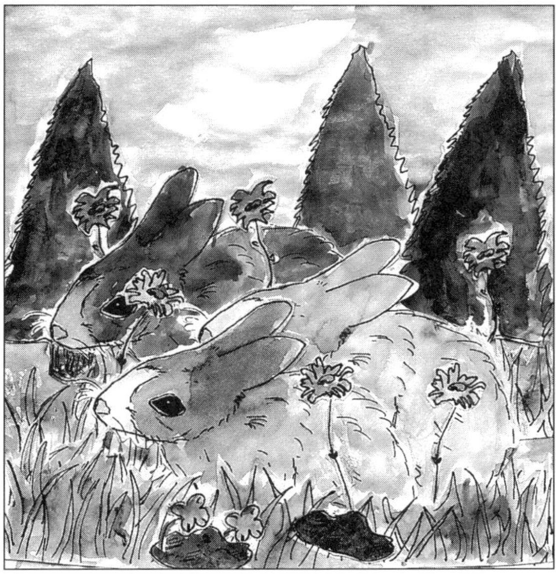

Rabbits, cut-and-pasted photocopies with watercolor, Noni Brynjolson, age 11

Fig. 4.23. Elements of the picture are crowded together and overlapped. Even beginners will be able to understand the concepts of "in front of" and "behind."

Enrichment

- Making multiple images is an ideal way to develop images for any media or technique. The initial focus on drawing will help students develop a strong image that they can use with other media. Using cutouts allows for discussion of depth and perspective. (See chapter 3.)
- Cutouts allow students to easily integrate cutout pieces of their stories or poems for use as illustrations. Using cutouts means that students may only have to draw their main character once and redraw the background, or draw one background and paste in different character drawings. Making multiple drawings to illustrate stories is easy when photocopies are used. These cut-and-paste illustrations may then be photocopied (to look like one smooth piece of paper) and colored with pencil crayon (figs. 4.24 and 4.25).

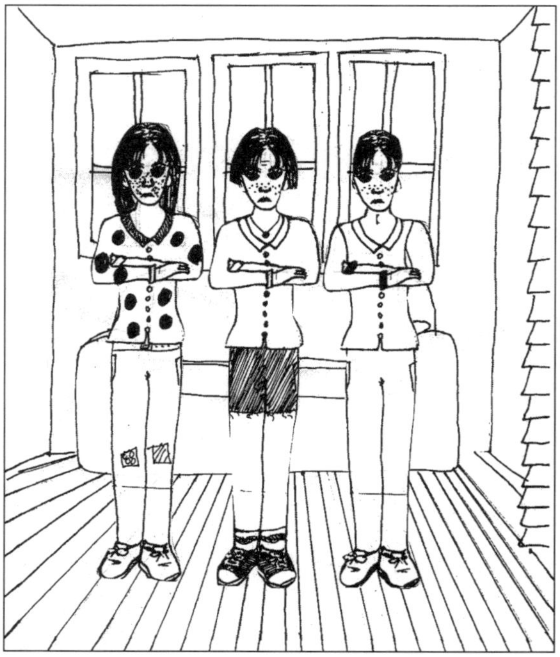

photocopies, cut and paste, Noni Brynjolson, age 11

Fig. 4.24. These three characters are photocopied from the same original drawing. Their hair and clothing have been cut or drawn over to vary their appearances.

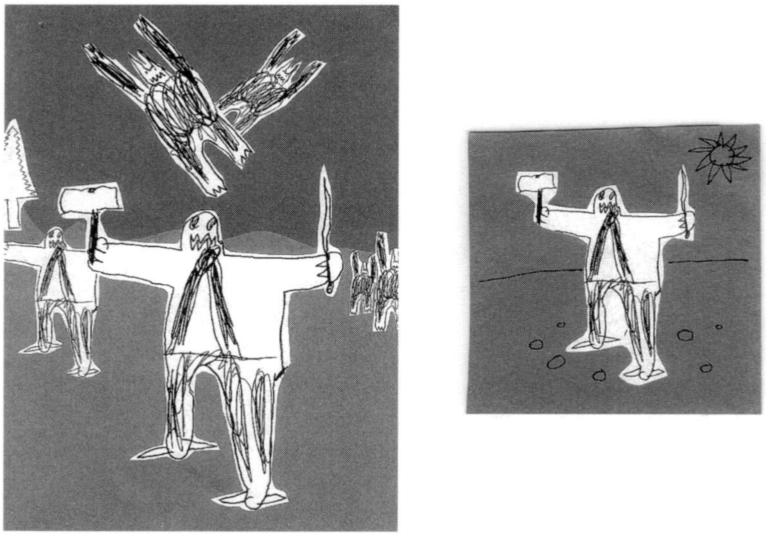

cut-and-pasted photocopies on colored paper, 7-year-old student, Luxton School

Fig. 4.25. For students, the big advantage of using a photocopier is that it is easier for them to illustrate a story. The student who drew these images used many photocopies of his scary characters to produce one full-size illustration. The other illustrations in his book may be quite small and simple—like the 2 1/2" (6 cm) size combination of photocopy and drawing on the right.

- Teachers of young students can use cutout multiple drawings for math (counting, number groups, addition), class stories with lots of characters, or a class mural (for example, "our trip to the zoo"). Enlarge drawings to 11" x 17" (28 cm x 43 cm), cut out, and paste on large paper.

- Try juxtaposed drawings with cutouts. Take a cutout of a subject and place it in an unlikely setting. Some examples are a dog driving a taxi, a shark in the refrigerator, and an apple wearing a suit. Resulting images may be surprising, horrific, or humorous (fig. 4.26). You can find many juxtaposed drawings in magazine ads. Look at *Changes* or paintings by René Magritte, a French surrealist artist, for other examples.
- Try integrating photo montage, using magazine photo cutouts. The use of selected pieces of photos glued into the picture can add interest; however, it is a very slow process to have students flipping through magazines to find the "right" picture! See *8 O'Cluck* for ideas.
- With good-quality paper and permanent pens, students can use watercolor techniques on their original drawings. To preserve a copy of the original drawing in case of a painting disaster, make sure the drawing has been photocopied first. Additional copies could be traced onto watercolor paper. Just tape the papers to a window for easy viewing. (See chapter 11.)
- Ideally, the photocopies of students' original drawings, or the photocopies of their finished multiples, will be used with a variety of the other art techniques and approaches described in other chapters. Since students will have invested a great deal of effort into the initial drawings, it makes sense to get maximum use out of the drawings. Photocopying is also a valuable way to demonstrate how different the same image can look when given different treatments. For other examples of this, look at the series of paintings by French impressionist painter Claude Monet of haystacks or Rouen Cathedral; or a series by Canadian painter Michael Snow called "Walking Woman." Students could also research how a similar subject or the same fairy tale is handled by a variety of artists or children's book illustrators. Students may want to work on their photocopies "in the style of" a particular artist or illustrator. (See page 117.)
- Multiples can be used in an extreme way. Photocopy and cut out, or trace, dozens of copies to use as border designs or in crowd scenes. One example might be a flock of flamingos.

Tip: Encourage students to mix colors. For a three-dimensional effect, use sharp pencil crayons and press slightly harder near the edges of objects. Place a piece of nylon window screen under the paper to produce an interesting surface pattern.

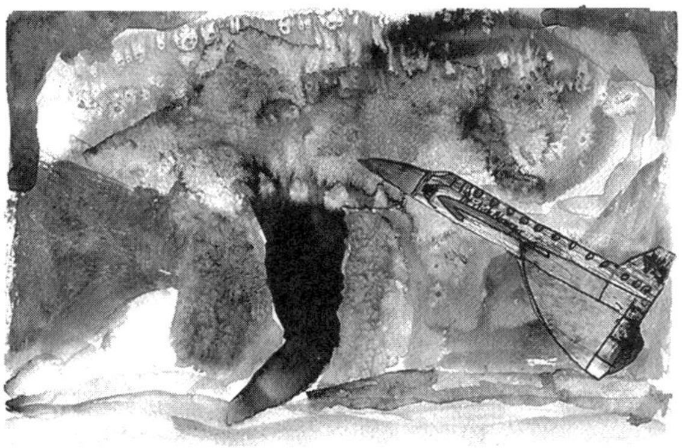

Jet and Tornado, paper cutouts with watercolor, pencil crayon, and ink, Alec Scarth Watson, age 9, St. John's Ravenscourt School

Fig. 4.26. Alec used watercolor to paint his background, and added his drawing of a jet plane heading for disaster.

Vocabulary (see appendixes for definitions)

compressed charcoal	*line*	*soft "chalk" pastels*
contour	*line qualities*	*texture*
contrast	*look-drawing*	*value*
crosshatching	*pattern*	*value chart*
cut and paste	*shadow*	*vine charcoal*
hatching	*shape*	
highlights	*smudge*	

5
Interesting Subjects

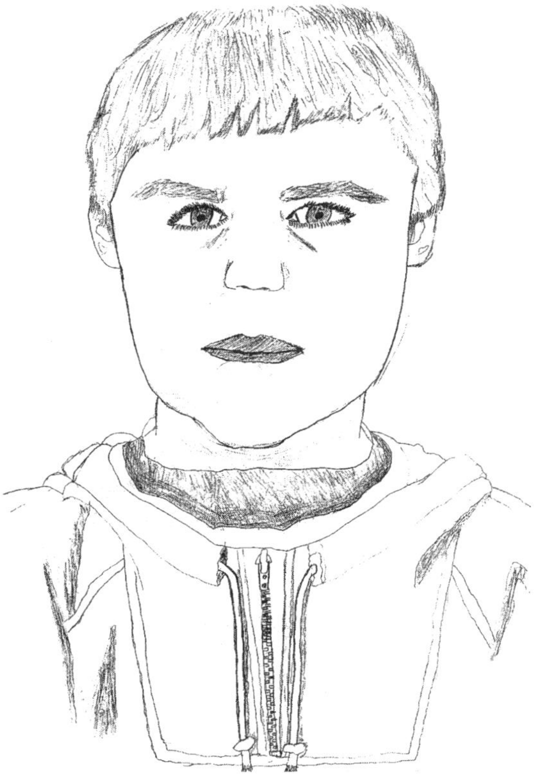

Self-portrait, ink and soft pastel, pencil on paper, Robert Shindruk, grade 5–8 class, San Antonio School

Fig. 5.1. Robert drew the contours of his face very carefully, then shaded in some of the darker values of the folds in his sweatshirt.

Introduction

Some subjects, such as people and portraits, seem to be particularly challenging to draw. Part of the challenge is to put aside what we assume a subject looks like, and to draw the visual information presented to our eyes. Portrait and figure drawing are dealt with in some detail in this chapter.

Drawing imaginary creatures presents a different kind of challenge. Instead of simply recording visual information, the artist composes an image of imagined or partially remembered fragments, reassembling a new creature. Because there are no eyewitnesses to these creatures, there is no right or wrong way to represent such creations. Yet, in order to make the creations convincing, the artist must borrow from experience in drawing a variety of animals, people, and objects, or use visual references from a variety of sources and combine them into a single image.

Materials

- sketchbooks
- pencils
- erasers
- rulers
- pocket mirrors (ideally 6" to 8" or 15 cm to 20 cm square, with plastic edges, self-standing), one per student
- white photocopy paper, or Dessin (8 1/2" x 11" or 11" x 17"; 21.5 cm x 28 cm or 28 cm x 43 cm)

Books to Have Handy

Picture Books
Best Friends
The Magic Paintbrush
The Night Rebecca Stayed Too Late

Teacher References
Drawing on the Right Side of the Brain

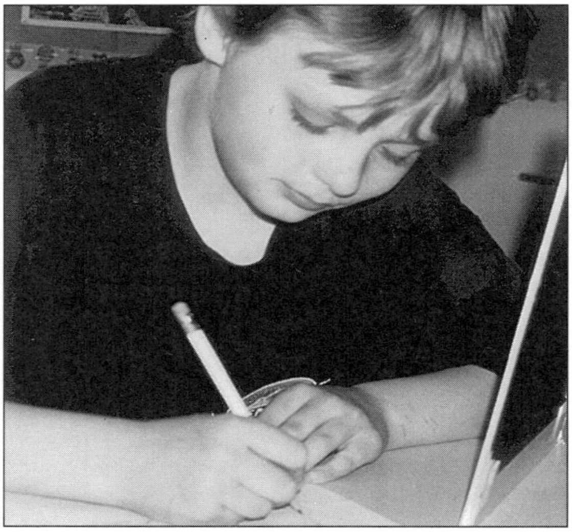

grade 5–8 class, San Antonio School

Fig. 5.2. This student has propped up a large mirror in order to see the contours of his face.

Tip: If students are shy of making faces in the mirrors, let them space themselves around the classroom (some may prefer to face the wall). This exercise helps students build positive self-image by making them aware that every face is different and that each has individuality. Depending on classroom dynamics, having students draw each other may not be appropriate, and it's sometimes hard to get a classmate to hold still.

Tip: To draw a fold of skin for the eyelid, shade slightly above the line and use an eraser to "soften" each end of the pencil mark.

Portrait Drawing

Portrait drawing involves learning to accurately represent facial features (eyes, nose, mouth, ears, hair), drawing the nuances of expression and personality, and combining all these elements in correct proportion.

Drawing people can be problematic. At a very young age, we begin drawing rough circles with dots for eyes and a line for a mouth. Later, we may add lines for arms and legs, a dot for a belly button, or marks for fingers and toes. As we get older, these marks become closer approximations to life—a triangle nose, oval eyes, and a longer torso. But they are still symbols rather than records of visual information. For students to progress beyond this symbolic drawing, they have to be encouraged to look carefully at their faces in the mirror or at a friend's face. Remind them to observe and record what they see, not what they assume a face looks like.

Preparation

Collect a pocket mirror for each student in the class. Tape over any jagged or cracked edges. Find picture books (see Books to Have Handy) or magazine photos with close-up faces that portray a range of expressions—the more extreme, the better.

Try the following drawing exercises first, so that you are comfortable demonstrating the techniques to your students.

Method

Before you introduce portrait drawing, distribute pocket mirrors to your students. Ask them to practice drawing parts of their own faces—eyes, noses, mouths, ears, hair—with varying expressions, in their sketchbooks (fig. 5.2). This exercise may take up an entire class lesson, or you may want to use short (10–15 minute) sessions for each part of the face. To have some fun, try introducing each part with blind contour drawing (see chapter 3).

Eyes

Start with the eyes (fig. 5.3). Remind students to look at the shapes of the white parts of the eye (triangles). Did they notice that the iris (the colored part of the eye) is round, or that eyelashes don't grow in straight lines, but "dip" in odd directions? Encourage them to draw in details like the tear ducts and the fold of eyelid above the eye. If students "shade in" the iris and pupil, notice the areas of light reflected on the surface of the eye. Have students draw a wide-open eye, a squinting eye, a partly closed eye, a "smiling" eye, and so on. For students struggling with the basic shapes contained in an eye, tell them to draw a triangle, a circle, and another triangle. Then encourage them to adapt these generalized shapes to suit the shape of their own eye.

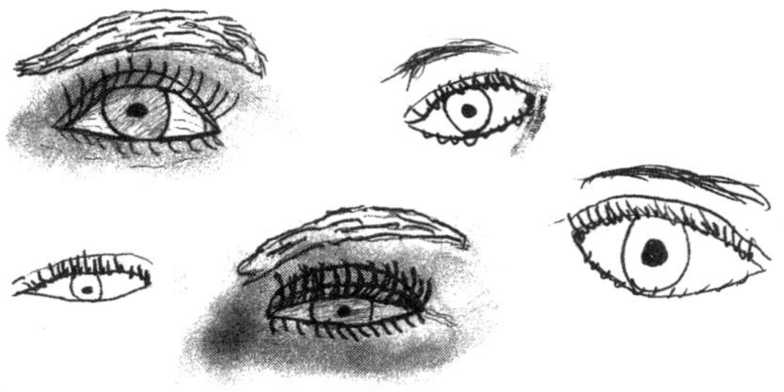

pencil on paper, grade 5–8 class, San Antonio School

Fig. 5.3. Eyes

Nose

Next try drawing noses (fig. 5.4). Have students draw a nose that is wrinkled, a nose on a face that is tilted slightly down, up, or turned to the side for a profile. Instruct students to hold the mirror straight in front of them—holding the mirror under the nostrils produces a very unflattering view! They should draw contour lines around the bottom of the nose only; the bridge of the nose is represented by soft shading on either side. If students are struggling with the basic shape of a nose, demonstrate that the bottom of a nose can be drawn with a letter "C," followed by a very curvy letter "M" (~), and another, backwards, letter "C." Then students can compare this shape with their own nose, and adjust their drawing.

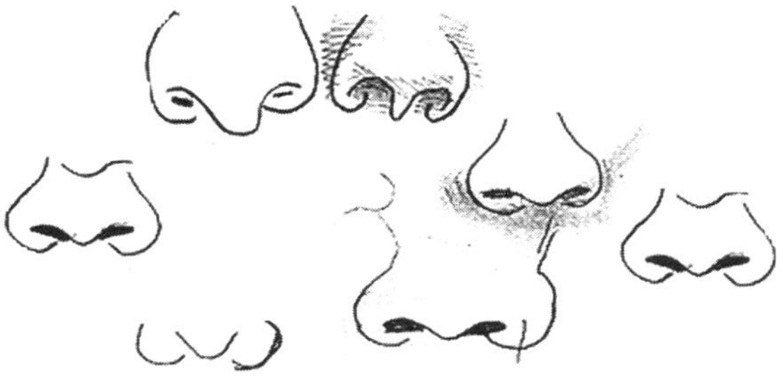

San Antonio School

Fig. 5.4. Noses

Tip: Shade areas of the face by making gentle, repeated pencil marks, or by "softening" dark lines with an eraser.

Mouth

Mouths can dramatically change shape with different facial expressions. A basic mouth shape might be an almost straight line (that dips a bit in the middle), a "volcano" shape for the top of the upper lip, and a "bowl" shape for the bottom line of the lower lip. Try drawing a closed mouth, an open mouth, a mouth with the tongue sticking out, a smiling mouth, a frowning mouth, and a mouth with teeth showing (fig. 5.5).

The line drawn between the upper and lower lip should be darker than the lines that indicate the edges of a color change above the top lip and below the bottom lip. Mouths aren't straight lines, they "dip." Add shading at the corners of the mouth. Teeth aren't square; each tooth has its own shape.

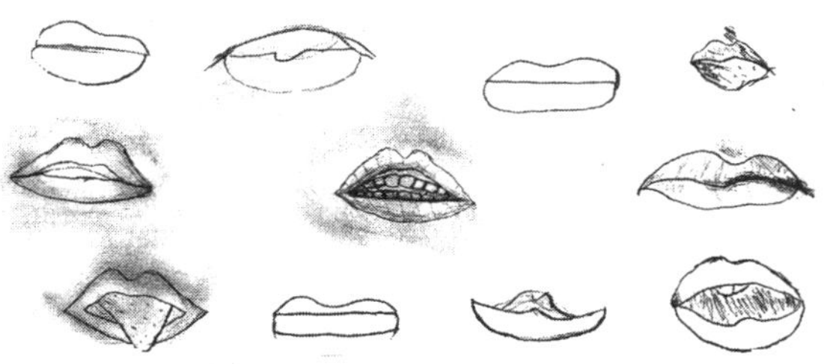

San Antonio School

Fig. 5.5. Mouths

Ears

Ears are a difficult study, with lots of overlapping lines. Try drawing a side view of a friend's ear. Soften the ends and edges of the overlapping lines with an eraser—a fold of skin is represented by a line that "fades out" gradually. When ears are viewed from the front, they stick out less than you think (fig. 5.6).

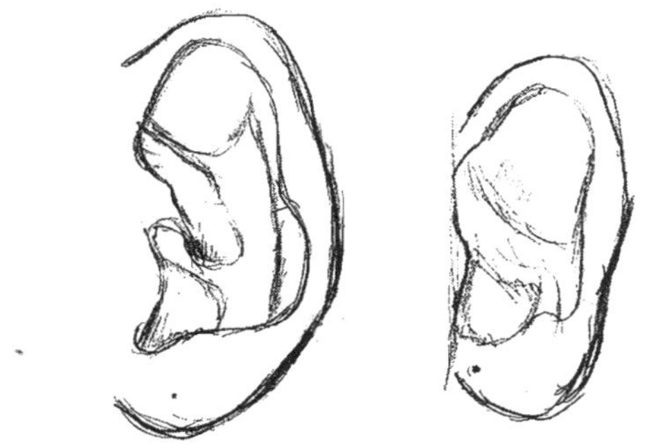

Noni Brynjolson, age 11

Fig. 5.6. Ears

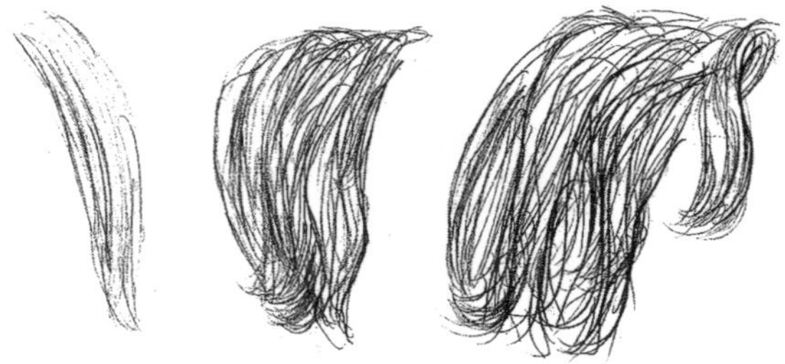

Noni Brynjolson, age 11

Fig. 5.7. Hair

Hair

Practice drawing hair (fig. 5.7). Hair can be an expressive part of the face as well. Hair may indicate mood. Some examples are morning hair (sleepy), hair standing up (fright). Hair might also indicate personality; for example, hair in a tight bun, long "flower child" hair, punky.

Draw "bunches" of hair rather than single strands. Pencil marks should indicate the length and direction the hair is growing. Soften or lighten pencil marks, or "draw" highlights into hair with an eraser (shade dark colors into the hair, then use the edge of an eraser to create highlights). Dark hair will require pencil marks closer together; look for light reflecting on hair that will require marks to be spaced slightly farther apart.

Proportion

Tip: An eye-width is a useful standard of measure. Students may want to measure an eye in their drawing with a ruler.

Before putting all the parts of the face together, introduce your students to the basics of proportion for drawing a face (fig. 5.8). This may require another whole lesson. Demonstrate on the chalkboard, then let your students practice in their sketchbooks. (Proportion can be a difficult exercise for very young students; you may want to skip to the next step.)

Draw a large oval. Draw one dotted line vertically down the center and one horizontally through the middle of the oval. This will serve as a guide to keep the eyes, nose, and mouth from being crooked or out of place. The oval and dotted lines are erased after the portrait is finished.

The basic rules of proportion are:

- eyes are located along the dotted line that runs horizontally, halfway between the top of the head and the bottom of the chin. This will look strange until the forehead and hair are allowed for!
- eyes are equal widths and are placed one eye-width apart. Measure this on your own face—there is a width of one eye between your eyes.
- the nose is one eye-width long, and one eye-width wide at the bottom
- the upper lip is about half an eye-width down from the bottom of the nose although this distance will vary
- the mouth, with a relaxed expression, equals the width from the inside of the iris in one eye across to the iris of the other eye
- the chin is just over an eye-width high although this distance will vary
- the edges of the face are less than an eye-width from the eye
- the height of the ears stretches from approximately the eye to the mouth. The ears will appear lower if the head is tilted up; higher if the head is tilted down.
- the neck is about as wide as the head; shoulders are far wider than the head

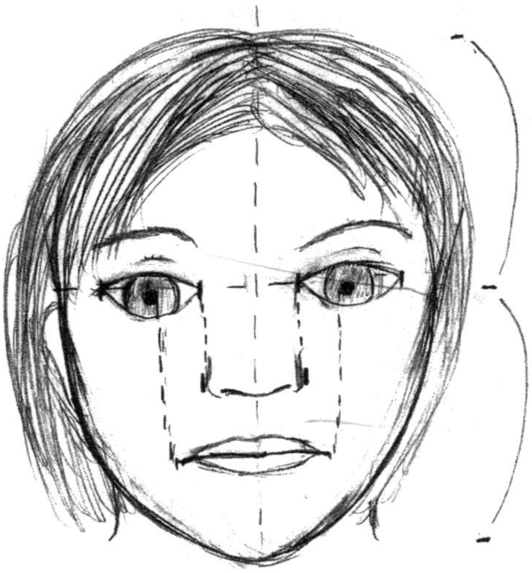

Noni Brynjolson, age 11

Fig. 5.8. An eye width is used to measure for the placement and size of facial features.

Tip: If something looks a bit odd in a student's drawing, it is probably a problem either with proportion (check the "rules"), or with the distance between the features (eyes, nose, mouth) and the edge of the face. Be gentle with your suggestions. Faces are hard to draw and distortions can add "character."

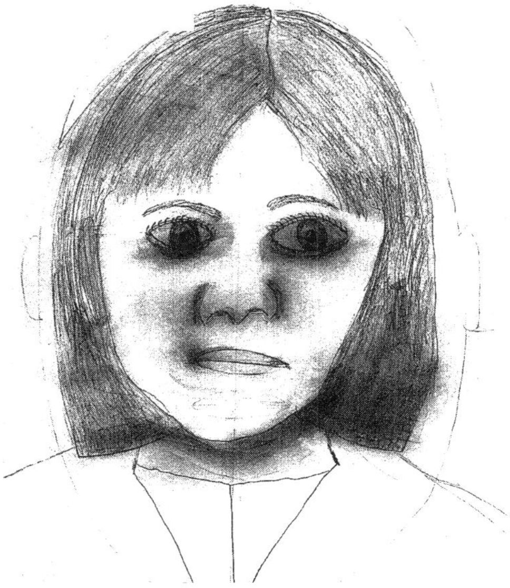

Self-portrait, pencil on paper, Ashley Smith, grade 5–8, San Antonio School

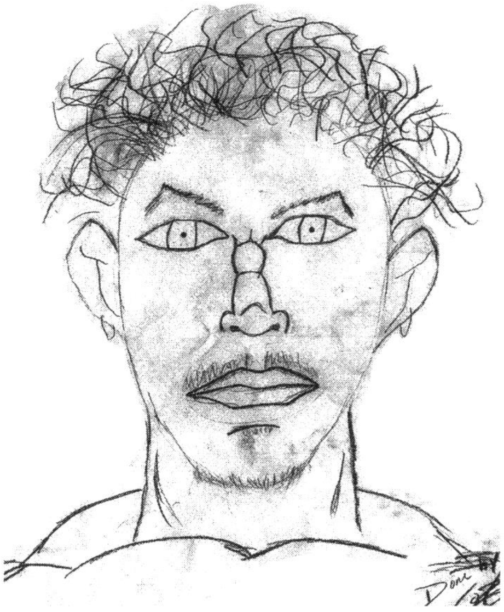

Self-portrait, pencil on paper, Vincent Bushie, age 16, Wanipigow School

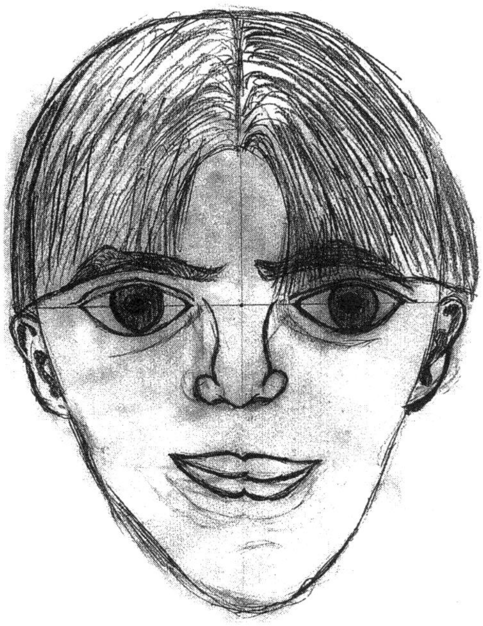

Self-portrait, pencil on paper, Kelvin Millen, grade 8, San Antonio School

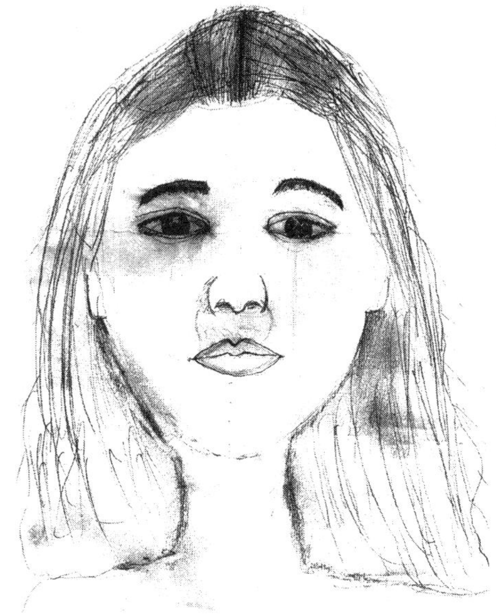

Self-portrait, pencil on paper, Aldeana Wood, grade 5–8, San Antonio School

Fig. 5.9. These students worked hard to reproduce the contours and some of the shading of their features. It is interesting to be able to see how students view themselves. These simple line drawings could be developed into more expressive or more finished portraits, which might reveal more about self-concept, interests, or state of mind. Remind students that large drawings allow for more accuracy and detail.

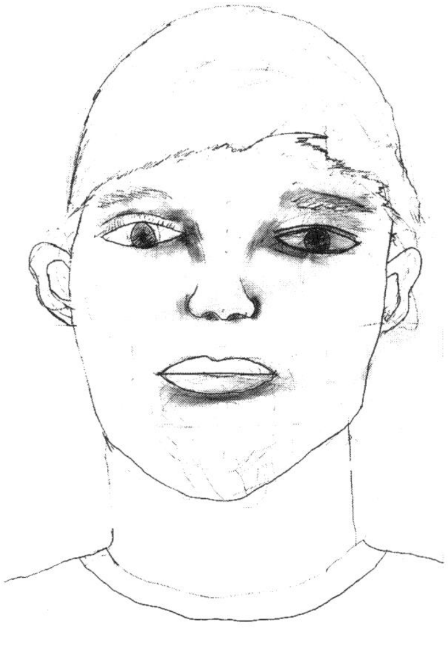

Self-portrait, pencil on paper, Ryan Johnson, grade 8, San Antonio School

Tip: Even black hair may have sunlight reflecting on one part of it to make it appear lighter. Faces will have shadowed areas. Look for shadows and areas of reflected light around folds on clothing.

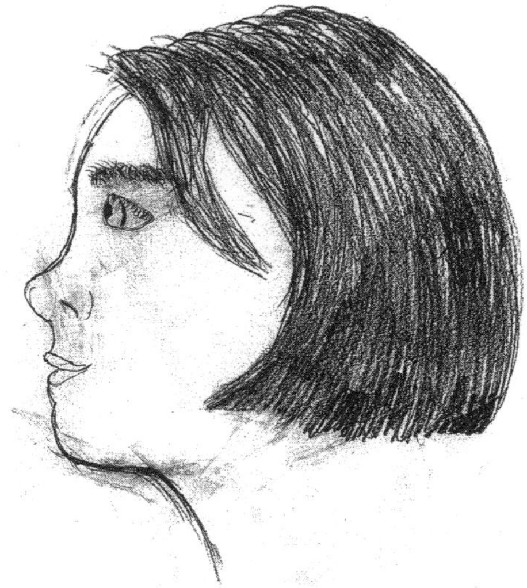

pencil on paper, Danna Slessor-Cobb, age 10

Fig. 5.10. When drawing a profile, it is important to notice the changed shape of the eye (almost triangular), the wide distance between the eye and ear, the wide distance between the ear and the back of the head, and the sloping line of the jaw between the chin and the neck.

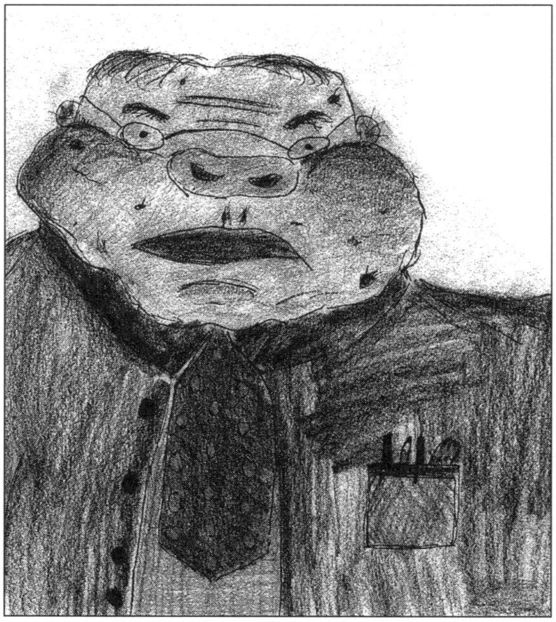

Mr.Hogg, pencil crayon on paper, Noni Brynjolson, age 11

Fig. 5.11. Caricatures or cartoons tend to break with the rules of proportion. Small, widely spaced eyes, a low forehead, and a pig nose give this fellow a unique character.

After the features are added in correct proportion, erase the oval and draw in a more accurate facial contour around the chin and jaw line.

Hand out larger sheets of paper when students are ready to put all the parts of the face together. Challenge them to come up with interesting and extreme facial expressions, or an expression that communicates something about how they feel. Suggest that they start with very gentle pressure on their pencils. That way, if they change their minds, lines will be easier to erase or can be easily darkened later. Drawing large allows for more accuracy and detail.

Enrichment

- Use this activity as an introduction to cartooning or caricature (fig. 5.11). Make the expressions of eyes, nose, and mouth very extreme. Try making them ridiculously large or small. Now put them together, breaking all the rules of proportion. Have fun!
- Students can draw a detail of their face on Dessin paper and practice "shading in" the darker values. If the drawing becomes too dark, students can "draw" highlights with their erasers.
- Ask students to create a self-portrait that tells something about who they are or what is important to them. Encourage them to bring favorite objects or images from home to draw or paste into their self-portraits. Ask them to draw themselves in their favorite places, or to give some clues to the viewer about what they were thinking or dreaming about. They can cover the drawing with layers of tracing paper to partially disguise what the original looked like, and they can redraw parts of the face.
- Advanced students might try a tempera-painted self-portrait (see chapter 9).
- To alter the self-portraits into interesting characters for illustration, use tracing paper and tape drawings onto a window with a second drawing paper over top to trace, or photocopy selected parts of the drawing. Look at a magazine or book photo for specific features such as beards, wrinkles, hats, and missing teeth. Work from imagination or from photos of lizards, mammals, or birds to create a space alien, mythical being, or mutant. You may want to disguise the character with a partial mask and create a superhero. Add an interesting background such as the inside of an alien space ship or the deck of a pirate ship.
- For a more advanced drawing class, work with sketching (or vine) charcoal and look at value. Value refers to the areas of reflected light and shadow in a drawing. Ask students to notice the areas of light and dark values on a face. Black-and-white magazine photos, or any other photo with bright light and dark

shadows, are the easiest subject for a value study. (See value in chapter 3.) If students are drawing "from life," values will be difficult to see in diffused light. Turn off the overhead lights and use sunlight or a single desk lamp to make reflected light and shadow more obvious (fig. 5.12).

- Students may begin illustrations by considering what expression and attributes they would like their character to have. Think of an extreme expression that communicates something about the situation in the story and alter the self-portrait to fit this character or feeling (fig. 5.13).

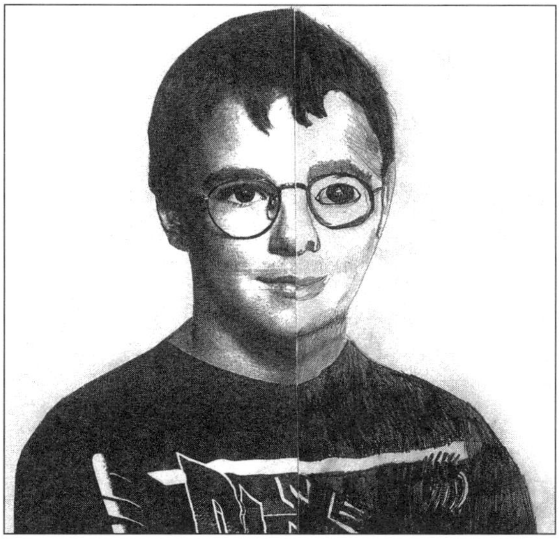

Self-portrait, photocopy and pencil on paper, Roger Rheault, age 11, Treherne Elementary School

Fig. 5.12. This student learned how to add light and dark values to a self-portrait by drawing from a photocopy. Student photographs were photocopied, cut in half, and students were asked to shade in the missing half, paying attention to values.

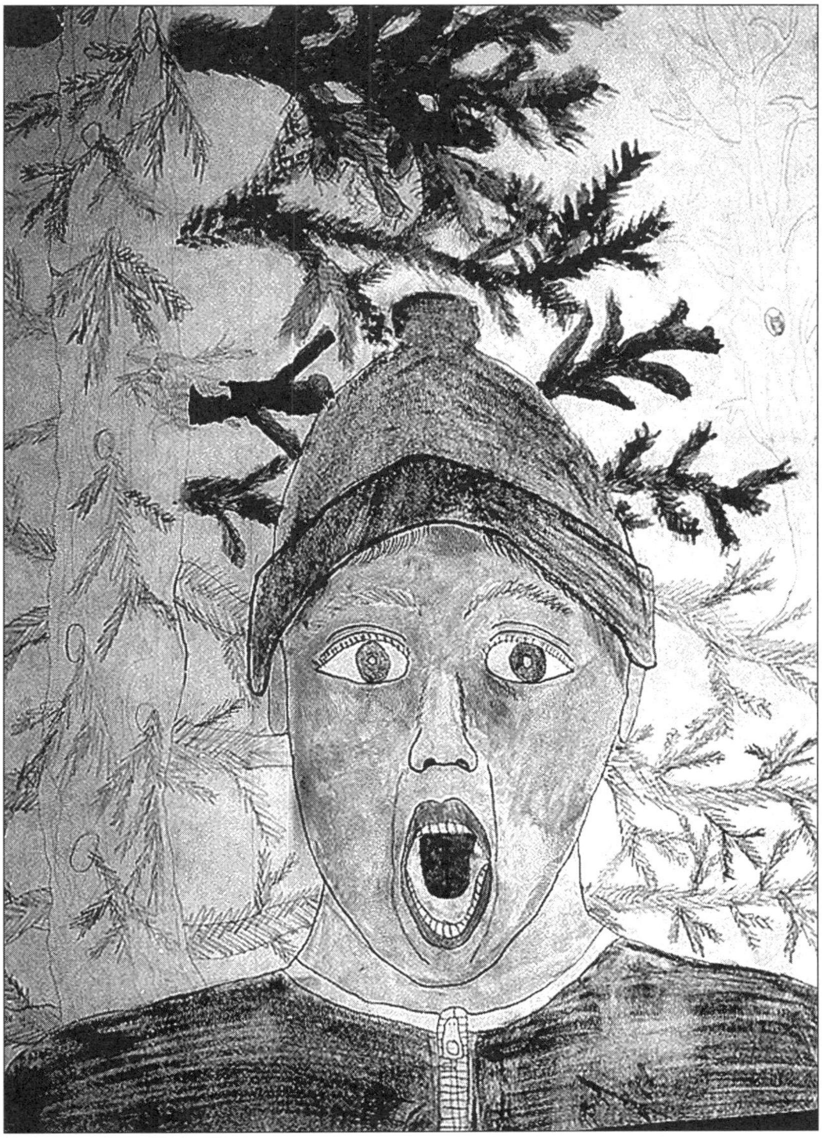

Self-portrait, pencil crayon on paper, grade 6 student, Matheson Island School

Fig. 5.13. This student used an extreme facial expression and added background and costume to his self-portrait to illustrate a scene from a survival story.

Materials

- sketchbooks
- pencils
- erasers
- rulers
- white photocopy paper, or Dessin or Mayfair, (8 1/2" x 11" or 11" x 17"; 21.5 cm x 28 cm or 28 cm x 43 cm)

Books to Have Handy

Picture Books
Amazing Grace
Batman comics
Best Friends
Calvin and Hobbes
The Night Rebecca Stayed Too Late
The Party

Teacher References
Drawing on the Right Side of the Brain
How to Draw Comics the Marvel Way

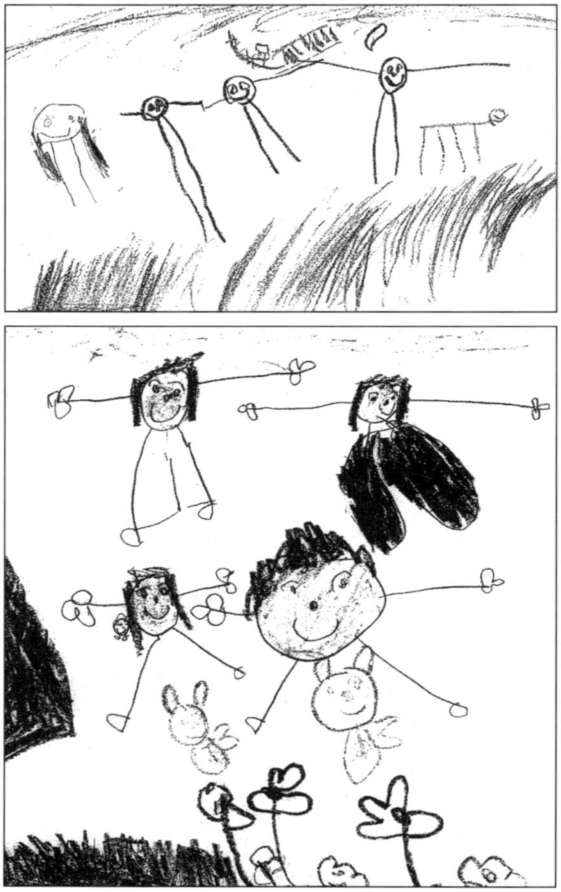

grade 1, Cranberry-Portage School

Fig. 5.14. These drawings were done the day before the lesson on figure drawing.

Figure Drawing

Figure drawing or "life" drawing is drawing people. People are often a favorite subject and learning to draw figures can help boost students' confidence with drawing in general. Figure drawing is also useful for studying movement and gesture.

Artists and illustrators commonly study figure drawing from nude models, or use movable wooden figurines to model active poses. Renaissance artists studied anatomy and muscle structure from partially dissected corpses. Students, starting at age seven or eight, can begin figure drawing by looking at photographs of athletes, dancers, or other children in motion, or they can pose for each other.

Figure drawing combines the challenges of proportion, movement, and detail.

Preparation

Figure drawing requires little preparation. You should, however, assemble materials and try the exercises first so that you can demonstrate them comfortably. Figure drawing can be taught as a series of short lessons: scribble or gesture drawing, geometric shape drawing, proportion, blind contour drawing, and lengthier combined drawings.

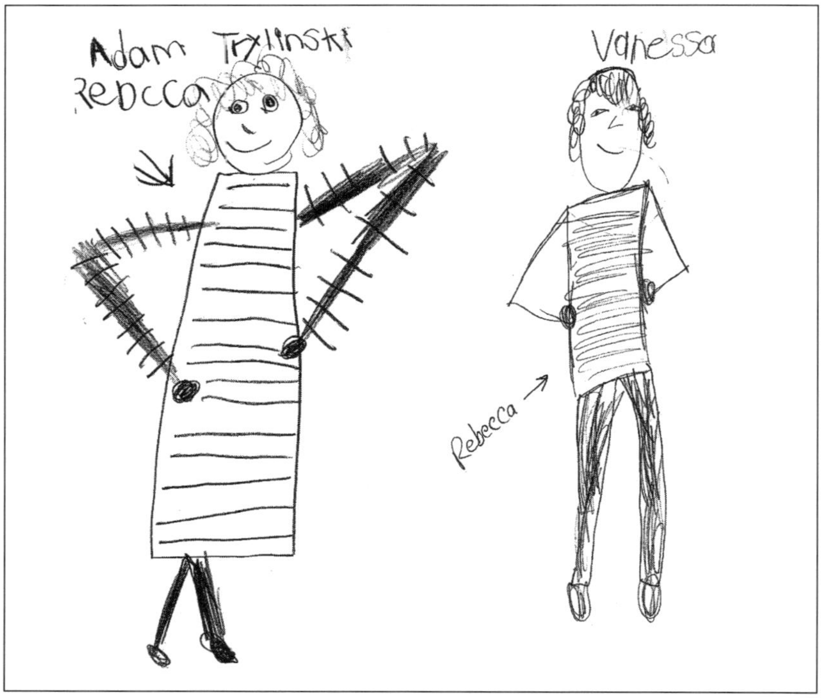

pencil on paper, grade 1, Cranberry-Portage School

Fig. 5.15. These drawings were done by students after instruction on how to draw people. Their earlier drawing styles were the result of lack of instruction, rather than a lack of developmental readiness.

Appropriate Subjects

Appropriate subjects for figure drawing include photos from sports magazines. These tend to be active poses, with figures running, falling, jumping, and so on. (see Books to Have Handy). Dance posters, brochures, and children's picture books are useful as well. Students may also pose for each other or use a movable figurine (fig. 5.16).

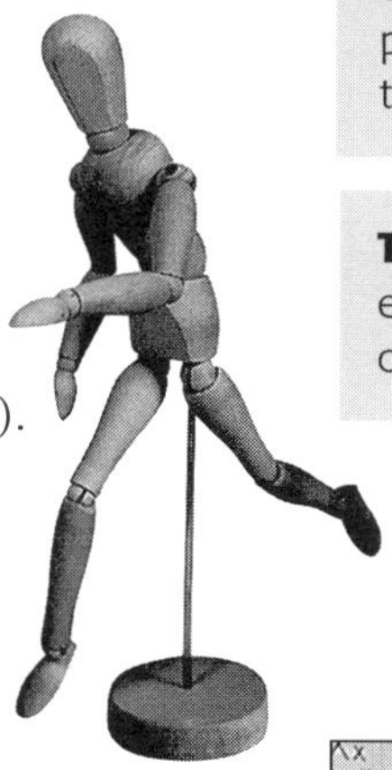

Fig. 5.16. Artists and illustrators use movable models such as this one to sketch figures in motion.

Tip: For self-conscious students, try having them pose for a short period right after recess, when they are still wearing their bulky outdoor clothes.

Tip: If you hold your pencil loosely, near the eraser end, you'll get a more relaxed scribble; try charcoal pencils or washable markers for variation.

Method

Students can try scribble-drawing to reproduce the shape of their model. This kind of scribble-drawing—capturing active poses that suggest movement—is called "gesture drawing." To introduce gesture drawing to your students, have the volunteers pose for each other at the front of the class, or sketch from active poses in photos. Look at *Amazing Grace* or Batman comics with your students. An active pose makes a more interesting illustration and communicates the action in the story (fig. 5.17). Keep the drawing time short (sixty seconds) for each pose and encourage gymnastic poses. (See scribble-drawing, page 30.)

Older or more advanced students may also try a negative space drawing: scribble in all the shapes around and between parts of the subject (fig. 5.18).

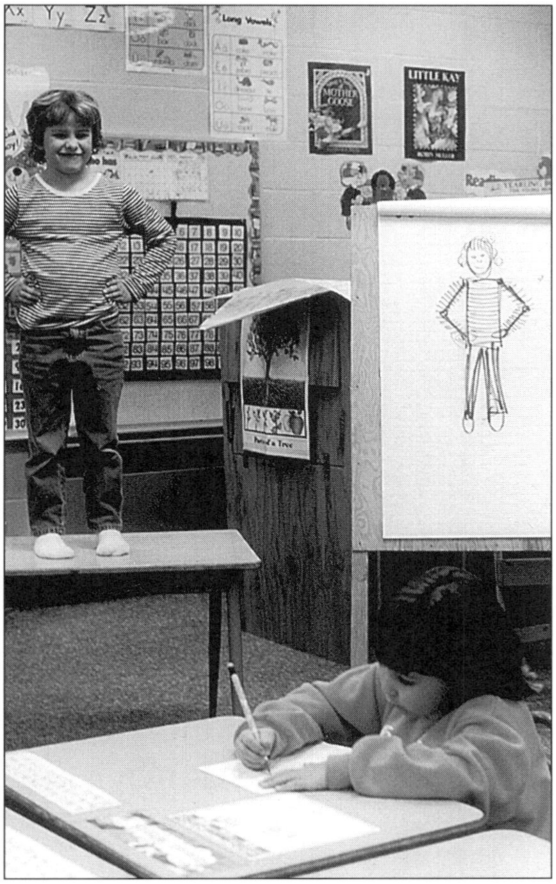

grades 1–2, Cranberry-Portage School

Fig. 5.17. The students in this class had fun posing for each other. Working with an older group, later in the year, the same class tried some of the extreme poses and contortions of Olympic athletes.

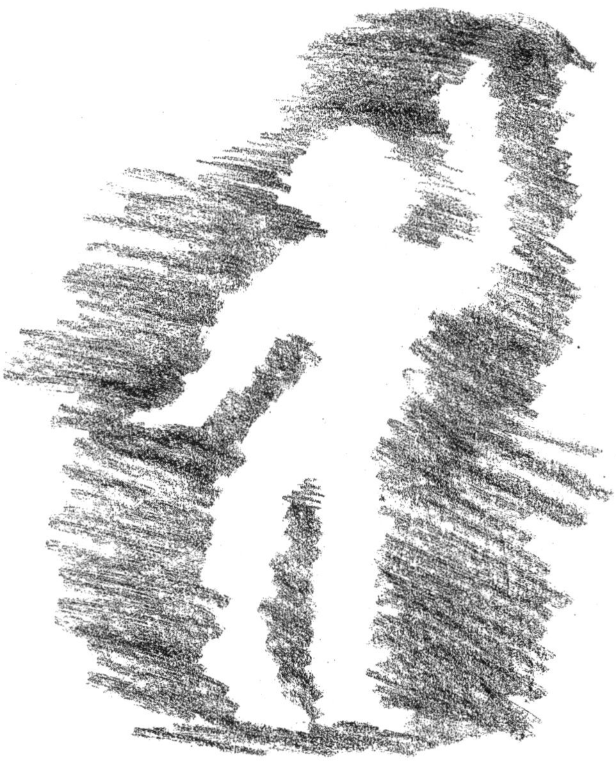

crayon on paper, Noni Brynjolson, age 11

Fig. 5.18. Noni scribbled in the negative spaces surrounding the figure, for a reverse image. Advanced students can try this exercise.

Tip: Negative space drawing will help your students see the shapes of spaces between parts of their subjects. The best poses for this are ones that "contain" some space (hands on hips, legs apart, and so on).

Tip: Think of arms and legs as long rectangles with circular joints. Think of the head as an oval and the shoulders and "trunk" of the body as rectangular. Hands can be tricky to draw—try to see them as a square shape with rectangular fingers and with the rectangle of the thumb attached to the side of the square.

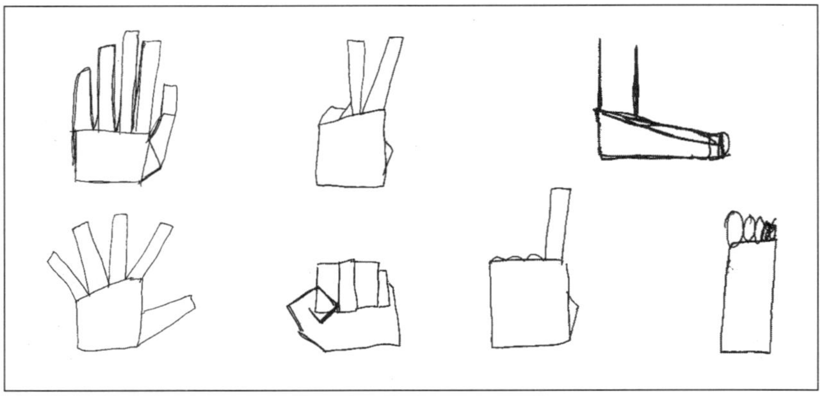

crayon on paper, Noni Brynjolson, age 11

Fig. 5.19. Complicated shapes such as hands and feet are easier to draw as geometric shapes.

The most basic approach to drawing the shape of a subject is to look for the geometric shapes contained in it (figs. 5.19 and 5.20). Ask your students: "What shapes do you see in the human form (circles, ovals, rectangles, and so on)?" Have students draw a geometric and simplified version of their models in their sketchbooks. Start with quick, two- to three-minute drawings.

Advanced or older students might be more comfortable defining these shapes as volumes—spheres, cylinders, rectangular prisms, or "boxes." Using three-dimensional volumes more properly describes the structure of the body, and will be helpful when drawing difficult poses.

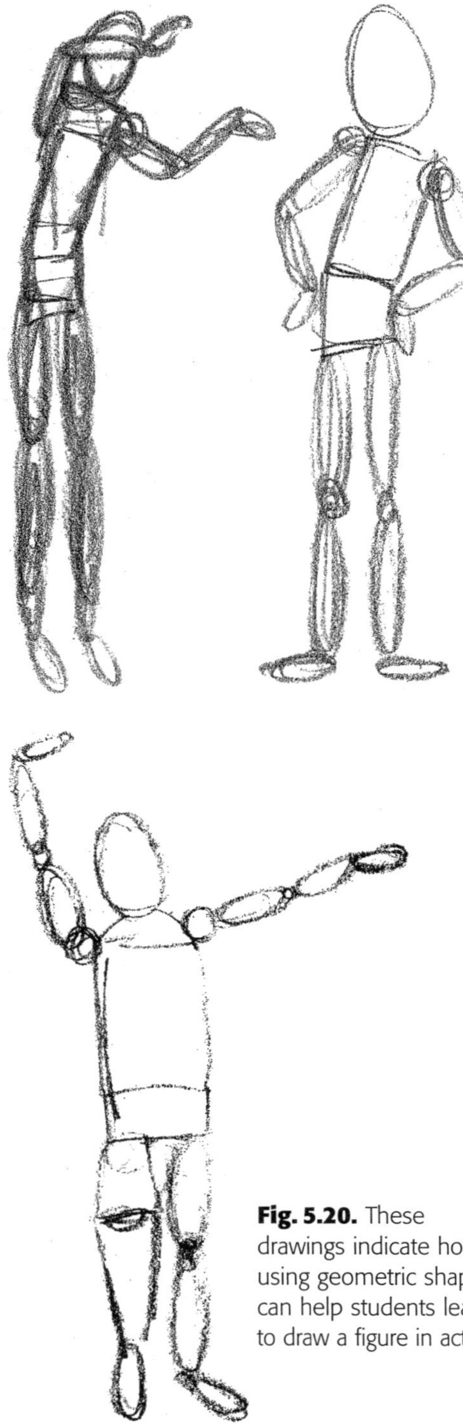

Fig. 5.20. These drawings indicate how using geometric shapes can help students learn to draw a figure in action.

crayon on paper, Noni Brynjolson, age 11

Basic Proportions of the Figure

Introduce your students to the basic proportions of the body (fig. 5.21). To demonstrate, invite a student to volunteer to stand at the front of the classroom.

- Measure how many times the height of the student's head fits into the measure of the body from top to toe (this will vary with the student's age). Young children may be only $4^1/_2$ "heads" high; adults are approximately 7 to $7^1/_2$ "heads" high.
- Notice that arms are longer than you'd think; fingertips reach down between the hips and knees.
- Hands and feet are larger than you might expect; a hand can stretch from chin to eyebrows.
- Notice that legs are long—the mid-way point of the body is near the hip. Look at the shape of the space between the arms and the body (it's very narrow).
- Look at a side view and notice how the arm hangs alongside the body and how the top of the shoulder forms an upside-down "U."

Have students do a quick sketch of a classmate or a figure from a magazine photo in their sketchbooks, noting the basic rules of proportion.

Challenge students to find interesting poses for their "models." Students may also try interesting views including close-up, distant, side, front, back, and top.

Ask students to do a blind contour drawing (fig. 5.22) of their subject (see chapter 3). Encourage them to notice things like the wrinkled edges in clothing, facial features, fingers, and feet. Allow five to ten minutes for a blind contour drawing. The result, if it is recognizable as a "human," may take on the qualities of a caricature or alien.

Students are now ready to begin their figure drawings on larger paper. Encourage them to continue with a relaxed, almost scribbly line (a scribbled line conveys action and is interesting to view). For a combination of approaches, draw the underlying geometric, or scribbled, shapes first to judge proportion and pose, then add contour lines on top for interesting line quality and detail. Students may then add texture, pattern, and value (fig. 5.23). (See chapter 3.)

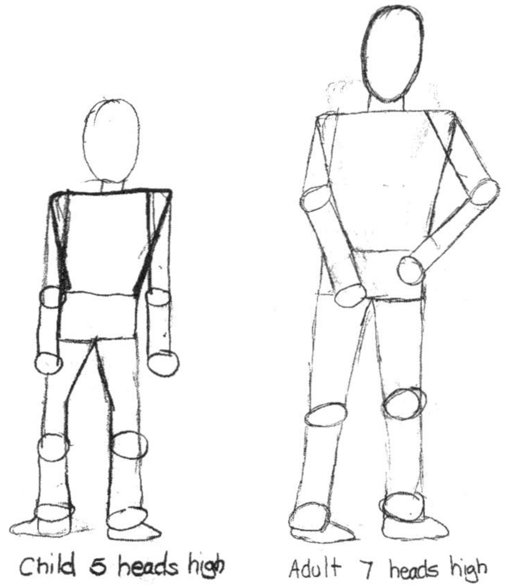

Danna Slessor-Cobb, age 10

Fig. 5.21. These geometric drawings show the proportion of the human figure. Adults are about 7 heads high. Children's heads are larger, relative to the size of their bodies. Arms should be drawn long enough so that fingertips reach halfway between the hip and the knee.

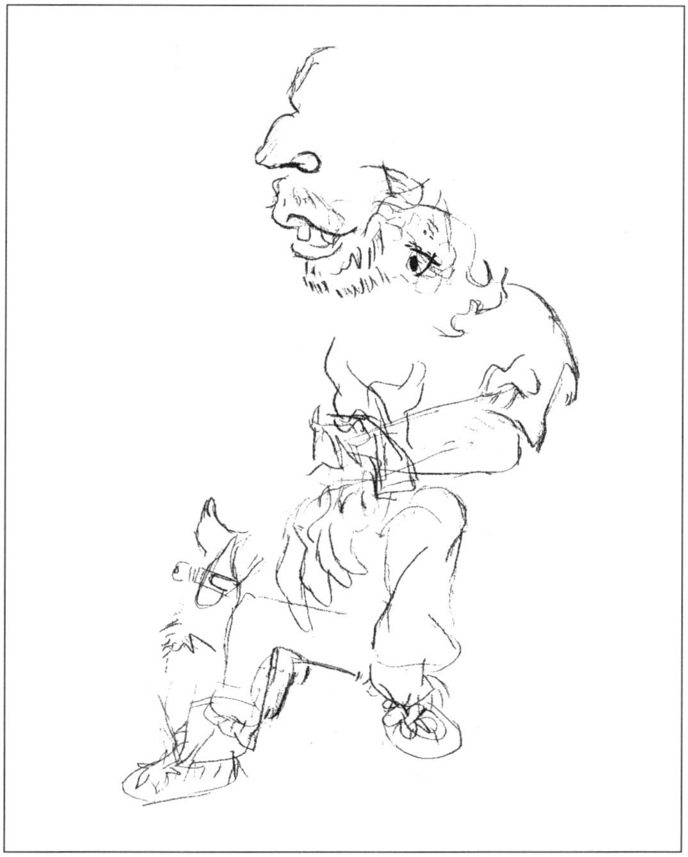

My Dad, pencil on paper, Noni Brynjolson, age 11

Fig. 5.22. Blind contour drawing produces a quirky, expressive result. Be prepared for lots of giggling when students look at their finished drawings.

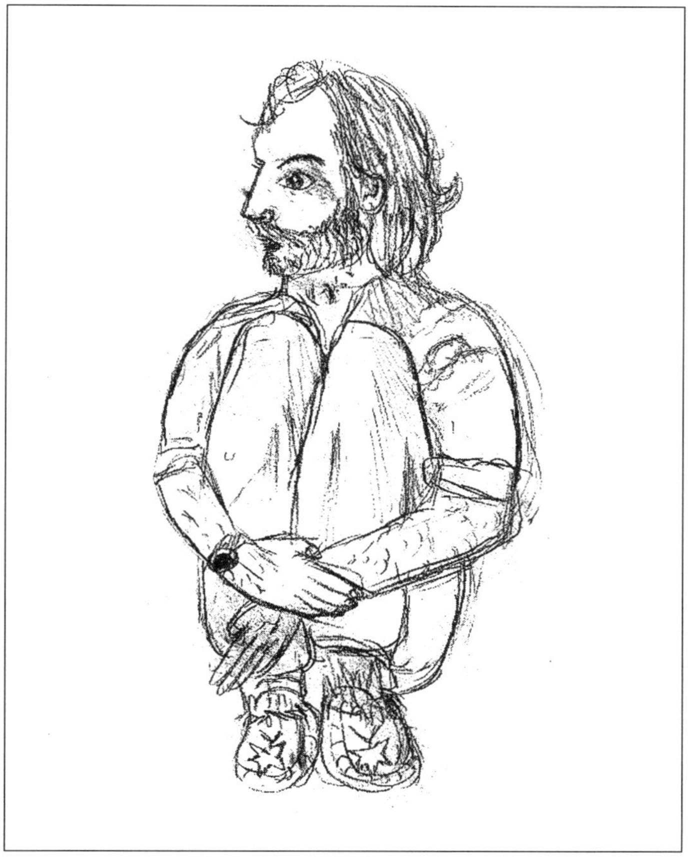

My Dad, pencil on paper, Noni Brynjolson, age 11

Fig. 5.23. Noni began by sketching in the geometric shapes, added a careful contour line, and finished the drawing by adding texture marks and darker values.

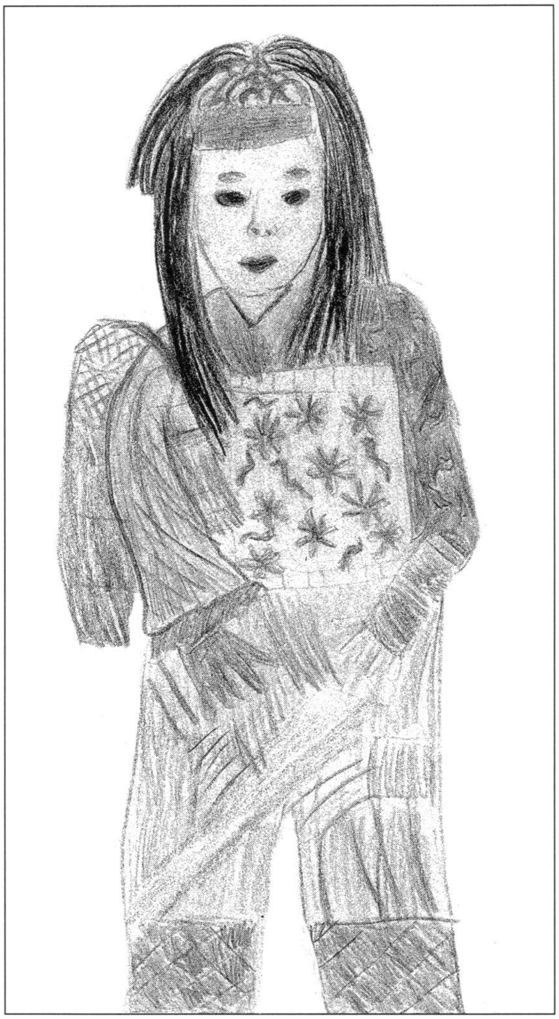

Samurai, pencil crayon on paper, Jessica Howison, grade 6, Luxton School

Fig. 5.24. This Samurai warrior provided an interesting study of a figure in costume.

Enrichment

- Students may wish to draw each other in costume, or design masks or wrappings that disguise part of the face or body (fig. 5.24).
- Try celebrity drawings of guest teachers, principals, visitors, or students on their birthdays; or visit a dance troupe in rehearsal or a basketball game to practice gesture drawing in students' sketchbooks.
- Similar drawing approaches will work with drawing animals "from life," if they are cooperative enough to pose for a minute or two at a time.

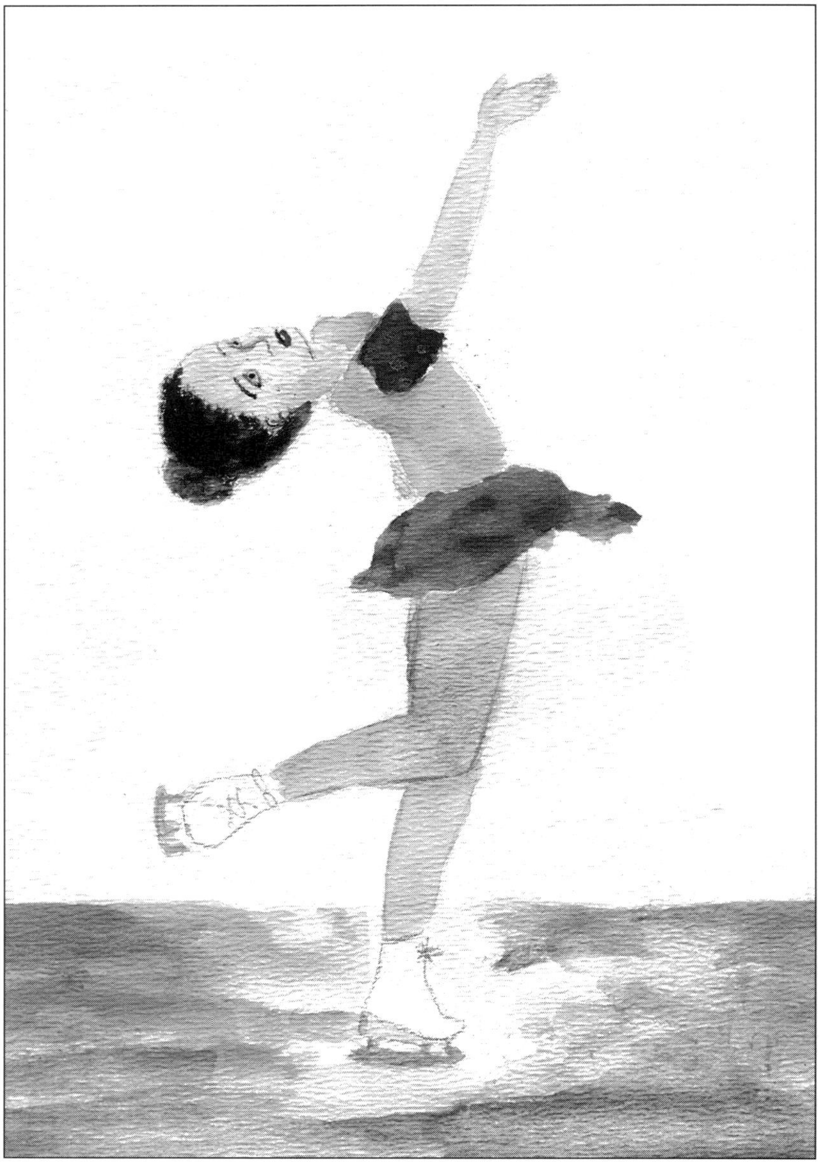

Figure Skating, pencil and watercolor on paper, Noni Brynjolson, grade 6, Luxton School

Fig. 5.25. The winter Olympics provided plenty of opportunities to study figures in action.

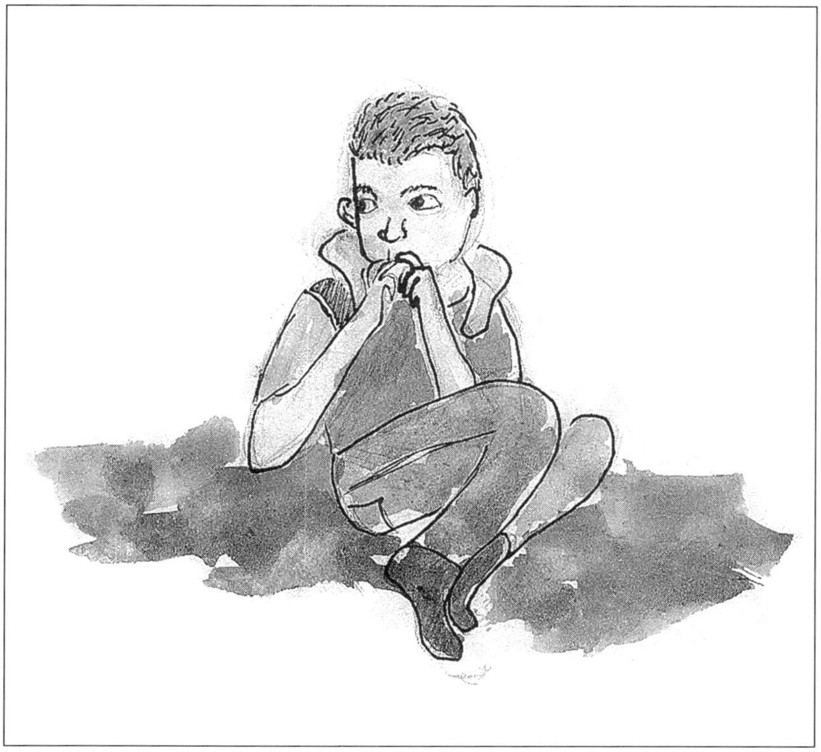

watercolor and ink, Noni Brynjolson, age 11

Fig. 5.26. This simple line drawing captures the pose and expression of the subject.

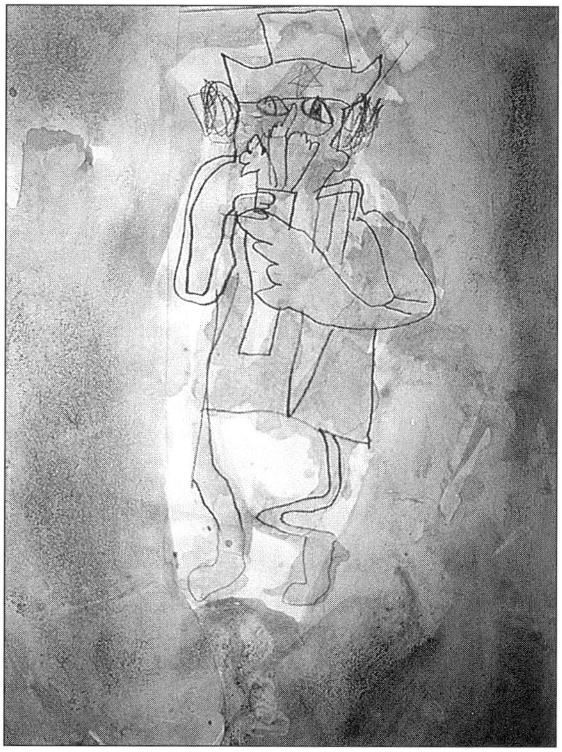

Man with Flowers, grade 1 student, Stanley Knowles Elementary School

Fig. 5.27. After a session on figure drawing, this grade-one student chose to draw a person from a magazine photograph. A simple question like, "I wonder who he will give those flowers to?" may prompt an explanation—and perhaps a story—from the student.

- If your VCR gives a clear picture on "pause," try drawing from videos of dancers, athletes, or children playing (fig. 5.25).
- Finish pencil drawings with pen and ink; with permanent pens and a watercolor wash; or cut out drawings and reassemble several overlapping images onto a colored sheet of paper for display (fig. 5.26).
- For illustrations, choose poses and (costumes) that fit the action in the story, or express something about the character (fig. 5.27).
- Add shading and reflected highlights (fig. 5.28). (See value in chapter 3.)

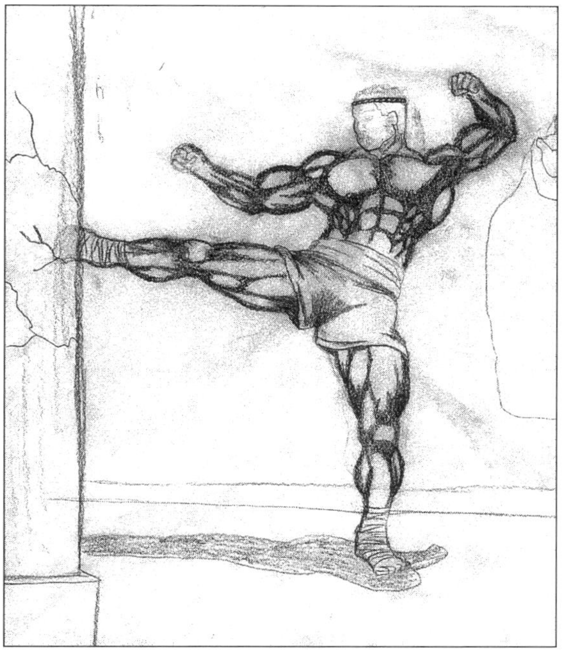

pencil on paper, Sherman Baptiste, age 15, Wanipigow School

Fig. 5.28. Learning to draw realistic figures—with accurate muscle structure and with darker values shaded in to produce a 3-D effect—is important to students like Sherman who want to draw superheroes.

Materials

- pencils
- sketchbooks
- erasers
- white photocopy paper (or Dessin or Mayfair), 11" x 17" or 28 cm x 43 cm
- felt pens, black, very fine-tipped, nontoxic (other media may be used to "finish" the drawings, see Part 4.)

Books to Have Handy

Picture Books
Dragon Feathers
Dragon
Dragons, Dragons and Other Creatures That Never Were
Have You Seen Birds?
Saint Francis
Where the Wild Things Are

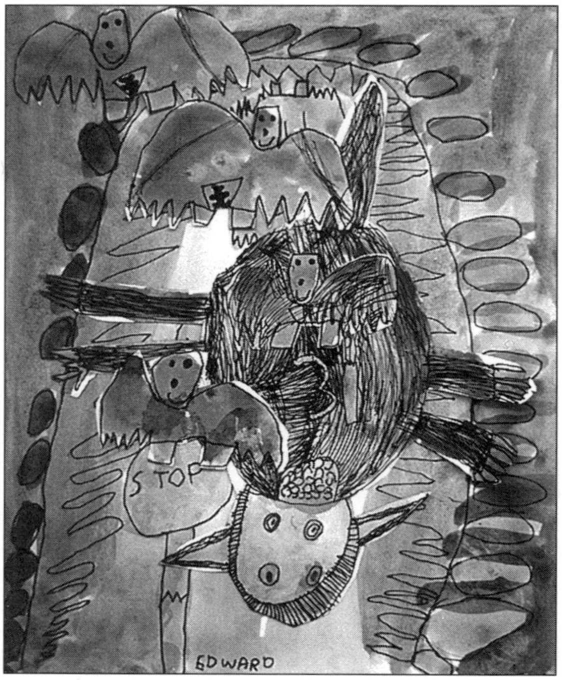

Wild Things, paint, ink, and collage, Edward, age 5, Pine Dock School

Fig. 5.29. These creatures were drawn with a fine-tipped, permanent marker, painted with tempera paint, then cut out and glued onto a drawn and painted background.

Tip: Some students may have the patience to draw a quick study of their creature in their sketchbooks and redraw a "good copy" onto a larger sheet of paper; younger students may want to work directly on their good copy.

Composite Creatures

Drawing composite creatures provides students with a method for developing look-drawing into fantasy or imagined subjects.

Many students spend hours copying comics, cartoons, and sports logos. By copying a well-drawn figure such as Batman over and over in a variety of poses, students can learn a lot about drawing anatomy, figures in action, foreshortening, and the conventions of comic-book art. To supplement this activity—and to gently nudge students into creating their own characters and scenarios—have students use the same creative process as other artists and writers: take pieces of familiar subjects and mix them with imagination.

Appropriate Subjects

Have students research a topic involving some kind of mythical or imaginary creature (fig. 5.30). Appropriate subjects might include dragons, Greek myths, space aliens, mutants, "wild things," or transformers, depending on the topic of study.

Preparation

Gather visual references relating to the description of the creatures. For dragons, for example, you will need photos of the following: animals with wings (bats, birds, insects), claws or talons (lizards, eagles), scales (fish, lizards) or feathers (birds), long bodies (snakes, lizards, dinosaurs), long tails (snakes), and so on.

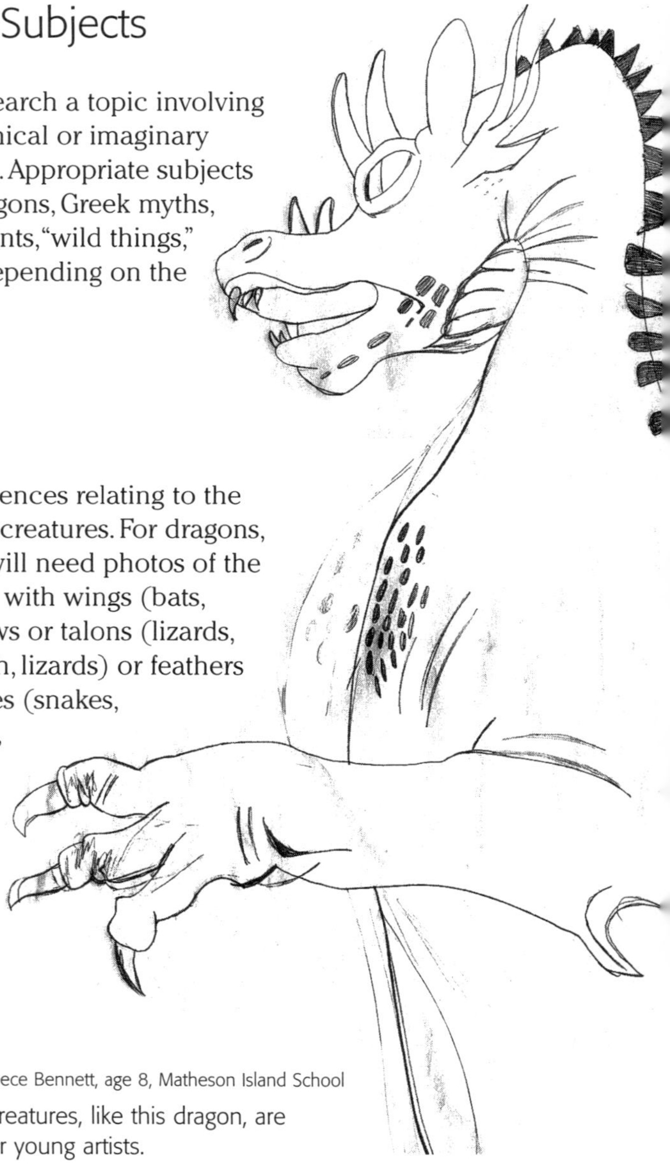

Dragon, pencil on paper, Reece Bennett, age 8, Matheson Island School

Fig. 5.30. Imaginary creatures, like this dragon, are compelling subjects for young artists.

Method

Look at *Dragons*, or other books on dragons, with your students. Point out to them how the illustrator "borrows" details from a variety of other animals to design his dragon. In *Dragons*, the illustrator's careful drawing style and the way he uses detail make these dragons appear real. Look through other books about dragons (see Books to Have Handy). Notice how every artist draws dragons differently. (If you are studying another topic, look at illustrations in books related to that topic.)

Challenge students to design their own creatures. Have them begin by drawing details from a variety of animals in their sketch-books: different kinds of eyes, wing shapes, animal feet, claws, and so on (fig. 5.31). Encourage them to "collect" parts of animals, and to not combine the parts into a creature until they've collected lots of possible options. For tips on how to draw, see chapter 3.

Ask students to pay careful attention to contours, textures, and patterns in their sketches (fig. 5.32).

After students have drawn a number of detailed parts in their sketchbooks, they can begin to design a composite creature on a larger sheet of paper. Remind students to work carefully; light pressure with pencil marks means lighter lines that are easier to erase. Encourage students to draw their creatures large enough to fill the page; to fit a long creature onto the page, the neck or tail may have to bend or loop around.

Take a look at the different pen marks used by the illustrators in *Where the Wild Things Are* and *Saint Francis*. Then have students trace over their pencil drawings with fine-tipped black markers. Students may also want to experiment with the pens in their sketch-books before outlining their good copy. (See chapter 4.)

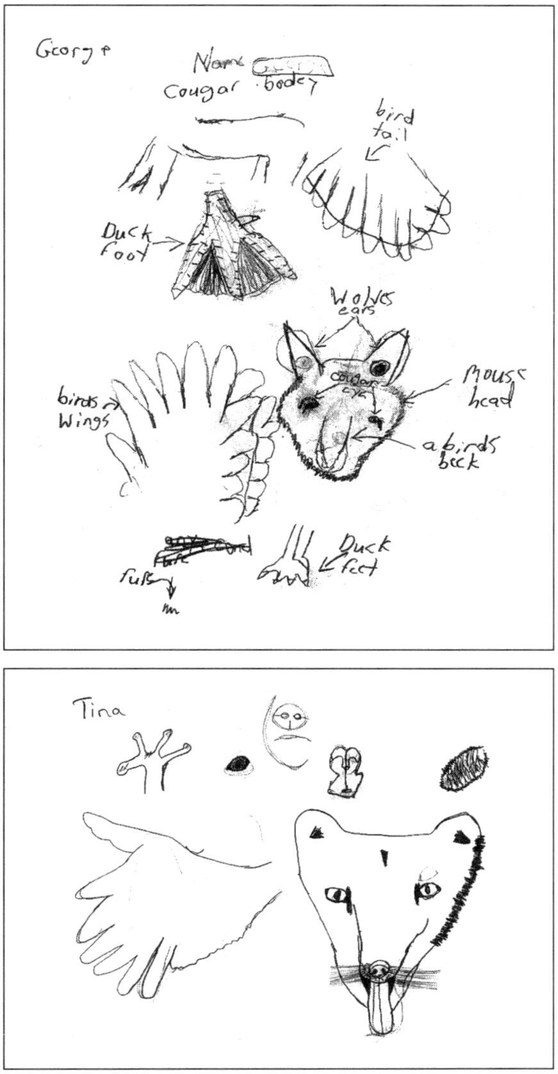

George and Tina, age 10, Wanipigow School

Fig. 5.31. Before composing a composite creature, it is important to make carefully drawn studies of animal parts.

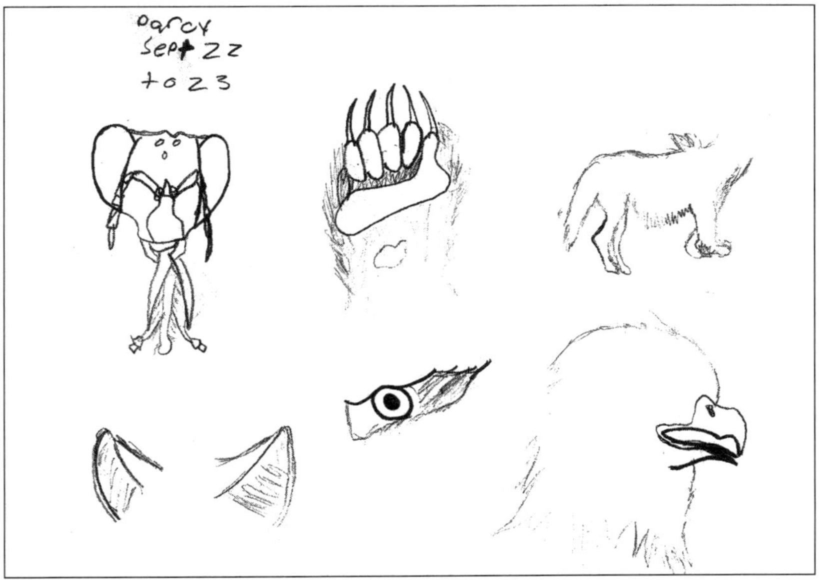

Darcy, age 10, Wanipigow School

Fig. 5.32. The jagged contour lines and repeated pencil marks indicate the furry and feathered textures of these animals.

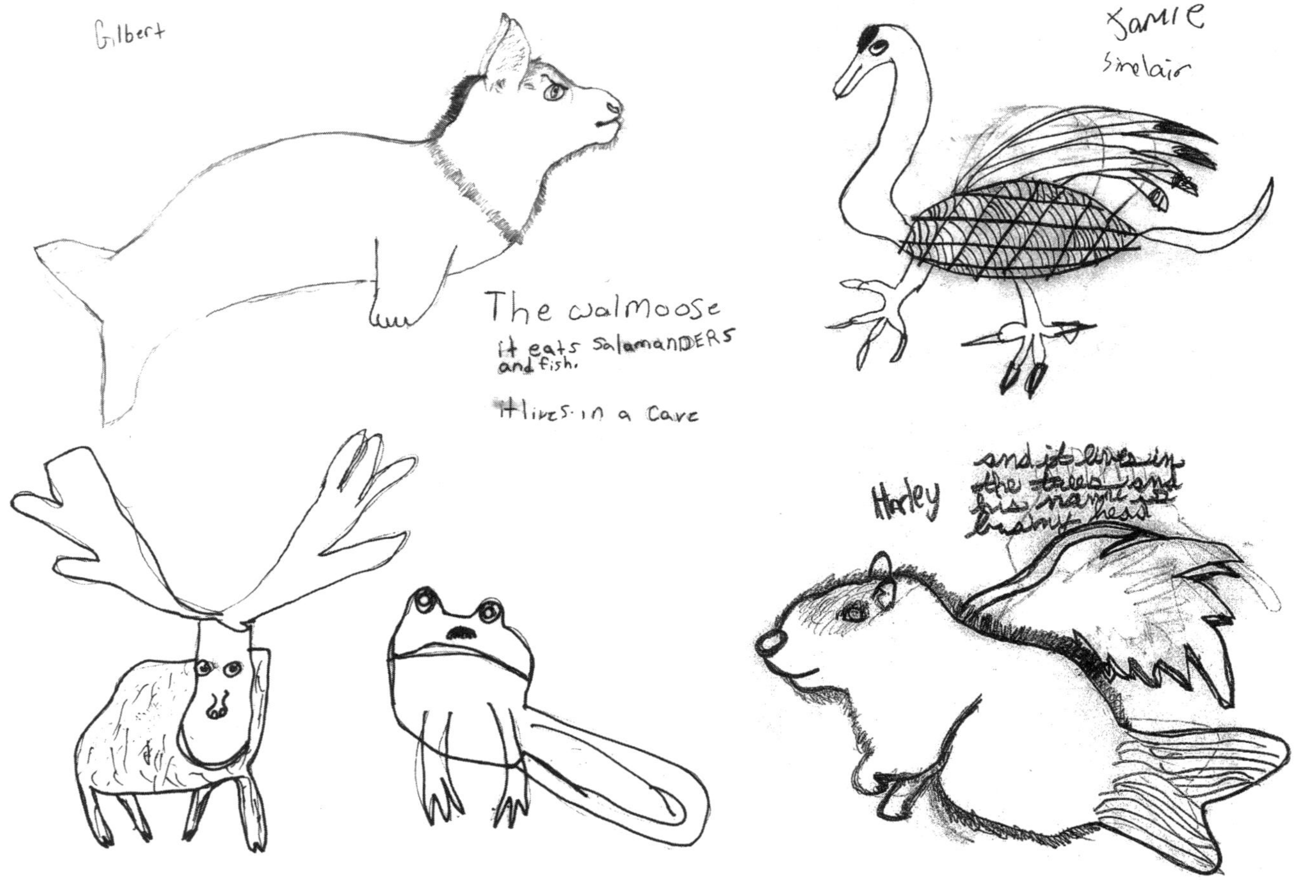

Composite Creatures, pencil on paper, Gilbert, Jamie, Jocelyn, and Harley, age 10, Wanipigow School

Fig. 5.33. After students designed these fantastic creatures, they were asked to describe them and use them as characters in a story.

Tip: Some students rush to draw an entire creature. To slow them down, you might want to ask them to sketch a given number of eyes, claws, bodies, and so on, before continuing. Advanced students may have strong visual memory, and may insist on designing their creatures by assembling, from memory, pieces of drawings they have done before. Be tactful with their efforts, and suggest that they look for two or three parts of their creature that may be improved by drawing from a visual reference.

Tip: Because most students are exposed to creatures regularly on television and video, you may have to (gently) insist that the creatures be the student's own design; that is, no Ninja Turtles, Batman, and so on. Explain that copyright laws protect those designs from being copied by others. Students may want to draw the copyright symbol (©) to protect their own work.

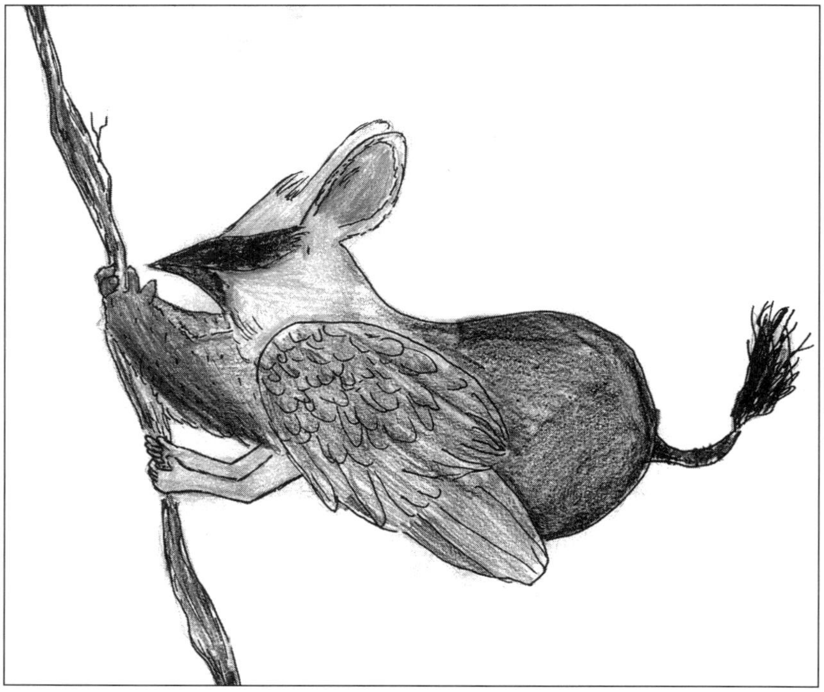

Chinchilkoalabirdamoose, nk and pencil crayon, Noni Brynjolson, age 11

Fig. 5.34. This is a finished composite creature, outlined with a fine-tipped marker and colored with pencil crayon. The name of this piece is fun, too!

Enrichment

- Use the creatures as characters in a story (fig. 5.33). (See chapter 6.) Challenge students to consider what environment, food, and character traits might best suit their character.
- Color may be added to drawings with pencil crayons (fig. 5.34). Pencil crayons should be sharp. Encourage students to press lightly and blend colors; for example, green can be varied by adding yellow, blue, or brown. The drawing will be more interesting if the colors are richer. Use dark blue, brown, or purple for darkening colors, rather than black. Too much black will make the colors all appear gray. Press slightly harder next to the outside contour lines, as darker edges next to the ink lines will make the subject appear more three-dimensional. Try placing a piece of window screen, plastic mesh bag, or other flat, fine texture under the paper when coloring, to provide a pattern resembling scales. (See chapter 10.)
- Decide how the creature will be posed (flying, sleeping, walking), and whether the view is close-up, distant, from above, from the side, front, or back (fig. 5.35). Advanced students might be interested in drawing these creatures in action, or from various viewpoints. A three-dimensional model would be useful. Use either a toy with a related shape that can be turned over and viewed from different angles (for example, a toy dinosaur from the back may give clues about drawing a dragon from the back), or sculpt the creature out of Plasticine, then bend and manoeuvre it until the desired pose is obtained, then draw.
- With young students, try a crayon or pastel "resist" picture of the creature. Draw the creature with crayon, pressing hard. Emphasize drawing the pattern or texture of the creature, not coloring. Paint over with watery tempera paint.
- Using the drawings as blueprints, students could try sculpting creatures out of Plasticine or clay, or constructing them out of recycled materials and a hot-glue gun, or papier-mâché.

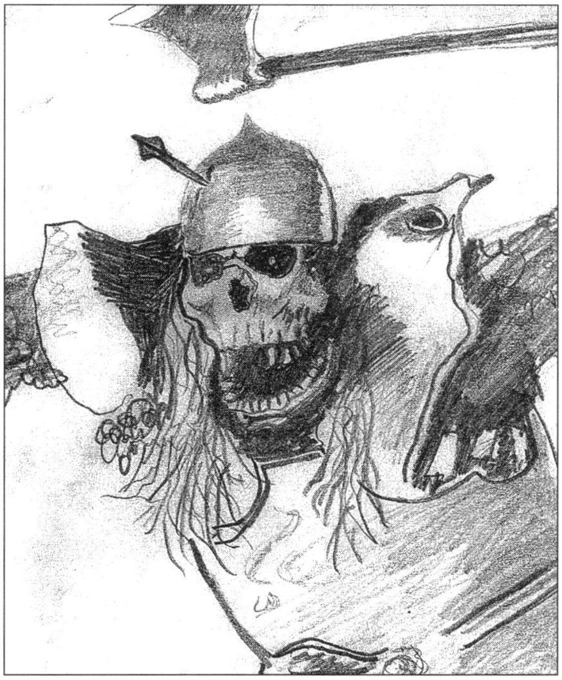

Wraith, Chris Bushie, grade 7–8, Wanipigow School

Fig. 5.35. The close-up of this nightmarish creature was drawn with attention to texture marks and light and dark values.

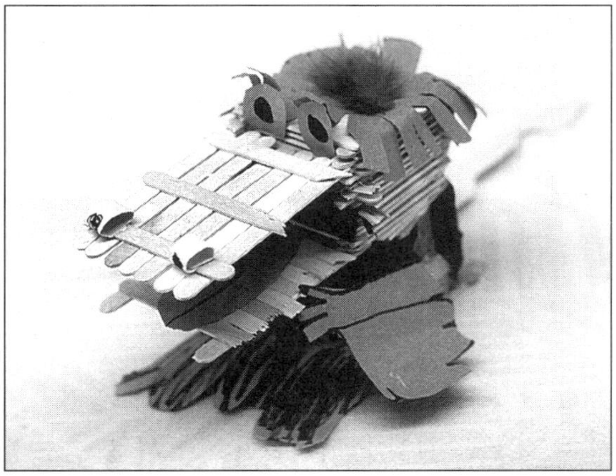

Mascot, mixed media, grade 5–8 class, Stevenson Island School

Fig. 5.36. This creature was constructed out of materials that were handy—Popsicle sticks, construction paper, and feathers.

Vocabulary (see appendixes for definitions)

anatomy	*figure drawing*	*profile*
background	*foreground*	*proportion*
blind contour	*gesture*	*self-portrait*
caricature	*line*	*shape*
composite	*look-drawing*	*texture*
contour	*overlapping*	*value*
disguise (costume)	*portrait*	*volume*
expression	*pose*	

Part 3
Illustration and Design

Illustration is important to the students' writing process and as a companion form of communication. In this section, you will show your students how to combine words and images, and how to use storyboards as part of the writing process. Shadow puppets (chapter 7) are another tool you can use to motivate your students to write. You can adapt these same processes for planning other art projects—a class mural, a poster, advertisement, comic book, large drawing, theater sets, and so on. (See Enrichment in each chapter.)

The drawing exercises in Part 2 described how to draw a subject and how to achieve an illusion of depth in a picture. Now you will introduce your students to the "grammar" of art—the organizing principles and design choices that artists and illustrators make in order to compose an interesting picture.

Motivating Students to Write

Looking at Picture Books

Illustrations are often thought of as "decorations" for text. The storytellers who read the books to young children—librarians, teachers, parents, and older students—rarely discuss illustrations. And yet, many richly illustrated picture books can be "read" silently, and their illustrations can even convey aspects of the story that are absent from the text.

Illustration is the most accessible vehicle available to pre-literate children for entering the story. If our goals are to interest and excite students in books, teach them that ideas and narratives can be expressed and respected in book form, and show them that "reading" books is an enjoyable activity (rather than a humiliating one), then we should be looking at the primary means of communication available to them—pictures—before gradually introducing text.

There are many examples of picture books that contain no words. (You might point out to your students that the illustrators still get credit as authors. The story line, although not expressed in writing, is present in the illustrations.) *Frog, Where Are You?* by Mercer Mayer, *Tuesday* by David Wiesner, and *The Little Mouse Trapped in a Book* by Monique Felix are excellent examples of wordless stories. You might show students the pictures silently at first, and then invite some discussion or description of what students thought was happening in the story. Introduce the idea of story sequence, perhaps as simply as beginning, middle, and end. Students might then develop their own story sequence in pictures (see chapter 6). Choose topics for these books that are exciting for students. "Spring" is a bland theme that may not capture their imaginations—remember that you are competing against 300 channels of satellite television! Try "undersea monsters," "tyrannosaurs," or an adventure story about the classroom's pet hamster.

Students may spend several sessions on wordless books—the best of which might be "published" (see Assembling Books, page 94). The goals here are to have students improve their ability to develop pictorial story sequence and to feel pride and competence in being an author/illustrator.

Studies have found that quality picture books stimulate language more effectively that the illustrations in many widely used basal series. Using a "Picture Potency Formula," winners of the Caldecott Medal for illustration were given a high rating for student response (Mavrogenes n.d., 239).

Creating a Narrative Sequence Through Illustration

If we stop to ask ourselves why we teach children to write, or what we value about their writing, we might say that writing expresses thoughts or ideas, conveys information, documents events, and allows us to invent stories or transform ordinary situations into marvelous ones. Why then would we ignore or discount the value of these qualities in students' visual communication?

Visual symbols are available to students from a very early age. Drawing is available to students as a form of communication long before students learn to write.

Visual communication is, in its own right, important to students. It is also an important bridge to the written word. At a certain point in a child's development, a story line or narrative sequence begins to accompany or dominate the drawing. These stories are spontaneous and allow children to role-play, to arrange and re-arrange models of reality in order to understand their world (Wilson and Wilson 1982, 102).

Encourage students to draw a story sequence or verbalize a story while they draw; this is an important step in the development of writing. Children learn that they can communicate while making marks on paper.

Wilson and Wilson (Ibid.) suggest practical ideas for encouraging storytelling and narrative sequence in children's drawings.

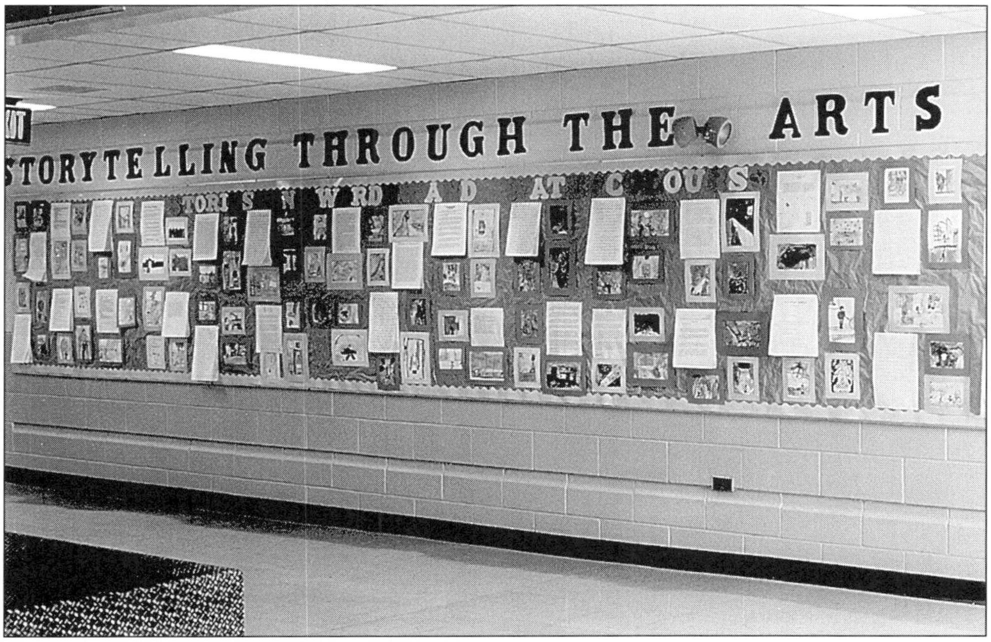

Fig. Pt. 3.1. Students at Niakwa Place School combined writing with illustration to tell their stories.

- To tell a story through drawing, some children may require prompting: "And then what's he going to do?" "I wonder what she'll meet in the forest?" "How does she get home again?"
- Suggest a general topic or theme that might trigger students' imaginations. Then provide students with a long strip of paper (a long strip of paper will encourage them to draw a number of scenes, one after the other).
- Suggest a specific topic or character.
- Invent a new character or superhero (see chapter 5). What personality of superpowers will they have?
- Give students a page with pre-drawn frames (see chapter 6).
- Read a story to the class. Discuss what they would change about the story. Encourage students to create their own versions.

All of these suggestions should be open-ended enough that students will be able to create their own story—one that is prompted but not completely guided by a model or by adult intervention. There is a fine line to walk between these two.

Once students have worked out the narrative in visual form, then writing becomes simply a matter of describing the illustrations or recording the verbal explanation of the pictures.

There are other exercises that use visual art or illustration as a springboard for creating writing, many of which are appropriate for older students.

- *postcards:* Students can draw or paint a landscape (see chapter 11) on a 6" x 6" (15 cm by 15 cm) card, and then write home, describing their trials and tribulations in reaching their (imaginary) location, and describing it to a friend or family. See *Stringbean's Trip to the Shining Sea* for examples of postcards combined with creative writing.
- *irrational images:* Many magazine photographs, advertisements, and picture books (see *The Mysteries of Harris Burdick*) contain humorous, impossible, or "irrational" images. Some other examples are an armchair in space, a hovering house, or Magritte's painting of a man with an apple for a head. These visual puzzles can challenge students to explain or write a mystery story about the image.
- *captions:* This is a popular exercise for introducing dialogue. Whiteout the caption boxes in cartoons and have students write their own words. Or try adding dialogue to a humorous or dramatic magazine photo, advertisement, or famous painting. "What was the Mona Lisa really thinking?"
- *cartooning:* Students who spend time drawing comic-book characters or caricatures can be encouraged to develop a story sequence and add text (see chapter 6). The text in comics often includes exciting sound-effect words such as "kaboom" or "POW" that might appeal to students (who can be encouraged to have fun making up some of their own sound-effect words). Comics also contain strong narrative sequence, dialogue, flashbacks, a narrator, synopsis, and other sophisticated devices that you may want to challenge advanced students to use.
- *puppets:* Puppets are one of the most powerful devices for developing story sequence. Puppets encourage both visual thinking and play (see chapter 7). Story lines emerge as students play together with puppets ("And then pretend my wolf went to the store and your princess was there…"). A variety of puppets can be used, but shadow puppets are especially effective because they translate easily into illustrations.

Illustration can provide an important bridge to literacy for students in several ways. Students may become interested in books and reading just by looking at engaging picture books. Creating a book and working with art materials can coax even reluctant writers into producing a story, and make them feel like "real" authors and illustrators. Working out narratives in storyboard form is important for young students and visual learners as a pre-writing exercise—adding the text then requires looking at the pictures and describing what is seen.

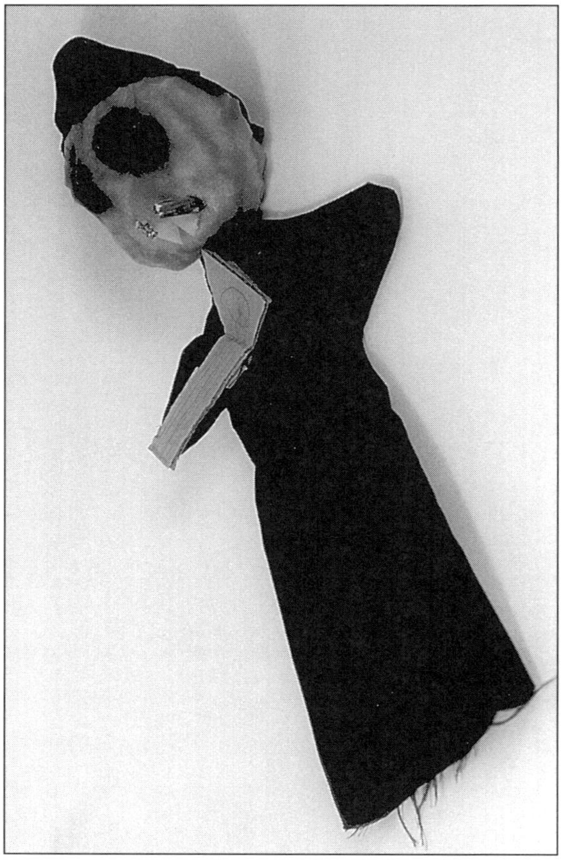

Rock and Roll Alien, cloth, foam rubber, paint, Iain Brynjolson, grade 3, Luxton School

Fig. Pt. 3.2. Puppets are a helpful device for developing a story sequence.

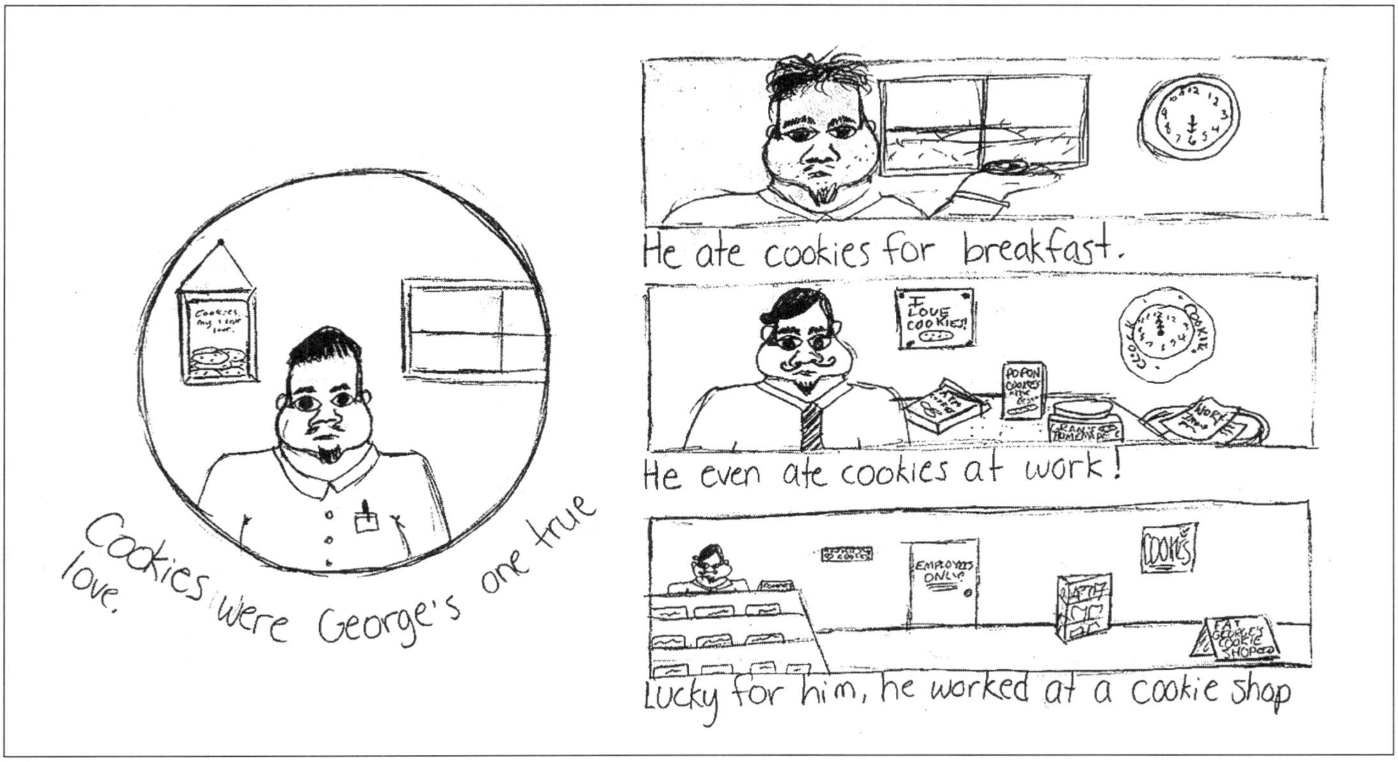

pencil on paper, Noni Brynjolson, age 11

Fig. Pt. 3.3. These thumbnail sketches reveal George's greatest passion. The story idea grew from the initial sketch of a well-fed character.

The Illustration Process

> Illustration, once regarded as a decorative appendage to children's books, has in recent years been elevated to the status of text. It is now common for educators to refer to children's "reading" the pictures in their storybooks and finding there a parallel story rivaling the written one. Illustration, as much an intellectual process as writing is, requires children to research their material and to think and feel with an artist's eye…Children learning to interrelate these two "languages" acquire inimitable insight into communication (Johnson 1997, 3).

The process of illustrating a story is similar to the writing process, and can be central to it. Visual information and imagery can contribute to the writer's imagination and assist in developing both narrative sequence and descriptive detail. The process that I use to develop text and illustration for a book is the same process that I use in the classroom. A summarized version of this process might go as follows:

A story usually begins with a topic or idea that catches the authors' interest. The story line is worked out by the authors in a story outline, or by authors/illustrators on a storyboard—a visual sequence that may consist of rough sketches of characters, settings, and action. The outlines or storyboards become the framework for developing the rough draft of the text. Authors research their stories, and illustrators research the visual elements of the story and gather visual references. Illustrators practice drawing different aspects of their subjects and settings, solve design problems, and decide what media will be used. Meanwhile, the text is rewritten and edited, and submitted to a publisher. When the text and illustrations are finished (and approved by the editors and art directors), a graphic designer uses a computer to lay out the text with the illustrations, and the books are assembled and printed.

Depending on the time available and your intentions for the project, writing and illustrating a story with students might take a few hours. A more elaborate approach might require a month. If you want to introduce the process of using storyboards and try a number of writing/illustrating projects in a short time, your end product might be a small, stapled booklet illustrated with simple line drawings. Once your students are familiar with the processes involved, you might take more time and produce a richly illustrated book over a period of several weeks.

Adapt the exercises that follow to fit your goals and to meet the needs of your students.

6
Composing a Whole Image

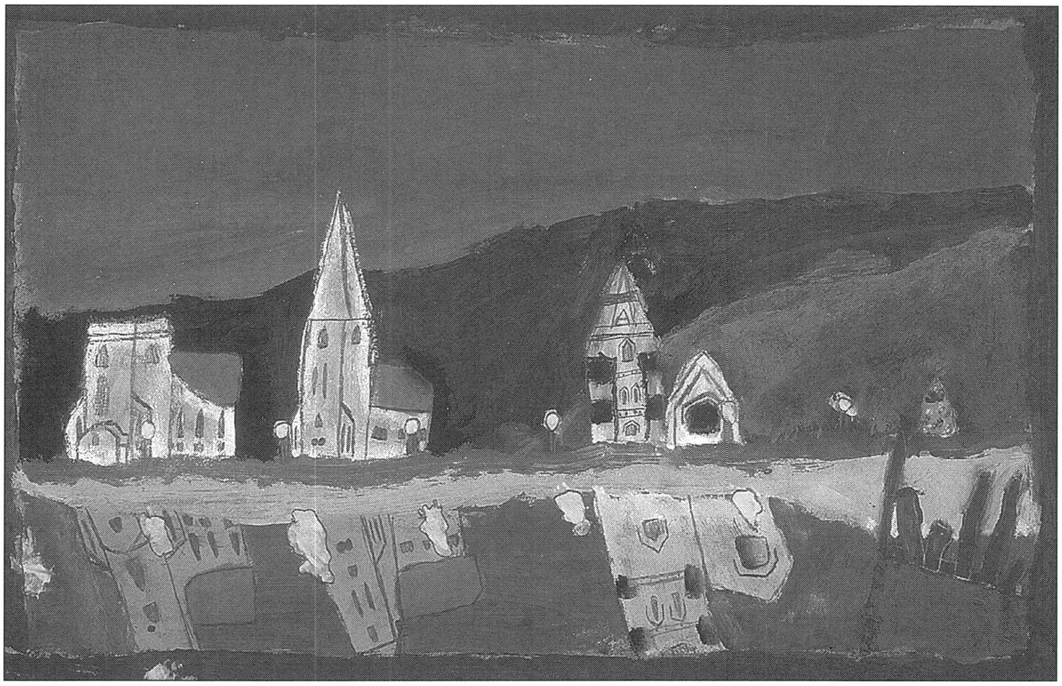

Reflections, tempera paint and pencil on paper, Johnny Yang, grade 6, Wellington School

Fig. 6.1. Johnny used strong composition in this landscape painting.

Introduction

In this chapter, you will introduce students to design and composition, and show them how to combine words with images to make a book.

Storyboards

A storyboard consists of a collection of sketches that may be very simple or very elaborate. Storyboards are a good starting point for visualizing a finished book, play, or movie.

Books to Have Handy

Picture Books
The Night Rebecca Stayed Too Late

Teacher References
Literacy Through the Book Arts
The Anti-Coloring Book series
Suddenly!

Preparation

Materials *for planning illustrations*

- sketchbooks
- scrap paper
- optional: storyboard planning sheets
- pencils
- erasers
- scissors
- glue or gluesticks
- books, magazines, photos, and so on (for reference)

Materials *for finishing illustrations*

- Dessin paper, or paper that fits your budget, cut to desired size (cut the paper fairly small, about 6" x 6" (15 cm x 15 cm), and glue illustrations into assembled books later)
- felt markers, black, fine-tipped
- pencil crayons
- optional: various media (watercolor, oil pastel, paint, collage, and so on)

Tip: A storyboard can become an interesting finished product in its own right. It may be a good model for a research project or a novel study.

Tell the students they are going to use a storyboard to plan the design and composition of a story. Students can make a storyboard in their sketchbook or use a pre-made storyboard planning sheet. If you use the planning sheet, distribute a photocopied page that has three empty boxes—entitled "beginning," "middle," and "end"—and lined spaces beside each box (for writing). Paul Johnson (1997) suggests using an even more structured format, which you might find useful with very reluctant writers. He outlines six boxes with an open-ended story line underneath each, with captions such as, "Draw a character in a house setting," and, "Character falls down hole. At the bottom is...?" The story line leads the character into an underground area, to adventure, and back home again. A similar approach is used in single frames in the Anti-Coloring Book series. The narrative is guided, but open-ended enough to allow for variation and student innovation.

A good example of pattern in writing is in the children's book *Suddenly!* The author uses a recurring device to provide unexpected plot twists.

Before your students begin, you will need to make the following decisions about the book (alone, or in discussion with students):

- the length and format; for example, booklet, concertina, postcard, hardcover, pop-up (see Assembling Books, page 94).
- the writing genre: poetry or story, mystery, adventure, fairy tale, western, imaginary journal, and so on
- the topic: some suggestions are country, animal, space, monsters, and oceans
- the design issue: borders, vantage points, shadows, and so on (see page 87–92)
- the art medium that will be used to finish the illustrations: some possibilities are paint, collage, printmaking, Plasticine, and watercolor (see Parts 4 and 5).

Try to have examples of each of these categories available to students as they begin their project.

Enrich the activity by giving students time to become familiar with their topic first—through posters and books; activities such as games, drama, songs, and cooking; handling objects and artifacts; and look-drawing their subjects. Students produce richer writing and stronger illustrations when they have access to this kind of "multi-sensory" exploration, become familiar with the visual forms (through observing and sketching), and have visual references available to them.

Method

Stage One

The first stage in illustrating a story is to study the manuscript or topic carefully and to begin to imagine what the characters, setting, and action might look like. A storyboard is very useful at this stage. Students can use their storyboards to:

- do practice drawings of their characters and settings
- plan the sequence of their illustrations (and story)
- consider design issues before they tackle their final copy

Storyboards may be undertaken as group projects or may be eliminated entirely for students with short attention spans.

If students have a pre-written story, encourage them to divide their story into scenes and to decide how many illustrations their story will require (or how many they can realistically complete in the time available).

Explain that they are going to begin with thumbnail sketches (fig. 6.2). A thumbnail sketch should be a quick scribble, shape, or line drawing. "Stick people" are fine. Discourage students from spending more than five minutes on a sketch; they will need to redraw these scenes later. Have them begin with a series of small sketches (maximum 4" or 10 cm).

Thumbnail sketches are also a good way for visual thinkers and less confident writers to begin a writing project, especially those who prefer to develop the narrative by describing the illustrations. Ask students to look at their quick sketches to make sure they have included characters, setting, and action in every scene: "Who is in

Tip: For students who want to use imaginary subjects, it helps to have them refer to related visual references rather than to have them copy another artist's version. For example, if they are going to draw dragons, look for photos of lizards, bird's talons, insect wings, and so on.

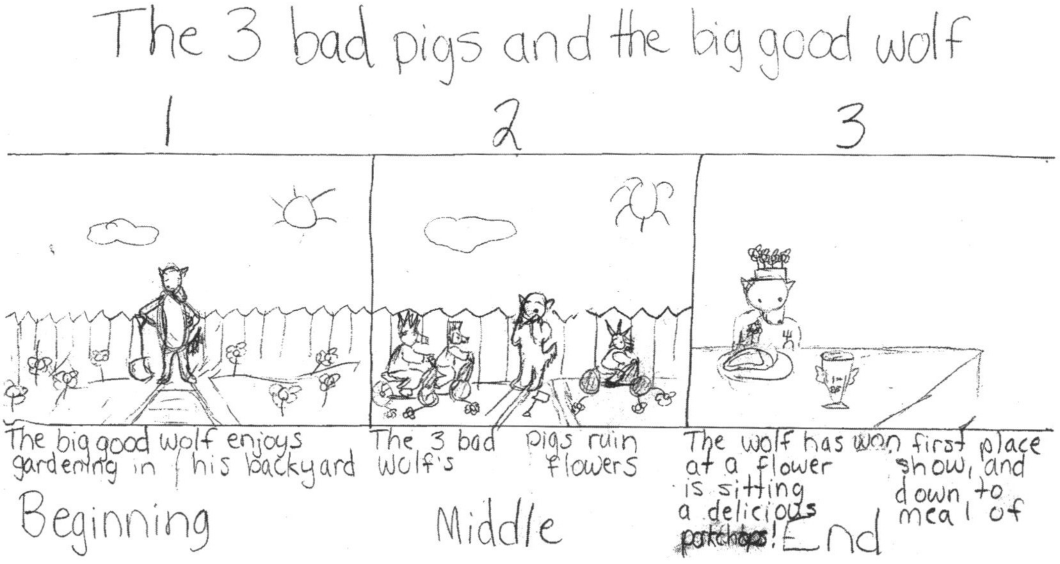

pencil on paper, Noni Brynjolson, age 11

Fig. 6.2. Thumbnail sketches provide the outline for illustrating, and sometimes writing, the story.

the picture?""Where are they?""What are they doing?" and if the students are stuck,"What will happen next?"

An argument can be made for establishing the format first, and having students work in that format for their storyboards. For example, if students are to work on a six-page story (two papers, folded in half, with a front and back cover), then folding two pages into a rough booklet for their storyboards might help them with the narrative sequences. They might find it easier to understand that they are working in a book format.

Explain to beginning writers that most story narratives start with a problem, and the problem is resolved at the end of the story. When the students are finished their sketches, do a quick pre-edit of their visual narrative.

Stage Two

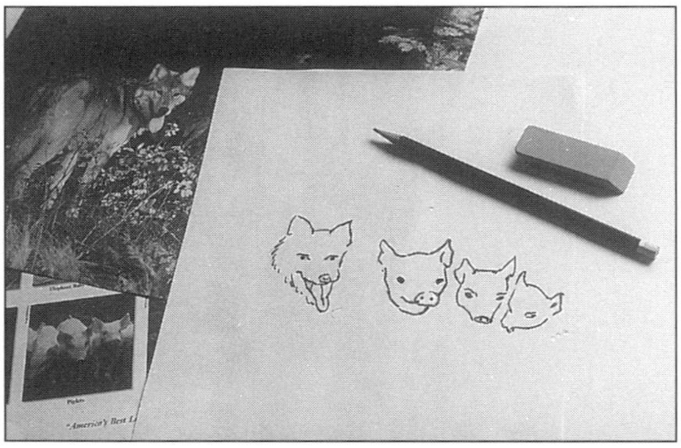

Fig. 6.3. Students produce stronger illustrations when they have visual references available to them.

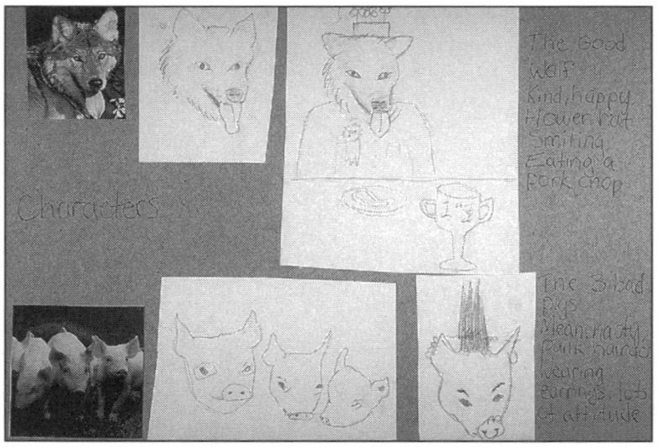

photographs and pencil drawings glued on cardboard, Noni Brynjolson, age 11

Fig. 6.4. Noni used visual references as she began a straightforward look-drawing of her subjects. She then used her imagination to transform the subjects into characters for her story. Elements of the background (house and flowers, for example) may also be included in a storyboard. Advanced storyboards map the progress—scene by scene—of the entire story.

The second stage in illustrating a story is to decide what the main characters, actions, and the settings will look like. It helps to have visual references—magazine photos, mirrors, calendar pictures, postcards, books (or any other visual resource)—available to give students something to look-draw (fig. 6.3). Students should feel free to add elements that make the characters or settings more interesting to look at. For example, in *The Night Rebecca Stayed Too Late* the cartoon bear began as a postcard photo of a black bear—the black leather jacket, haircut, and sunglasses were added from imagination. (See pages 67–68 for ideas on drawing figures in action, pages 60–64 for portrait drawing, and pages 60–61 for information on expressions.)

Students may want to take extra time to practice drawing their characters, settings, and action in their sketchbooks. Some of these practice drawings might be just details; for example, a tree rather than a whole background. This practice will result in the final images being much stronger. (See chapter 3 for tips to help with drawing difficult subjects.)

Students are now ready to introduce a design issue into their illustration. For students who are satisfied with their preliminary drawings, this may also be a good time for them to begin a rough draft of their writing.

As a special project, students may wish to make a storyboard for display or for easy reference for group projects such as stories, animation, and theater sets.

Tape drawings of the characters and settings onto a large piece of heavy paper (fig. 6.4). (Note: Students may want to use a small piece of masking tape rolled up on the back of each piece instead of paste. That way, they can change the sequence and arrangement of pieces.) If students are working from a draft or from finished text, they can paste in copied passages from the text that fit the rough illustrations.

Design

Design in illustration refers to how to fit the components of a picture together in a visually interesting and meaningful way with one another and with the text on a book page. Design issues are considered by artists and illustrators when they are deciding (a) how to communicate the layers of meaning and atmosphere of the story, and (b) how to make the illustrations aesthetically interesting.

It is important for students to learn these skills if they use computer graphics, and especially if they are interested in such areas as graphic design, engineering, architecture, fashion design, and advertising. Yet even apart from those specific interests, design issues exercise the broader skills involved in problem solving, of seeing something from a new angle (literally), and of spatial organization.

Before students begin their final illustrations, they, therefore, need to consider several design components or issues. You may want to make each of these design issues into a full-class lesson. Young students and those just beginning art should focus on one design issue per book.

Students can work out these design problems in their sketchbooks or on scrap paper and paste their most successful solutions onto their storyboards. When they feel comfortable with one design issue, they can move onto the next. Very advanced students may combine several of these considerations into one illustration.

Books to Have Handy

Picture Books

Animalia
Best Friends
Black and White
Changes
Effie
Have You Seen Birds?
How the Animals Got Their Colors
Jumanji
Nanabosho Dances
Owl Moon
Rumpelstiltskin
Simon and the Snowflakes
Strega Nona
The Baby Who Wouldn't Go To Bed
The Enchanted Caribou
The Magic Fan
The Magic Paintbrush
The Mitten: A Ukrainian Folktale
The New Baby Calf
The Night Rebecca Stayed Too Late
The Rebellious Alphabet
Way Home
Who Is the Beast?
Window
Would They Love a Lion?

Size and Shape

Have students consider the shape of the illustration and how the illustration fits the page. Look at *Animalia*. Ask your students what they notice about the shapes of the illustrations. Point out the following: some illustrations fill the whole page, some fill two pages (this is called a two-page spread), some are round with images that overlap the frame (a leg or a wing sticks out from the border of the picture), and some pages have more than one picture (like the pages in comic books).

In some books, all of the pages are shaped like the main subject of the book (for examples, see *The Magic Fan* and *Black and White*). Ask students to decide what shape their book pages and illustrations will be and how the shape of the illustrations will fit the pages (fig. 6.5) or have students sketch a scene in their sketchbook to fit a geometric shape or a shape that relates to their story.

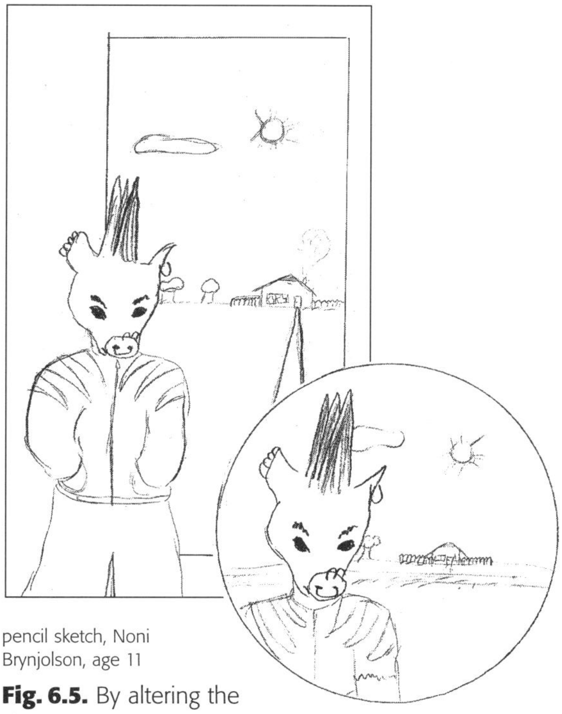

pencil sketch, Noni Brynjolson, age 11

Fig. 6.5. By altering the shape of her illustration, Noni adapted it to the space available on the page. The alteration also added visual interest.

> **Tip:** Encourage students to try several options before choosing one as a plan for a finished drawing: Ask them: "What would that picture look like if it was oval? Square? If the subject overlapped the edges of the frame?"

> **Tip:** Collage is an ideal way to approach the grouping design issue; students can physically move cut-out shapes around the page. (See chapter 4, page 53.)

(a)

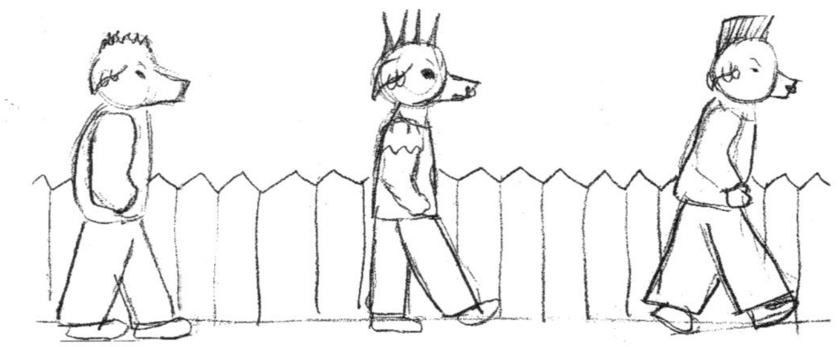

b

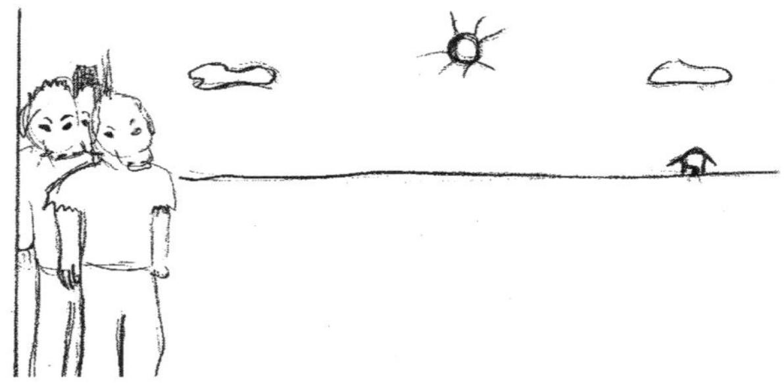

pencil sketch, Noni Brynjolson, age 11

Fig. 6.6. The figures are grouped differently in these sketches: **(a)** the figures are spaced evenly along the fence, **(b)** the figures are stacked in the corner.

> **Tip:** Encourage students to add a border. It will add a finishing touch to even the weakest work.

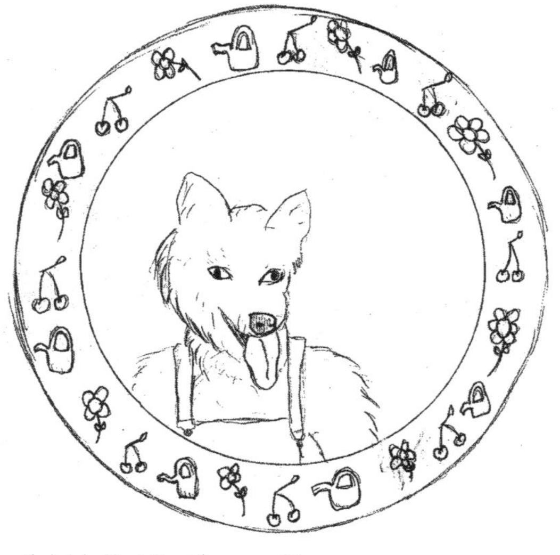

pencil sketch, Noni Brynjolson, age 11

Fig. 6.7. Noni added a border design to decorate the frame of her illustration.

Grouping

Explain to your students that how they group the shapes on the page affects the balance in their illustration. Shapes that are stacked vertically, overlap, or crowd onto one side of the page can make for interesting or dramatic contrast. Shapes spread evenly along a horizontal line, arranged in a radial pattern, or spaced evenly across the page form a more balanced, stable composition. Isolating one shape from the others will call attention to that one shape (fig. 6.6).

Borders

Students may consider a border design that will act as a frame around the outside of the illustration (fig. 6.7).

Look at *Animalia* with your students. Note the elaborate borders on some illustrations. Some borders are of text; others are a simple line. In *Nanabosho Dances*, the border designs are taken from Ojibwa beadwork and appliqué patterns that relate to the story. Look for books by other illustrators who use border designs. *The Mitten: A Ukrainian Folktale* is a good example of one.

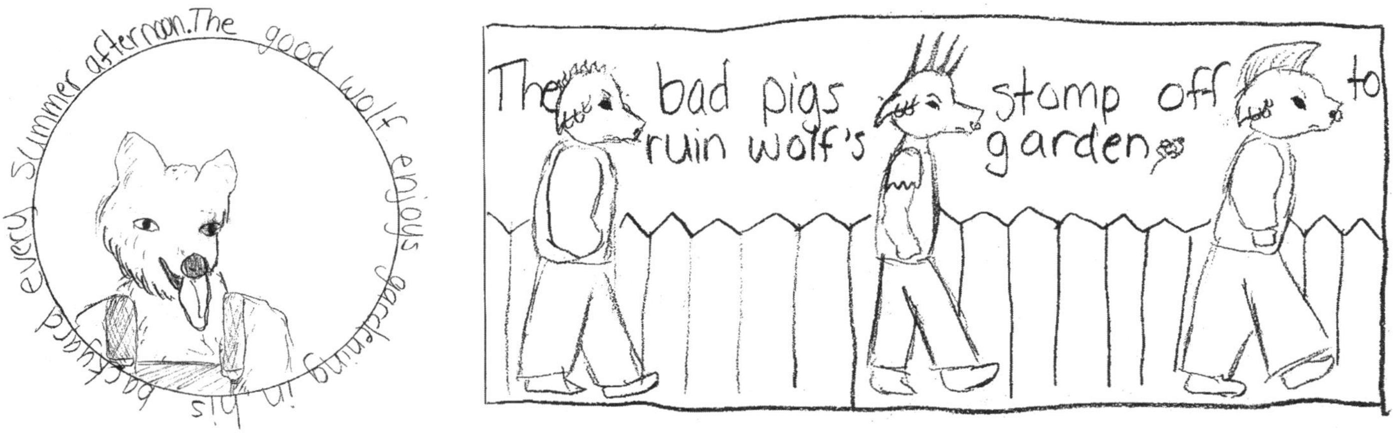

pencil sketch, Noni Brynjolson, age 11

Fig. 6.8. Here are two imaginative examples for incorporating text with an image.

Fitting Pictures and Words Together

With your students, look at *Animalia*. Discuss how the text fits together with the pictures. Look for words beside the picture, words as a frame for the picture, words that are hidden on objects inside the picture (for example, on a picture of a book inside the illustration), and even words hidden backwards on a mirror.

In some books, the text becomes fully integrated with the illustrations; two examples are *The Rebellious Alphabet* and *Rumpelstiltskin*. Challenge students to find an interesting way to fit, or hide, the words in their illustration (fig. 6.8). Ask them: "What if the words were in the middle of the page, with the pictures around the outside?" or "How could the words fit inside the picture?"

Also have students try different kinds of lettering (fig. 6.9). Look at the lettering used in *Animalia*. Some letters are elaborately designed and some are a variety of colors and shapes.

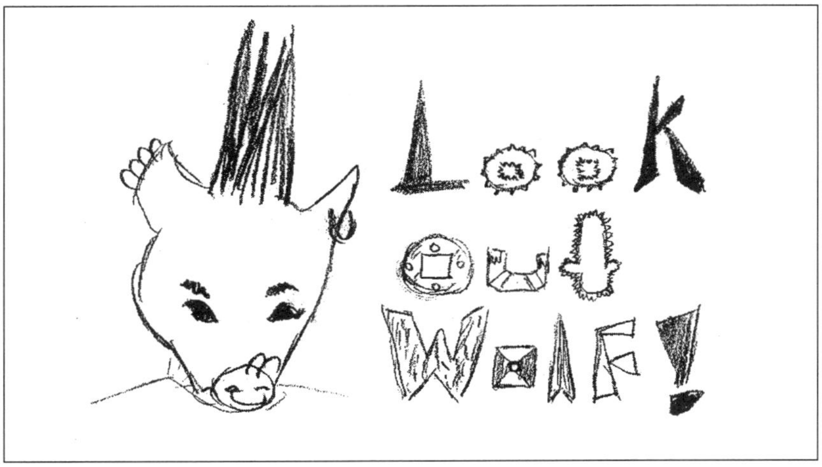

pencil sketch, Noni Brynjolson, age 11

Fig. 6.9. Students may use conventional lettering—block letters, balloon letters, computer fonts—or design their own interesting script.

Tip: Computer fonts may provide some interesting options for size and typeface style for students' texts.

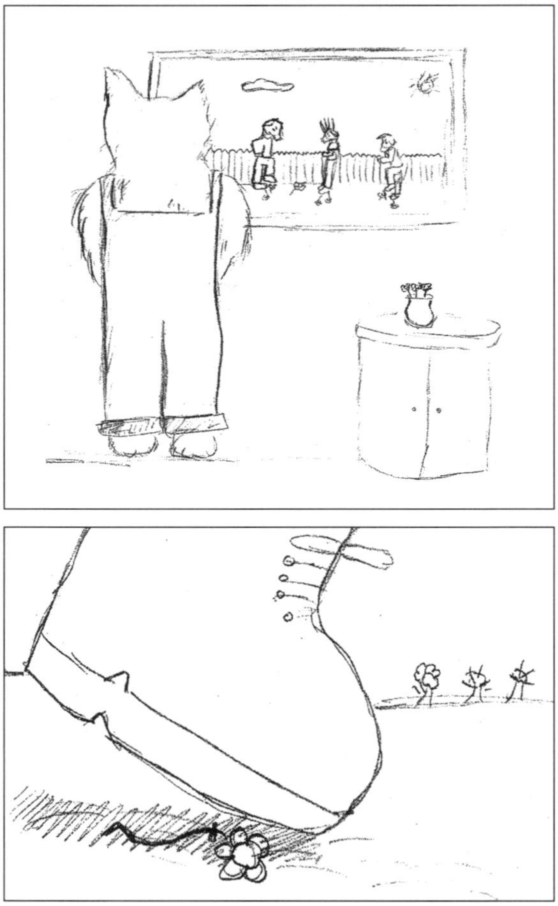

pencil sketch, Noni Brynjolson, age 11

Fig. 6.10. A view through a window (left) and a close-up of a boot (right) are two solutions to the problem of finding interesting vantage points.

Tip: When students are looking for an interesting vantage point, they may find it easiest to work from small, three-dimensional objects; for example, toy dinosaurs. Such objects can be turned around to expose the required view. Objects like oranges can be cut open to show, for example, a cross-sectional view.

Vantage Point

The vantage point is the place from which a scene or subject is viewed. Ask your students to consider what vantage point they might like to use in their illustrations (fig. 6.10).

Look at *Have You Seen Birds?* and *Effie* with your students. Have them identify different vantage points in the books. They might talk about a view from above ("bird's eye view"), below, close-up, distant, side, back, and front. Challenge students to try drawing their subject from a new—and interesting—angle.

Advanced students could also try one of the following, unusual, views:

- distorted (as seen through water, heat waves, or thick glasses)
- magnified
- aerial
- cross section
- close-up
- from a distance
- through something (looking from inside or outside, looking through an opening or between objects)
- x-ray
- transparent (ghostly—so the background shows through)
- exploded (pieces of the subject)
- simultaneous (different views as if seen at one time)

Movement

Dramatic gestures and expressions add interest to illustrations (fig. 6.11), and can communicate the actions and emotions of the characters in the story.

Look at *The Night Rebecca Stayed Too Late* or *Best Friends* with your students. Ask them to find expressions and poses that give them clues about how the characters are feeling and what is happening in the story. Challenge them to redraw their characters in more active poses, or with extreme facial expressions that communicate their characters' roles in their story. One method for drawing figures in action is to make a movable template—a traceable cutout with movable joints—of their subject. The students can then change the pose of their subject from one illustration to another by tracing the template in various poses. Later, students may want to decorate the template and use it to illustrate the front cover of their book (see chapter 7).

Students can achieve a sense of movement in their illustrations by:

- using diagonal lines, and drawing objects that are leaning; for example, a stack of tea cups about to fall over

- having the subject lean into the movement. For example, people and animals tend to lean forward when they are running and when they are walking into the wind.
- using brilliant and contrasting colors; for example, fiery orange instead of pale peach (see Part 4)
- using multiple outlines. For example, draw around the outside of the subject three or four times, then erase lightly to soften the edges. The result is like a blurred photograph.
- repeating shapes; for example, a sequence of a frog hopping across the page
- having several frames on one page, each showing a progressive phase of movement. For example, a car gets smaller in each picture, until it disappears over the horizon.
- making repeated, active, or jagged marks rather than a smooth, continuous line while drawing (see *Would They Love a Lion?*)
- accounting for how wind will affect a moving object. For example, draw a horse with its tail and mane sticking straight out rather than hanging down.

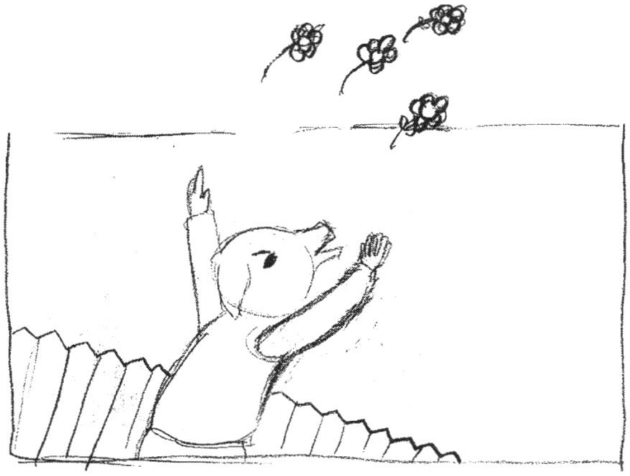

pencil sketch, Noni Brynjolson, age 11

Fig. 6.11. An active pose by the main character, a diagonal fence line, and the flowers leaving the borders of the drawing have created a sense of movement in this sketch.

Tip: Sports magazines are a good place to look for figures in action. Small hand-held mirrors are good for drawing facial expressions.

Humor and Detail

Humor and detail in an illustration make it more interesting. A viewer will likely take a second look to catch all the visual "jokes" in the background of the picture (fig. 6.12).

Look at *Changes* and *Window* with your students. Ask them what they notice happening from page to page (a chair turns into a gorilla, a rural landscape becomes urban). Have students consider what they might introduce into the backgrounds of their illustrations to add humor or interest. Ideally these changes or visual subplots will relate to their story.

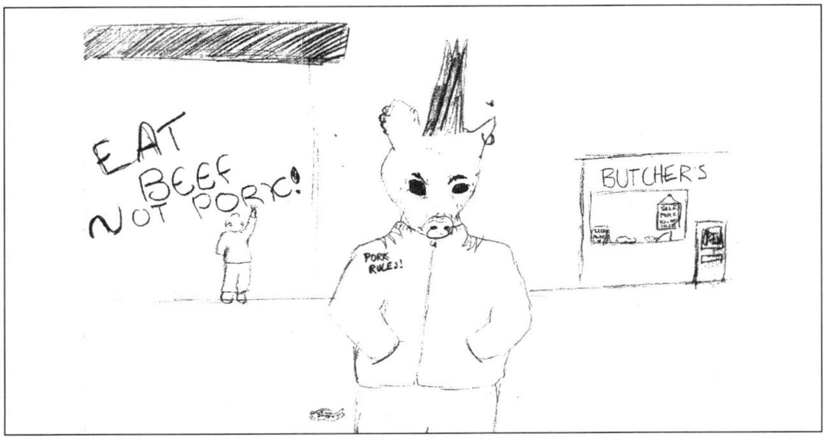

pencil on paper, Noni Brynjolson, age 11

Fig. 6.12. Humor and detail in the background of this picture almost guarantee that the viewer will take a second look.

Scale

Students might consider the scale of their subjects, and how to convey the sense of relative sizes in the illustration (fig. 6.13). See, for example, *The Baby Who Wouldn't Go to Bed*.

Look at *Effie* with your students. Ask them to consider how the illustrator fits the ant and elephant onto the same page, and what views give us clues about their "scale" or relative sizes. Many considerations affect the scale of an object in a picture:

- *Comparison.* Compare the size of an ant to a blade of grass. Drawing these subjects next to each other gives us a clue about the relatively small size of the ant.
- *Partial View.* Fitting only part of an elephant on a page is a device to indicate that the elephant is too big to fit on the page.
- *Vantage Point.* A view from above might make an ant look small; a view from below will make the elephant appear larger.
- *Foreshortening.* A foreshortened view of an elephant's trunk will give a sense of size or length (the trunk is wide at the tip where it is closest to the viewer, and it "recedes" into a faraway distance of the elephant's head—just like the road in the single-point perspective drawing). (See chapter 3, page 39.)

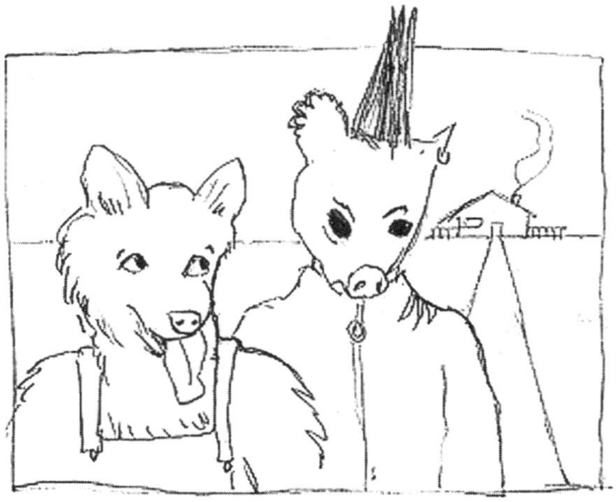

pencil sketch, Noni Brynjolson, age 11

Fig. 6.13. Relative sizes suggest the scale of these characters. The single-point perspective and overlapping introduce an element of depth.

Tip: Explain to students that some images appear higher up in their field of vision because there is more ground between them and things that are far away. Have them notice that people sitting next to them appear larger, whereas people across the room appear smaller and higher up in their field of vision. This might be a good opportunity for a science lesson on optics (how the eye receives an image).

Atmosphere

The atmosphere or mood of an illustration should express the action or emotion in the story. Often, atmosphere foreshadows things to come. Atmosphere can be determined by many things:

- the time of day
- light source
- placement of shadows
- the season
- the weather
- the inclusion of specific kinds of objects
- the landscape

Look at *Owl Moon* for moonlit pictures and *Have You Seen Birds?* for different seasons. For night scenes, look at *Way Home*. Check *The Night Rebecca Stayed Too Late* or *The Magic Paintbrush* for interesting shadows. Ask students to think about the mood of their story. Have them consider what atmosphere they want to create (fig. 6.14)—a dark, windy night for Halloween; a rainy afternoon for a sad event; firelight for a dramatic scene; a sunrise sky for a hopeful ending (see chapter 8 for information on color and atmosphere).

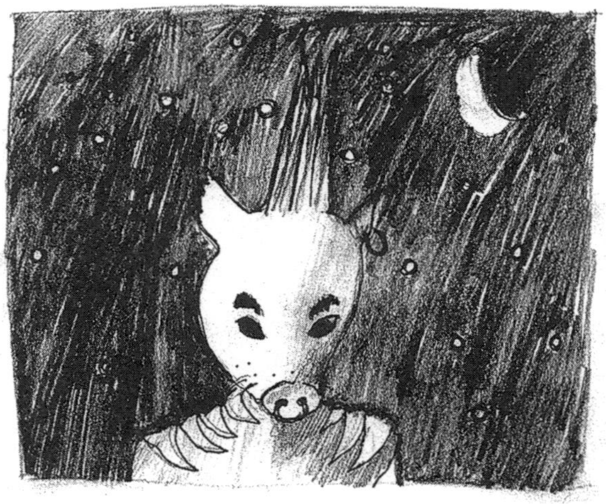

pencil sketch, Noni Brynjolson, age 11

Fig. 6.14. The night sky and shadow lend atmosphere to this sketch.

The "Good" Copy

To this point, students have been working on their storyboard copy of their illustrations. Now it is time for them to transfer the drawings from the storyboard, or from their practice drawings in their sketchbooks, to a new piece of paper. There are a few ways to do this. They can:

- redraw their picture
- trace parts of the drawing onto the clean paper; tape the drawing onto a brightly lit window or use an overhead projector to make the drawing easier to see
- photocopy the drawings, then cut and paste the characters or settings into the illustration (see chapter 4)
- use the practice drawings and storyboards as a guide and create a media-based copy to minimize redrawing. Students could use cutouts, collage, paint, and so on (see Parts 4 and 5).

The illustrations do not have to be large, unless students intend to create an oversize book. A 4" x 4" (10 cm x 10 cm) illustration fits nicely onto a book page, with text.

Although students are encouraged to spend time practicing the drawing of their subject, it is not necessary to be able to draw in a "realistic" style in order to make beautiful illustrations. Look at *Would They Love a Lion?* or *Rumpelstiltskin* with the students. Although the drawing is very beautiful in each of these books, the characters are drawn quite simply. Perhaps students would consider simplifying the drawing of their characters rather than attempting realism. If your students are experiencing difficulty with a drawing, and you don't have time for a "how-to-draw" session, suggest that they simplify the view. This can be done by "cheating": drawing the character from the back, placing hands in pockets, drawing an enlarged detail rather than the whole subject, or overlapping easy-to-draw objects in front of difficult ones. You may even find examples of "cheating" in published picture books.

It may also help to try a media-based approach. Cut paper, textured paint, collage, and shadow puppets are more forgiving for less experienced artists and can provide a strong image even if the initial drawing is somewhat weak (fig. 6.15).

Have students choose which media they will want to use to finish their illustrations. Illustrations may be left as pencil drawings, or simply outlined with black felt markers and colored with pencil crayons. However, a wide variety of other media may be used. Look through children's picture books with your students. See if they can guess what media or technique the illustrator used to make the illustrations. (Some books with interesting medium or technique are: *Best Friends*, watercolor and ink; *Effie*, Plasticine; *The Enchanted Caribou*, shadow puppets; *The Magic Fan*, acrylic paint; *Window*, collage and paint; *How the Animals Got Their Colors*, cut paper.) Refer to chapters 4, 7, 9, 11, 13, and 14 for ideas on how to use another medium to finish the illustration.

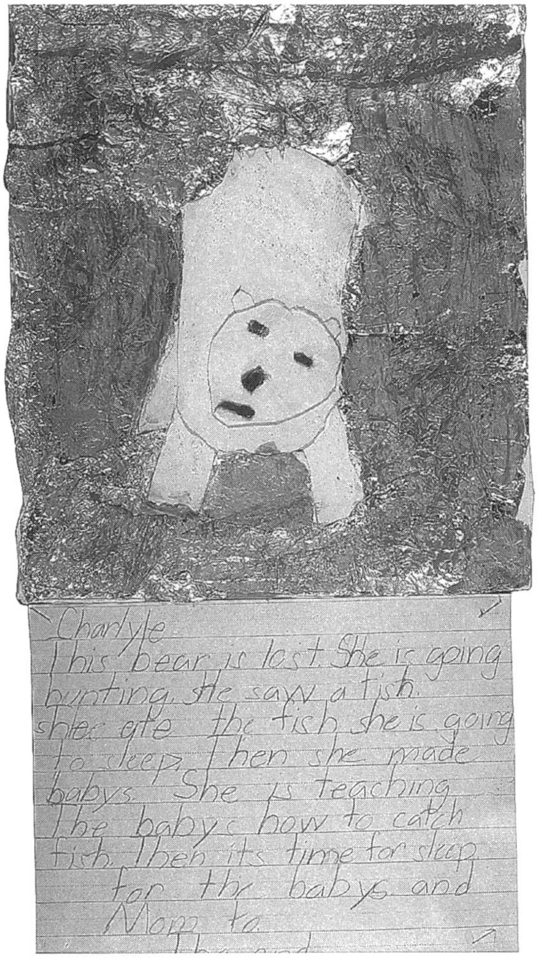

Bear Is Lost, mixed media, Charlyle Cabungcal, grade 2, Wellington School

Fig. 6.15. Charlyle's simple sketch became an interesting collage of cut-out cardboard shapes, surrounded by painted tinfoil.

Tip: Not all the illustrations need be full color or full size. Choose the most exciting or interesting scenes for the full-size pictures.

Tip: Drawing a series of pictures is hard work. Some students may become tired or lose interest (especially if the initial drawings were done slowly). There are many ways to make the task simpler: (1) use smaller paper (6" or 15 cm square, cut out and glued onto larger paper with the text); (2) make most of the illustrations black and white; (3) photocopy or trace characters from sketchbooks and paste into illustrations (see chapter 4).

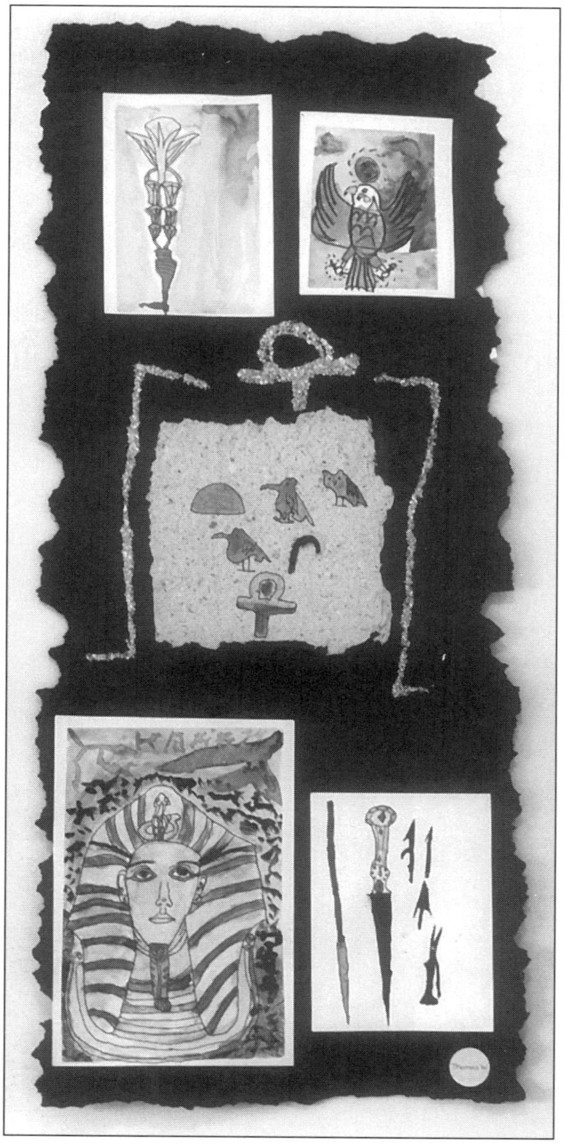

Egyptian Scroll, Thomas B. Weirich, grade 3, St. John's Ravenscourt School

Fig. 6.16. Thomas's class researched ancient Egypt. They then made watercolor paintings and drew hieroglyphics on handmade "papyrus" paper. These were then assembled into a scroll rather than into a book.

Assembling Books

Making a book can be as simple, or as involved, as you want it to be (figs. 6.16 to 6.19). The advantages of making the illustrations separately from the text are:

- a variety of "messier" media, such as paint, collage, and printmaking, can be used with illustrations
- text can be incorporated with the illustrations in an interesting way, not just as a strip across the bottom of the page
- if students make a "mistake" while drawing or writing, a new piece of paper can be easily substituted. Use hand-lettering or cut out pieces of computer-printed text to add to the story. Students may want to print on a separate piece of paper, and glue it into their book page later.

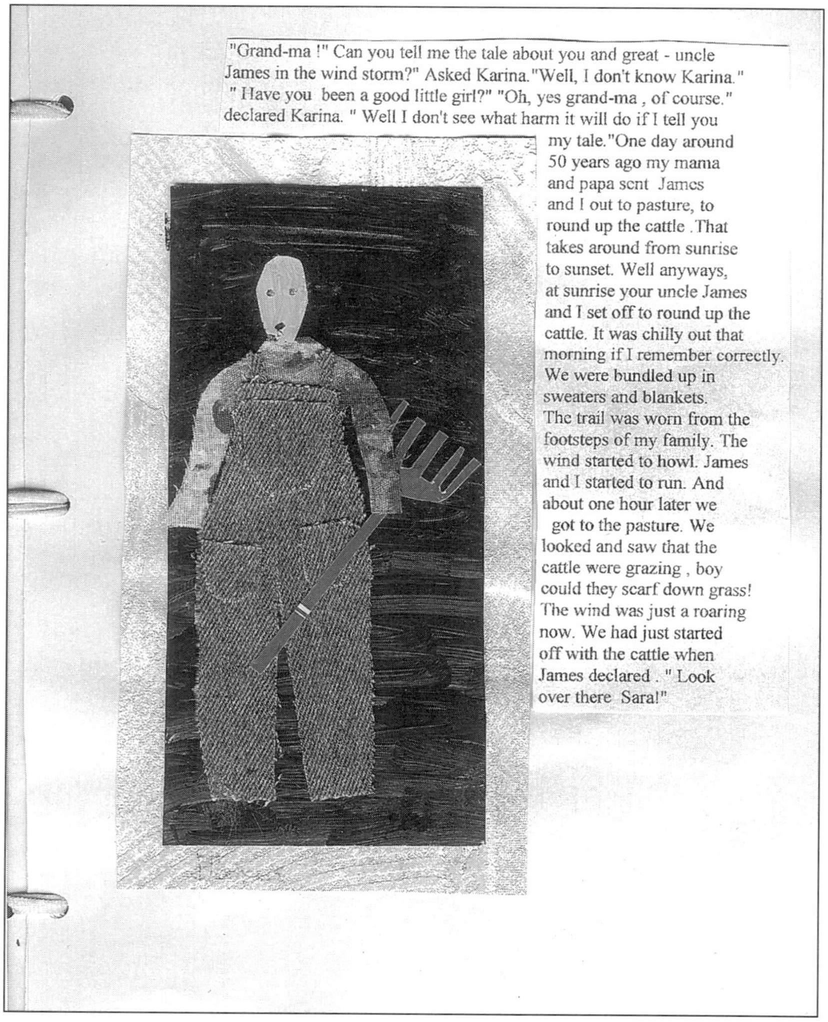

Sara's Story, mixed media, Alicia Elgert, age 11, Ecole Prince Charles

Fig. 6.17. The text on this page was formatted on the computer to wrap around Alicia's illustration.

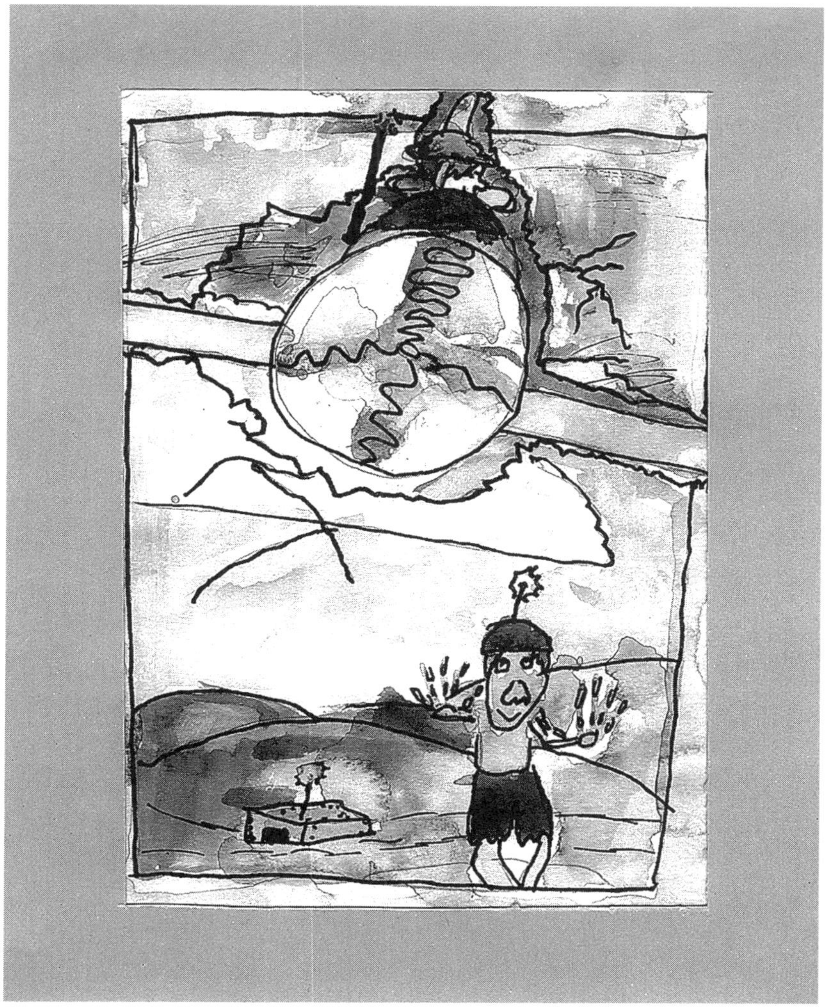

Air Attack, watercolor and ink, Philip Neufeld, age 10, Niakwa Place School

Fig. 6.18. Small illustrations can be "framed" with a colored paper matte before being glued onto the book page.

The choices students make about the sizes and shapes of their illustrations (see page 87) will determine the size and shape of their book.

A "book" can be as simple as a piece of paper folded in half. To add more pages, fold more pieces of paper. Stapling along the side rather than through the center allows extra pages to be added on later.

Colored Manila file folders make excellent book covers. Trim the folders to size (page size plus ½" (1.5 cm) margin). Stitch or staple pages together and use bookbinding or hockey tape to reinforce the "spine" along the outside of the central fold and attach the cover.

To make a hardcover book, cut three pieces of cardboard—two should be the size of the book page (plus ½" (1.5 cm) margin), and one should be the height of the book page (plus ½" (1.5 cm) margin). The width should accommodate the thickness of the book (¾" or 2 cm). Attach the pieces with durable tape (duct tape, hockey tape, or bookbinding tape). The pieces can be covered with a single piece of plain or patterned cloth, or decorated paper, folded over around the edges of the cardboard. Stitch or staple the book pages together

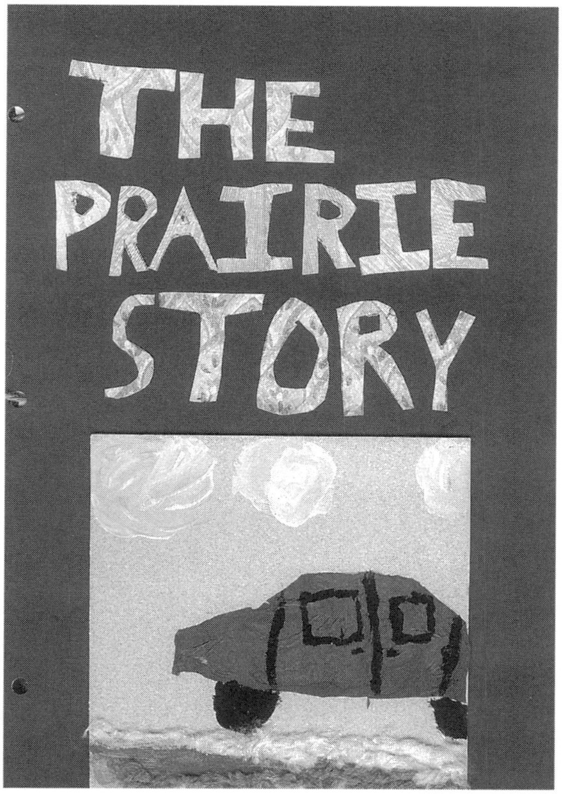

The Prairie Story, mixed media, Becky Nielsen, age 11, Ecole Prince Charles

Fig. 6.19. Becky used a colored file folder for the cover of her book. She constructed and painted the cover illustration separately, then glued it onto the cover. Finally, she put the book together with a hole-punch and string.

and attach to the cover with more tape. To cover the folded edges and the tape, glue in "end papers" and decorate or leave plain.

There are a range of other options for book formats. Perhaps the most interesting of these options are the concertina, origami, and pop-up books designed and described by Paul Johnson (1993). These books are objects of art, simple to make, and can be integrated easily with the storyboard process.

Enrichment

- Storyboards may be used to plan large or complex art projects. Murals and theater sets are planned using the processes described in this chapter, and combined into one class storyboard. This storyboard is then used to break the project into parts and delegate tasks. Murals and theater sets may be drawn, painted, and assembled as separate pieces by individuals or by small groups of students and combined later. Posters or advertisements can be completed using storyboards, and then working on larger paper with a variety of media to "finish" the illustration.
- Students can look for elements of design in other illustrated children's books. Ask students what they notice in the work of various illustrators. Students could try sketching details or impressions of the illustrator's style in their own sketchbooks.
- Have students look critically at a variety of new picture books, then consider all the elements of design. Next, have them, as a group, decide on who they think should win an illustration award. Send a letter to the winning illustrator to let him or her know of the students' decision. One school I visited did just that and received a gracious reply from the illustrator (I'm sure he was very flattered). What a great way to get students looking critically at visual art!
- Have a book launch in the school library for students who have completed ("published") their books. Students can read to classmates. Invite guests, and serve snacks. Add a blank page in the back of students' books for readers' comments.
- Invite local illustrators and authors to present their work.
- Visit a print shop to see how books are printed and assembled.
- Have a special place of honor in your classroom or school library for completed ("published") books (fig. 6.20).
- Have advanced students consider the *principles of design*. These principles describe the placement or grouping of the shapes, lines, textures, values, colors, and/or medium used within a work of art. They provide a language for looking at and understanding visual art—cave art, architecture, advertising art, Renaissance art, modern art, and so on.

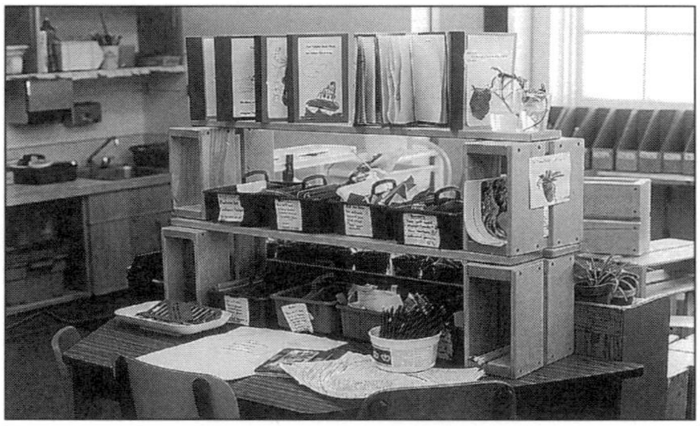

Teachers: Andrea Stuart and Donna Massey-Cudmore, Wolseley School

Fig. 6.20. Set up a classroom illustration center. The center can include labeled activity bins, a place to display finished books, and a quiet space where students can go to illustrate their stories.

The principles of design—unity, rhythm, contrast, balance, emphasis, motif, and movement—may be introduced gradually. For example, a grade-two student can begin to work with symmetrical patterns. These principles of design can be used as a tool for discussing the "grammar" of visual art. They can also become the basis for exercises, as students work with cutout images to play with these design principles in their sketchbooks. By grade eight, students should be thoroughly familiar with these principles:

- *Unity:* Unity refers to the integrity of an image; that is, whether or not it "holds" together. The elements repeat or relate well to provide harmony to the image (fig. 6.21). In *Effie*, for example, unity is provided by the medium—all the images are made entirely of Plasticine. In *Strega Nona*, unity is provided by the repetition of simple, geometric shapes and consistent, dark outlining.

- *Rhythm:* Elements placed at intervals throughout the picture create rhythm (fig. 6.21). In *The New Baby Calf*, the fence posts and lines in the fields create a regular rhythm; an irregular rhythm is created by the placement of hills, trees, and animals.
- *Contrast:* A variety of elements within an image will provide visual interest (fig. 6.22). In *Would They Love a Lion?*, the variety of lines add visual interest to the illustrations. In *Jumanji*, the strong differences between light and dark values in the pictures make the pictures more dramatic.

- *Balance:* Each element in an image carries "visual weight" that can be balanced in several ways (fig. 6.23, page 98):
  - *symmetry:* one part of an image is a mirror image of another. In *The Magic Fan*, for example, the shape of the illustration is the same from the left-hand page to the right.
  - *asymmetry:* each side of the image is "different but equal." In *Who Is the Beast?*, for example, the tiger's detailed face and bright pattern is balanced by the large, brightly colored and patterned leaves and flowers.
  - *radial:* the design moves outward from the center in a spiral or wheel, creating a mandala. See *The Magic Paintbrush* on the page where "Nib" is escaping from the dungeon.
  - *crystalline:* elements are placed in an overall pattern. In *How the Animals Got Their Colors*, the elements are spread, more or less evenly, across some pages for a "wallpaper" effect.
- *Emphasis:* Emphasis refers to the focal point or outstanding element in the image (fig. 6.24, page 98). In *The Magic Paintbrush*, a natural focal point (the scene under the bridge) is created by the lit figures near the bottom of the page. A second focal point (the moon) is framed by the archway and pointed to by the crossbeams.

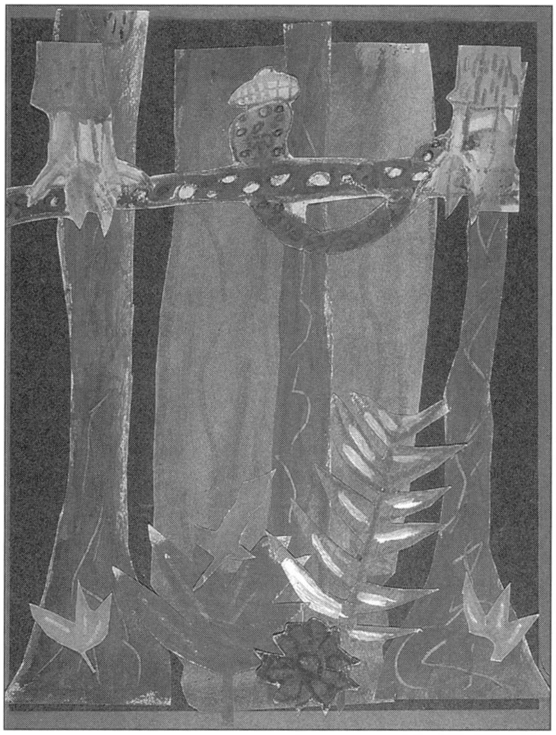

paint and collage, Samantha Edwards, age 9, South Oaks School

Fig. 6.21. The three tall trees create a *rhythm* across Samantha's collage. Her use of cutouts throughout helps to *unify* the composition.

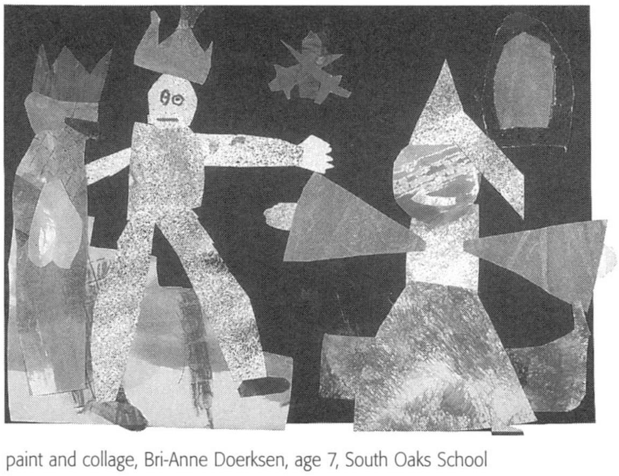

paint and collage, Bri-Anne Doerksen, age 7, South Oaks School

Fig. 6.22. There is strong *contrast* between the light figures and dark background in Bri-Anne's illustration. This contrast makes the image interesting to look at.

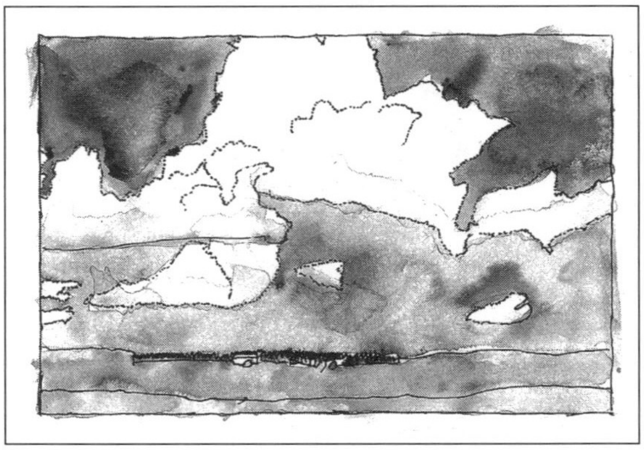

watercolor and ink, Charlie Cabuncal, grade 4, Wellington School

Fig. 6.23. In Charlie's landscape painting, the large white clouds are *balanced* by the strip of detail and the dark color on the horizon.

- *Motif:* This refers to the commonality of elements throughout the picture (fig. 6.24). In *How the Animals Got Their Colors,* the jagged (zigzag) edges on many of the shapes form a motif (repeated shape) that unifies the image.
- *Movement:* Repetition of images, flowing lines, soft edges, and diagonal lines create a sense of movement. The placement of elements can lead the viewer's eye through the picture (elements placed in a spiral pattern, zigzag, curves, and so on) (fig. 6.25). In *Simon and the Snowflakes,* the row of birds leads the eye across the page. In *The Magic Paintbrush* (the scene where "Nib" is brought before the king), the line along the boy's body and along his arm leads the eye inwards, toward the central figure. (See page 90.)

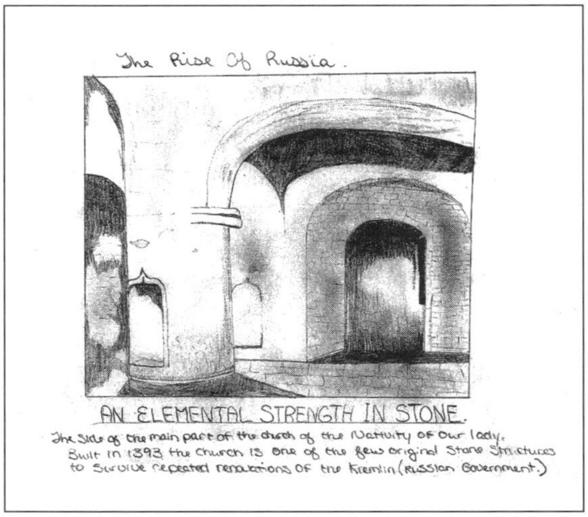

pencil on paper, Alia Millen, grade 8, San Antonio School

Fig. 6.24. In Alia's sketchbook drawing, the successive archways *emphasize* the focal point on the right side of the drawing. The repeated archways also provide a *motif.*

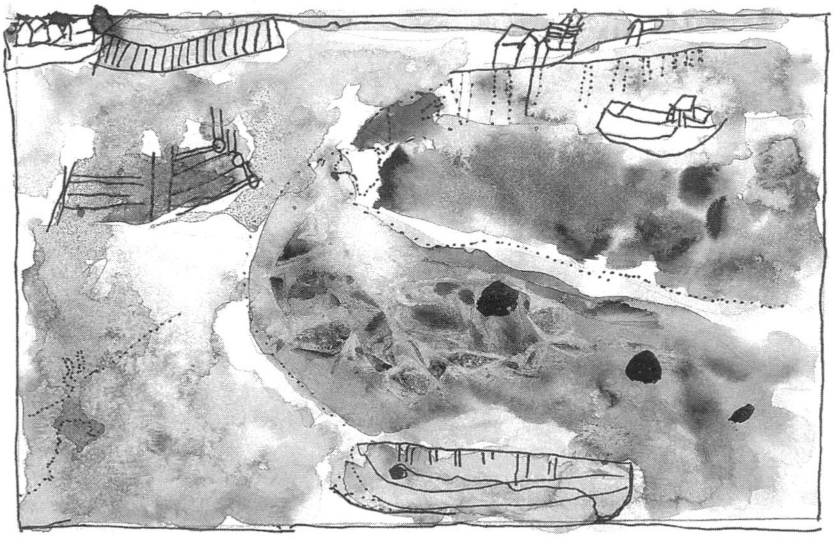

watercolor and ink, William, grade 4, Wellington School

Fig. 6.25. The wobbly and dotted lines, curved shape of the water, irregular paint marks, and repeated boat shapes give William's illustration a sense of *movement.*

Vocabulary (see appendixes for definitions)

atmosphere	*illustration*	*setting*
balance	*line*	*shape*
character	*manuscript*	*storyboard*
composition	*motif*	*text*
contrast	*movement*	*thumbnail sketch*
depth	*pose (gesture)*	*unity*
emphasis	*rhythm*	*vantage point*
expression	*scale*	*visual reference*
font	*scene*	

7
Shadow Puppets

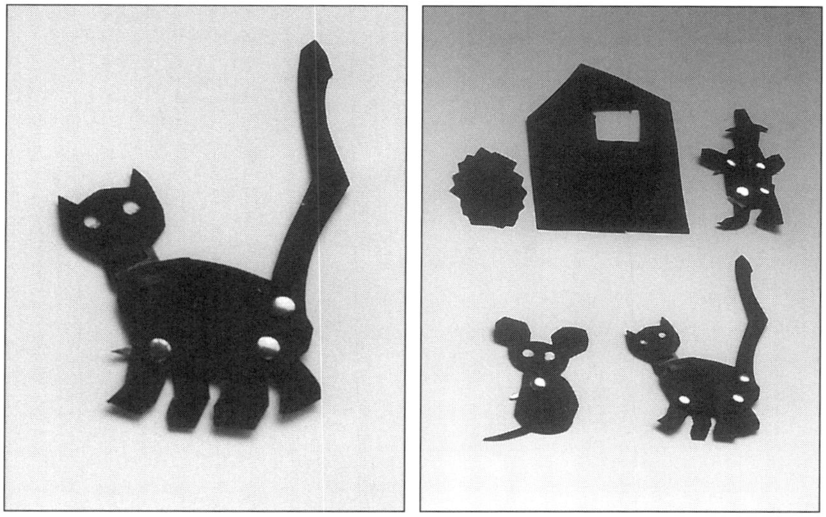

Darlene Paranaque, grade 3, Prairie Rose Elementary School

Fig. 7.1. Shadow puppets engage students' interest and are effective in helping them develop story scenarios. Students can also use the puppets as illustrations for their finished stories.

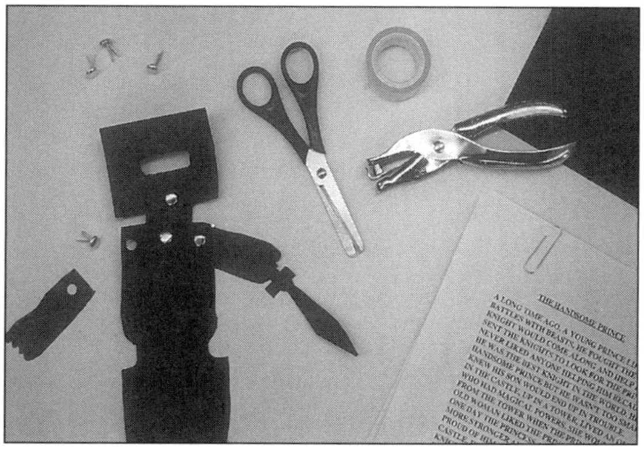

Fig. 7.2. These are some of the materials you will need to make shadow puppets. To make movable parts, cut out the pieces separately, punch with a hole punch, and attach with brass paper fasteners.

Introduction

A shadow puppet is a flat, cutout figure with movable parts, made from paper. Some shadow puppets are very elaborate. Traditional Indonesian shadow puppets, for example, have intricate designs carved into the paper and are waxed to be translucent. The puppets described in this chapter are much easier to make, and have been adapted for use in the classroom. While Indonesian puppets are used behind a back-lit paper screen to act out a story, you will find an overhead projector is a simple solution for the classroom.

Shadow puppets are especially effective as a device to develop story narratives through play. Shadow puppets allow for visuals to be developed before the stories. Students with beginning or weak writing skills, in particular, may find it easier to describe aloud the actions of their shadow puppets than to develop a story directly into print.

Materials

- construction paper, black
- single-hole punches (at least one per four students)
- scissors
- brass paper fasteners
- overhead projector(s)
- Scotch tape
- clear plastic

Books to Have Handy

Picture Books
The Enchanted Caribou
How the Animals Got Their Colors
The Shadow Puppet Book

Tip: To help students who want to create imaginary animals such as dragons, find related visuals (bird's talons, bat wings, lizard skin, and so on). (See Composite Creatures, chapter 5.)

Tip: Some students may produce pieces that are too small or narrow for the hole punch. Encourage them to work larger, and to solve problems with Scotch tape and grafts of larger pieces of paper taped on.

Appropriate Subjects

Many subjects are appropriate for shadow puppets: animals, composite creatures (page 72), dinosaurs, and athletes are just a few. Shadow puppets work well for profiles (side views) of movable subjects.

Preparation

Decide on a topic for puppets. Gather materials and visual references. Decide on the story genre—adventure, legend, fantasy, mystery, and so on—and how students will approach the writing component (see chapter 6, page 84).

Method

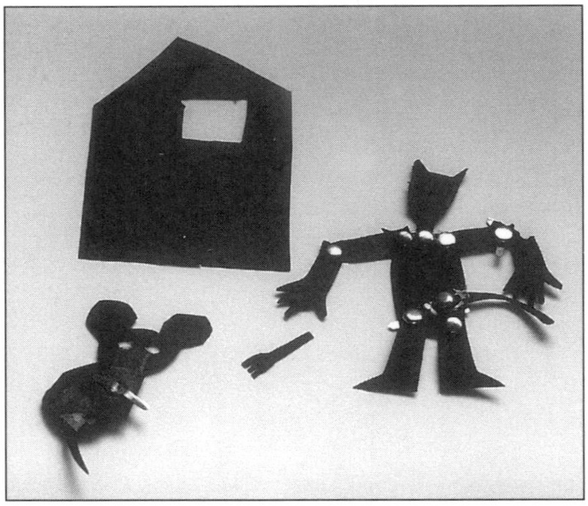

Darlene Paranaque and Chantal Del Carmen, grade 3, Prairie Rose Elementary School

Fig. 7.3. Darlene and Chantal created some interesting characters. Notice that details—like the fingers and the fork—were cut out, not drawn.

Introduce your students to shadow puppets by looking at *The Enchanted Caribou*. This book is illustrated entirely with shadow puppets. The last page shows how the puppets were constructed with movable parts.

Have each student pick a particular animal, character, mythical beast, or some other subject that relates to a classroom theme or study topic. Have visual references available in the classroom so that students can become visually familiar with the subject. Discuss the body shapes of the students' subjects; if necessary, look again at visual references such as magazine or calendar photos or books.

Explain how the different parts of the body of the subject (legs, tail, wings, and so on) need to be cut out separately to allow for movable parts. Demonstrate how to make movable parts: take two pieces of paper; with a hole punch, punch a hole in each piece; attach the pieces with a brass fastener.

Set up an overhead projector. Put some pencil marks on a piece of paper and use the projector to display the paper on the wall or screen. This demonstration will show students that pencil lines do not show up! Eyes and other details have to be cut out for them to appear on the wall (fig. 7.3).

Distribute black construction paper and scissors to your students. Encourage them to try out their puppets on the overhead projector as they work. That way, they will be able to see the shadow shapes reflected on the screen.

As students finish their first shadow puppets, look again at *The Enchanted Caribou*. Point out how each picture contains several characters as well as background elements. Discuss with your students what they can do to make a whole picture. Ask leading questions like: "What kind of a place would this dinosaur live in? What did it eat? What might be close to it, or far away in the distance? What is it doing?"

Decide on what writing process students will use. The story narrative will emerge through puppet play (with more or less prompting), and students will require a format for recording the story.

Some options are:

- Young or impatient students might play out a story on the overhead projector—alone or with a small group of students—until they can decide on a beginning, middle, and end. They don't have to be able to verbalize the entire story at this point. You may have to prompt them with questions like: "What happens first?" "What will he eat?" "Where is she going?" After the illustrations are complete, the students can write or dictate the story to accompany the illustrations.
- Have students try the initial puppet play on the overhead projector, and then make an outline, story web, storyboard (see chapter 6), or quick rough draft of the story before completing the illustrations.
- Stress the idea that stories have a beginning, a middle, and an end. Have students produce three thumbnail sketches, then decide which scene comes first, which comes second, and which comes third. Ask them to describe what happens in each scene.
- Shadow puppets are good for demonstrating the characters, settings, and action in a story. After students make characters from shadow puppets, prompt them with questions about where their characters would live, or where they would travel to. Have them cut the background pieces out of black paper.
- Stories need a problem and a resolution. Make up scenarios for the students: If their shadow puppet is alone on the white screen, perhaps she has nowhere to live, or has no friends, or no food. Ask them how their puppet will find these things (fig. 7.4).

When students have completed all their shadow puppets (for example, T-Rex attacking a hapless diplodocus) and background elements (volcanoes, trees, pteranodon, grass, clouds, and so on), and have written a beginning, middle, and end to their stories, they are ready to tell their stories to their classmates, using the puppets in a play or as illustrations. Have them try one, or a combination, of the following approaches:

- Use the overhead projector as a shadow-puppet screen.
- Attach wooden slats to the puppets' movable parts—slender pieces from a bamboo window blind will do. Construct a shadow-puppet theater; hang up a white sheet, and use an overhead projector or gooseneck lamp behind it as a light source.
- Use the puppets as stencils. Trace the puppets in a variety of poses onto paper. Outline the background pieces (trees, stars, houses, and so on) with a black pen, and add color with tempera paint, watercolor paint, or pencil crayons.
- Trace the shadow puppets in a variety of poses onto colored construction paper (fig. 7.5), and use paper cutouts to decorate a story (see *How The Animals Got Their Colors* for ideas).
- Make illustrations directly from the shadow puppets. You can do this by exposing the shadow puppets on Solargraphics or light-sensitive blueprint paper (see page 102).

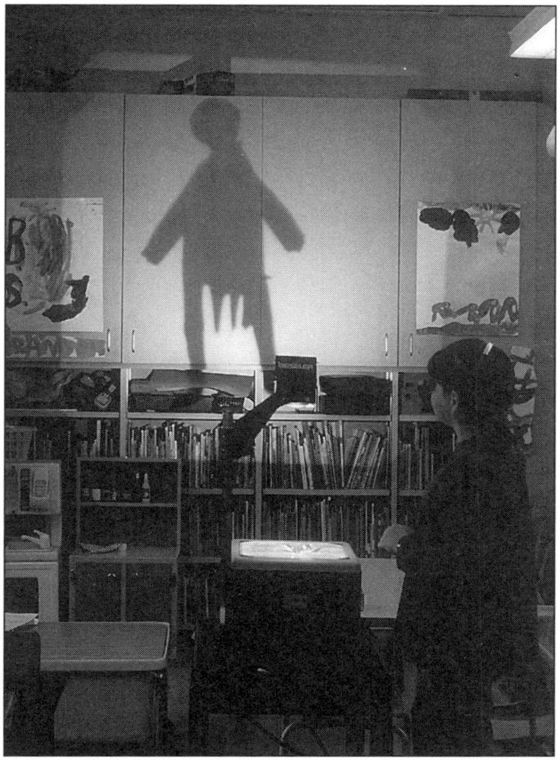

Janine Lea, grade 3, Pine Dock School

Fig. 7.4. Janine admires her puppet's shadow on the cabinets. Encourage students to test their puppets on the overhead projector as they work. Ideally, groups of students will gather at the projector and small scenarios will emerge: "Pretend my cat is chasing your bird"; "...and then my bird flies away and hides in a tree"; "We need to make a tree!" Instant characters, action, and settings are created in these sessions.

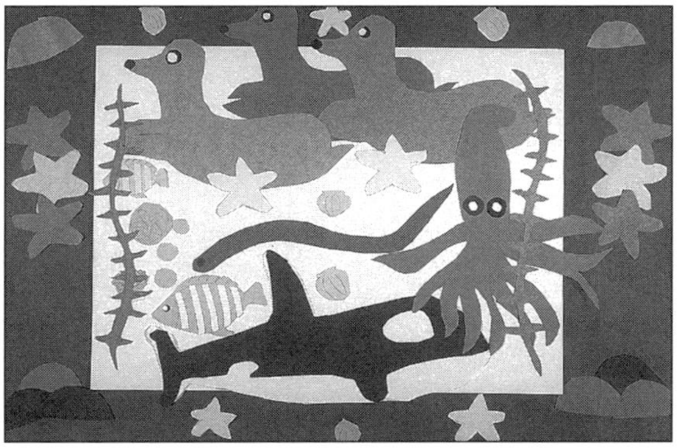

Maria Juliana Rufo, grade 3, Wellington School

Fig. 7.5. Students can easily change their shadow puppets into paper cutouts. Trace puppets onto a variety of colored papers. Encourage them to trade pieces for a variety of characters in one picture. Decorate with more cutout shapes for details, pattern, and a border design.

Materials

- Solargraphics, or similar brand of sun-sensitive paper (more expensive, but easier to develop) or light-sensitive blueprint paper, 8 1/2" x 11" (21.5 cm x 28 cm) (ask for "fast, blueline" paper)
- goose-necked lamps (several), with 100-watt bulbs, and extension cords (indoors); or outside in a shady area on a windless day
- shadow puppets (pages 99–101)

for Solargraphics

- a tray of water

for blueprint paper

- plastic pail, large (5 gallons or 12 l+), that has not been used for bleach (bleach and ammonia are a toxic combination)
- household ammonia, one bottle *
- nylon window screening (approximately 14" or 36 cm square)
- duct tape
- garbage bag, large, black
- string (enough to tie around pail)
- funnel

Tip: Keep light-sensitive blueprint paper in its dark, air-tight, protective envelope. These papers are time-sensitive, and should be used within several months of purchase.

Solargraphics and Blueprint Paper

Solargraphics or blueprint paper can be used to make book illustrations from shadow puppets.

Preparation

Keep Solargraphics or blueprint paper in its dark, protective envelope and pull out sheets only as needed. When students have their puppet and background pieces organized, remove one or two sheets per student from the envelope. Have students write their name on the white side, then place—colored side up—on a table under a lamp that is turned off. Students can then quickly arrange their shadow puppets on the paper before turning on the light.

Method

Exposing Solargraphics and Blueprint Paper

Turn on the light. Make sure the light bulb is about 8" (20 cm) from the paper. Expose the paper for about four to five minutes (fig. 7.6). Turn the light off and slide the puppet pieces off the paper. The puppet pieces should leave a definite silhouette, and the exposed paper should be almost white.

Quickly pop the exposed paper back into the envelope. Keep the paper in the dark until you are ready to develop them.

Developing Solargraphics Paper

You will need a tray of tap water. In dim light, place the exposed Solargraphics paper in a tray of water for two or three minutes, or according to package instructions. Remove when the image becomes clear. Hang to dry. Flatten dry papers under heavy books.

Developing Blueprint Paper

Develop blueprints after students have gone home for the day (fig. 7.7). Use a large, well-ventilated room (I use a garage). You may want to

* Ammonia is a toxic substance (and it stinks). It is a good idea to develop the blueprints away from school, in a well-ventilated room, or outdoors. (Caution: Direct sunlight on the pail, or papers will ruin prints.)

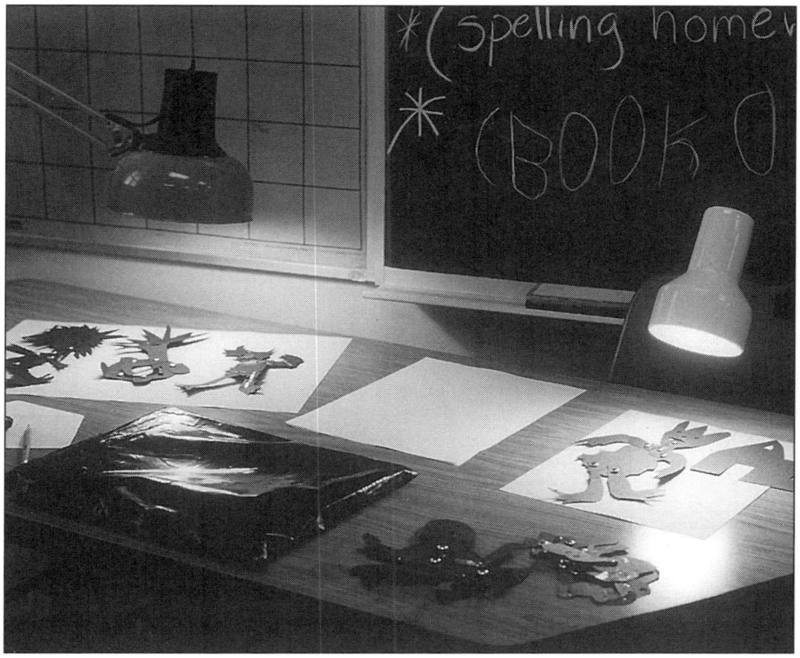

grade 3 class, Prairie Rose Elementary School

Fig. 7.6. Expose shadow puppets on Solargraphics or blueprint paper under a 100-watt light bulb. Although the process looks tricky, it is very forgiving. Keep the exposed paper in a dark wrapper until they are developed.

> **Tip:** Because only a few students will be working with the lamps at the same time, the other students can be involved in rewriting and developing their stories. It is helpful to have another adult or older student in the classroom to help coordinate the activity.

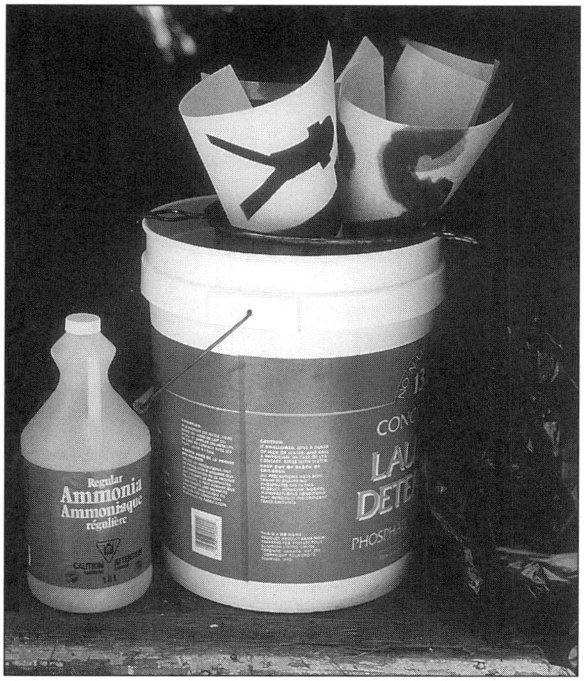

Fig. 7.7. Find a dimly lit and well-ventilated area and develop blueprints in a pail partially filled with ammonia. Support the paper on a piece of screen and cover the pail with a garbage bag—it is the fumes from the ammonia that develop the prints. Developing takes about 15 minutes, but the paper may be left in the pail overnight.

wear goggles, rubber gloves, and a ventilation mask. Place the window screen across the inside of the pail, several inches (centimeters) from the bottom, and tape in place. This screen becomes a "shelf" and is to keep the blueprints above the ammonia. Use a funnel to pour about half a bottle of ammonia down the inside of the pail. Try to keep the screen dry. Cover the pail with the garbage bag.* Loosely roll up the blueprint paper, yellow side out, and place into the pail on top of the screen. Make sure the blueprint paper stays dry, and above the ammonia; it is the fumes from the ammonia that develop the prints. Quickly close the garbage bag over the pail and secure with string. The pail should be large enough to hold about twenty papers at a time.

Blueprints take fifteen to thirty minutes to develop; however, leaving them in longer won't damage them. They are ready when they have turned a deep blue-violet color and no green or yellow streaks remain (fig. 7.8, page 104). Blueprints are now permanent. They no longer need to be kept in the dark.

When you return the Solargraphics or blueprint paper to your students, have them assemble text and illustrations into book format.

---

* If you are working outside, you may have to work in the evening or use several garbage bags to keep the pail sufficiently dark. Bright daylight will overexpose the paper and cause the image to disappear.

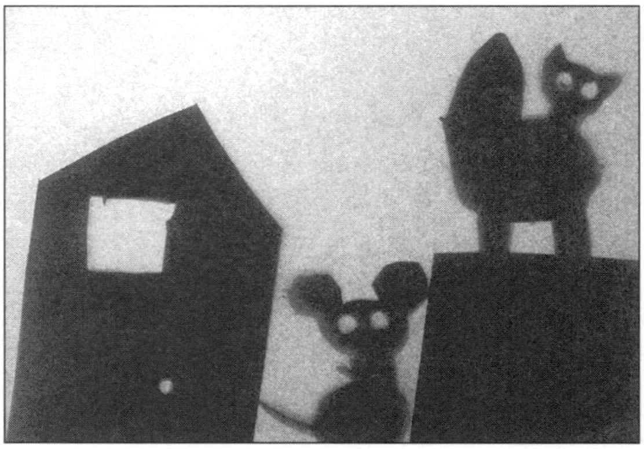

Darlene Paranaque and Chantal Del Carmen, grade 3, Prairie Rose Elementary School

Fig. 7.8. (above and right) These finished prints contain a wide range of light and dark violet-blue tones.

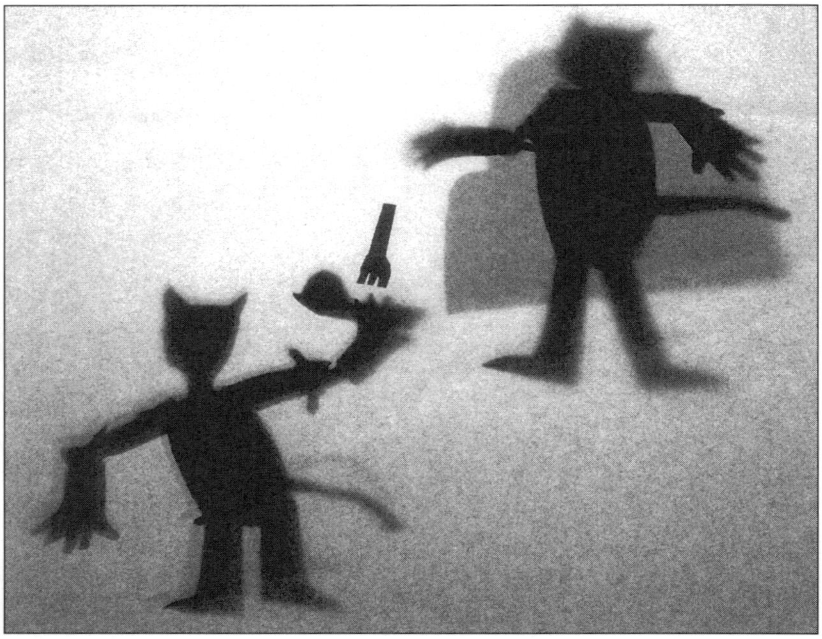

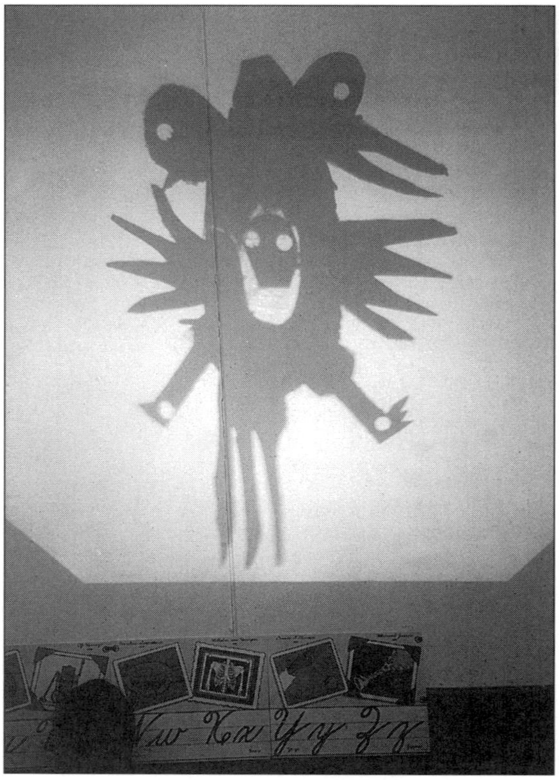

Shaman Puppet, Nicole Selkirk, age 7, Pine Dock School

Fig. 7.9. Nicole's inspiration for making her puppet came from prints by Inuit artists. The shaman's face is inside the two-headed bird image. The whole creature folds into an egg shape and can "hatch" into the more complicated image.

Enrichment

- Make shadow puppets that can change from one kind of creature to another—transformers, shamans, magical beings, and so on. Construct shadow puppets (pages 99–101) and make more than one head. Attach both heads with the same brass fastener and fold one at a time out of sight over the body; attach wings and arms to the same fasteners; make a tail that folds out; and so on. This idea will also work for creatures hatching out of eggs, growing, and so on.
- Put pieces of clear plastic in cut-out windows of black paper, then attach pieces. This works well for small pieces; for example, the iris in an eyeball, an x-ray view of stomach contents. They will look like they are "floating." Try drawing on the plastic with overhead projector markers.
- Attach sticks or wires to pieces to make "proper" shadow puppets. Construct a simple screen out of white paper. Then cut a hole for a window in a large cardboard box and tape the paper over it. The box may be decorated to look like a puppet theater. Students will need to work in groups to present their stories this way, and may need coaching on developing their characters' voices and voice projection.

Vocabulary (see appendixes for definitions)

blueprint	*profile*	*setting*
character	*props*	*shape*
light-sensitive paper	*resolution*	

Part 4
Working in Color

After students have become familiar with drawing, design, and the process of developing an image, they are ready to learn about working in color. By now students have the knowledge they need to make decisions about shape, line, texture, pattern, value, space, and design in their artwork. Working in color gives them new choices about color mixing, complementary and analagous colors, cool and warm colors, intense or reduced colors, transparency and opacity, brush marks, paint chemistry, viscosity, technique, and so on. Color can be used expressively, and can be experimented with in isolation from other considerations.

There are also good arguments for jumping into color media very early in your school art program. Paint, collage, and Plasticine are fun, tactile media to work with. They encourage exploration of and enthusiasm for visual art. Students may learn valuable lessons about color mixing and viscosity while finger painting in kindergarten. You may integrate the techniques for working in color with the basic exercises in previous chapters.

Someone once referred to some colors of paint as "juicy," "sour," or "sweet." Other people talk about some colors as being "depressing," "calming," or "happy." Color can evoke a visceral or emotional response in the viewer. So, too, can the "act" of painting. There is a certain pleasure to pulling a paintbrush, or fingers, through the pudding-like consistency of thick paint. For both of these reasons—to experience a vivid range of colors and to get the proper paint consistency—it is an advantage to use good-quality materials.

The experience of painting and the end product will be enhanced if you avoid chalky colors and runny or lumpy liquid paint. Paint chemistry has recently improved tempera paints—true colors are now available in block and liquid forms. Relatively inexpensive watercolor paint is now available in small tubes; these provide more intense color than student paint boxes. Plasticine varies tremendously from sticky, unworkable goop or old crumbly lumps, to quality brands that stay pliable for months and don't stick so persistently to table tops. Of course, you may have to find your own—often financial—balance between "making do" with what is in the school supply cupboard and ordering new materials. Many of the exercises for working in color can—like collage—use recycled or found materials.

8
The Basics of Color Mixing and Color Theory

Introduction

In this chapter, you will find information on the basics of color mixing and color theory. Use this chapter as a reference for chapters 9–11. If students encounter problems with color media, you can also use this chapter to look for solutions.

The exercises may be adapted to the age and ability of your students. Those from about grades two and up might benefit from actually painting a color wheel to learn to predict how colors will interact. Making a color wheel may also be a good introductory exercise for older students who are inexperienced in art or who lack confidence with painting—a color wheel is a "safe" exercise that requires no drawing skills.

Younger students might simply be presented with trays of paint that contain only the three primary colors (red, yellow, and blue), plus black and white. Experimenting with these colors may lead them to "discover" how to mix the secondary colors, tints, and shades. Nursery and kindergarten students might find only yellow and red paint at the painting easel one day and notice that, when the colors are mixed together, they make orange.

Students can make a color wheel and practice mixing colors using any color media—oil pastel, pencil crayons, crayons, paint, and so on. Paint, however, is the preferred medium. The colors mix thoroughly to make secondary colors more recognizable and uniform (see chapter 9 for tips on painting).

The exercises that follow are a good introduction to the messy, liquid qualities of paint. They also provide students with a good introduction to the routine of using paint in the classroom. This is a good time to establish:

- where in the classroom painting supplies are kept
- routines for student access to materials and clean-up

It is also a good time to delegate specific clean-up jobs to the students. This will make the tasks less stressful and ensure that painting remains an enjoyable and frequent activity in your classroom (see appendix B).

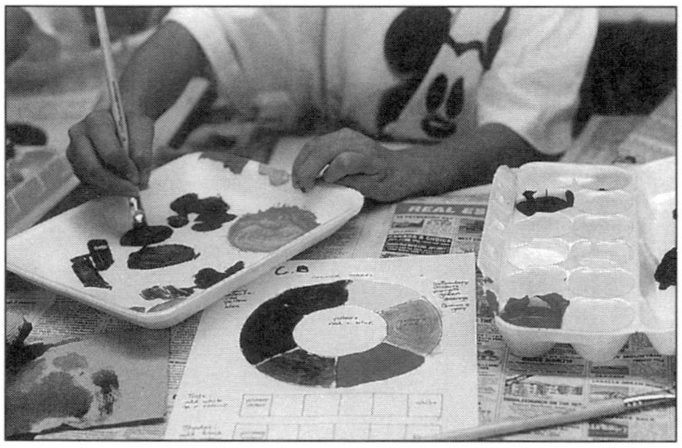

Fig. 8.1. Painting a color wheel with liquid tempra paint. Some brands of red paint contain a yellow pigment; students may end up mixing a violet that is almost brown. The problem can be solved by buying a "cool" red paint. **See color plate.**

Introduce your students to colors and color mixing by first familiarizing them with primary colors. Then have them work on mixing secondary colors, tints, and shades. The three primary colors are red, yellow, and blue. Secondary colors—orange, green, and violet—are those that result from the mixing of two primary colors:

red + yellow = orange
yellow + blue = green
blue + red = violet

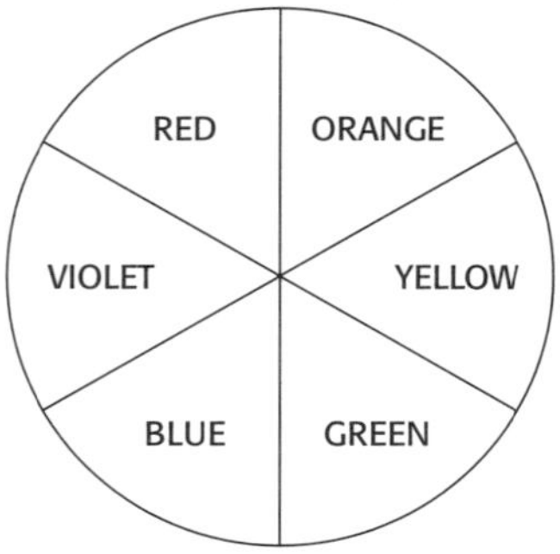

The Color Wheel

Show students how to draw a color wheel. Make a donut shape on a piece of paper. Divide the circle into six parts and pencil in the names of the primary and secondary colors in sequence. The sequence is: red, orange, yellow, green, blue, and violet. Explain to students that they are going to paint their color wheel these six colors, but they are going to use only red, yellow, and blue to do so.

Students should get into the habit of mixing colors on palettes before painting the colors on the color wheel (fig. 8.1). This gives them more control of whatever color they are mixing. When mixing the colors, make sure they start with the lightest color and gradually add in small amounts of the darker color. For example, when they are mixing yellow and blue, have them start with yellow and add a small amount of blue. Remind them to clean off the paintbrush before dipping it into a new color. This way, they will avoid polluting the colors.

If your students are older or advanced, explain that colors next to each other on the color wheel are *analagous*. For example, yellow, orange, and red are analagous colors. These colors harmonize easily in a painting—if they are similar enough they "blend in" when next to each other (fig. 8.2). Colors opposite each other on the color wheel are called *complementary*. For example, red and green are complementary colors; so are yellow and violet. Placed next to each other in a painting, complementary colors "stand out" and call attention to each other.

Brown is made by mixing any two complementary colors (red + green; orange + blue; yellow + violet) together. Brown is a difficult color to mix. If the mixture is too green, add a touch of red. If it is too orange, add a touch of blue. If it is too yellow, add a touch of violet. Balance the color with a touch of its complement until an acceptable brown is achieved.

More advanced students can also practice mixing *tertiary* colors. Tertiary colors are those that result from combining a primary color and a secondary color together. They include yellow-green and blue-violet.

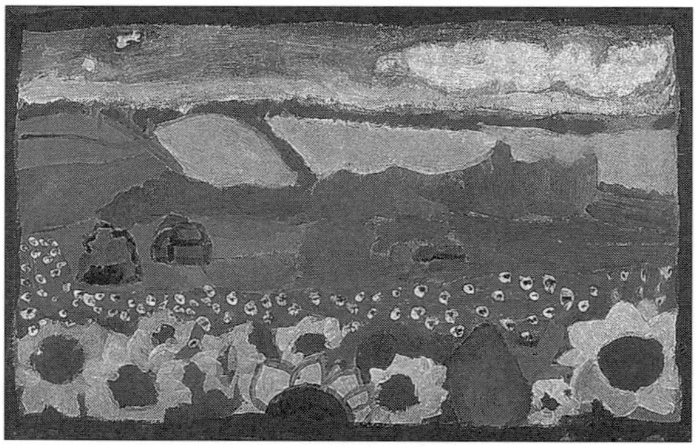

Sunflowers, Sophorn Nhem, grade 6, Wellington School

Fig. 8.2. Sophorn used an analagous color scheme of yellow, green, and blue for her field of flowers. **See color plate.**

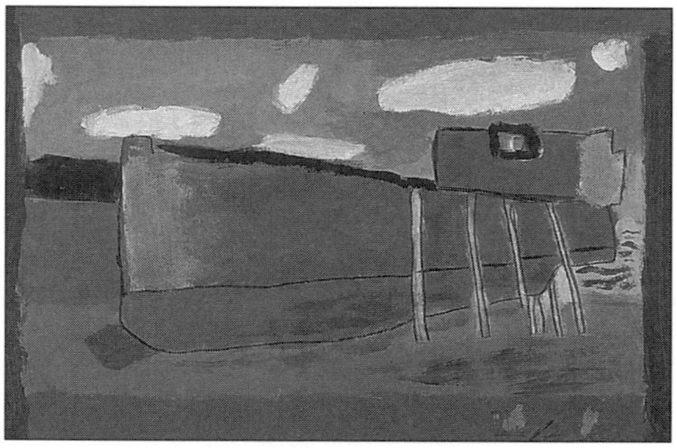

Dry Dock, Steven Bothelo, grade 6, Wellington School

Fig. 8.3. Steven used a complementary color scheme of red and green, and strong contrasts in white and black, for his painting of a boat. He outlined with black pencil crayon after the paint was dry. **See color plate.**

Students who are genuinely color blind may be able to mix secondary colors—especially if the paint tray is labeled—but may have trouble with more subtle mixes. Usually color blindness is limited to a specific combination of complements; for example, confusion of red with green or violet with yellow. There is little value in insisting on accuracy with students who are color blind! Depending on the situation and the students' preferences and personality, you may provide them with specific formulas (or premixed paint), or you can accept their accidental combinations as simply their way of seeing.*

Tip: Some varieties of red paint are actually orange and, when mixed with blue, make brown rather than violet. You will need a "cool" red, or you will have to "cheat" and provide purple paint.

Tip: For bright, solid colors, it is important not to have too much water mixed with the paint. Dry brushes on paper towels before dipping into liquid paint; use a minimum of water with block paints. Some brands of paint are much brighter, and have a thicker consistancy, than others.

Tints and Shades

When students understand primary and secondary colors, introduce them to tints and shades. Tints are colors in which white has been added to make the color a lighter value. Shades are colors in which black, or another dark color, has been added to make that color a darker value.

Tell your students they are going to practice making tints. Have them draw a long rectangle and divide the rectangle into five parts. Begin by painting white in the first box. Next pick a single primary color and mix white on the palette with a small amount of that color. Paint this mixture in the second box. Now add a bit more of the primary color to the mixture on the palette and paint that into the third box. The colors become progressively darker, from white at one end of the chart to the pure primary hue on the other end—from a lighter to a darker value (fig. 8.4).

Students can now practice making shades. Again, have them draw a long rectangle and divide the rectangle into five parts. Now pick a single primary color. Begin by painting the first box with the primary color. Next mix the primary color on the palette with a very small amount of black, and paint this mixture into the second box. Now add a bit more black to the mixture on the palette. The colors will become progressively darker, from the primary color at one end of the chart to black at the other end—from a medium to a very dark value (fig. 8.5).

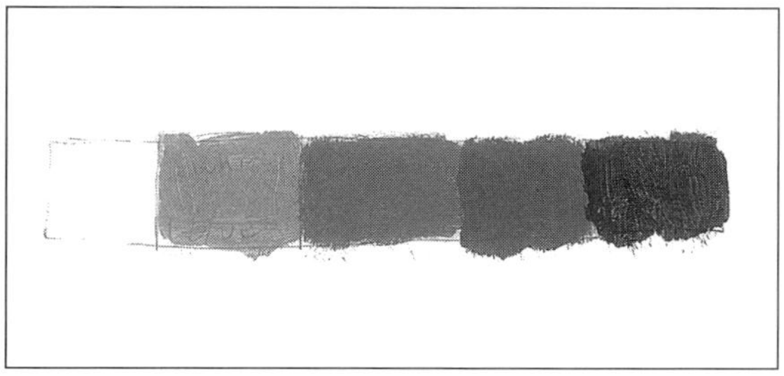

tempera paint, Charlene Moneyas, age 14, Wanipigow School

Fig. 8.4. To make a tint, start with white paint. Add a chosen color a small amount at a time until a "true" color is achieved. The result should be a gradual transition from light to dark. **See color plate.**

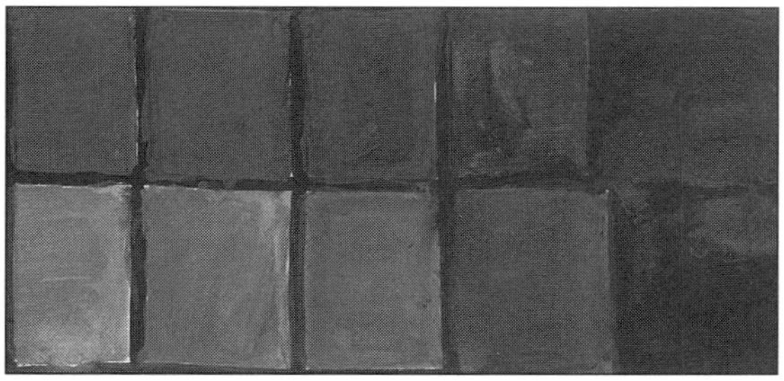

tempera paint, Noni Brynjolson, age 11

Fig. 8.5. To make shades, begin with a chosen color. Add black a small amount at a time. The result is a gradual transition from light to dark. **See color plate.**

Tip: Adding black to a color will make the color quite gray and dull. To achieve a darker shade, try adding another dark color (for example, blue, violet, or brown) instead.

* A color-blind classmate of mine in a university-level painting class happily painted everything in shades of blue and yellow, with interesting results.

Enrichment

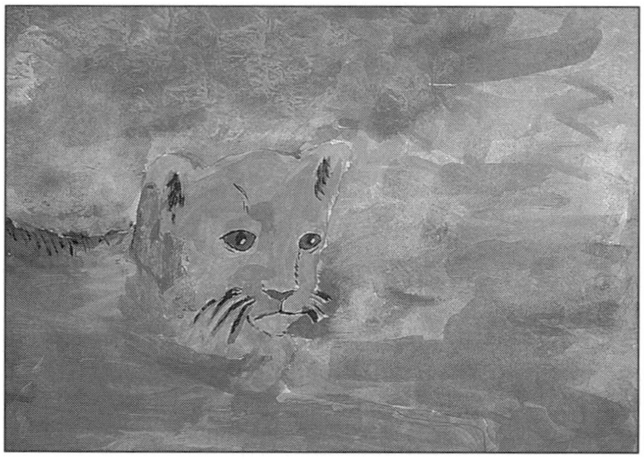

Lion Cub, block tempera on paper, Noni Brynjolson, age 11

Fig. 8.6. Noni used a range of warm colors in her painting. **See color plate.**

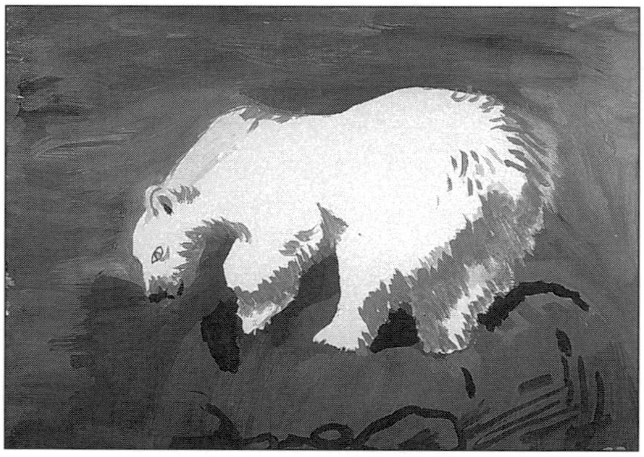

Polar Bear, block tempera on paper, Danna Slessor-Cobb, age 10

Fig. 8.7. Danna used a range of cool colors for her polar bear. **See color plate.**

- Introduce advanced students to the following color schemes. Use as color-mixing exercises (using boxes or charts similar to the ones used for tints and shades) or in paintings to create subjects that contain only the desired colors. Alternatively, you could limit the range of paint colors that students may use. The color schemes may also be useful when looking at and discussing visual information such as advertisements, paintings, and illustrations.

  - *"warm" and "cool" colors.* Warm colors are yellow, orange, and red (fig. 8.6). Cool colors are blue, blue-violet, and blue-green (fig. 8.7). Within each color, there may be a range from warm to cool. For example, red may vary from a fiery orange-red to a cooler violet-red. Yellow may be a warm orange-yellow or a cooler (more acid) green-yellow.

  - *monochromatic color.* This means that only one color has been used. The color may be more or less transparent (more or less water may be added to paint to allow more or less of the paper to show through) or the color may be tinted or shaded, but only one color is present. (An entire painting may be composed of only tints and shades of the same color.)

  - *intense or brilliant color.* These are brilliant hues that are pure or unmixed. Intense color can be emphasized by arranging several analagous colors (for example, blue, blue-violet, and violet) to butt up against a complementary set of colors (for example, orange, yellow-orange, and yellow). This creates an image with a rich variety of colors, set against the "shock" of their complements.

  - *reduced color.* Colors are reduced by mixing them with their complement, or by mixing them with a small amount of brown or gray. The resulting colors are muted, and the result is a more subtle color range (fig. 8.8). When a small amount of one color is added to every color in the paintings, it helps unify the colors.

  - *color and space.* Intense colors, warm colors, and complementary colors tend to attract the viewer's eye, causing the object to appear nearer. Reduced colors, cool colors, and analagous colors tend to "recede." In this way, colors can be used to create a sense of space or depth in a picture (see chapter 3, page 39). Practically speaking, this means that a red barn in a landscape painting will appear closer (stand out), unless the red is "reduced" with a small amount of green, "cooled" with a bit of blue, or surrounded by analagous colors such as orange and yellow autumn fields or trees.

- Skin tones may be challenging colors to mix. Skin tones range in color from tinted peach or tinted brown to a nearly black blue-brown. For very light skin tones, mix yellow with some red and white. For browner skin, mix a rich, reddish brown, and tint slightly with white. Add more yellow or red as necessary. For very dark skin tones, mix brown with a touch of blue, and shade slightly with black. Notice that all skin tones will appear to be a lighter value where they reflect light, and will appear darker where a shadow falls.
- Look at a variety of houseplants for an interesting color-mixing exercise. Have students make a "jungle scene" by drawing and painting large leaf shapes. Young students may paint each piece separately and cut and paste them to achieve the overlapping shapes seen in a jungle. Students may discover hundreds of variations on the color green; for example, tinted, shaded, warmed, cooled, intense, and reduced.

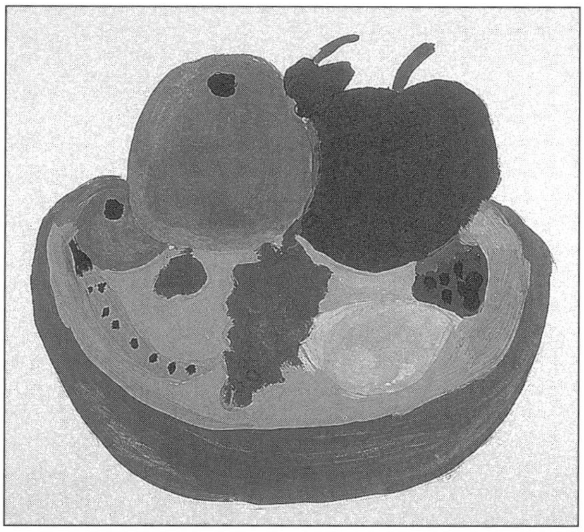

Bowl of Fruit, block tempera on paper, Danna Slessor-Cobb, age 10

Fig. 8.8. This painting was done using reduced colors. Every color was mixed with a small amount of its complementary color to produce an overall brown or gray effect. **See color plate.**

Vocabulary (see appendixes for definitions)

analagous colors	*intense colors*	*secondary colors*
background	*monochromatic color*	*shade*
color spectrum	*mural*	*space*
color wheel	*palette*	*tertiary colors*
complementary colors	*pigments*	*tint*
cool colors	*primary colors*	*warm colors*
hue	*reduced colors*	

9
Learning to Paint

Introduction

In this chapter, the basics of handling paint and the "tempera" technique (using thicker paint with little water and layers of color) are introduced. (See chapter 8 for introductory exercises on color mixing and color theory.)

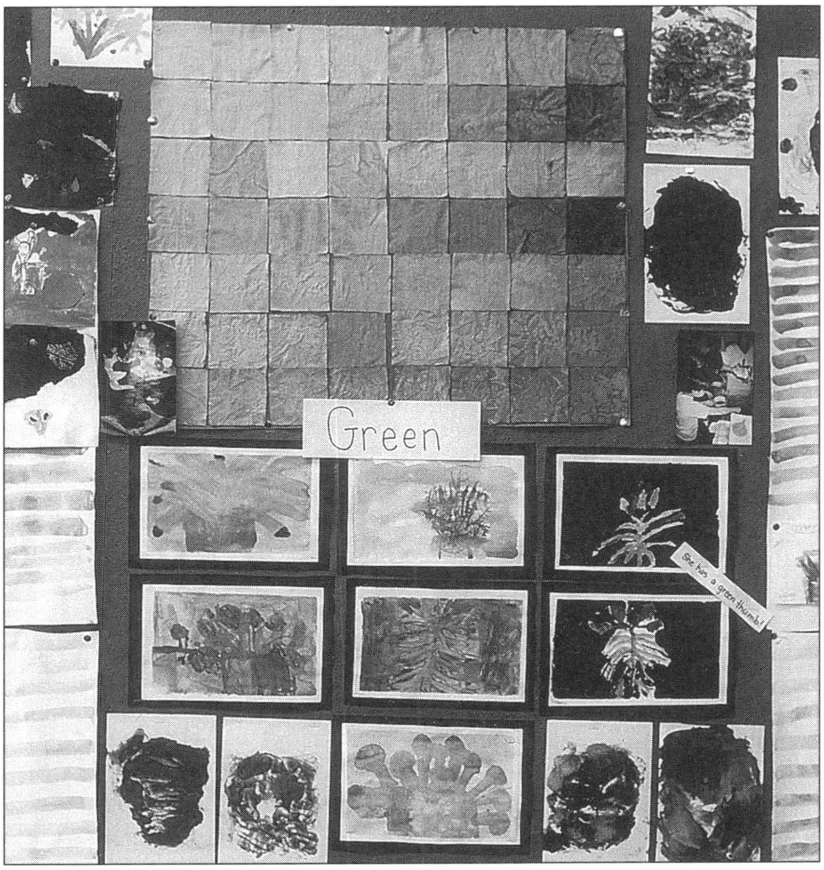

Green, grade 1 class, Wolseley School

Fig. 9.1. This display of student work was a result of work by two teachers, Donna Massey-Cudmore and Andrea Stuart, who teach art as a well-integrated part of their curriculum. The graph at the top is a math exercise. Students measured varying amounts of yellow and blue food coloring, using an eye-dropper to count drops onto pieces of paper towel. The results were then pieced into a graph. **See color plate.**

Books to Have Handy

Picture Books

The Cremation of Sam McGee

Josepha

Teacher References

Paint!

Painting

Tempera Paint

Materials

- pencils
- optional: white chalk
- erasers
- paper, 8 1/2" x 11" (21.5 cm x 28 cm)
- tempera paint blocks, or liquid tempera ("cool" red, yellow, blue, white, black) one set per two to four students
- paintbrushes, assortment of flat-head (square-tipped) (1/2" to 3/4" (1.5 cm to 2 cm) sizes)
- water and water containers
- paper towels
- Kleenex
- heavy paper (Dessin, Mayfair, bristol board, or brown butcher paper) 11" x 17" or 28 cm x 43 cm
- palettes
- newspapers (to cover tables)
- painting smocks (paint may stain clothing)

Tempera paint is a versatile medium that can be used in a variety of ways. Tempera paint, like artists' gouache, is fairly opaque. However, it can be mixed with more water for a "wash" of watery paint that lets pencil or permanent pen lines show through. This may be a good way to introduce painting to students who are more comfortable with drawing media.

Tempera paint may also be combined with other color media. Draw first with oil pastel or crayon, and paint over it with tempera —the oil or wax will resist the paint, and the drawn designs will show through. Use thick tempera paint on top of collage or to decorate masks and sculpture. Paint on burlap, rocks, pieces of wood, or cardboard boxes. Coat tempera paint with a gloss finish such as PVA to brighten colors, give a shiny finish, and preserve the otherwise powdery surface.

Appropriate Subjects

Tip: Have paper towels or tissues handy to "erase" spills if mistakes happen or paint is dripped across a page. Paint can be erased by gently dabbing the area with a clean, wet brush and then with a paper towel. When the spill is dry, paint over with thick paint tinted with white.

To start, choose fairly straightforward subjects in a simple setting. Help students find visual references. Look for magazine photos, postcards, objects, books, and so on that have clear pictures of their subject in a setting and that have an interesting color range. As starting exercises, try landscapes from calendar photos or close-up photos of animals from wildlife magazines. Ideally, the pictures will relate to topics being studied by the class. Avoid scenes or subjects that have too much black. Remind students that they will be reducing their subjects to simple shapes; the more detail, the more difficult the subject.

Preparation

Tip: Set the black paint aside until near the end of the session. This will encourage students to mix other dark colors to achieve shades and will prevent black from mixing with other colors and turning them gray. Use black last.

Set out materials (see appendix B) and prepare the palettes. For liquid tempera, try putting color in Styrofoam egg cartons and using plastic lids or Styrofoam trays as palettes for color mixing (egg carton lids may be closed to keep paint for up to two weeks). For block painting, set out paints in standard plastic trays or individually in tuna cans, and have Styrofoam trays or plastic lids available to use as palettes for color mixing. Place books and irreplaceable photos inside large Ziplock bags to protect them from paint splatters.

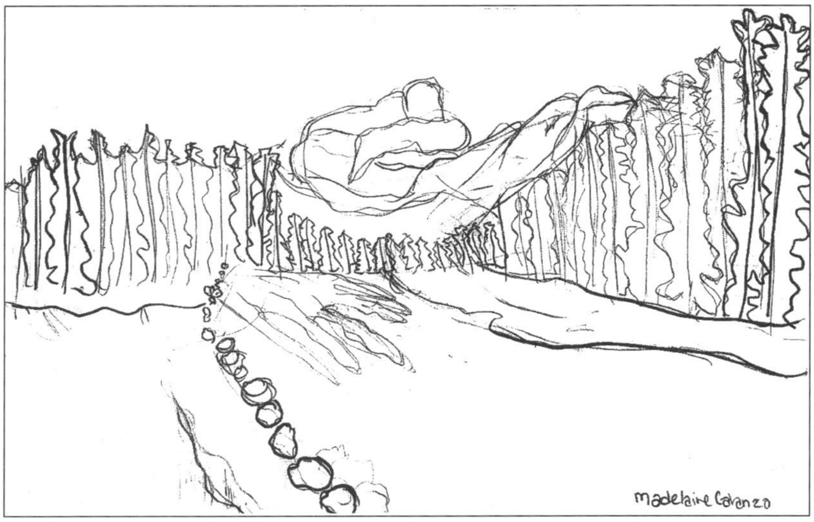

pencil sketch, Madelaine Calanza, age 11, Wellington School

Fig. 9.2. Madelaine made this sketch in preparation for painting. The landscape has been reduced to its most fundamental shapes.

Method

Look at *The Cremation of Sam McGee* with your students. Make sure they note the wavy bands of color in the sky and snow. The color of each band is very similar to the one next to it. Pick one picture and ask the students how many different blues they can see. Now look at the sky on the cover of *Josepha*. The wavy bands of clouds and variety of colors are similar to those done by Ted Harrison in *The Cremation of Sam McGee*. The drawing in each book is quite simplified—every subject is reduced to its most basic shapes.

Discuss some of the differences between the two books. One difference is the clean lines between colors in Harrison's work and the rougher edges in *Josepha*. Students may choose to handle edges either way—with a clean edge or with brush marks overlapping the areas of color. Point to different areas of each picture and ask which colors the artist might have mixed to make that particular color.

To begin, have students make a simplified drawing of their subjects on a large piece of paper, using pencils or white chalk (fig. 9.2). Tell them to draw in only the basic shapes; avoid detail and shading in. Some students may first wish to try a few quick practice drawings in their sketchbooks to get a feel for their subject and to decide which elements of the background will fit into their drawing. Ask students to divide up large areas of their backgrounds with "wavy lines" and irregular shapes. These might correspond roughly to shapes of clouds, shadows, or color changes in their photographs.

Students are now ready to begin painting. Arrange desks or tables so that students can easily share paint materials. Have them look carefully at their subjects for areas of reflected light and shadow that appear to change the color of their subjects. Remind students to pre-mix their colors on their palettes and to use a rich variety of colors, tints, and shades.

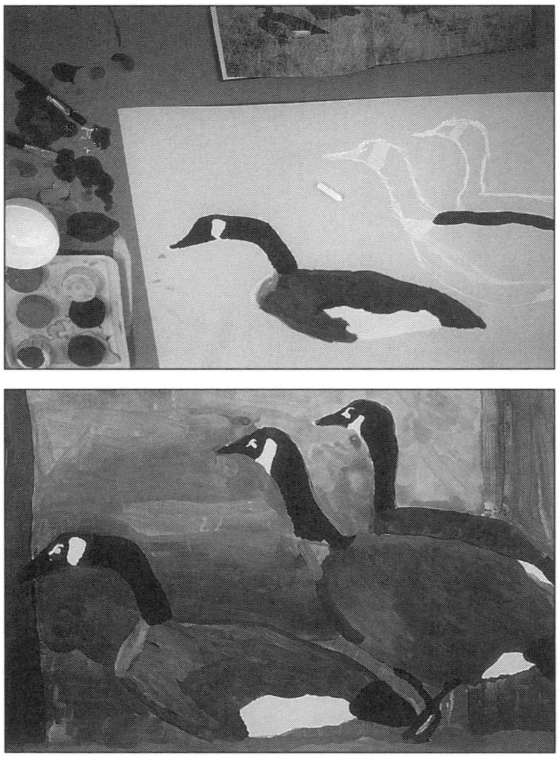

Canada Geese, Jamie Scott, age 13, Matheson Island School

Fig. 9.3. Jamie began his picture by drawing with chalk onto a large, colored piece of Bristol board. He worked carefully to match the colors and values of his reference photograph. **See color plate.**

Have students mix the colors they will want to use (see chapter 8) (fig. 9.3). Even advanced students will find it useful to mix small color swatches on scrap paper or newspaper to match the colors in their subject before they start their painting. This serves as a reminder to mix colors rather than to use them straight from the container. Remind students to wash their brushes and dry them before using a new color. Suggest that they start with the lightest colors (whites and tints) and use darker colors, especially black, last.

Suggest to your students that they avoid painting small details (eyelashes, for example). It is much easier to add in fine details later with a colored pencil, chalk, or oil pastel (fig. 9.4).

Students may wish to experiment with a variety of brush marks. Demonstrate how a paintbrush is pulled rather than pushed, so that the bristles remain together. Light pressure, or turning a square brush edgeways, will produce a fine line. More pressure will produce a thick line. Paint can be dabbed on in dots or in overlapping marks. Brush marks can swirl to convey movement, or their length and direction can correspond to the texture of an animal's fur.

Rich layers of color can be achieved by allowing one color to dry and then painting over top with other colors to add highlights, shadows, textures, or pattern. As advanced students "finish" their paintings, help them look for details (especially light reflections, shadows, and textures) that they may have missed. Often a few light reflections—the gleam in an eye or the sparkling on water will help to add life to their painting.

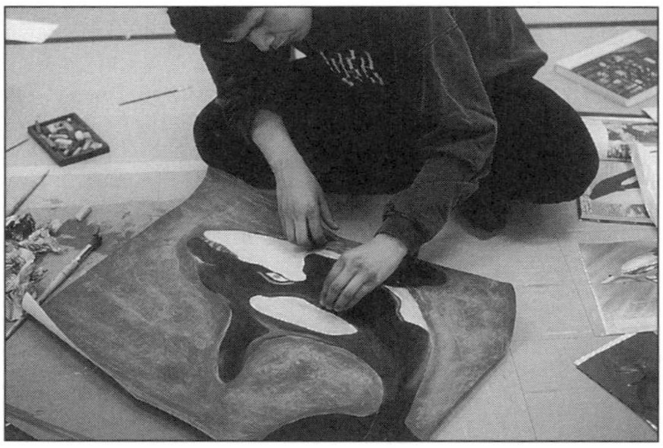

Killer Whale, Bradley Mowat, grade 7, Matheson Island School

Fig. 9.4. After the paint dried, Bradley added some details and highlights with soft (chalk) pastel.

Enrichment

- Students can combine techniques with look-drawing by cutting out their drawings, and gluing them onto painted backgrounds.
- Have students try using a deliberate color scheme for their entire painting: monochromatic; analagous; complementary; warm colors; cool colors; tints; shades; reduced colors; intense colors (see chapter 8, page 110).
- Students might try the color schemes systematically. Have them make a simple sketch, then photocopy it several times. Encourage them to paint a different color scheme on each photocopy. Compare the different effects of each approach. Alternatively, set up simple arrangements of still-life objects such as flowers, fruit, toy dinosaurs, or stuffed animals. For each lesson, pass out only the desired colors of paint, or discuss with students which color scheme may be appropriate for their subjects.
- Coat finished tempera paintings with PVA or acrylic gloss for a shine and brighter color.
- Have students look at paintings by other artists. Examine what kinds of colors, brush marks, and subjects they painted. Advanced students might like to try a painting "in the style" of one of these artists to learn more about brush handling and color sensibilities (fig. 9.5):

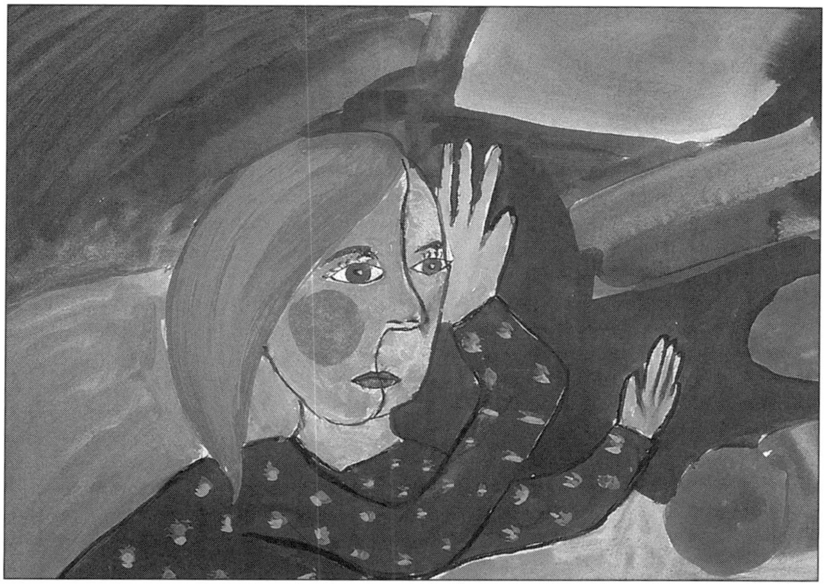

block tempera on paper, Noni Brynjolson, age 11

Fig. 9.5. Noni made this painting after a visit to a Picasso exhibit.

- Try an entire painting made of small dots of color. This approach is called "pointillism." See paintings by Seurat for examples.
- Artists such as van Gogh, Monet, and The Group of Seven, painted in the "impressionist" style. They used loose, overlapping marks to represent the light and colors in an image.
- Jackson Pollack painted in the "expressionist" style. He used brush marks and drips of paint to decorate the surface of his paintings.
- Have students paint a mural or large painting. Use sturdy brown butcher paper and large house-painting brushes. Also try very small paintings (6" x 8" or 15 cm x 20 cm) with tiny (#6) brushes. Mix sand, laundry starch, egg yolk, or other materials with the paint to vary its texture and transparency. Paint with different brushes (thick, thin, long-handled) or use sticks, sponges, homemade paintbrushes, rollers, and so on, for a variety of marks.
- See chapters 10 and 11 or look at the books *Paint!* (for beginners) or *Painting* (for advanced students) for other painting projects and information on how to use other types of paint.

Vocabulary (see appendixes for definitions)

analagous colors	*hue*	*palette*
background	*impressionism*	*pointillism*
complementary colors	*intense colors*	*reduced colors*
expressionism	*monochromatic color*	*shade*
gouache	*mural*	*tint*

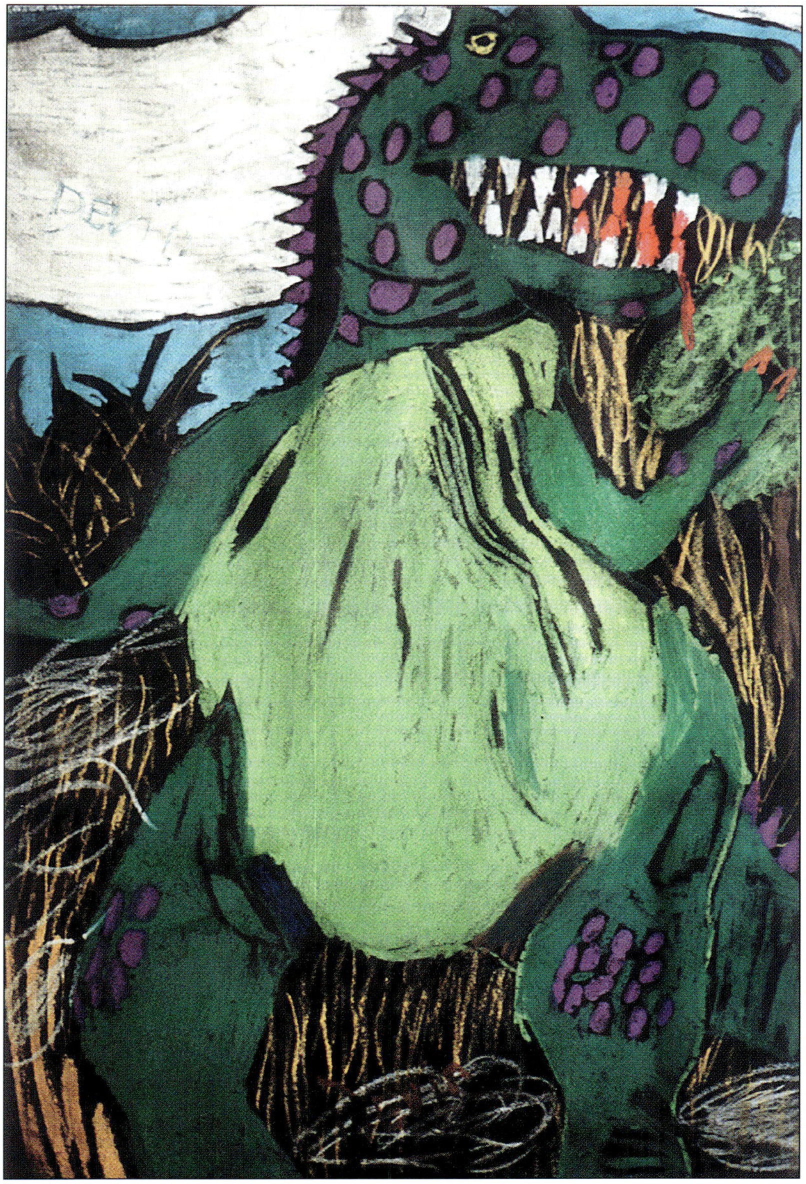

oil pastel and ink on paper, Devin Scott, age 9, Matheson Island School

Fig. I.2.

Any of the drawing exercises in this book can be adapted for use with color media. This dinosaur was drawn with oil pastels and then painted over completely with India ink. Excess ink was then washed off under a tap. The final image has a black outline that contrasts well with the bright color of the oil pastels.

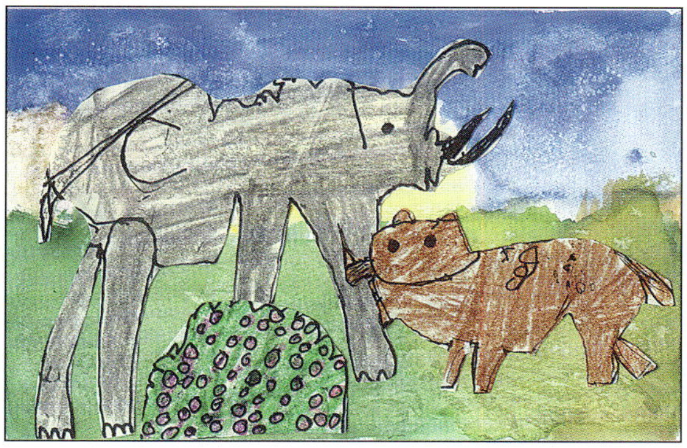

from ***Rhino and Elephant Go Swimming,*** photocopy cutouts on watercolor background, Mark Savage, age 6, Elm Creek School

Fig. 4.19.

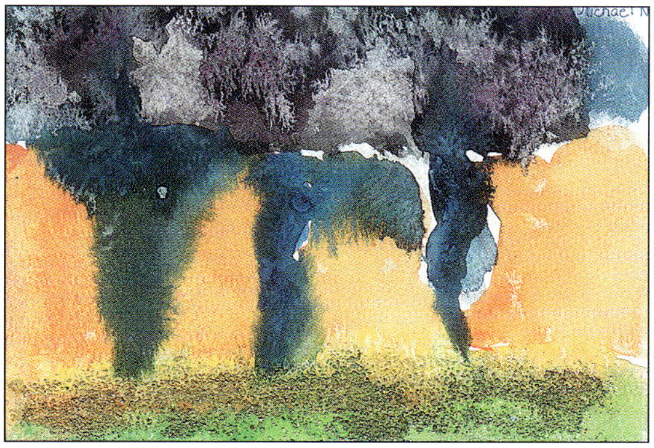

Tornado, watercolor, Michael Noh, age 9, St. John's Ravenscourt School

Fig. 11.6.

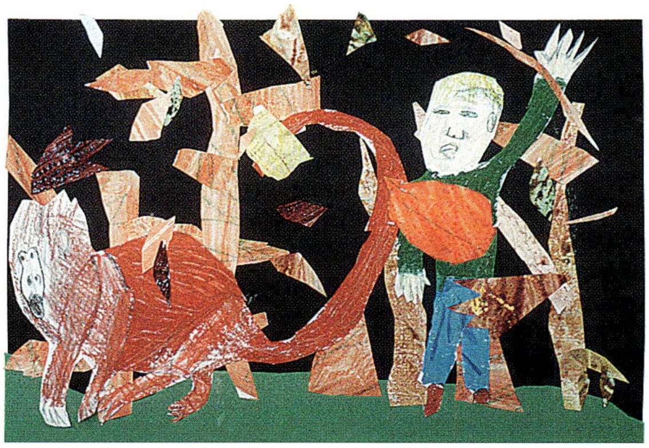

In the Jungle, painting and drawing, cutting and pasting, grade 2 student, Matheson Island School

Fig. 10.16.

In these three mixed-media pieces, students drew and painted the images separately, cut the images out, and combined them to make a picture. Cutting and pasting allows students to make choices about where to place the parts of their image, and it encourages them to consider which pieces might be in front of or behind other pieces. Cutting and pasting is also a good technique to use for illustration, when introducing *character* and *setting*.

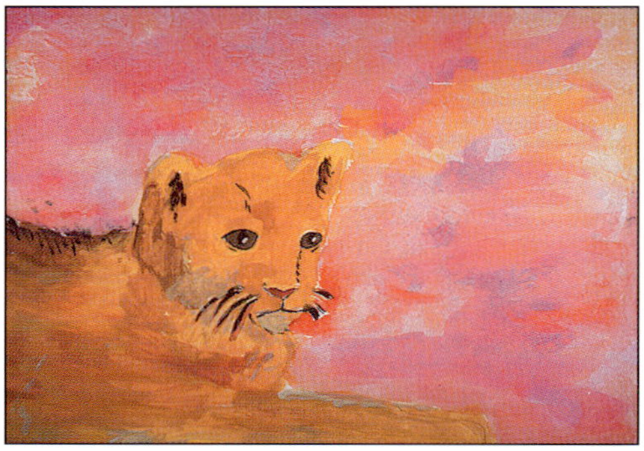

Lion Cub, block tempera on paper, Noni Brynjolson, age 11
Fig. 8.6.

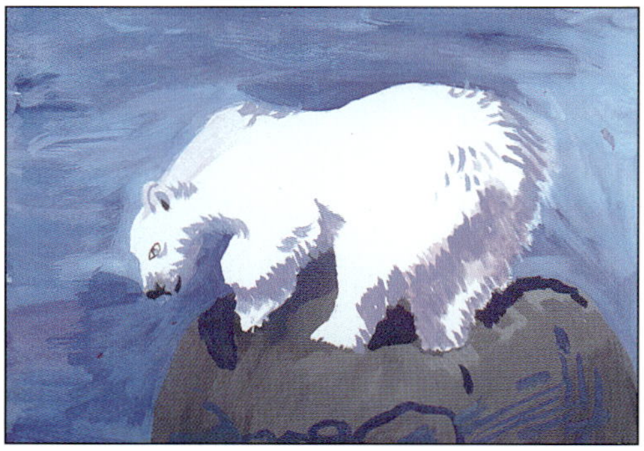

Polar Bear, block tempera on paper, Danna Slessor-Cobb, age 10
Fig. 8.7.

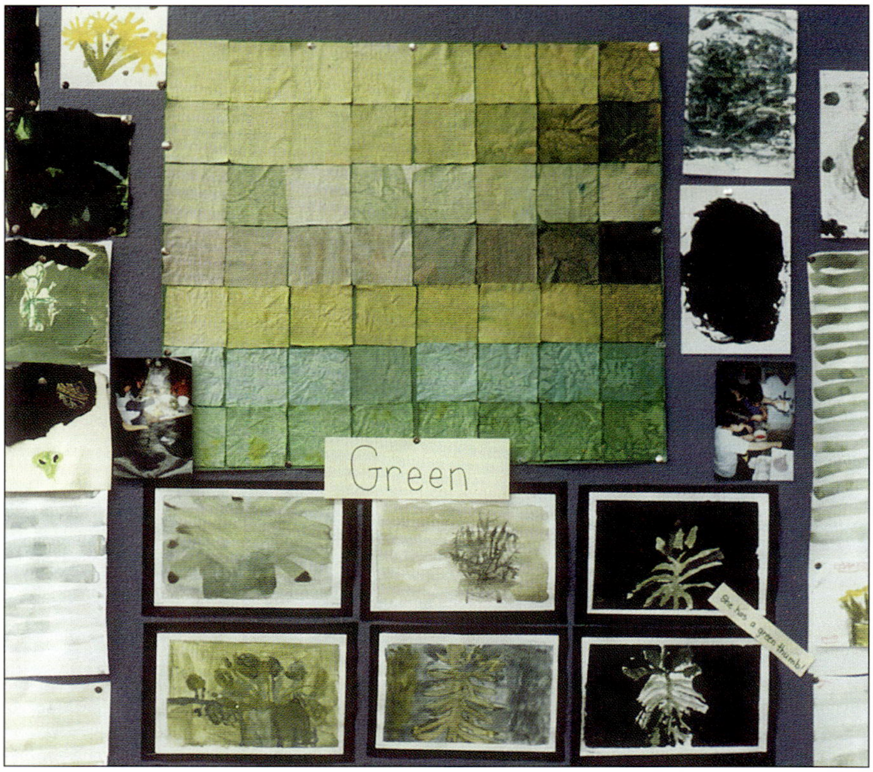

Green, grade 1 class, Wolseley School
Fig. 9.1.

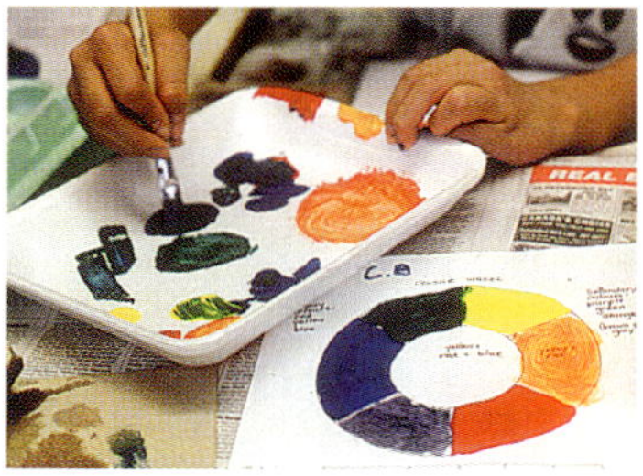

Fig. 8.1.

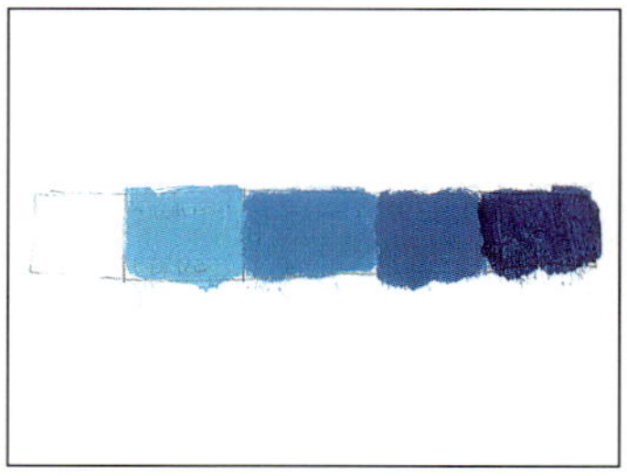

tempera paint, Charlene Moneyas, age 14, Wanipigow School
Fig. 8.4.

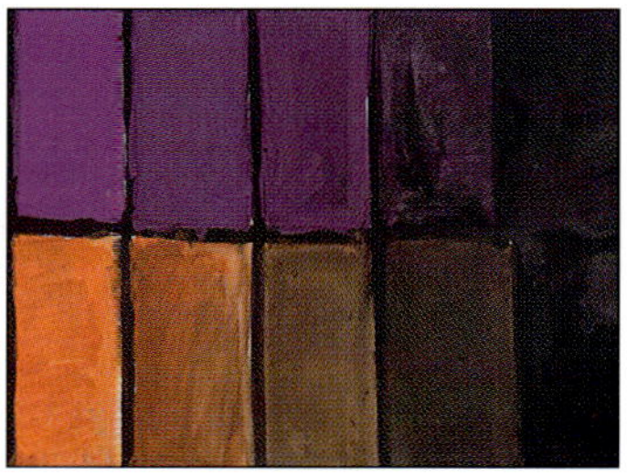

tempera paint, Noni Brynjolson, age 11
Fig. 8.5.

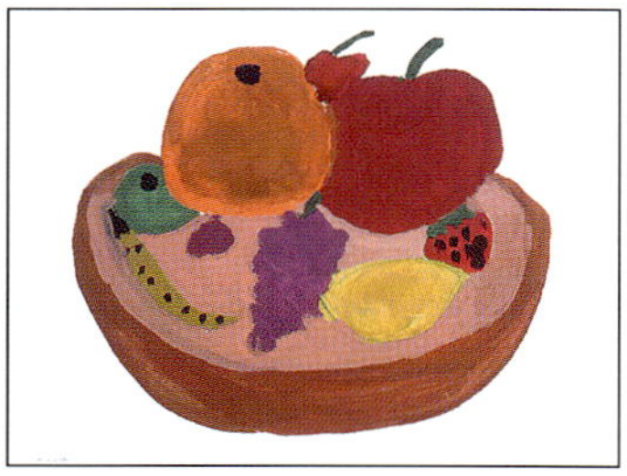

Bowl of Fruit, block tempera on paper, Danna Slessor-Cobb, age 10
Fig. 8.8.

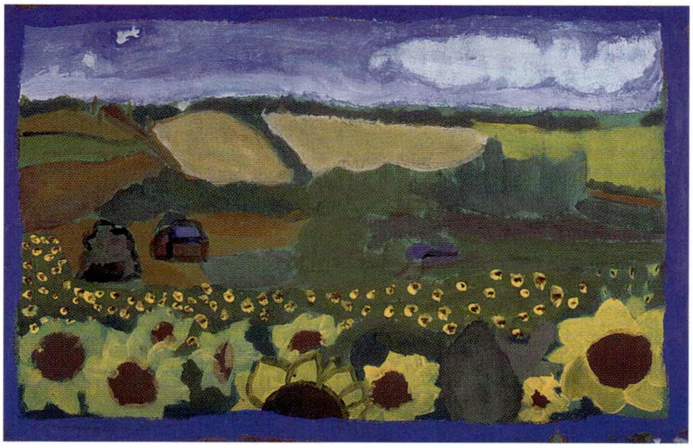

Sunflowers, Sophorn Nhem, grade 6, Wellington School
Fig. 8.2.

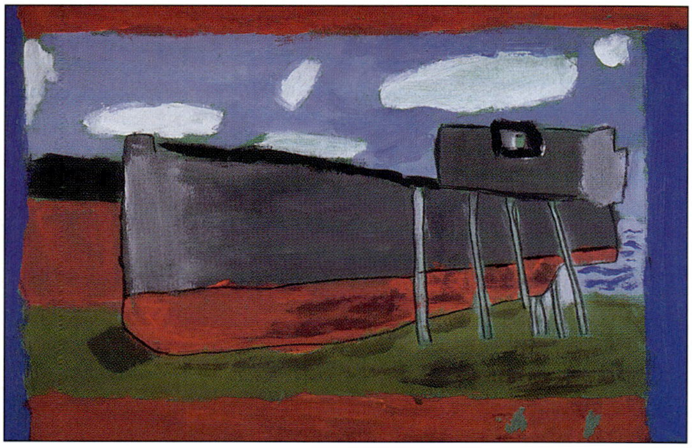

Dry Dock, Steven Bothelo, grade 6, Wellington School
Fig. 8.3.

Students need to gain confidence with mixing secondary colors, tints, and shades before they can use more sophisticated color schemes. Good quality tempera paints can provide bright, opaque colors for mixing.

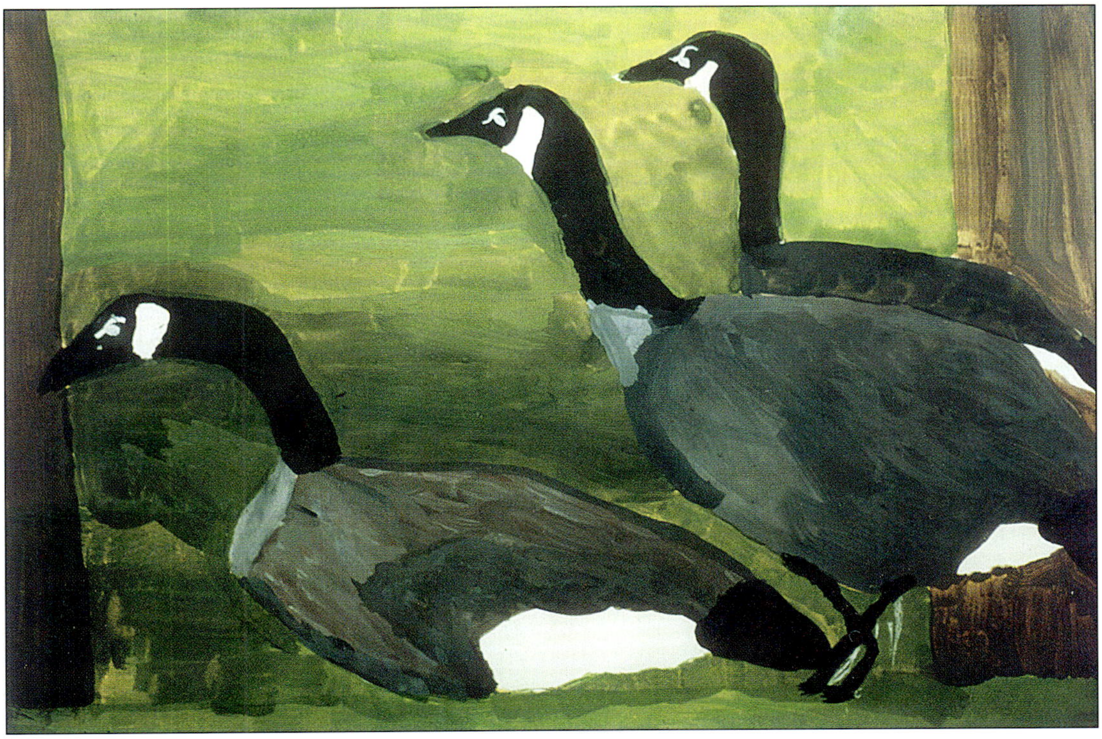

Canada Geese, Jamie Scott, age 13, Matheson Island School

Fig. 9.3.

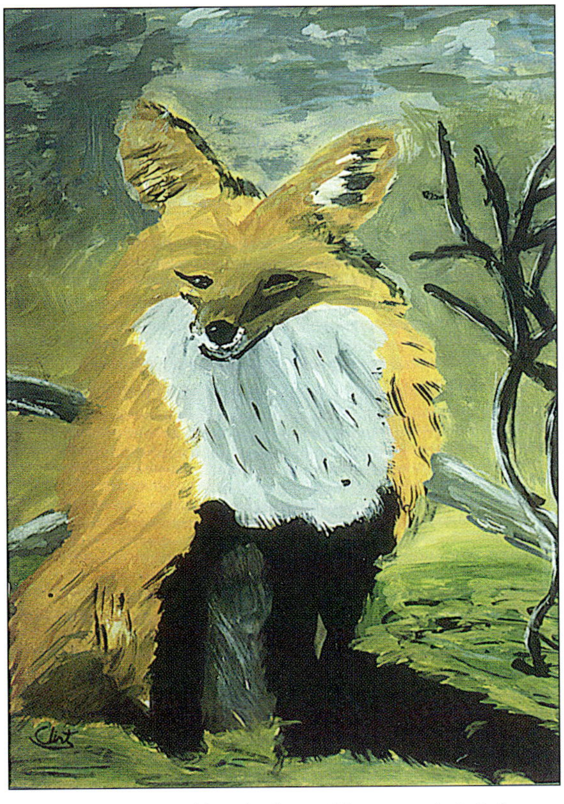

tempera paint on Bristol board, Clinton Whiteway, grade 4–8 class, Matheson Island School

Fig. 2.9

The students who made these images practiced mixing the colors they saw in their reference photographs before they began painting on large sheets of Bristol board.

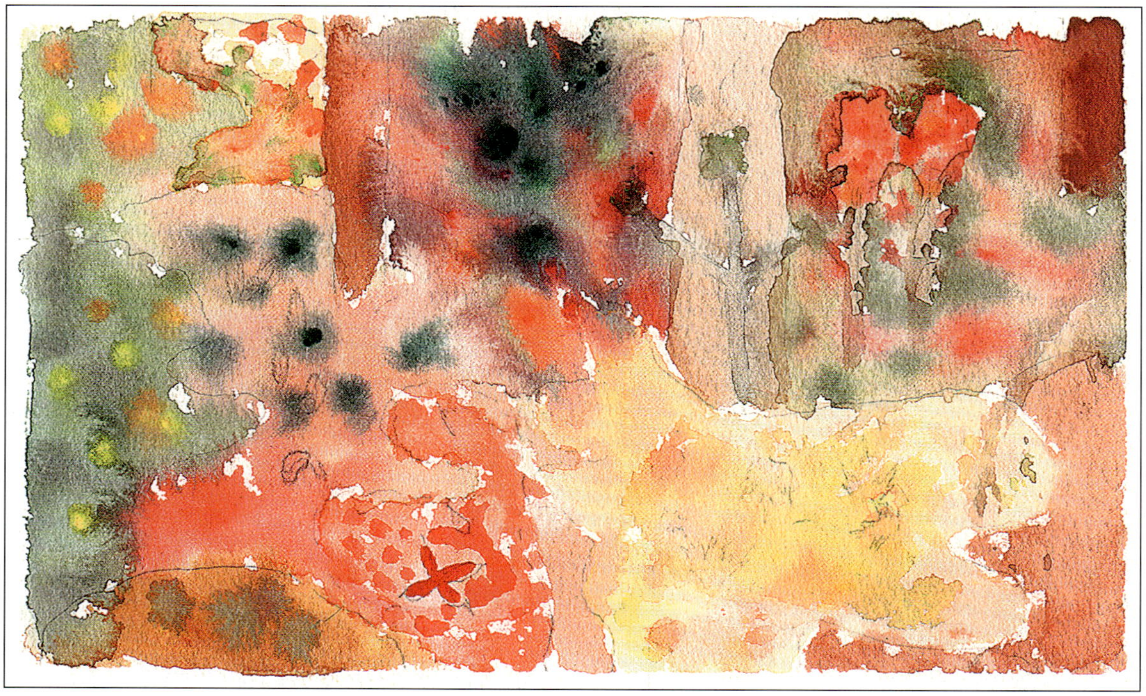

Autumn Forest, watercolor, Tyler Hammerstedt, grade 8, San Antonio School

Fig. 11.1.

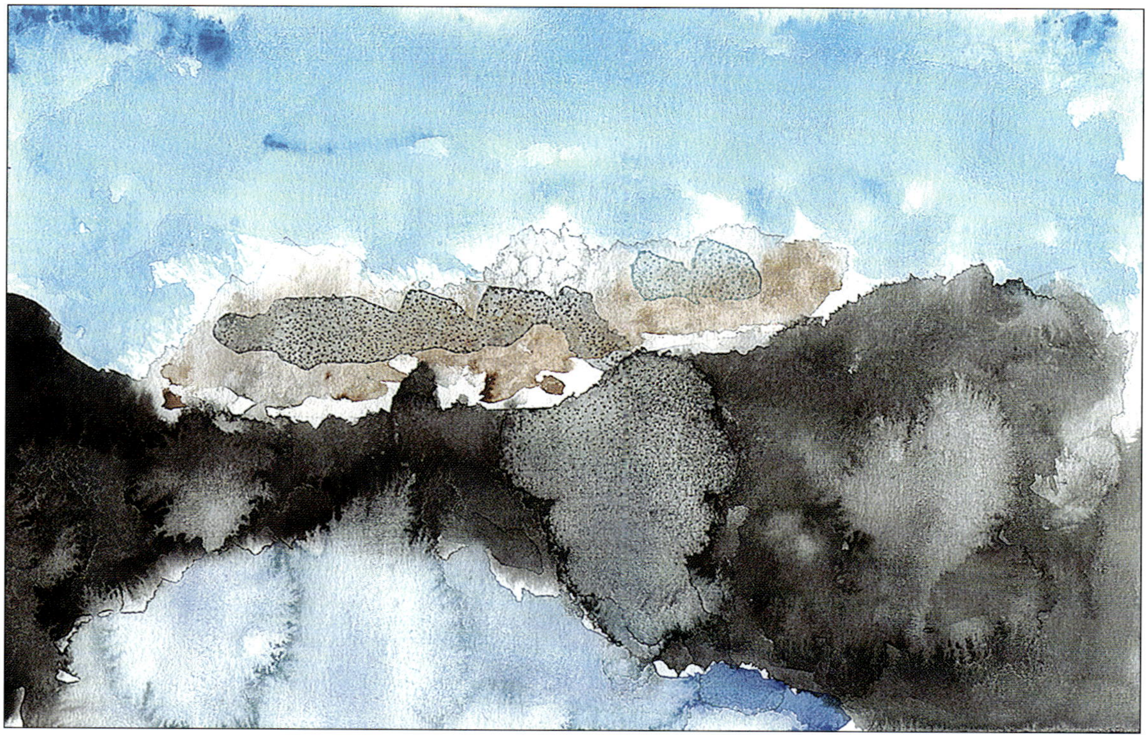

watercolor, Eden Jerao, grade 5, Wellington School

Fig. 11.3.

Watercolor is a quick, versatile medium that can be combined easily with drawing. It is ideal for illustration projects. The "special effects" that are possible with watercolor paint can produce a successful image even if the initial drawing is weak.

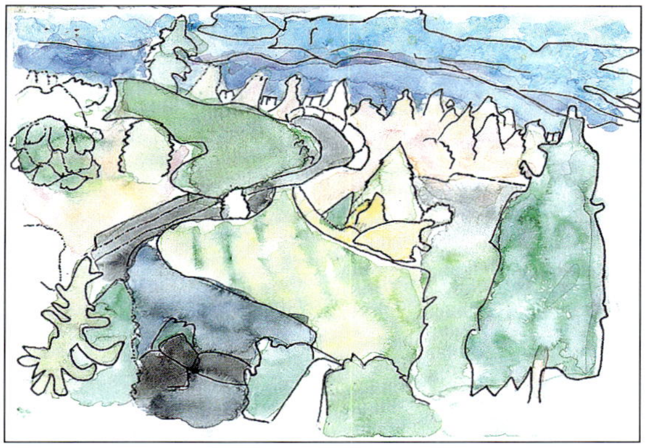

watercolor and ink, Eden Jerao, grade 5, Wellington School

Fig. 11.8.

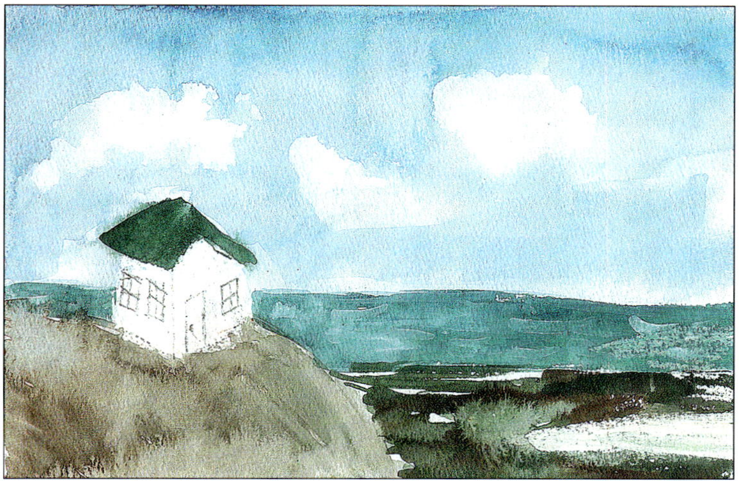

watercolor, Noni Brynjolson, age 11

Fig. 11.4.

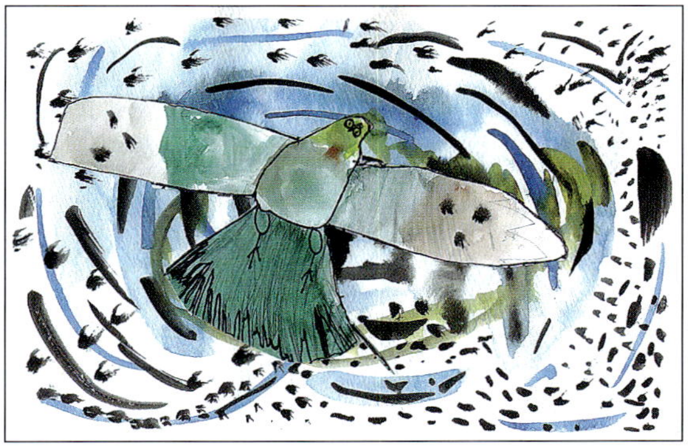

watercolor, cut and paste, Riley Gray, age 8, St. John's Ravenscourt School

Fig.11.10.

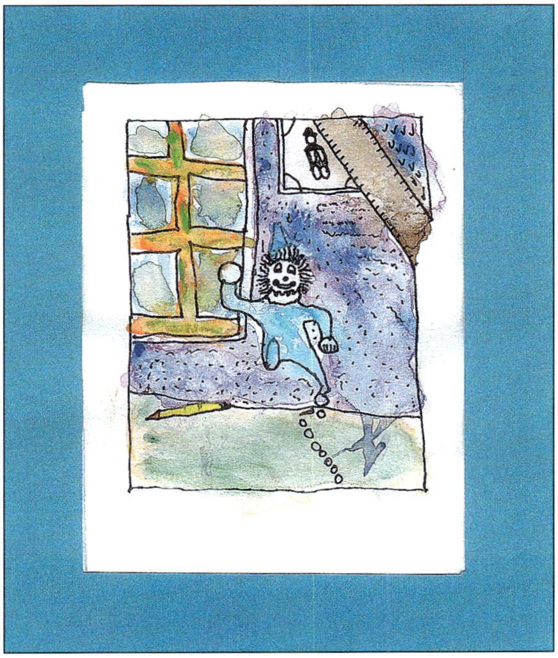

illustration for ***Tale of the Pompom,*** watercolor and ink, Shannon Barbour, age 9, Niakwa Place School

Fig. 11.11.

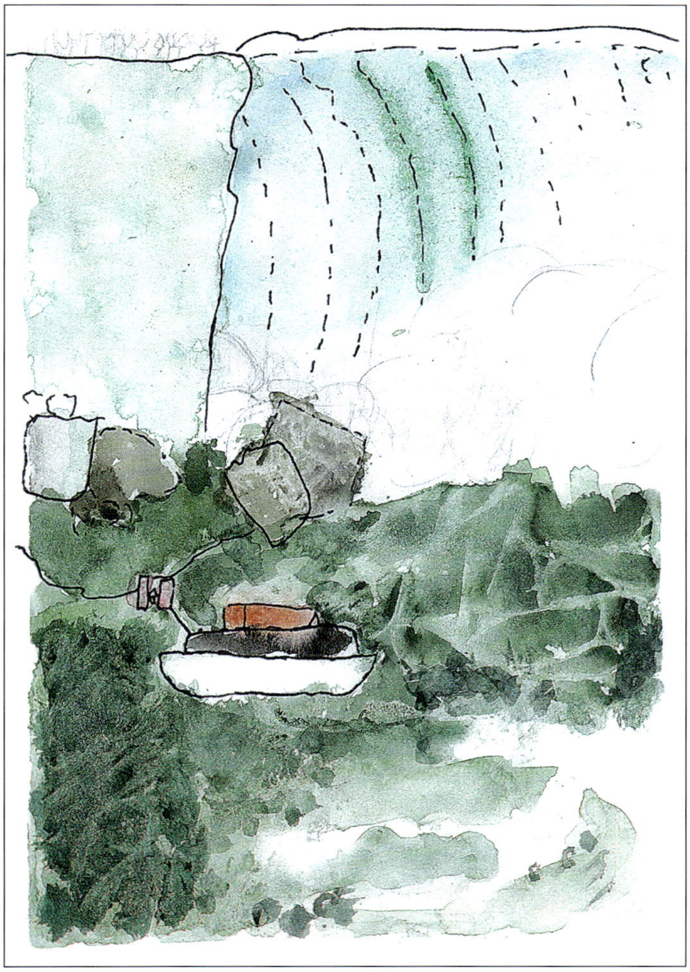

Waterfall, watercolor, Laura Chantharangsri, grade 5, Wellington School

Fig. 11.7.

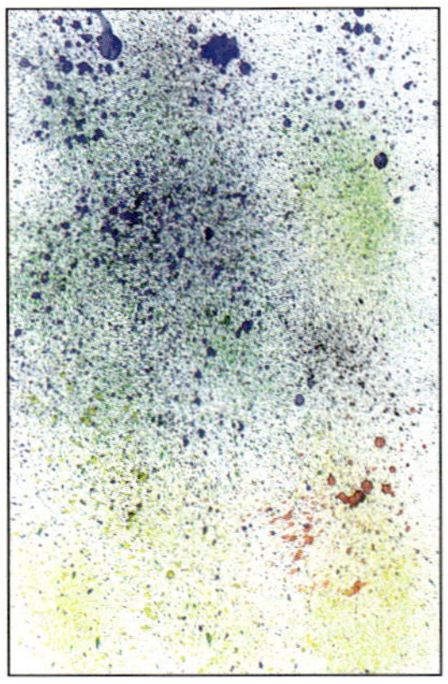

kindergarten class, Luxton School
Fig. 10.3.

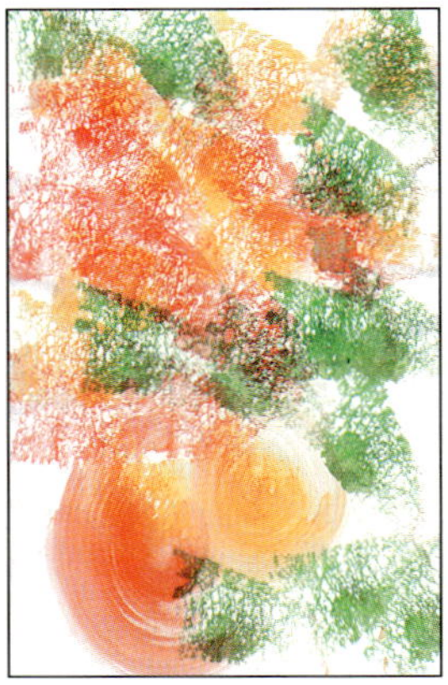

kindergarten class, Luxton School
Fig. 10.5.

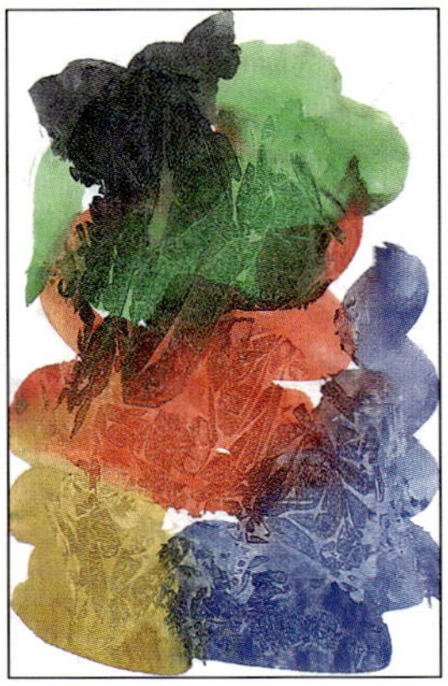

kindergarten class, Luxton School
Fig. 10.7.

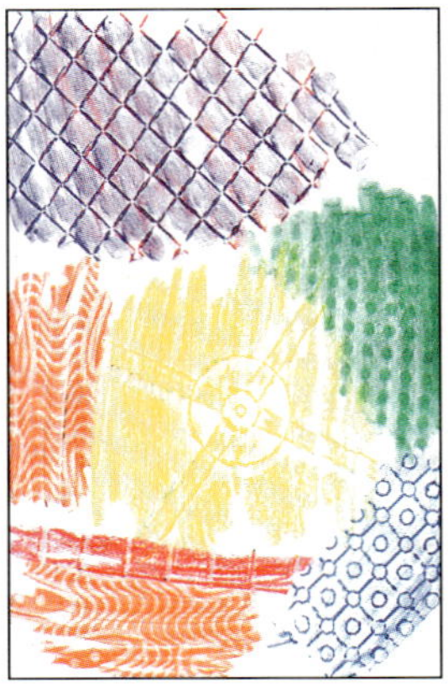

kindergarten class, Luxton School
Fig. 10.9.

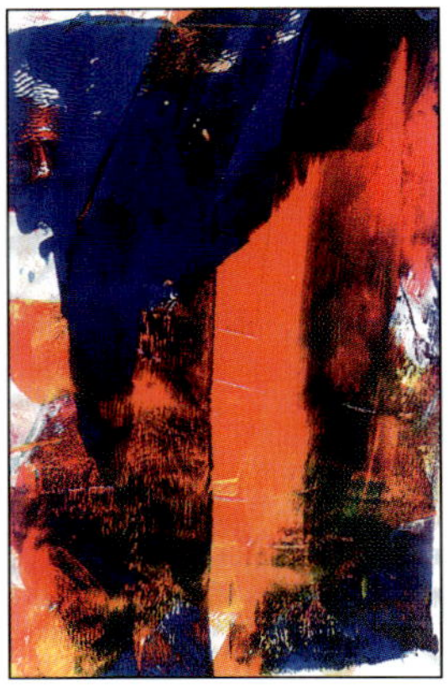

kindergarten class, Luxton School
Fig. 10.11.

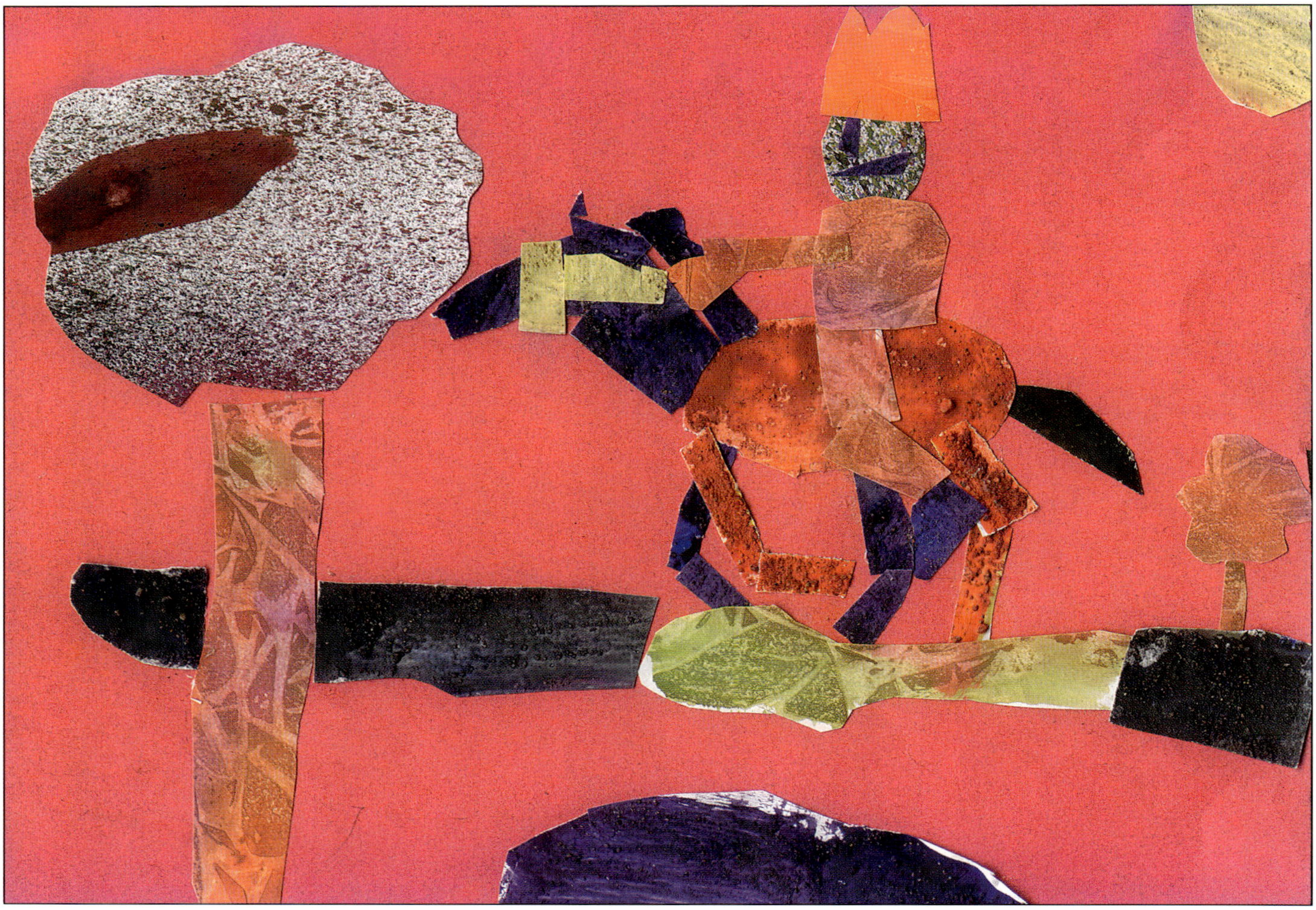

The Prince, paint, cutting and pasting, Joel Dyck, age 8, South Oaks School
Fig. 10.14.

Students need an opportunity to explore the endless variety of marks that can be made with paint. The accidental color mixing and patterns that result can be very beautiful.

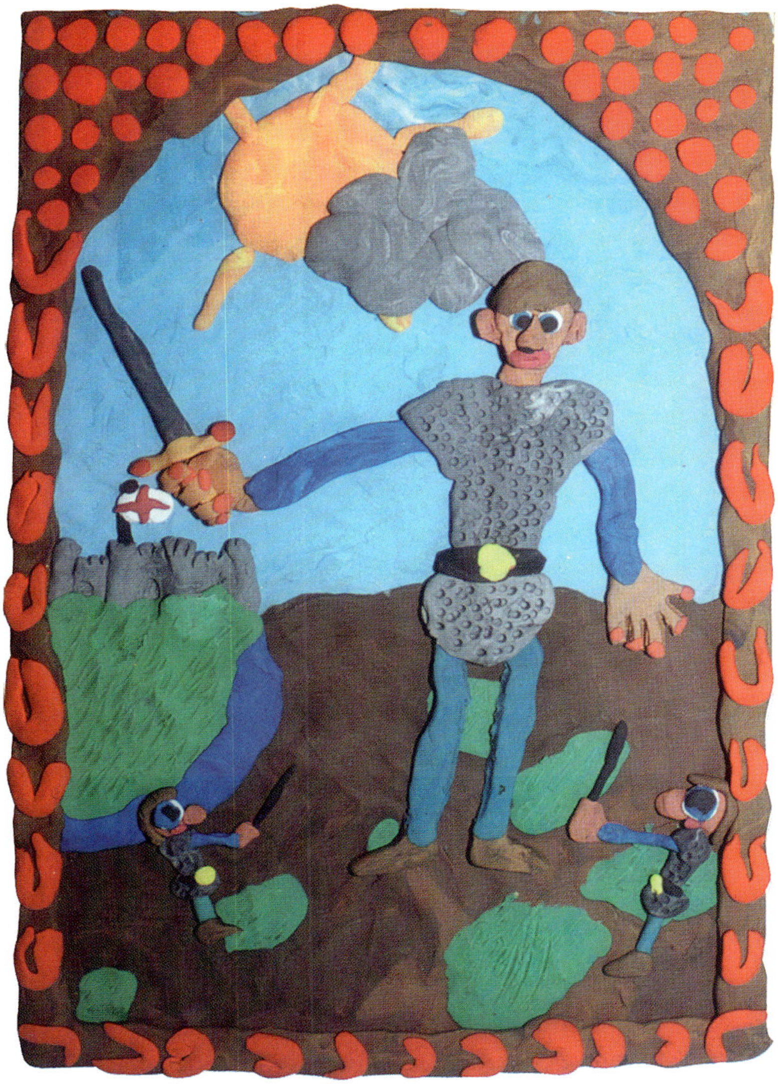

Medieval Knight, grade 8 student, Treherne Elementary School

Fig. 13.7.

Plasticine is a tactile medium that allows students to make images in relief. Although Plasticine is often thought of as "kids' stuff," it is possible to build sophisticated images, with intricate pattern and detail, and subtle color.

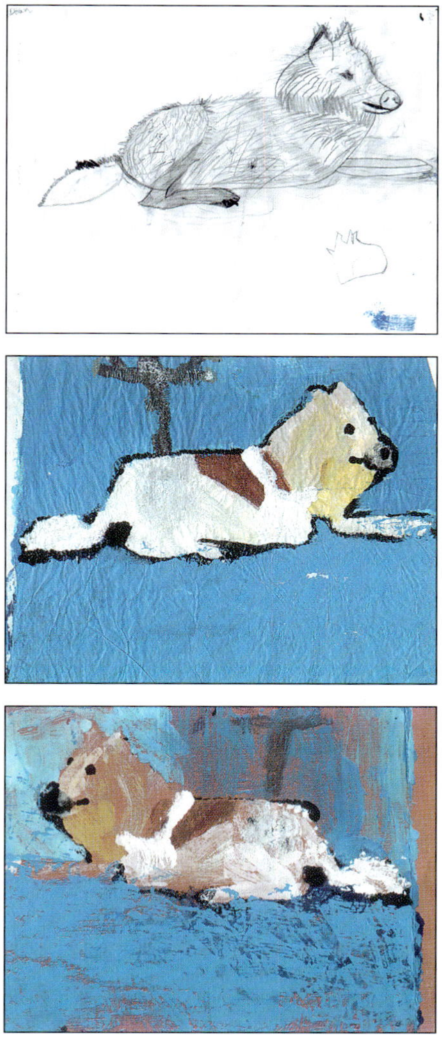

Wild Dog, pencil on paper, paint on wax paper, and monoprint, Dean Savage, age 10, Elm Creek School

Fig. 12.5.

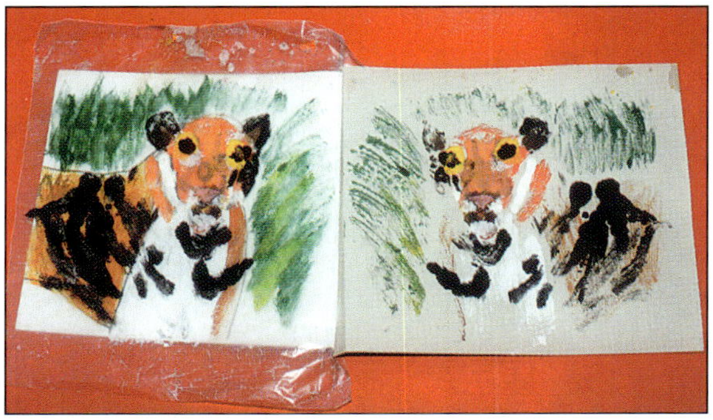

Tiger, monoprint in progress, grade 5 student, Elm Creek School

Fig. 12.1.

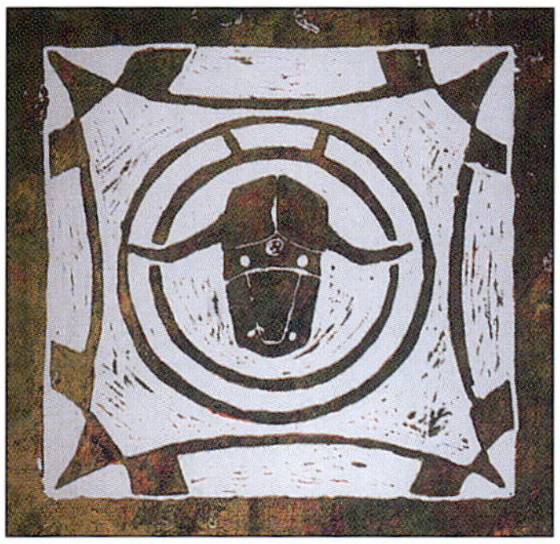

The Native War Pig, linocut print, Ryan Bride, grade 7–9 class, Australia

Fig. 12.13.

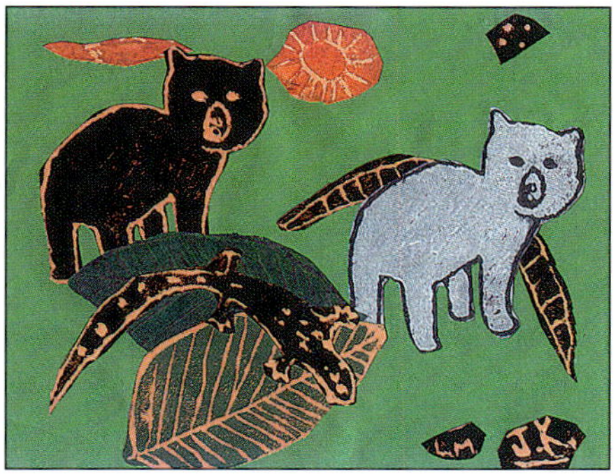

Bears and Salamanders, Jonathon Kulchyski and Laura McPherson, grade 4–5 class, San Antonio School

Fig. 12.11.

Printmaking techniques allow students to experiment with an image. They can produce a number of different color combinations and effects from their initial drawing.

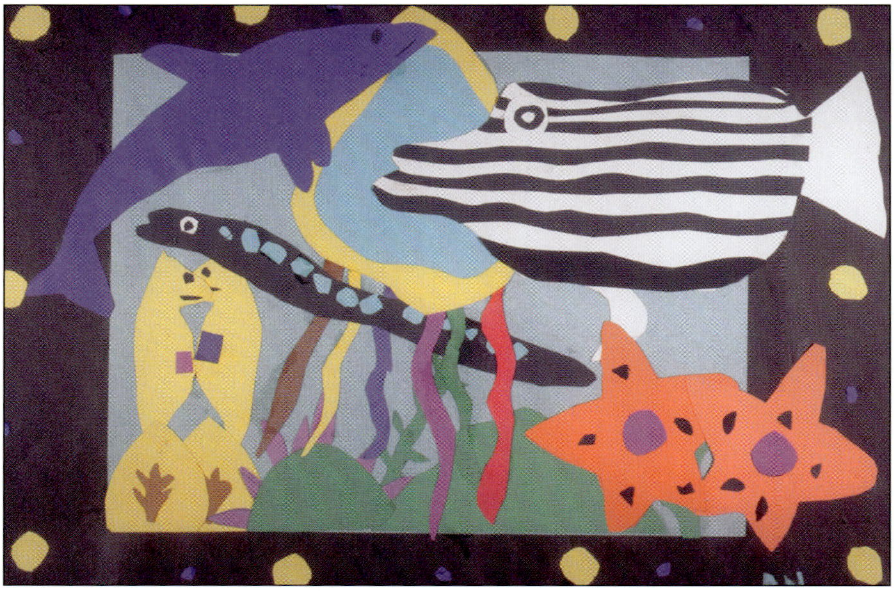

Tropical Fish, cut-paper collage, Dong Nguyen, grade 3, Wellington School

Fig. 14.5.

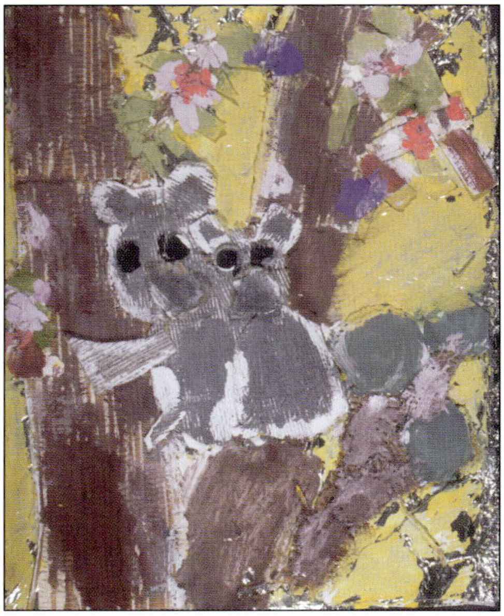

Kaola Bears, mixed media, Channa Tach, grade 2, Wellington School

Fig. 14.7.

Collage techniques allow students to explore a variety of found objects and materials and transform them into images. Collage requires problem solving in order to reproduce the shapes, textures, patterns, values, and colors of subjects using only scrap materials. Students also gain experience working with a variety of tools and materials.

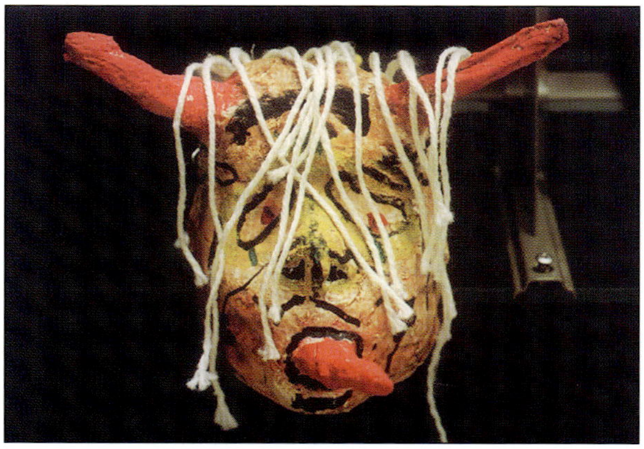

grade 6 student, Sun Valley School

Fig. 15.8.

Masks can be made with paper, papier-mâché, or plaster wrap. Making masks produces opportunities to discuss or dramatize ideas about disguise, character, or transformations. Working on masks is a good introduction to working with three-dimensional form.

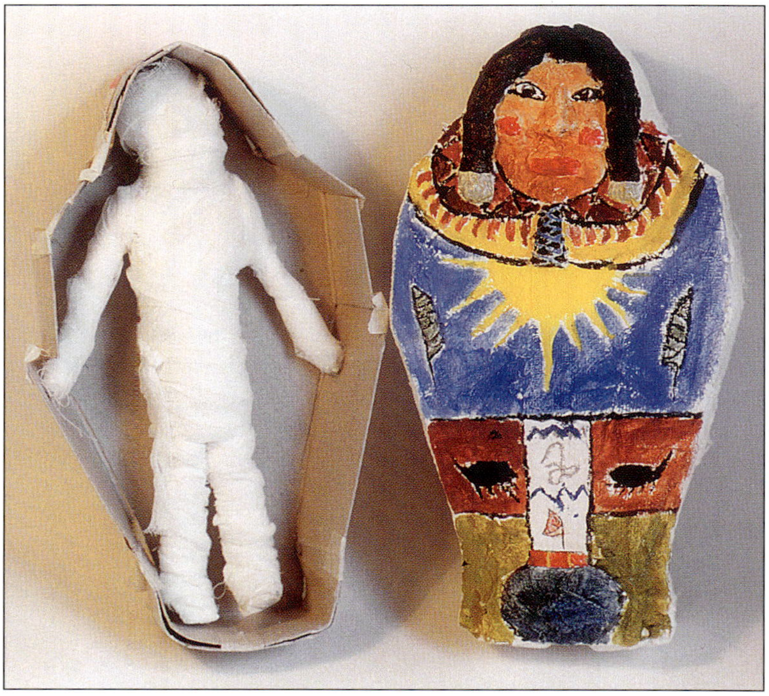

Mummy and Sarcophagus, plaster wrap, gauze, cardboard, paint, Noni Brynjolson, grade 6, Luxton School

Fig. I.1.

The enrichment exercises offered in this book provide suggestions for adapting the art techniques to fit the ages and abilities of your students, and to be relevant to the curriculum. This student constructed a mummy and sarcophagus as part of her study of ancient Egypt.

10
Exploring Paint with Beginners

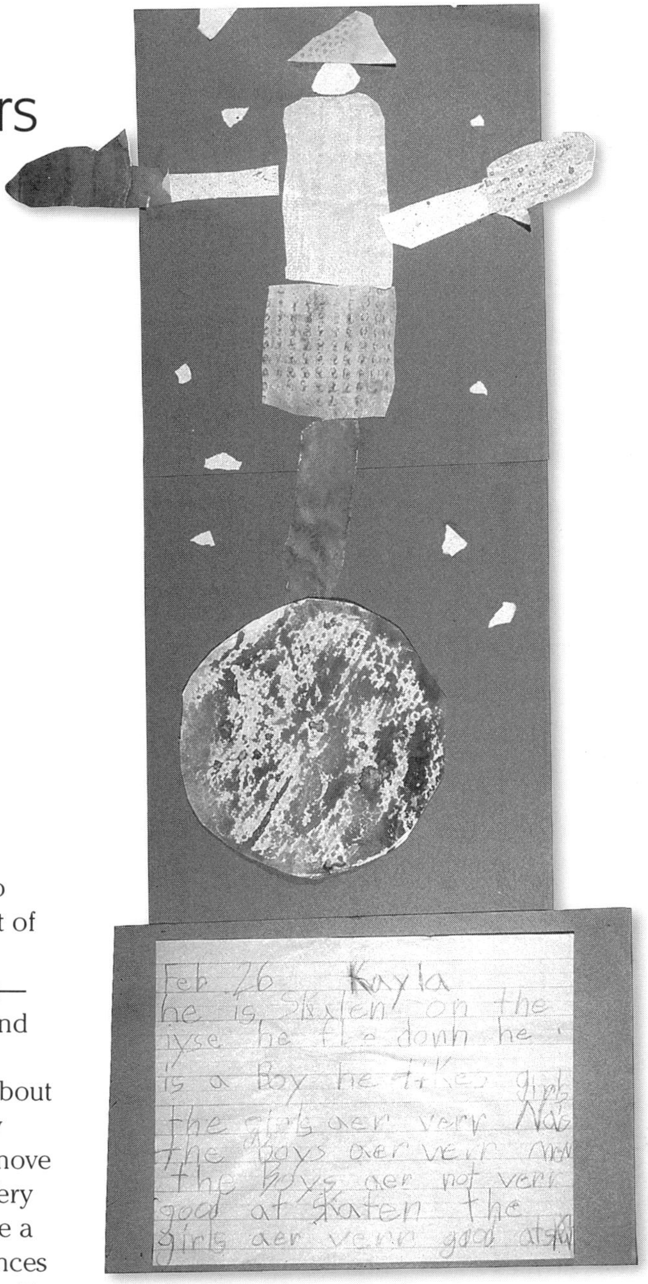

Skating, Kayla Boychuk, grade 1, Wellington School

Fig. 10.1. By combining explorations in paint with cutting and pasting, young students can use paint freely and still end up with a clean-looking image.

Introduction

The painting techniques that follow are probably not new to most early years teachers. Painting should be a regular part of classroom activity.

Students should have daily access to materials for painting—either an easel set up in a quiet corner with a supply of paint and paper or an accessible cupboard of supplies near a table.

During nondirected painting time, students are busy learning about how to handle paint, how paint drips, and how colors mix. They experiment with their grip on the paintbrush, and learn how to move their arm, wrist, and hand in order to make a variety of marks. Very young students may talk to you as they paint. They may describe a person, a house, or an event as they give their thoughts, as experiences form, and as they work out relationships and scenarios on paper. To students, dialogue and communication through the visual symbols in their paintings are important. Studies show that students spend twice as long at a drawing or painting activity if an adult is present to offer conversation and encouragement (Brittain 1979). Learning to communicate through visual symbols has obvious importance as a pre-writing exercise.

Young students are not troubled if their painted symbol of an object does not correspond to its actual appearance. Their satisfaction derives more from the act of painting than from the aesthetic qualities of the finished product. Adults may compliment these paintings, and see some of them as "pretty," but what they value in the painting is not likely to correspond to the students' original intentions or values.

Books to Have Handy

Picture Books
The Mixed-Up Chameleon (and other books written and illustrated by Eric Carle)
Who Is the Beast?

Teacher Reference
Paint!

Tip: Spread out extra newspapers. There will be lots of wet paper and you will need lots of drying space. Print students' names on the newspaper, or on each painting. This will make paintings easier to sort later.

Tip: For easy clean up, have a pail of soapy water available to collect paintbrushes, rollers, toothbrushes, and so on. If you don't have a sink in the room, have an empty pail available to dump used paint water, and another pail of water for washing hands.

In this chapter, you will find:

- exercises students can do to explore painting techniques freely and still produce the kind of recognizable, "finished" image that is valued by adults and older students
- some combined approaches that allow students to handle a variety of painting tools, scissors, and glue
- a technique for using students' beginner-level paintings to make book illustrations

Students will explore paint techniques and learn how to combine their paintings with cutting and pasting. This media-based approach is based on books by Eric Carle. Although the activities are most suited for younger students, older students will also have fun experimenting with different colors, textures, and patterns.

Preparing for Painting

Spread newspaper on tables and, depending on what technique you are going to use, prepare the materials. You can do the painting exercises in one of two ways: (1) Try painting techniques one at a time over several days, each as a separate art activity, or (2) Set up several centers around the classroom (you will need extra adults for this) and be prepared for one hectic session!

Explain to students that they will not be painting "pictures" today. They will be experimenting with paint and trying to fill a whole page with interesting colors and patterns. Demonstrate the techniques before your students try them. Ask students to keep their paintings. They can use them later for cutting and pasting (see page 126).

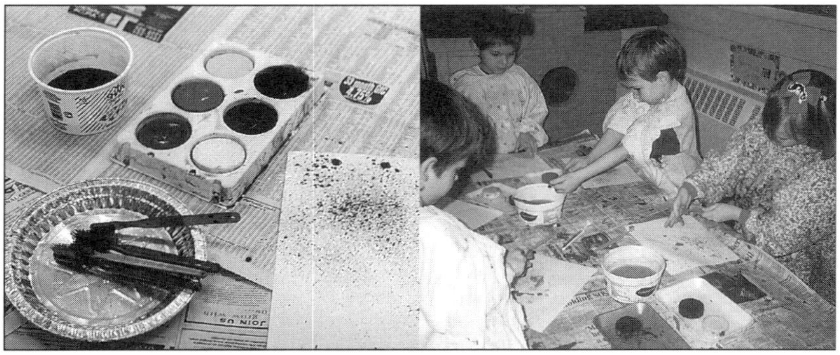

kindergarten class, Luxton School

Fig. 10.2. Splatter painting with block tempera paint

Materials

- photocopy paper, white or colored, 8½" x 11" (21.5 cm x 28 cm) (several per student)
- tempera block paints (red, yellow, blue, black, white. Optional: orange, green, purple, brown), several sets
- water and water containers (preferably with wide, flat bottoms)
- toothbrushes (one per student)

Splatter Painting

Splatter painting will end up looking like spray paint. For use with cut and paste, simply splatter paint onto blank paper with a toothbrush. For more finished pieces, have students make their own stencils from cut paper, or set objects (leaves, a toy spider, hands) on a piece of paper and splatter paint around them. The stencils or objects leave a blank space on the paper, surrounded by splatter painting. (This is a good companion exercise for teaching about shape and negative space, page 30.)

Method

Dip the toothbrush in water and rub on paint blocks. With the thumb or index finger, flick paint onto the paper to produce a "spray paint" effect. Encourage color mixing. This can be done by rubbing the toothbrush on more than one color, or by splattering layers of a variety of colors (fig. 10.2).

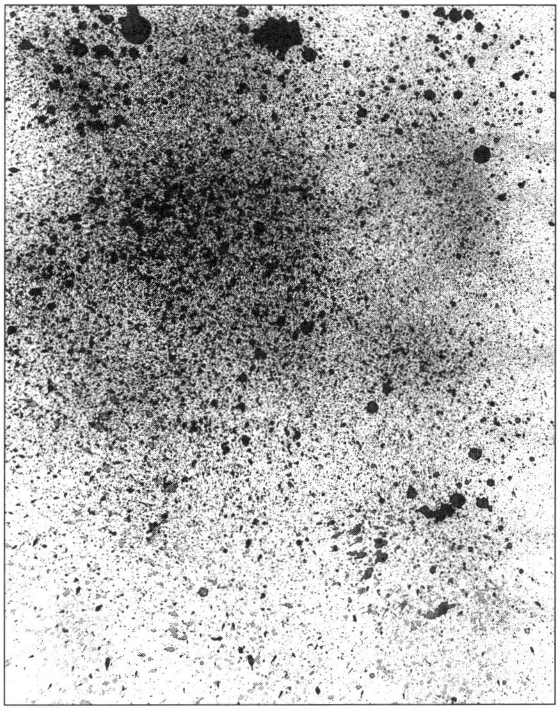

kindergarten class, Luxton School

Fig. 10.3. Splatter painting with block tempera paint. **See color plate.**

Tip: Make sure students point the toothbrush down at the paper and not at their face. Tap excess water off of brush before rubbing it on paint.

Materials

- photocopy paper, white or colored, $8\frac{1}{2}$" x 11" (21.5 cm x 28 cm) (several per student)
- tempera block paints (red, yellow, blue, black, white. Optional: orange, green, purple, brown), several sets, or small amounts of liquid tempera in shallow trays
- water and water containers (preferably with wide, flat bottoms)
- sponges (use large sponges cut into 3" (8 cm) pieces)

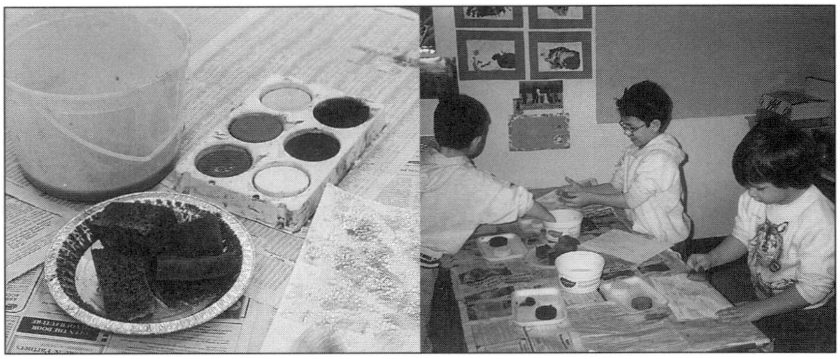

kindergarten class, Luxton School

Fig. 10.4. Sponge painting with block tempera paint

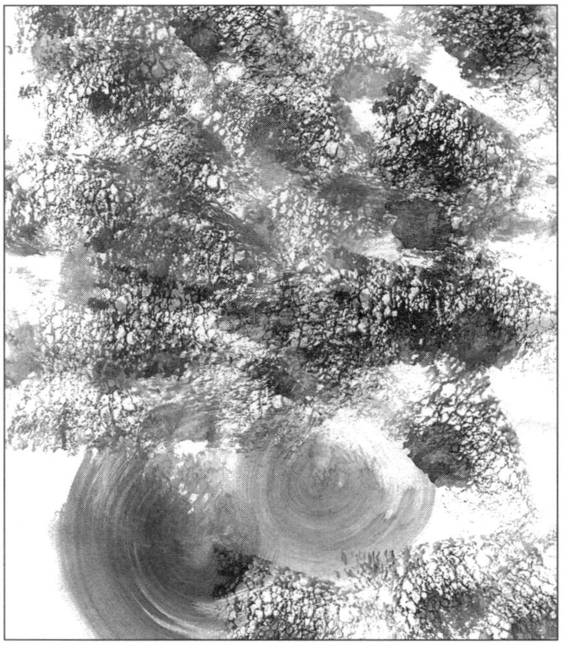

kindergarten class, Luxton School

Fig. 10.5. Sponge painting with block tempera paint. **See color plate.**

Tip: To avoid puddles on the paper, squeeze excess water out of sponges first. Encourage students to "use muscle" as they wring out their sponges.

Sponge Painting

Sponge painting leaves interesting marks behind on the paper. Like plastic-wrap techniques (see Impress Painting, page 123), sponge painting has come into vogue as a technique for decorating walls and furniture. For more "finished" images, sponge painting can be used with stencils (page 121) or with sponges that have been cut into a variety of geometric shapes. It can also be used like tanagrams (page 31) and to make patterns (page 31).

Method

Wet the sponge and rub on paint blocks. Press onto the paper, using an up-and-down motion. Encourage color mixing: dip the sponge into more than one color, or layer the colors on the paper (fig. 10.4).

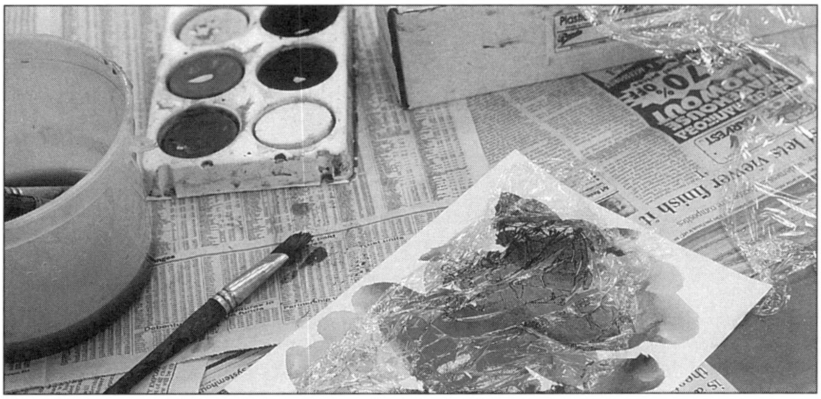

kindergarten class, Luxton School

Fig. 10.6. Impress painting with block tempera paint

Materials

- photocopy paper, white, 8½" x 11" (21.5 cm x 28 cm) (several per student)
- tempera block paints (red, yellow, blue, black, white. Optional: orange, green, purple, brown), several sets
- water and water containers (preferably with wide, flat bottoms)
- plastic wrap (pieces of Saranwrap), or bubble-wrap, leaves, other flat objects
- large paintbrushes (#12)

Impress Painting

Impress painting is normally a watercolor painting technique. Impressing objects into wet paint leaves an interesting variety of marks in wet tempera, and in acrylic paint as well.

Method

Paint quickly on paper, with any mixture of colors, to fill the page. Press wrinkled plastic wrap into wet paint—the wrinkles will produce a pattern in the paint. When the paint is dry, pull the plastic wrap off the paper (fig. 10.6).

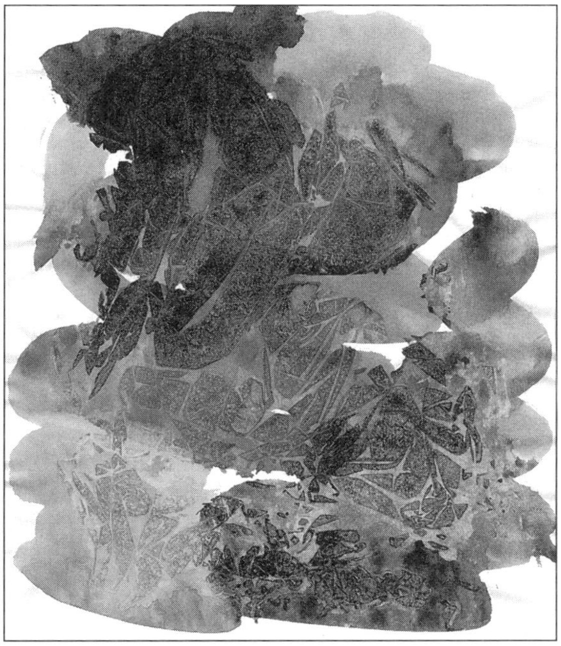

kindergarten class, Luxton School

Fig. 10.7. Impress painting with block tempera paint. **See color plate.**

Tip: Call impress painting "speed painting"—the paint must be very wet; avoid excessive brushing. For other interesting patterns, use objects such as bubble-wrap plastic, keys, and leaves pressed into the wet paint.

Materials

- photocopy paper, white, 8½" x 11" (21.5 cm x 28 cm)(several per student)
- tempera block paints (red, yellow, blue, black, white. Optional: orange, green, purple, brown), several sets
- water and water containers (preferably with wide, flat bottoms)
- wax crayons (pieces of old crayons without wrappers are best)
- an assortment of flat objects with rough or bumpy texture (window screen, sandpaper, rubber-soled shoes, plastic netting, Lego block bases, Pegboard, and so on)
- large brushes

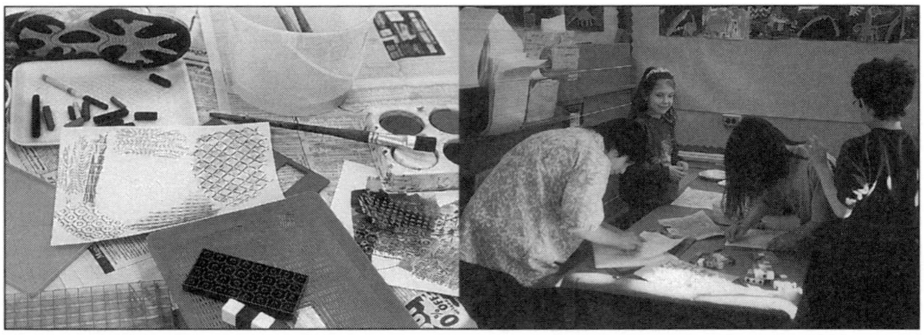

kindergarten class, Luxton School

Fig. 10.8. Crayon rubbings

Crayon Rubbings

Rubbing over various surfaces is a good way to explore texture and pattern (see page 34). Challenge students to find objects that have hard, rough, or bumpy surfaces—they can use objects found in the classroom, in a natural environment, or at home.

Method

Review texture with your students. Remind them that texture is how something feels when you touch it. Have students touch their hair, the table top, the carpet, the bottom of their shoes. Ask them to think about how each texture feels. Note that each object on the table has a rough or bumpy texture.

Now place the paper over a textured object and hold down firmly. Rub the side of a crayon over the paper, pressing hard. With a large brush, paint over the rubbing; the wax crayon will resist the paint (fig. 10.8).

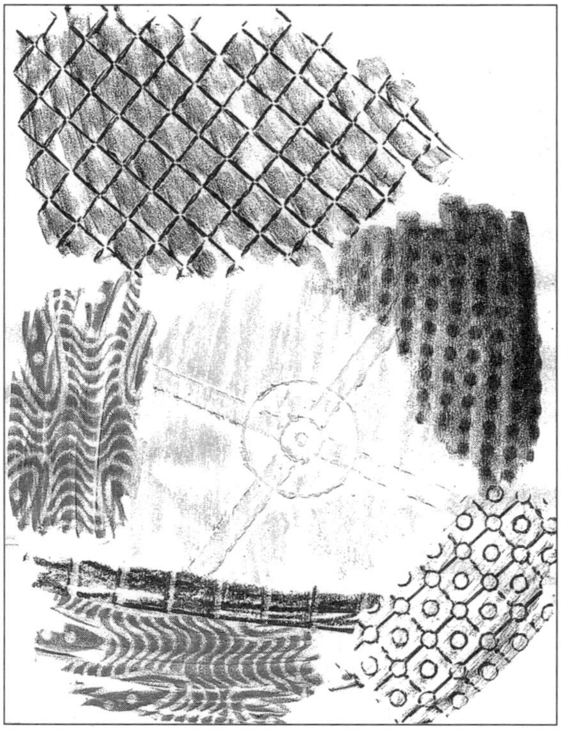

kindergarten class, Luxton School

Fig. 10.9. Crayon rubbings. **See color plate.**

Tip: Sometimes the paint may completely cover the crayon. Some reasons this could happen are: (1) the paint is too thick (add more water to the paint, and repaint the area; dab the painting with a wet brush or a paper towel to remove the thick paint), (2) the brush has been rubbed back and forth over the crayon image excessively (dab the image with a paper towel), or (3) the crayon was applied too lightly (try another rubbing, pressing hard with the crayon).

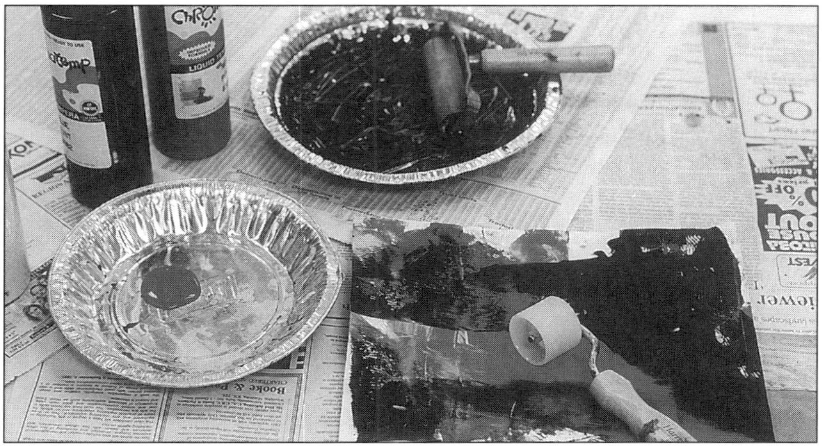

Fig. 10.10. Roller painting

Materials

- several soft rollers (brayers), 4" to 6" wide (10 cm to 15 cm) (These are soft, rubber, printmakers' rollers. Small, wall-painting rollers may be used instead.)
- liquid tempera paint (small amounts of red, yellow, and blue in shallow trays)
- photocopy paper, white, 8½" x 11" (21.5 cm x 28 cm) (several sheets per student)

Roller Painting

Painting with a roller has a very different feel from painting with a brush. Roller painting is a good technique for filling in large areas of color—a mural, background for display, or repainting a wall.

Method

Dip the roller into paint and roll it back and forth on the paper. Layer and mix colors on the paper. Wash rollers thoroughly after use (fig. 10.10). Students can make their own stencils. Cut shapes out of old file folders and go over them with a roller dipped in paint. The stenciled area will remain blank.

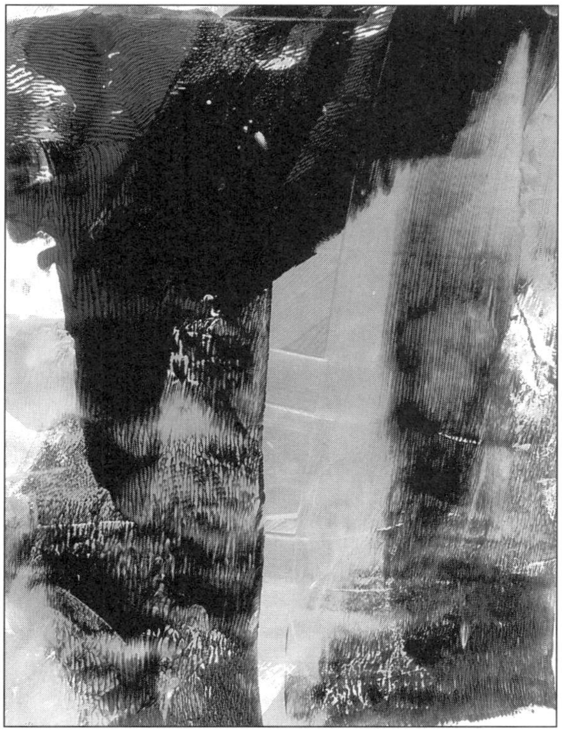

kindergarten class, Luxton School

Fig. 10.11. Roller painting. **See color plate.**

Materials

- photocopy paper, white, or colored construction paper, 8½" x 11" (21.5 cm x 28 cm)
- scissors (one pair per student)
- painted paper (gathered up from previous sessions)
- glue or gluesticks

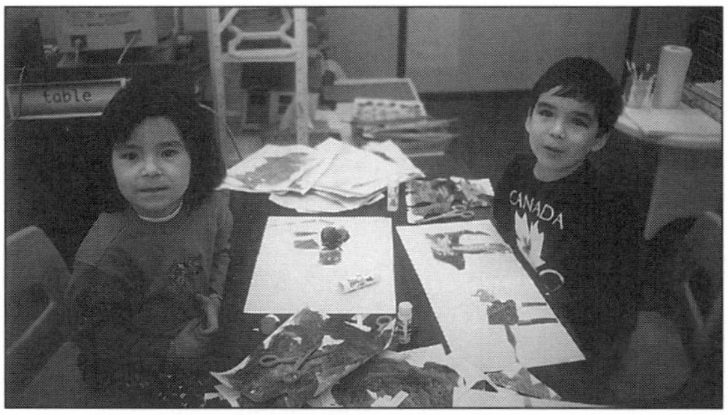

cutting and pasting, kindergarten students, Disbrowe School

Fig. 10.12. Students can begin cutting out shapes and arranging them on paper.

Tip: Don't give students glue until after they have arranged most of their pieces. It is easier to introduce the idea of overlapping and putting large background pieces underneath the main subject *before* the pieces have been glued.

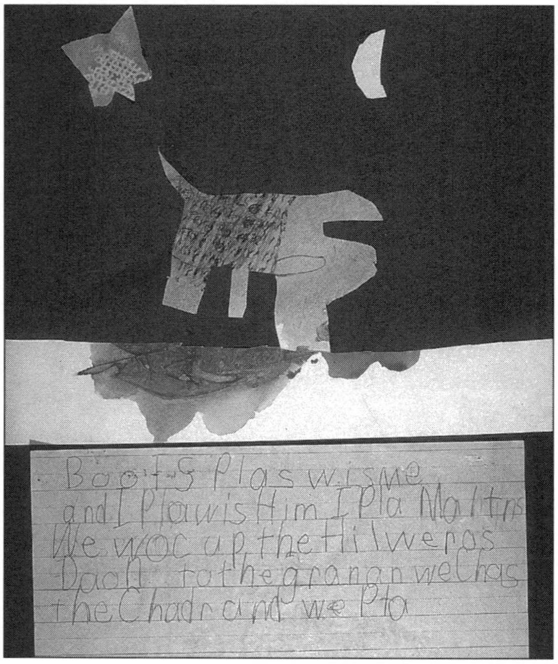

Boots Plays With Me, paint and cutting and pasting, Charles Harvey, age 7, Wellington School

Fig. 10.13. Charles looked at his picture and began to imagine walking up hills with a dog, and racing back down.

Cutting and Pasting

In this exercise, students use their paintings from the previous sessions to make cut-and-paste pictures or book illustrations. This technique is based on Eric Carle's picture books. Carle must have great fun experimenting with paint colors and effects before cutting and pasting pieces for the characters and settings in his illustrations.

Appropriate Subjects

For early years (N–1), a simple subject such as an animal, "my house," or a car is enough. Subjects with obvious geometric shapes are easiest. For older students, find visuals similar to those in *Who Is the Beast?* that show a rich variety of patterns and colors and complex, overlapping shapes.

Preparation

Explain overlapping to your students. To do this, you will need visual references such as magazine photos, calendar photos, and library books. Examine pictures that relate to a current topic of study; for example, an animal surrounded by jungle leaves, a person in a crowd, a car on a busy street.

Method

Look at *The Mixed-Up Chameleon* (or other books by Eric Carle). Notice how Carle's illustrations look like students' paint samples! Explain how Carle used scissors to make his pictures; each part of the subject is cut out separately and placed behind or in front of another piece. Show students how the edges of shapes can indicate texture. Notice how in some places Carle cut a jagged edge around the edge of a furry cat or along the top of the grass.

Look at examples of students' subjects and discuss what shapes students will need to cut out to make their subjects—for example, a jelly-bean shape for a bear's body, rectangles for legs. Demonstrate this method, showing students that small cutouts can even be used for details like whiskers. Make sure there are no pencils or markers on the tables; student will use these rather than cutouts when they are available.

Tell students they are going to be cutting out shapes from one of their paintings (fig. 10.12). Ask them to choose their most beautiful painting, or to pick the one with interesting colors and patterns. Demonstrate how light-colored or white pieces don't show up well on white paper. Suggest they use brighter colored pieces, or paste their pieces onto colored construction paper.

Have students cut out shapes, then arrange these shapes on the paper. Show them how to glue down the background before they glue down the objects in the front of the picture.

Some older students may wish to draw the subject first. Ask them to draw on the back of their painting. That way, when the shape is cut out it can be flipped over and the pencil marks won't show. Hand out the glue and have the students affix their shapes to the paper (figs. 10.13 and 10.14).

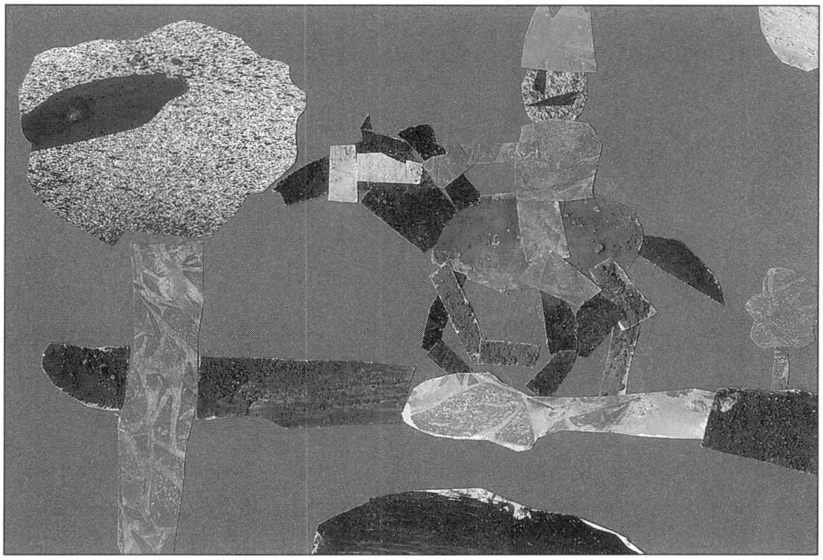

The Prince, paint, cutting and pasting, Joel Dyck, age 8, South Oaks School

Fig. 10.14. Joel used his patterned papers to illustrate one page in a class book. **See color plate.**

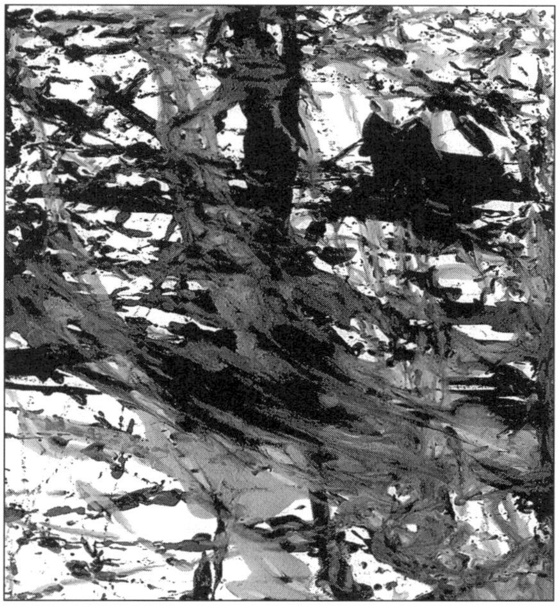

Fig. 10.15. A student placed paper, a few drops of paint, and a marble into the bottom of a lettuce dryer.

Enrichment

- Have students try other painting techniques to produce the paint sample papers:
  - *string painting:* Fold a piece of paper in half. Place a dab of paint and a piece of string inside the fold, close, and pull out the string. The string will move the paint to make interesting marks on the paper.
  - *washable marker:* On a piece of paper, make a variety of lines with washable marker. Paint over with water and watch the colors run together.
  - *marble painting or golf-ball painting:* Place a piece of paper, a marble (or golf ball), and a dab of paint in the bottom of a pan or lettuce dryer. Roll the pan from side to side (or turn the handle of the lettuce dryer). The marble (or the golf ball) will leave paint tracks on the paper (fig. 10.15).

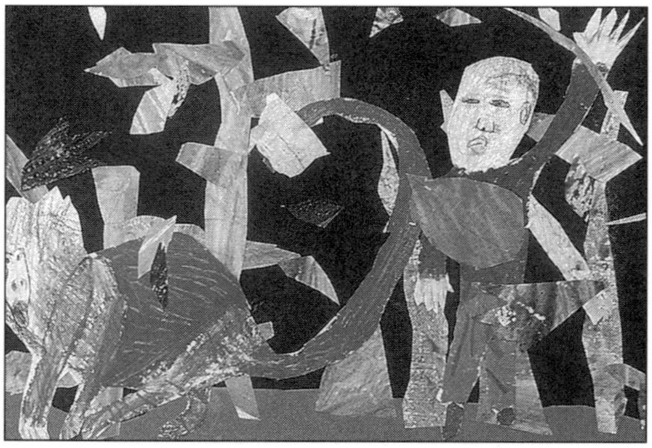

In the Jungle, painting and drawing, cutting and pasting, grade 2 student, Matheson Island School

Fig. 10.16. This student combined painted pieces with drawing. He drew the boy and the monkey with pencil, colored with oil pastel, then cut and pasted them into his picture. The overlapping leaves and figures show that this student understood and could visualize an object being "in front of" or "behind" another.
See color plate.

  - *sand:* Mix sand with liquid tempera paint. This will make the paint thicker and give it a rough surface texture. Encourage students to mix colors together on the paper.

- Watercolor technique may be used on paper to make a background to paste pieces on: dissolve half a tube of Pentel brand watercolor paint in a half cup (125 ml) of water. Paint onto Dessin paper. For a grainy surface or "snowflake" pattern, sprinkle small areas with sand or salt before paint dries completely.

- Young students can use their cut-and-paste pictures as the basis for a story, writing (or dictating) to describe the illustrations they have already made (fig. 10.16). As an alternative, suggest to your students that they try a series of three simple illustrations to show the beginning, the middle, and the end of their story. You may need to prompt them: "Your picture shows a cat walking on a fence. What happens next?" or "The cat is in a mud puddle! How did it get there? How will it get out?"

Vocabulary (see appendixes for definitions)

background	*impress painting*	*shape*
brayer	*overlapping*	*splatter painting*
collage	*pattern*	*texture*
cut and paste	*rubbings*	*watercolor*

11
Watercolor Techniques

Autumn Forest, watercolor, Tyler Hammerstedt, grade 8, San Antonio School

Fig. 11.1. Tyler began with a simplified pencil sketch, then used wet-in-wet watercolor techniques for his landscape painting. **See color plate.**

Introduction

Students tend to think of watercolor paint as a "real" art medium. If students have used tempera paint as a regular part of their art activities since nursery school (or even since the beginning of the school year), they may appreciate a new challenge, or a sense of having "graduated" to new materials.

Watercolor paint allows students to:

- work with new materials and paint techniques
- combine drawing and painting
- produce small painted images quickly for illustration

* The author has used inexpensive Pentel brand with success. The cost for paint and paper for a class (at the time of writing) worked out to about $22, with enough paint left over for three or four painting sessions. Some other types of watercolor paints will work with these techniques (test them ahead of time).

Materials

- watercolor paints, student-grade (one set of watercolor tubes)*
- watercolor paper, or Dessin paper, torn or cut into small rectangles (cut large papers into one-sixteenths, or approx. 6" x 8" (15 cm x 20 cm))
- soft brushes (½" or 1 cm in size)
- masking tape (several rolls)
- Kleenex
- water and water containers
- salt (in salt shakers)
- sand (small amount of dry sand)
- plastic wrap (Saranwrap)
- palettes (Styrofoam trays or plastic container lids), one per two or three students
- optional: white wax crayons (or oil pastels)
- felt markers (fine-tipped, black, permanent, nontoxic)

Books to Have Handy

Picture Books

A Promise Is a Promise
Owl Moon
Saint Francis
The Third-Story Cat
Would They Love a Lion?
The Yesterday Stone
Stringbean's Trip to the Shining Sea

Tip: You can substitute food coloring (diluted somewhat with water) for watercolor in a "wash." When diluted, colors are painted over an entire picture or page of writing on regular paper. Food coloring has bright, accurate color for color mixing and works with crayon-resist—draw first with a white or colored crayon, and then paint over with diluted food coloring. However, salt and sand will not produce the "special effects" with food coloring that they do with watercolor paints.

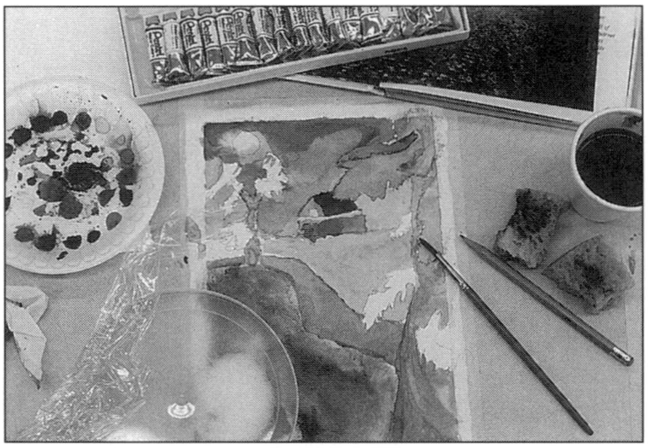

grades 6–8, San Antonio School

Fig. 11.2. Materials needed for watercolor. **See color plate.**

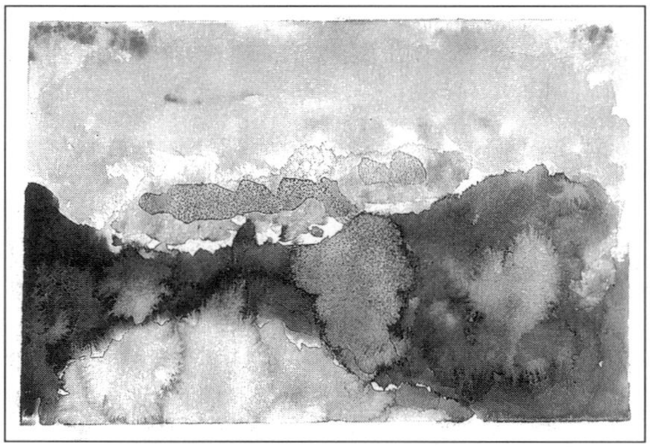

watercolor, Eden Jerao, grade 5, Wellington School

Fig. 11.3. Using the wet-in-wet technique produces irregular edges. **See color plate.**

Tip: Paper will "pill," or roughen, if it is brushed too much. Just dab the colors on the paper, rather than brush back and forth. Quality watercolor paper (Strathmore, Arches, or Windsor-Newton) will not pill as easily as less expensive brands.

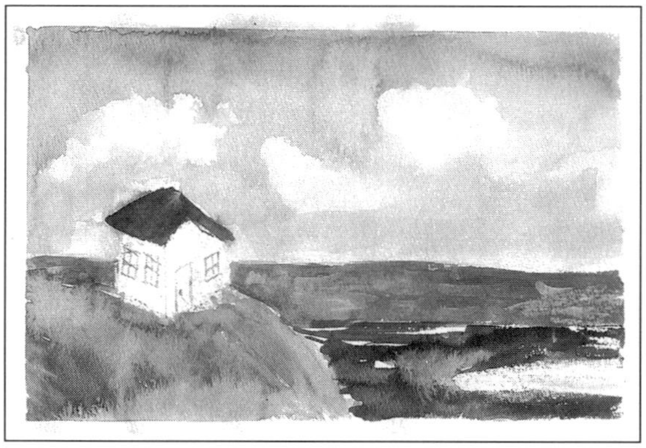

watercolor, Noni Brynjolson, age 11

Fig. 11.4. Noni used crayon-resist for the house and the surf in this picture. She made clouds by using Kleenex to lift the blue paint off areas of the sky. **See color plate.**

Watercolor

Watercolor is an ideal medium for illustration. It is a much more transparent medium than tempera paint is, and it can be used overtop pencil or permanent pen drawings. Watercolor techniques—wet-in-wet, salt, or impressing objects—result in beautiful marks and effects, even if the original drawing is weak. This makes them success-oriented techniques for students.

Watercolors take a very short time to paint and to dry. That, combined with the small size of paper used—expensive paper is torn or cut into roughly 6" x 8" (15 cm x 20 cm) pieces—make it an ideal medium for producing the quick series of images required for an illustration project. Watercolor can provide brilliant color and, when dry, can be drawn over with pencils, pencil crayons, or pastels.

Appropriate Subjects

A simple subject in a landscape—an animal in a field, a sailboat on a lake—is an appropriate introduction to watercolor painting.

Preparation

Put small dabs of each color of paint (except white) around the outside of the palettes.* Only a very small amount of color is required. Explain to students that because the color is very concentrated, this is enough paint for about twenty paintings! As the paint dries out, it may be used again with a wet paintbrush. Fill water containers half full and set out other materials.

Students can tape their pieces of watercolor paper to the tables; this will keep the papers flat while the students work on them. Tape all four edges evenly. The tape, when peeled off later, will create a white border around the edges of the painting.

Basic Method

Have students look at *Owl Moon*, *Would They Love a Lion?*, *A Promise Is a Promise*, and *The Third-Story Cat*. Notice how the colors in the illustrations run into each other (look especially at the last illustration in *The Third-Story Cat* and at the skies in *A Promise Is a Promise*).

With younger or less experienced artists, you may want to call attention to the horizon line in the pictures: the ground comes halfway up the page, and the sky often comes halfway down; the sky is not just a strip of blue at the top of the page.

---

* White is not usually used in watercolor painting because watercolor paint is such a transparent medium. To achieve white or light values, add more or less water to the paint to allow more or less of the white paper to show through.

Now you can introduce painting with watercolors to your students. Begin with a very simple landscape painting: sky and ground. Demonstrate the general techniques for applying watercolors:

- Brush water onto the top half of the paper (sky). Explain that with watercolor the water is applied before the color. (This is called "wet-in-wet" technique.) Make sure the paper is thoroughly wet—remove puddles by touching them with a Kleenex (fig. 11.3).
- Ask your students what color the sky might be (is it sunny? sunset? nighttime? stormy?). Gently touch the brush to the appropriate paint colors, and then to the paper—the paint colors are "touched" to the paper rather than brushed together. Remember that only a very small amount of paint is required. Wash out the brush before dipping into a new color. If the paper is wet enough, the colors will run and pool on the paper in interesting ways.
- Make clouds or "erase" paint by scrunching Kleenex and touching or tamping the wet paint (fig. 11.4). Produce a "snowflake" effect by sprinkling salt onto wet or damp painted areas (fig. 11.5).
- Now paint water on the bottom half of the paper. Add "ground colors" (blue-violet for snow; greens and yellows for grass; brown and gray for rock, and so on). Sprinkle on a small pinch of dry sand (fig. 11.6), or press wrinkled plastic wrap (fig. 11.7) into the wet paint and leave on paper until dry. Some of the sand will stick to provide a rough or gravelly surface. Plastic wrap will leave marks resembling leaf, rock, or wave patterns.
- Mix colors by dabbing them next to each other on the paper, rather than on the palette. Rich mixtures of color are the result of using more than one color in a given area. Try adding small amounts of analagous (similar) colors into each area; for example, add small amounts of yellow or brown into green; add violet into blue. (See chapter 8.) You may need to wet the paper again before adding a second color.
- You may want to use white crayon or oil pastel on small areas of the paper that are to remain white (the wax or oil will resist the water paint). But draw with them first while the paper is still dry. Use white crayon marks for white areas of the subject, light reflections, snow on a tree branch, and so on.
- Allow your paper to dry, then pull the tape off the edges slowly.

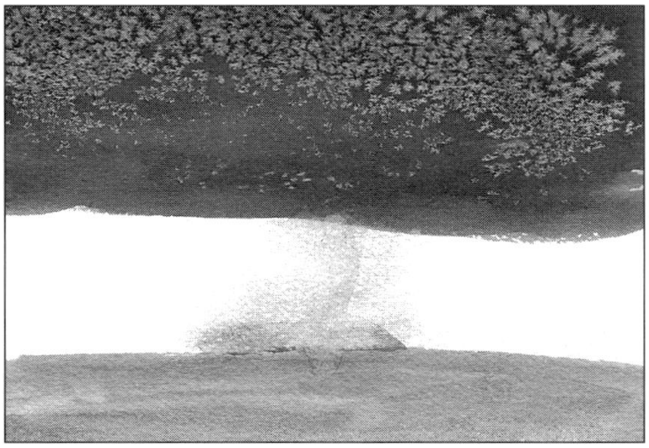

watercolor, David Marantz, age 9, St. John's Ravenscourt School

Fig. 11.5. David produced a snowflake affect by sprinkling salt in wet watercolor paint.

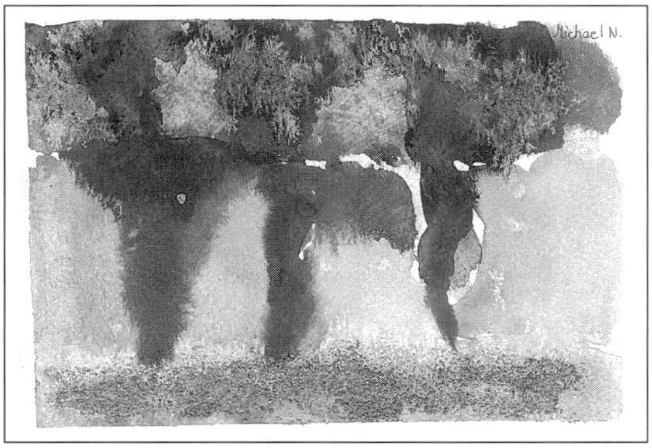

Tornado, watercolor, Michael Noh, age 9, St. John's Ravenscourt School

Fig. 11.6. Michael added texture by sprinkling sand into the watercolor paint at the bottom of his picture. **See color plate.**

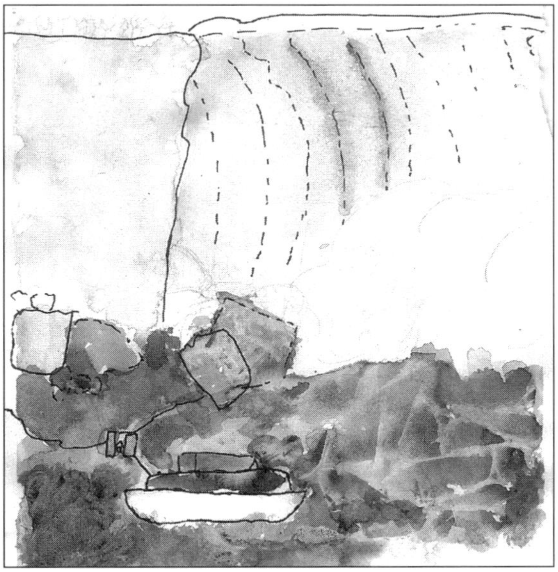

Waterfall, watercolor, Laura Chantharangsri, grade 5, Wellington School

Fig. 11.7. Laura pressed wrinkled plastic wrap into the wet paint to produce a wave-like effect. Impressing other objects—bubble-wrap, leaves, plastic mesh, and so on—will produce other interesting effects. **See color plate.**

Combining Drawing and Watercolor

After students have tried the techniques on a simple landscape (sky and ground), show them some variations they can do to produce a finished image or illustration.

Choose a subject and gather visual references. Because students have begun with a landscape, the subject may be a simple object, animal, or person in a landscape. Alternatively, students may be painting an illustration project (see chapter 6).

Look at *Would They Love a Lion?* and *Saint Francis* with your students. Notice the wonderful, wobbly, broken quality of the pen lines and how the color overlaps the lines (fig. 11.8). This is a good time to remind your students not to worry about "coloring over the lines." Some white edges and overlapping colors lead to beautiful watercolor effects. The white edges of unpainted paper throughout the painting resemble light reflections, and help to keep the image from looking "muddy" and overworked.

Have students draw, or trace, one of their line drawings directly onto a blank piece of watercolor paper with a pencil. Avoid shading in areas with a pencil. If desired, use black or brown, fine-tipped, permanent, nontoxic markers to trace over the pencil lines (see chapter 4) and then paint over with a wash (a watery layer) of watercolor paint. Start with the sky and other large areas (fig. 11.9). Very small areas and details may be washed over with watery paint, painted with a very small brush, or left blank, to be colored with pencil crayons later when the paper is dry.

Remind students to include salt, sand, Kleenex, and plastic-wrap techniques in areas where the effects will be appropriate to the image.

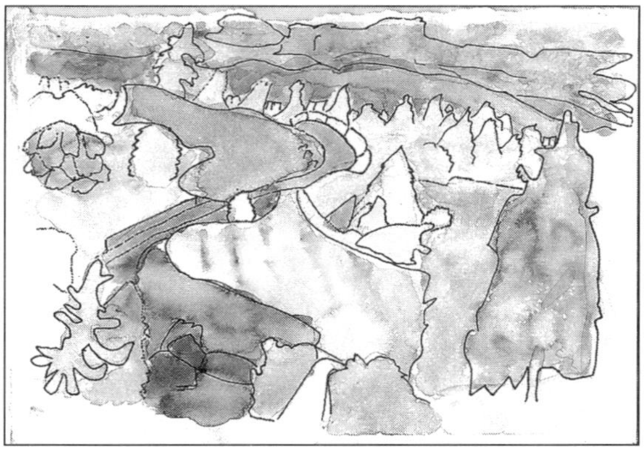

watercolor and ink, Eden Jerao, grade 5, Wellington School

Fig. 11.8. Eden looked carefully at the reference photo, then drew contour lines with a fine-tipped black marker. This approach resulted in interesting, irregular shapes and an almost abstract image. **See color plate.**

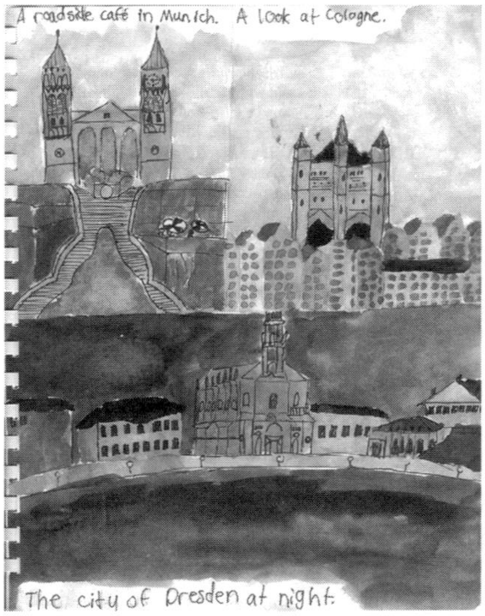

research project on Germany, watercolor and ink, Noni Brynjolson, age 11

Fig. 11.9. Watercolor and pen drawings allow for fine detail and a quick wash of color.

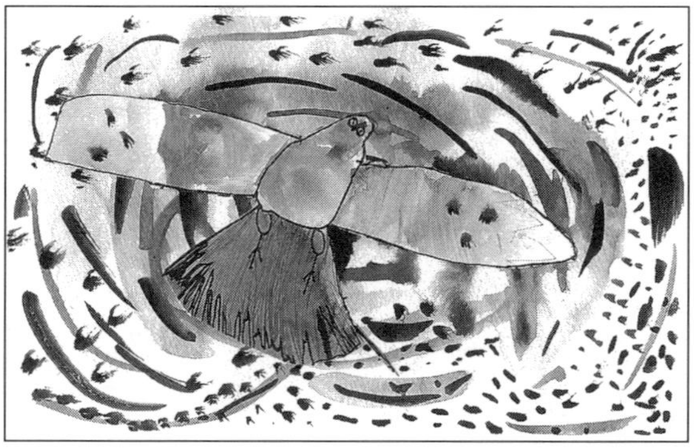

watercolor, cut and paste, Riley Gray, age 8, St. John's Ravenscourt School

Fig. 11.10. Riley drew and painted the bird separately, then cut and pasted it onto the swirling background. With cutouts, students can use watercolor techniques freely in the background, and still add in a carefully drawn subject or character. **See color plate.**

Enrichment

- Add cutouts (see chapter 4, page 53). Since students have begun with painting a landscape (or background), it makes sense for them to draw a subject or character separately, cut it out, and glue it to their painting. They can then produce a number of images easily and quickly (fig. 11.10) and glue them into a prepared story.
- When using watercolor for illustration, students can work on very small paintings (even 4" (10 cm) square) (fig. 11.11).
- Many objects produce interesting patterns when pressed into wet paint. Encourage students to try "bubble-wrap" plastic, leaves, paper towel, Lego, shoe soles, and so on.
- Have advanced students paint with only the three primary colors of watercolor paint. Layer the colors to produce secondary colors. Use yellow first in all areas that will be yellow, green, or orange and allow to dry. Add red ("cool" red) in areas that will be red,

violet, or orange. Paint over with blue any areas that are blue, violet, or green. Brown or gray areas will require layers of all three colors. This technique is called "glazing," and can be used with other paint colors as well (see chapter 8 for other paint color combinations). Look for glazing in *Would They Love a Lion?*.

- Use dry-brush techniques for night scenes or other scenes that require dark colors. Students might paint in most of the scenes with the wet-in-wet technique, let the paint dry, and then use slightly thicker watercolor paint (including white paint), gouache, or tempera on top to add more solid forms, light colors, and details with a drier brush. Interesting, irregular brush marks can be produced with an almost dry paintbrush.
- Have students use pencil crayons, chalk pastels, or oil pastels on top of dry watercolor paint, to add form and detail. Look at *The Yesterday Stone* for extensive pencil drawing on top of watercolor paint.
- Have students make postcards. The 6"x 8" (15 cm x 20 cm) watercolors of landscapes make perfect postcards. This might be the basis of a writing project—send a postcard home from an imaginary journey or mail art correspondence with students from another school or another city. (See *Stringbean's Trip to the Shining Sea* for examples of postcards combined with creative writing.)

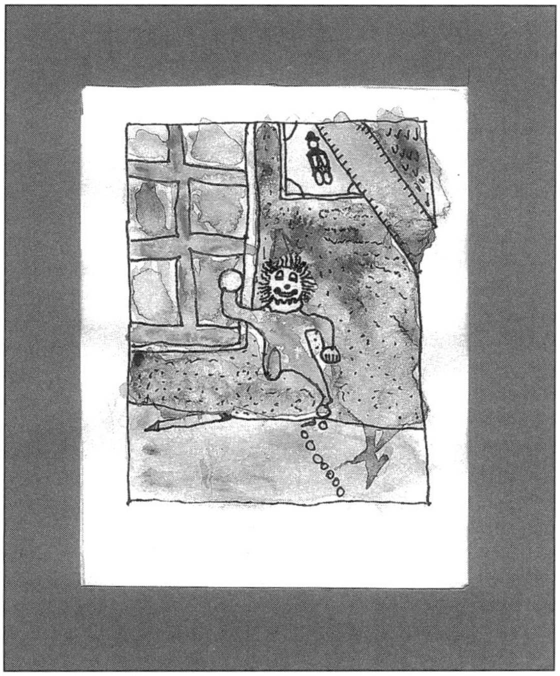

illustration for ***Tale of the Pompom,*** watercolor and ink, Shannon Barbour, age 9, Niakwa Place School

Fig. 11.11. This watercolor painting is only 3 1/2" x 4 1/2" (9 cm x 11 cm), an ideal size for a series of book illustrations. Shannon matted the illustration with a piece of colored paper (to frame it) before gluing it onto a book page. **See color plate.**

Vocabulary (see appendixes for definitions)

background	*landscape*	*watercolor*
characters	*palette*	*wet-in-wet technique*
glazing	*primary colors*	
gouache	*secondary colors*	
horizon line	*setting*	
illustration	*wash*	

12
Printmaking

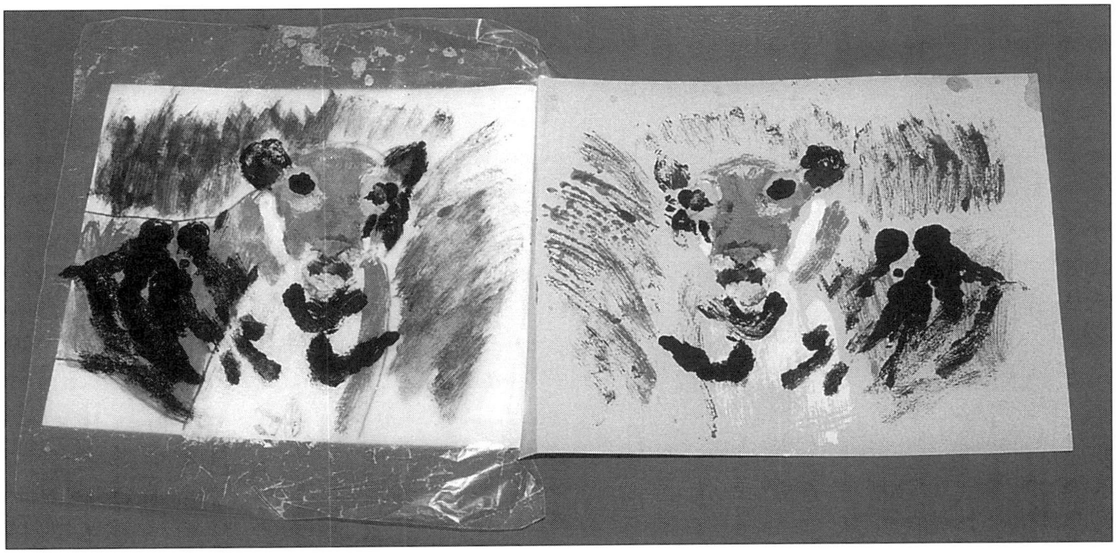

Tiger, monoprint in progress, grade 5 student, Elm Creek School

Fig. 12.1. A monoprint produces a mirror image of the original drawing. Paint is applied to wax paper and transferred to construction paper. The resulting image has interesting, obvious brush marks and soft edges. **See color plate.**

Introduction

Two kinds of printmaking—monoprints and relief prints—are discussed in this chapter. Printmaking provides variations of an image; students can take the same image through several distinct states. Printmaking provides them with opportunities to:

- take a simple drawing and experiment with a variety of colors and marks
- produce multiple images
- use familiar materials in a new way
- problem solve with reverse images, and with contrasting colors and values

Books to Have Handy

Picture Books
The Lazy Bear
(these are not monoprints, but some of the paintings of the bear have a similar texture)

Monoprints

Materials

- white photocopy paper, 8½" x 11" (21.5 cm x 28 cm)
- pencils
- erasers
- wax paper (one roll)
- stapler and staples
- "soft" paper (white or gray construction paper) or drawing paper (Mayfair or Dessin) 8½" x 11" (21.5 cm x 28 cm)
- acrylic paint (small amounts of red, yellow, blue, black, white) or a very good quality liquid tempera paint ("chromatemp")
- paintbrushes, flat-head (½" or 1.5 cm)
- water containers (with wide, flat bottoms to prevent tipping)
- plastic lids or Styrofoam trays (for palettes)
- paper towels
- newspaper to cover tables (lots of table space required)
- painting smocks (paint may stain clothing)
- a pail of soapy water (for washing brushes)

Monoprints are closely related to painting. With a monoprint, students begin with a drawing that includes texture, pattern, and value. Students end up with three versions of their original image—a drawing, a painting on wax paper, and a reverse printed image with exaggerated brush marks and soft edges. Making monoprints requires some care and patience, and is recommended for students in grades four and up.

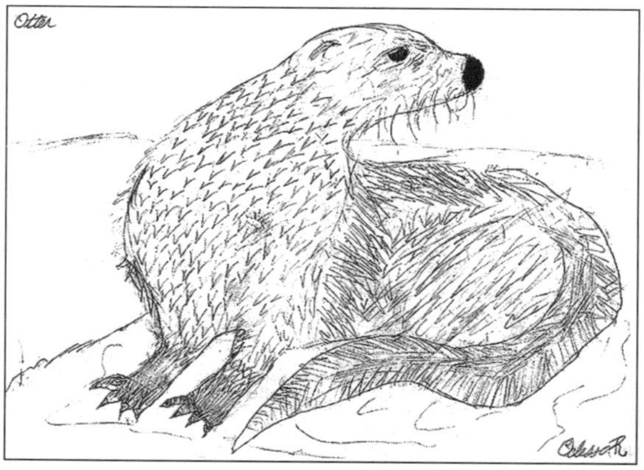

Otter, pencil on paper, Odessa Redekop, age 10, Elm Creek School

Fig. 12.2. Odessa's drawing has interesting contours and lots of texture. It is ready to be assembled into a "wax-paper sandwich"—with the drawing face up on the bottom, the wax paper in the middle, and the construction paper on the top.

Appropriate Subjects

Appropriate subjects for monoprints have easy-to-recognize shapes, interesting textures and patterns, and contrasting colors between the main subject and background (for example, a red fox in front of green foliage). Close-up calendar photos of familiar objects or animals are ideal for visual references.

Preparation

Have students select a visual reference (calendar or magazine photo, for example) and complete a pencil drawing (fig. 12.2) that includes texture or pattern, and values (see chapter 3).

If students are unfamiliar with color mixing, set aside the drawings and have them work on mixing secondary colors, tints, and shades (see chapter 8).

Have students practice mixing colors that occur in their reference photo—they may fill a piece of scrap paper with small color swatches as they try to find the exact mix of colors, tints, and shades represented in their photo.

Tip: Students will need to refer to their photograph while painting. You may want to use laminated or disposable photos, place books inside large Ziplock bags, or prop the books and photographs on nearby ledges to protect them from paint splatters.

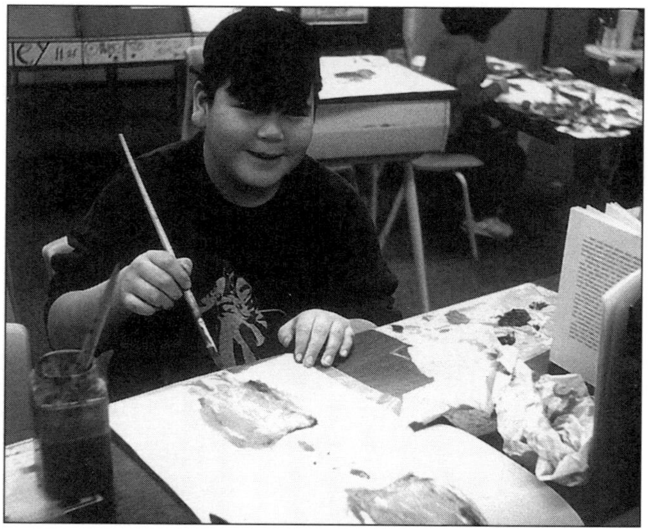

Fig. 12.3. This student is applying small amounts of acrylic paint to the wax paper covering his drawing.

Eagle, grade N–8 class, Disbrowe School

Method

- Lay a sheet of wax paper over the drawing (which is face up), then lay a sheet of construction paper over the wax paper. Staple the top or left sides together (whichever falls on the long side of the papers). Voilà—wax-paper sandwich!
- Fold back the construction paper layer and paint on the wax paper (the drawing will show through as a guide). Start on a piece of the background, rather than on the main subject (fig. 12.3).
- Apply acrylic or tempera paint in small areas at a time, and then carefully lay the construction paper back down onto the paint and rub gently (fig. 12.4). The paint will transfer from the wax paper to the construction paper.
- Repeat this procedure, painting and transferring a small area at a time. Care should be taken about the length and direction of brush strokes, as the strokes produce a pattern on the printed side.
- Leave the "sandwiches" open to dry thoroughly before storing. This prevents the layers from sticking together as they dry.

Monoprinting produces a soft-edged image with exaggerated brush marks (fig. 12.5). It is similar in appearance to the painted illustrations in *The Lazy Bear.* Some students become frustrated by the lack of exactness in the printed image. You might calm them by calling this exercise an experiment with a soft-focus image—and by reminding them that their more precise pencil drawing is still intact and protected by wax paper. For students who are very concerned about their original drawing, photocopy the original and let them use the photocopy for their wax-paper sandwich.

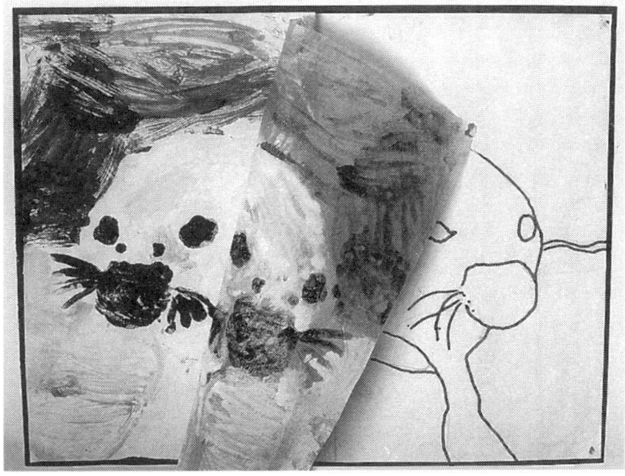

Seal, monoprint, Noni Brynjolson, age 8

Fig. 12.4. This finished print shows how the papers were assembled. Enough of the drawing showed through the wax paper for Noni to use it as a guide for her painting. She applied a small amount of paint and folded over the construction paper. When she rubbed the paper with the heel of her hand, the paint transferred to the construction paper (on the left).

Tip: If the paint "blotches," the paint is too thick or the paintbrush is too wet. Dry the brush on a paper towel before dipping it in paint, then apply a thin layer of paint. If no paint transfers, the paint has dried too quickly. Paint a smaller area with a bit more paint and "print" immediately. Wash brushes thoroughly with soapy water after use with acrylic paint!

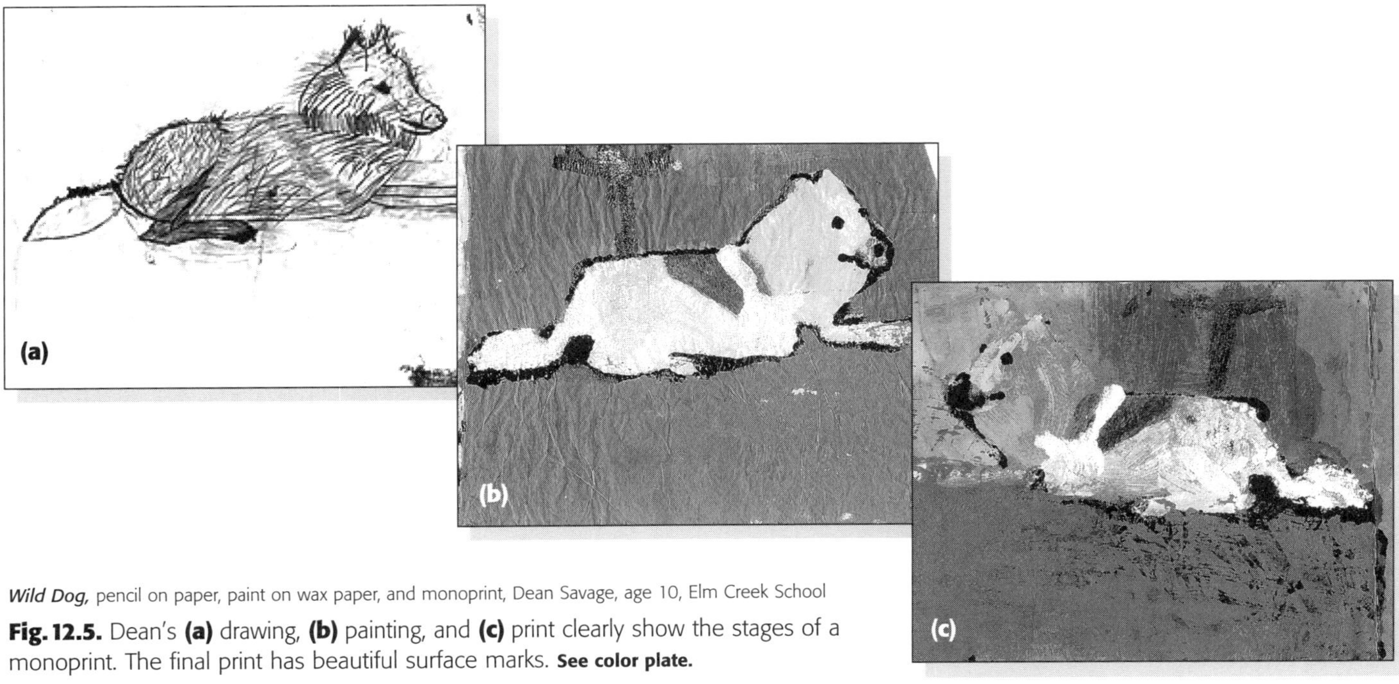

(a) **(b)** **(c)**

Wild Dog, pencil on paper, paint on wax paper, and monoprint, Dean Savage, age 10, Elm Creek School

Fig. 12.5. Dean's **(a)** drawing, **(b)** painting, and **(c)** print clearly show the stages of a monoprint. The final print has beautiful surface marks. **See color plate.**

Enrichment

Monoprints are a time-consuming way of producing an image. Here are some shortcuts that may be helpful if this method is to be used for a series of illustrations:

- Have younger students make monoprints by painting directly onto an object with a paintbrush or soft rubber roller (brayer), covering the object with paper, and rubbing gently. Suitable objects will have an interesting surface texture. Try a large, partly frozen fish, variously shaped leaves, halved vegetables (peppers, squash, mushrooms, for example), small flat toys, machine parts, and so on. This exercise is an interesting way for young students to produce a "clean" image or patterns for border designs.
- Make small monoprints (6" x 6" or 15 cm x 15 cm) with a close-up view of the main subject.
- Use monoprints as a border design or frame for pencil or ink drawings.
- Use the original drawing, the wax-paper image, and the monoprint, and modify each to use as a separate illustration.
- Use the monoprint technique for painting the background, then cut out the original or photocopied drawing of the main subject and glue onto the finished background (fig.12.6).
- Use the original drawing and make several versions, experimenting with a different color scheme each time (see chapter 8). Just replace the wax paper and construction paper for each version.
- Printmakers in their studios use a plate of Plexiglas over a drawn or painted image, fasten the printing paper along one edge of the Plexiglas, and fold it back. They use acrylic paint or oil paint for color. This provides a more stable, see-through painting surface. If pieces of Plexiglas or Mylar (sheets of plastic from the overhead projector) are available, students may even use this as a color-mixing exercise; place the photograph directly under the Plexiglas or Mylar and match the colors to print on their papers. Plexiglas may be washed and re-used. Pre-test the brand of acrylic paint you have, to ensure that it will adhere to the Plexiglas or Mylar.

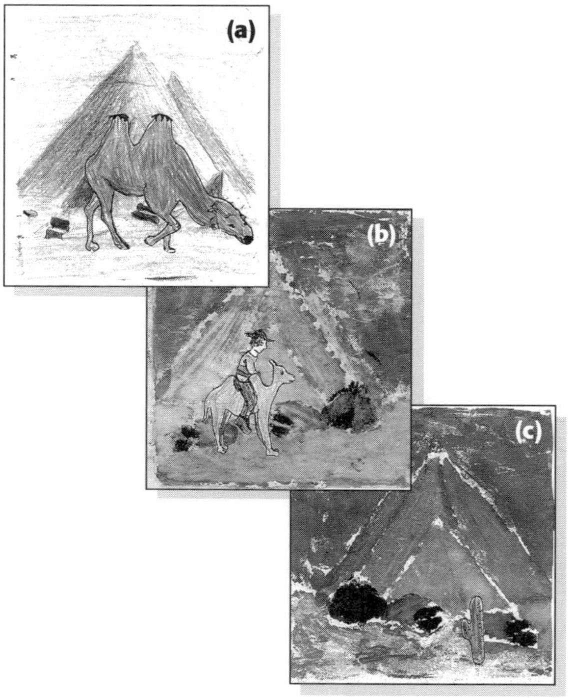

Desert Scenes, Noni Brynjolson, grade 6, Luxton School

Fig. 12.6. These three scenes show how **(a)** the original drawing, **(b)** the wax paper, and **(c)** the completed monoprint are all used as backgrounds for illustrating a story with cutout drawings.

Relief Prints

Relief prints are suitable for students in grades one and up. The method described here requires carving a line into a Styrofoam plate with a pencil. The line will remain uncolored as paint is rolled onto the plate with a brayer, and is transferred to paper. This project generates enthusiasm—and mass production—as students experiment with contrasting colors and roll their brayers through paint.

Students can use their relief prints as multiples (see chapter 4), cut and pasted, in a sequence of illustrations or pictures that have crowds, herds, or flocks.

Appropriate Subjects

Have visual references available for students to look-draw. Appropriate subjects are those that are easily recognizable; for example, leaves, flowers, animals, and fruit. A single subject, drawn fairly large, is preferred. Advanced students may try more difficult subjects such as landscapes, human figures, or shoes; these may need to be somewhat simplified so they can be drawn onto the Styrofoam plate. See *The Cremation of Sam McGee* or *Strega Nona* for examples of drawings with simplified shapes.

Preparation

Cover two long tables with newspaper. Set out materials. Have students cut off the "lip" from the Styrofoam plates or trays so they will have a flat surface to work on.

Method

- Students can practice drawing a simplified version of their subjects in their sketchbooks. When they are satisfied with the results, have them redraw their image onto a Styrofoam tray with a felt marker (the marker won't scratch the tray; mistakes can be wiped off with a damp paper towel and won't show up in the finished print).
- Next have the students draw over the lines with a sharp pencil. Make sure they press hard enough to carve evenly into the surface of the tray (small holes aren't a problem).

Materials

- pencils
- sketchbooks
- felt marker, fine-tipped, washable
- Styrofoam trays or plates (must be smooth with no bumps, imprints, or scratches)
- scissors
- acrylic paint or block-printing ink (one color, black, is sufficient for the first effort; red, yellow, blue, black, and white are required for color prints)
- soft brayers (these are printmaking "rollers"; soft rubber produces better results; four to six brayers are required per class, as students can take turns)
- construction paper, white or assorted colors, 8½" x 11" (21.5 cm x 28 cm)
- newspapers to cover tables with several layers (fold them over when they become full of wet paint)
- paper towels or rags
- painting smocks (paint and ink may stain clothing)
- optional: printmaker's baren (a rounded wooden object used for rubbing paper in order to transfer the paint or ink to the paper. The back of a wooden spoon or the heel of the hand can be substituted.)

Books to Have Handy

Picture Books

The Loon's Necklace
The Cremation of Sam McGee
Strega Nona

Tip: Acrylic paint is easy to work with. It dries quickly, allows multiple-color prints, is less expensive than block-printing ink, and can be used with other projects. Block-printing ink has a good consistency, but may take several days to dry and is more difficult than acrylic paint to remove from brayers.

Tip: To solve drawing problems, see chapter 3. If a student has found the initial drawing difficult, trace the drawing, or an enlarged or reduced photocopy of the drawing, onto the Styrofoam plate (by laying the drawing under the tray on an overhead projector), rather than redrawing. The light from the projector will help the drawing to show through the Styrofoam plate.

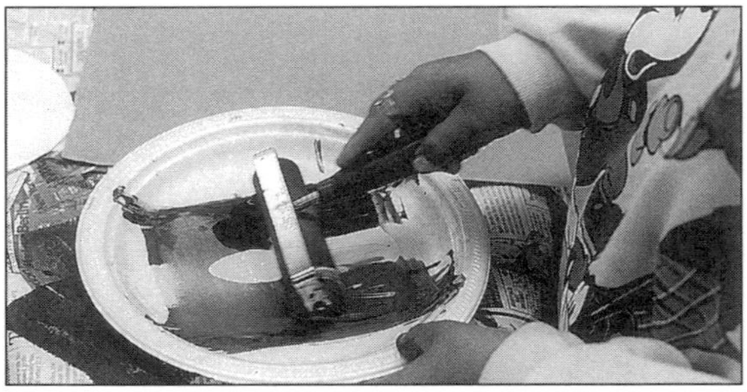

grade 4–5 class, San Antonio School

Fig. 12.7. This student is spreading paint evenly on the brayer. The paint will then be rolled onto a carved Styrofoam plate.

Tip: Too much paint, or "globs" of paint on the brayer, will fill in the grooves in the tray and produce a poor print (clean excessive paint from the plate with a paper towel and an old pencil). Too little paint will produce a poor print, or will cause paint to dry too quickly and stick to the paper.

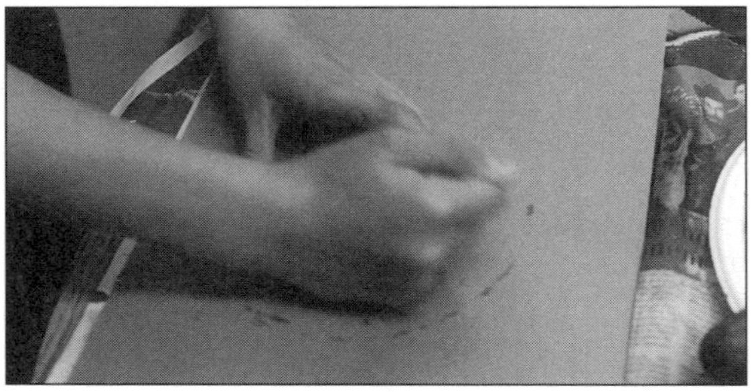

grade 4–5 class, San Antonio School

Fig. 12.8. The paper is placed over the Styrofoam plate and rubbed evenly with the heel of the hand.

Tip: Work quickly. If the paint becomes too dry it may stick to, or tear, the paper. Clean torn paper off of the plate with water, dry the plate with a paper towel, and try again.

- Demonstrate the printing process to students:
  - Squeeze a small amount of paint onto a clean tray. Roll a brayer (a roller used for spreading ink) through the paint in several directions until the brayer is evenly coated (fig. 12.7). Now roll the paint onto the student's carved tray (called a "printing plate") until the tray is evenly coated.
  - Quickly move the plate to a clean area (the second covered table), cover with a piece of paper, and rub with the heel of the hand (fig. 12.8), or a baren, in a circular motion. Rub the entire surface evenly, paying attention to edges. It is important to hold the paper still; avoid letting it slide on the surface of the tray. Peel off the paper and view the print (fig. 12.9). Students may have success on their first attempt, or it may take several tries to get exactly the right amount of paint.
- Let students try printing with a variety of paint colors, on a variety of colored papers. Add small amounts of white paint to colors that are to be printed on dark paper.

  For a "rainbow roll," squeeze small amounts of two colors onto a tray. Roll the brayer repeatedly in one direction only, until it is evenly coated. Now roll the brayer onto a Styrofoam plate, rolling in one direction. The two colors will remain distinct, with some mixing in the center.
- Older students can carefully cut out their Styrofoam piece, and print it separately, to produce a "clean" looking print. Younger students can cut out the finished print and glue it onto a contrasting color of paper (fig. 12.10).

A plate may be cut into two or three simple pieces for a three-color "jigsaw" print. Roll one color onto one of the pieces of Styrofoam, set it carefully on a paper, press down, and remove. Repeat, with different colors, on the second and third pieces. Each piece should fit together like a puzzle.

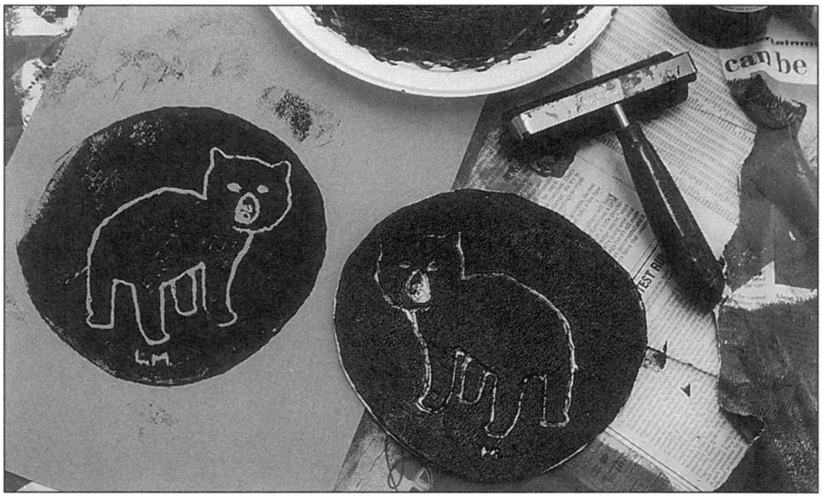

grade 4–5 class, San Antonio School

Fig. 12.9. Paint has been transferred from the Styrofoam plate to the paper.

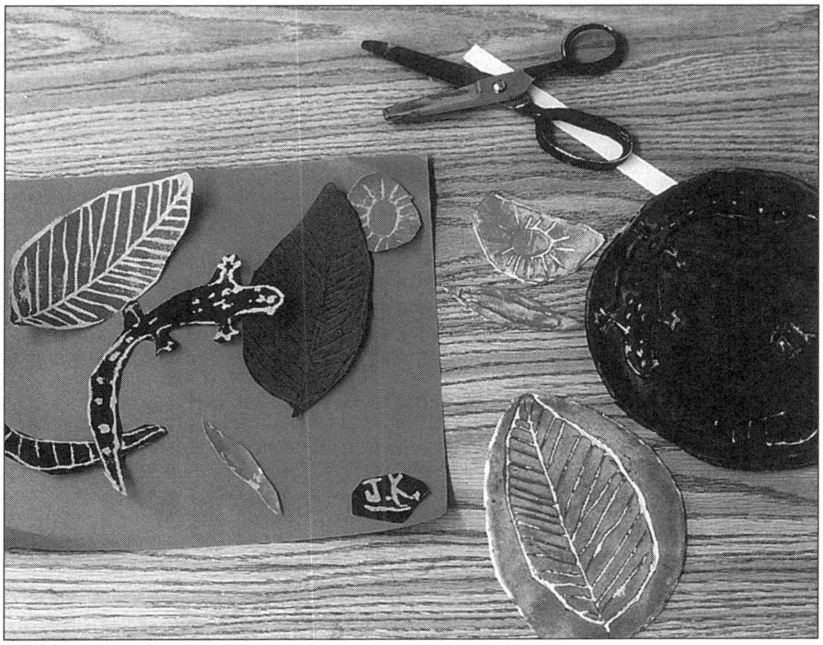

Salamander, Jonathon Kulchyski, grade 4–5 class, San Antonio School

Fig. 12.10. When Jonathon finished his prints, he cut them out and arranged them on a clean piece of colored paper.

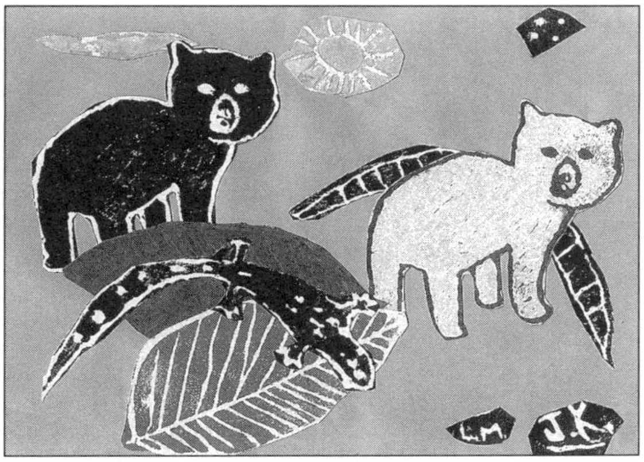

Bears and Salamanders, Jonathon Kulchyski and Laura McPherson, grade 4–5 class, San Antonio School

Fig. 12.11. Prints by both Jonathon and Laura were cut and pasted into one picture. These bears were printed with different colors of acrylic paint, on different colors of construction paper, from the same printing plate. **See color plate.**

Enrichment

- Cutting and pasting the finished prints will produce a clean-looking image. Cut carefully around the prints, arrange, and paste on colored paper (fig. 12.11). Before producing layered images, look at *The Loon's Necklace*. Note which parts of the illustrations are relief prints and notice where the cutouts overlap. Now have students use their own additional cutouts of colored construction paper and scrap papers painted with a brayer to make interesting color samples to cut and paste.
- Use the cut-and-paste method (above) to make illustrations. The printed cutouts can be used as the main characters, while the background elements can be cut out of colored paper. Students can trade pieces with each other, or work cooperatively to produce illustrations with multiple characters ("Will you trade me a leopard for a whale?") (fig. 12.12). This method solves the problem of having to redraw the characters in every illustration. Students may use this technique as a starting point for writing (see chapter 6).

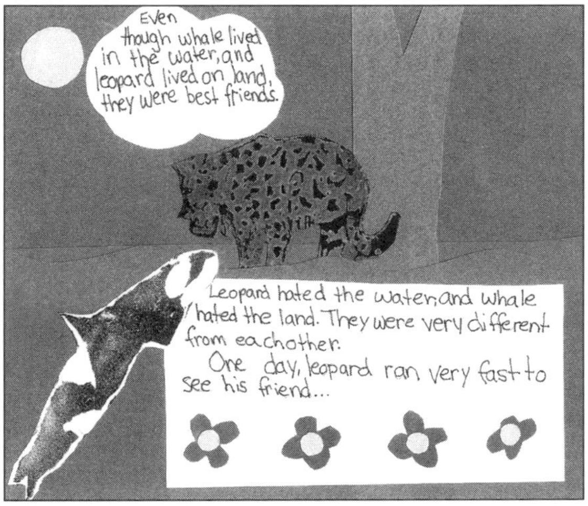

illustration from ***Whale and Leopard,*** relief prints, cut and paste, Danna Slessor-Cobb and Noni Brynjolson, age 9

Fig. 12.12. Danna and Noni put their cutouts together to produce a story with two characters. Cut-out prints are a versatile way to illustrate a story. Here, even the words are cut-out pieces of paper.

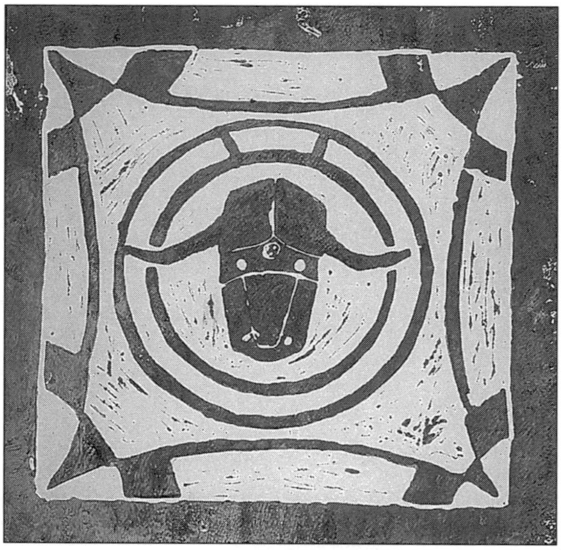

The Native War Pig, linocut print, Ryan Bride, grade 7–9 class, Australia

Fig. 12.13. Ryan rolled a brayer in several colors of printing ink to produce this multicolored linocut print. The number "3/5" indicates that this is the third print of a five-print series. **See color plate.**

- Make linocuts (fig. 12.13). Use lino-carving tools* to carve a design into a piece of smooth linoleum—warming lino slightly on a hot-plate will make it easier to cut. You can also use similar block-printing materials that may be softer and cut more easily than lino. Have students experiment with a variety of tools and try making a variety of cutting marks such as hatching, cross-hatching, and dots. Roll on paint or ink and print (as with Styrofoam prints). This technique works well with any subject or style that has pattern (a spotted leopard or striped tiger, for example).
- Try carving out Plasticine for relief prints with young students. Use a rolling pin to flatten Plasticine onto a table, outline an image with a pencil, and carve out areas with a dull tool (a pencil, plastic knife, or wooden clay tool that won't damage table tops). Print as above, rubbing gently.
- Take prints directly from assorted flat objects that have interesting shapes or surface patterns (for example, leaves, machine cogs, a partly frozen fish). Roll the paint on with a brayer and print as a relief print.
- Make a collograph. A collograph is a printing plate made from a variety of objects glued onto stiff cardboard. Glue a variety of nearly flat objects (string, cardboard cutouts, and so on) onto cardboard. Roll paint or ink on with the brayer, cover with paper, and rub gently with the heel of the hand. This is a good way to explore the surface texture of various objects.

Vocabulary (see appendixes for definitions)

baren	*illustration*	*secondary colors*
bench hook	*linocut*	*shade*
block printing	*monoprint*	*texture*
brayer	*pattern*	*tint*
collage	*printing plate*	*value*
collograph	*relief print*	

* Caution: Cutting tools are sharp. The tools should be used only by older and more experienced students (perhaps in grades five and up, in a settled classroom). Demonstrate how to cut in a direction away from the body, with no fingers in line with the cutting tool. For more control, keep the heel of the hand on the table while cutting. You can reduce the chance of injury by using a bench hook, instead of fingers, to hold the lino. A bench hook is a piece of plywood that has a strip of wood nailed on each end (one on the top, the other on the reverse side on the bottom) to hook over the edge of a table. It provides a stable edge to push against for carving. Slips may occur, however, so have a first-aid kit on hand.

Part 5
Working in Relief

This section is about working in relief—with Plasticine images, collage, and masks.* Low-relief means working close to the picture plane (the surface of the picture) rather than with a three-dimensional model. A collage may be raised several inches (or centimeters) above the backing it is glued to, but it still functions as an image rather than as a sculpture or model of the subject.

Relief media are especially suitable for very young students and for students inexperienced in art. Working in relief:

- uses media that are tactile, plastic, and easy to manipulate
- provides many opportunities to experience and learn vocabulary that has to do with texture, shape, and spatial relations (inside, outside, above, through, and so on)
- teaches building and modeling that help young students develop large and fine motor skills and coordination
- provides opportunities for problem solving—for example, how to attach pieces and how to choose suitable materials
- teaches how to handle basic tools such as scissors, stapler, tape, glue, and paintbrushes
- encourages imaginative play, allowing students to deliberately transform an ordinary object into something different and exciting. This is a good skill and experience for modern children whose entertainment—television and Nintendo—is typically very passive. Even the fact that students can have some transformational power over a small part of their environment can be a revelation, even therapy, for them.

For older students, working in relief provides them with the opportunity to incorporate what they know about drawing, design, and color into three-dimensional work. It also allows them to innovate and experiment with new media.

---

* Other three-dimensional media not dealt with here—puppet-making, plaster-casting, mobiles, modeling, clay, building with cardboard or wood—are worthwhile and effective projects for the classroom. Parents and teachers are encouraged to seek out the references on page 187 for specific information on these techniques.

13
Plasticine Images

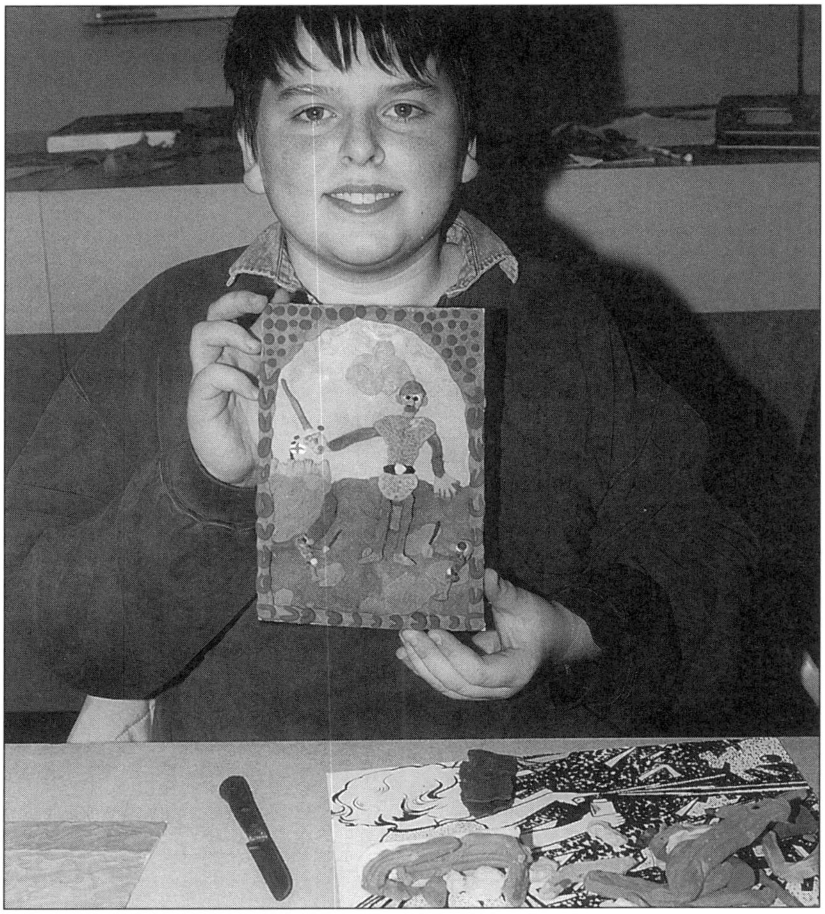

grade 8 student, Treherne Elementary School

Fig. 13.1. Students can develop very sophisticated images with Plasticine.

Materials

- sketchbooks
- pencils
- erasers
- scrap paper
- cardboard, stiff (cut into 6" x 8" or 15 cm x 20 cm pieces)
- Plasticine (red, yellow, blue, white, black;
- optional: purple, green, orange, brown) paper plates or cardboard (for distributing Plasticine)
- modeling tools (objects with a variety of blunt, sharp, serrated, and pointed ends)
- textured objects (burlap, buttons, tinfoil, and so on) for impressing into clay
- spatula (for lifting finished pieces onto background)

Books to Have Handy

Picture Books
Effie
Have You Seen Birds?
The Party

Teacher Reference
Working with Plasticine

Tip: Plasticine must be fairly fresh; it crumbles and becomes harder with age. Check out different brands—some remain fresh longer than others. A few seconds in a microwave oven might soften Plasticine enough for small hands.

Introduction

Working with Plasticine allows students to:

- both sculpt and carve away material to build an image
- apply what they know about color to a new (plastic) medium
- gain experience with modeling tools and techniques

Plasticine

Plasticine is a versatile modeling medium. It is easy to model forms, impress textures, and change the work by adding to and carving away. When colors are mixed, a wide palette or range of colors can be achieved. Fine detail and pattern can be incorporated. For young children, Plasticine can provide a bridge from the real, three-dimensional world to a flat, pictorial, two-dimensional surface. For more advanced students, Plasticine can provide a bridge from familiar drawing and painting into sculptural work.

Appropriate Subjects

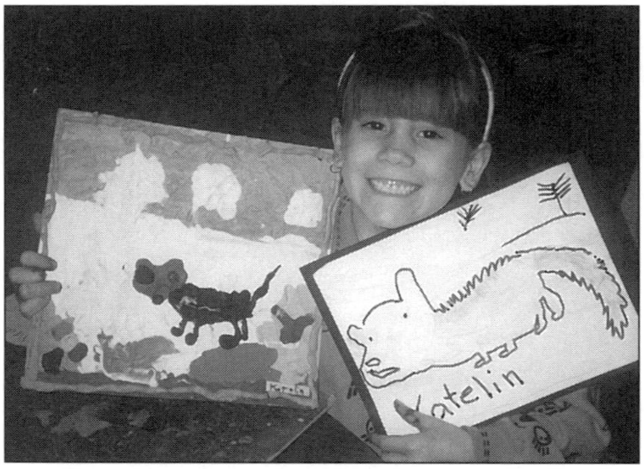

grade 1 student, Luxton School

Fig. 13.2. This student did a practice drawing before starting her Plasticine picture.

Students will require a visual reference for their item or scene (for example, photograph, magazine or calendar photo). Appropriate subjects are single, easily recognizable animals or objects, close-up, in a simple setting. Interesting and slightly more difficult subjects will have many small parts or patterns. These can be added as separate pieces of Plasticine (such things as fishes' scales, birds' feathers, and tigers' stripes) and overlapping elements (a tree branch across the front of the picture, a tiger partially hidden by leaves).

Preparation

Demonstrate drawing techniques to students (see chapter 3). Set out Plasticine on paper plates—some of each color per plate. Students can work in groups of three or four in order to more easily share materials.

Method

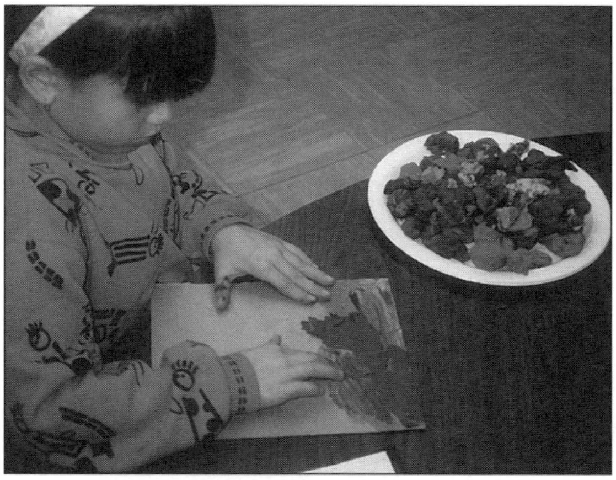

grade 1 student, Luxton School

Fig. 13.3. This student began her picture by spreading Plasticine across the top half of the cardboard to represent the sky.

This is a three-part exercise. First, students will draw their main subject and background. Second, they will spread the background colors of Plasticine onto the cardboard. Finally, with Plasticine, they will construct the main subject and details and add them into the picture. You may want to divide this project into several sessions.

1. Initial Drawing

Have students practice drawing the shapes of their main subject and background in their sketchbooks or on scrap paper (fig. 13.2). Students can study the shapes they will need when they model their subject out of Plasticine. For an intensive drawing class, or if students are struggling with their drawings, see chapter 3 (especially shape, pattern, and texture).

2. Applying Plasticine to the Background

Divide the class into groups of three or four students. Distribute a piece of cardboard to each student and give each group a variety of colors of Plasticine on a paper plate.

Look at *Have You Seen Birds?* with the students. Discuss how the illustrator used Plasticine to make the sky first, the ground second, the main subjects third, and how the foreground details were added last. Point out the overlapping edges to prove this point. The tree branches in the front of the picture are really on top of the other Plasticine pieces. It is much easier to construct the background (for example, the entire sky) before placing the foreground elements on top (overlapping the background). It is more difficult to "fill in" with Plasticine around fixed subjects.

Look at sky colors in the book. Demonstrate, with small pinches of Plasticine, how to mix light blue (white + blue), midnight blue (blue + black), sunset colors (yellow + red = orange, white + red = pink, and so on) (fig. 13.3). Look at various cloud shapes (long and thin, round, animal-shaped) in the pictures. Point out that the sky takes up a big portion of the page in some pictures, not just a strip across the top of the page.

Show students how to spread Plasticine over the top half of their cardboard a small piece at a time (fig. 13.4): warm each piece in your hand and spread it onto the cardboard with your thumbs or with flat-tipped tools. Covering half the cardboard with Plasticine is hard work for young students. This might be enough for one day's art session!

Look at the ground in *Have You Seen Birds?*. Notice that the ground covers a large portion of the page, not just a strip across the bottom. Explain to students that the horizon line may be flat or "hilly." Talk about the four seasons and how the seasons can be indicated by different colors in the ground; for example, green grass or white snow. Demonstrate how to mix some of these colors. Explain that there is more than one color of green—yellow-green, blue-green, for example—and that "white" snow may have blue or violet shadows. (See chapter 8.) Have students fill in the ground areas on their cardboard with Plasticine (fig. 13.5).

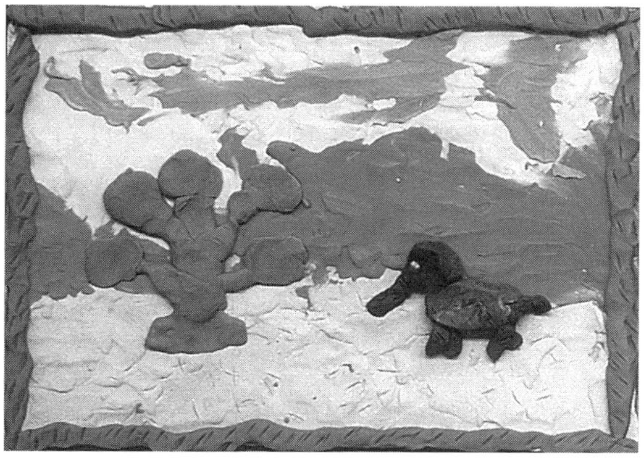

Elephant, grade 1 student, Wanipigow School

Fig. 13.4. This student mixed swirling colors to make a beautiful sky.

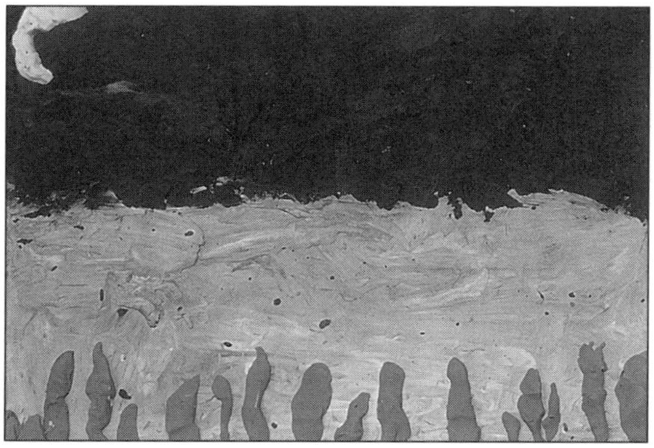

Plasticine on cardboard, grade 1 student, Wanipigow School

Fig. 13.5. A finished background for Plasticine illustration. The student who is making this is ready to add the main subject and details.

3. Constructing the Subject and Details

Students are now ready to construct their main subject of Plasticine (fig. 13.6). In *Have You Seen Birds?*, notice that the birds (especially the owl) are made out of more than one piece and more than one color of Plasticine. Talk to the students about the forms of Plasticine they will need to construct their subject. Demonstrate how to roll fat "worms" (cylinders) and thin "worms," how to flatten balls for circles, and so on. Flatten a piece of Plasticine to cut out a straight-edged shape with a plastic knife.

Have students build their main subjects separately from their background. That way, they can make changes to the size, shape, and color of a subject without destroying the background they have already made. Subjects can be built on a piece of scrap paper (then peel the paper off the back), or else built on a table top and lifted off with a

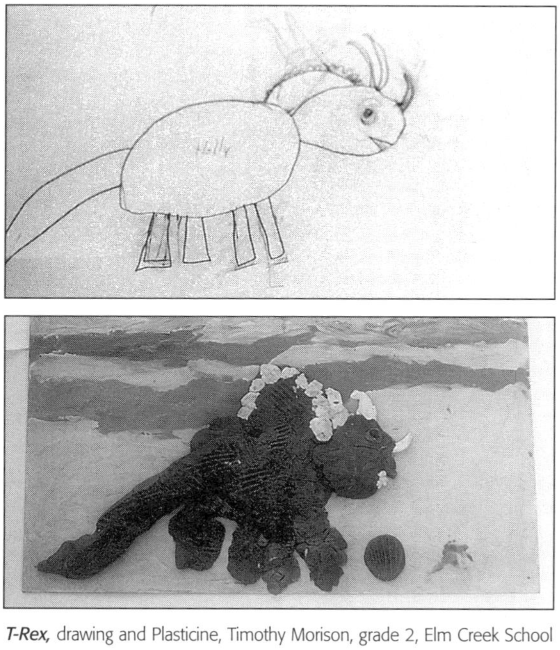

T-Rex, drawing and Plasticine, Timothy Morison, grade 2, Elm Creek School

Fig. 13.6. Timothy looked at his drawing to create this T-Rex stalking through a forest.

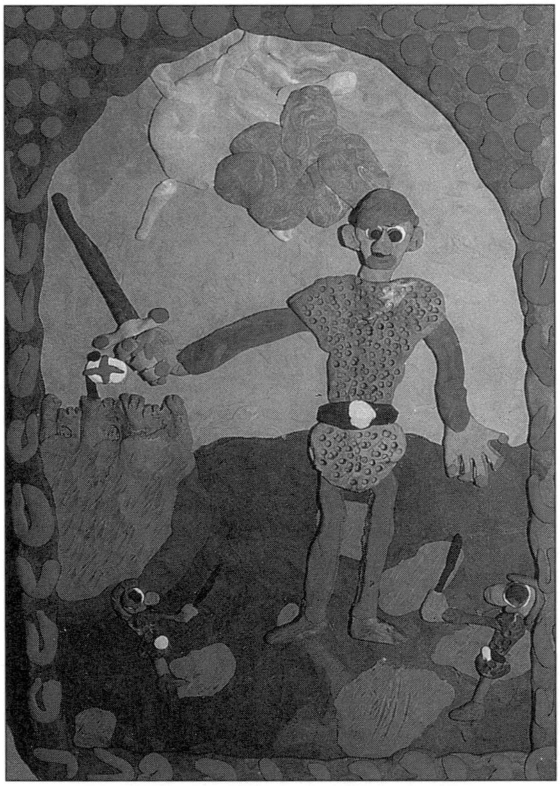

Medieval Knight, grade 8 student, Treherne Elementary School

Fig. 13.7. This student has added texture to the knight's chain mail and finished the illustration with a decorative border. **See color plate.**

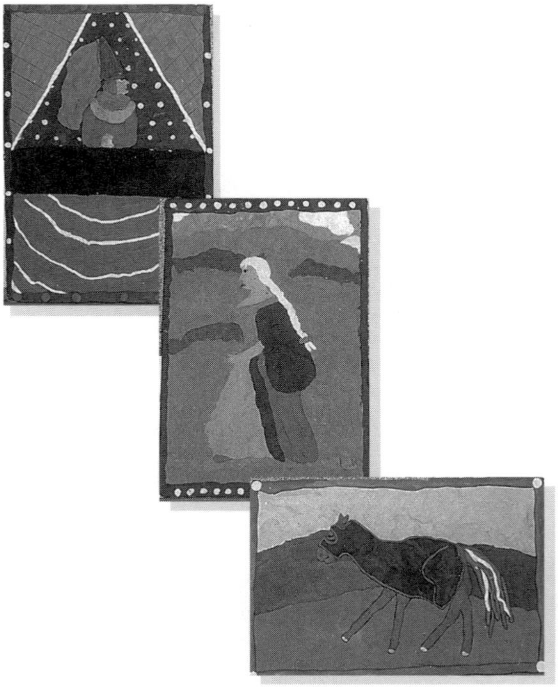

Plasticine on cardboard, grade 8 students, Treherne Elementary School

Fig. 13.8. The finished Plasticine images may be photographed to make a richly illustrated book.

spatula. In both cases, ensure that the Plasticine is not spread too thinly. You may want to try this ahead of time—some brands of Plasticine are too sticky to remove once they have been attached to a table top.

When students have completed their subjects in Plasticine, and have placed them onto their backgrounds, invite them to take one last look at *Have You Seen Birds?*. Point out surface texture (for example, lines scratched onto wings for feathers) and detail (footprints in the snow, snow on the tree branch, and so on). Students can achieve texture marks by impressing objects, such as a small piece of burlap, gently into the surface (fig. 13.7). Their final product will benefit from this kind of attention to detail. Include small shapes of different colors to build a pattern, and add details such as buttons on clothing and a white dot to show reflected light in an animal's eye. Also notice the borders (a long, thin "worm" of bright color) around the outside of the picture.

When Plasticine works are finished, you can display them as they are (use a hot-glue gun or paper punch to fasten a string on the back), or photograph them for students to use as illustrations in stories and displays (fig. 13.8).

Enrichment

- In both *Have You Seen Birds?* and *The Party*, the illustrator uses interesting vantage points (for example, close-up, from above or "bird's-eye view," from below, front, and back). Challenge students to try an interesting vantage point in their own Plasticine illustrations (see chapter 6).
- For illustration projects, keep in mind that making Plasticine images is hard work! Make cardboard pieces much smaller (4" x 4" or 10 cm x 10 cm) for a series of illustrations.
- Have students incorporate objects such as hair, feathers, bits of colored foil, or dried flowers into their Plasticine scene. See the caterpillar in *Effie* for an example of this.
- Students can construct a three-dimensional scene inside a closed environment; for example, a shoebox with a painted interior. They can move or change the characters to act out a story. Some students may want to go one step further. If you have access to a stop-action video camera, you can do primitive animation ("claymation"). Students will need to consider the light source (a desklamp, for example) and shadows for the photography. (See page 37.)

Vocabulary (see appendixes for definitions)

background	*modeling tools*	*texture*
detail	*pattern*	*vantage point*
foreground	*shade*	
horizon line	*shape*	

14 Mixed Media

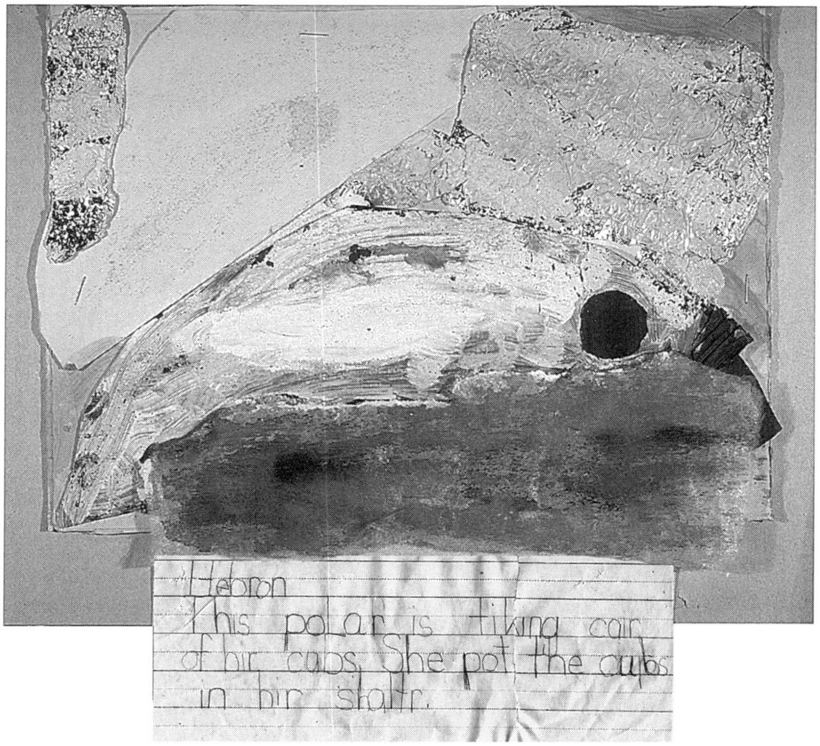

Polar Bear, mixed media collage, Hebron Sinclair, grade 1, Wellington School

Fig. 14.1. Hebron used blue vinyl, tinfoil, cotton batting, sand, and paint to give this simple image an interesting surface texture.

Introduction

Working in mixed media—with collage, or a combination of textured paint and collage—allows students to:

- experiment easily with composition (see chapter 6)
- explore a variety of textures, shapes, patterns, and colors
- learn to view collected objects or items from their environment as possible art materials
- learn to use a variety of basic tools (scissors, glue gun, and so on)
- problem solve how to represent their images with a variety of found or recycled materials

Materials *for planning illustrations*

- pencils
- erasers
- sketchbooks

Materials *for collage*

- masking tape
- white glue
- hot-glue gun (and refills)
- scissors (including some good, sharp ones)
- heavy cardboard (approximately 11" x 17", 28 cm X 43 cm or larger)
- miscellaneous items (when introducing collage, or working on specific subjects, it may be worthwhile to offer only one category of item at a time. You may change these lists to suit your topic or the availability of materials.)
- natural items (these items are good for landscapes and animals): small stones, twigs, dried leaves and flowers, tree bark, moss, shells, fur or fake fur, horse hair, small (bleached) bones, sand, straw, seeds, beans, rice, and so on.
- machine parts (try building robots or space shuttles with these materials): tinfoil, small machine parts, computer components, telephone cable wire
- plastic packaging, plastic pop bottles, bottle caps, candy wrappers, washers and screws, and so on.
- fabric: fabric scraps, quilt batting, cloth ribbon, lace, seam binding, buttons, fake fur, yarn, embroidery thread, tassles, felt pieces, beads, junk jewelry, and so on. Try making people, interior scenes, or landscapes with this material.
- paper (cut paper can be used for any subject—it allows for straight-edged precision and pattern for buildings, people, animals, and plants): textured or patterned wallpaper samples, paint chip samples, construction paper, origami paper, colored photocopy paper, newspaper, magazines, handmade paper, painted papers, paper doilies, and so on.

Books to Have Handy

Picture Books

Alexander and the Wind-up Mouse
Button
8 O'Cluck
How the Animals Got Their Colors
Snowballs
Smoky Night
The Dragon's Pearl
The Paper Crane
The Snowy Day
Weaving of a Dream
Who Is the Beast?
Window

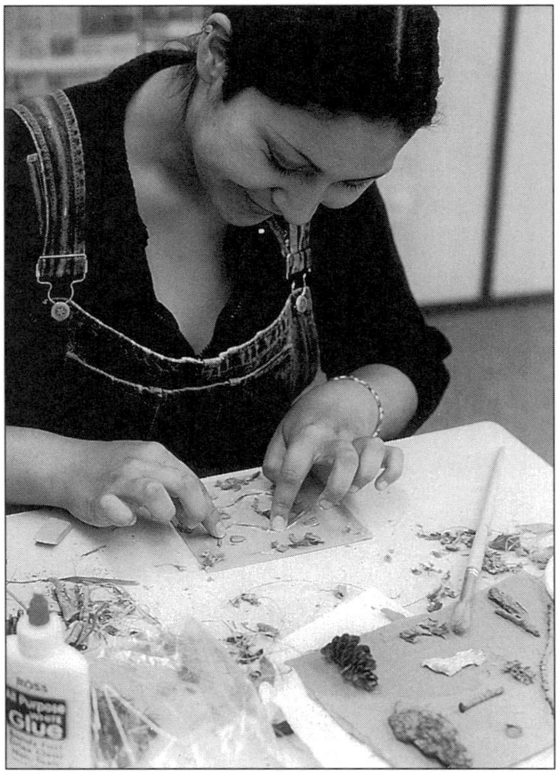

grade 8 student, Stevenson Island School

Fig. 14.2. This student is constructing her image from a variety of natural materials.

Collage

A collage is an image made from miscellaneous—often scrap or recycled—materials. The materials are cut and glued onto a backing and, sometimes, painted. Collage is a tactile medium that can provide an opportunity for teaching about texture, pattern, shape, and/or color. If materials are selected with care, collage can provide a "no fail" exercise that can teach some basic elements of art in a nonthreatening way—students can produce a beautiful image even if their drawing skills are weak.

Appropriate Subjects

An appropriate subject is a single, recognizable image in a setting, for example, a spaceship on an alien planet or an insect on a branch. More difficult subjects and settings have interesting surface textures, shapes, colors, and patterns. Some examples might include a goat on a junk pile; a tiger in a jungle with overlapping leaves and flowers; an elderly person in a sweater, with a quilt.

Find visual references for students' subjects and settings. Magazine or calendar photos, toy animals arranged in a "forest" of houseplants, books, and postcards make good references.

Preparation

Suggest to students that they begin a simple subject in a setting. Collect materials. Also collect several empty boxes or trays to hold the loose materials and scraps as students work. An object, live subject, or replica may be a good subject for young students—they can actually touch a guinea pig, for example, and then touch the collage materials to decide which one "feels furry like a guinea pig."

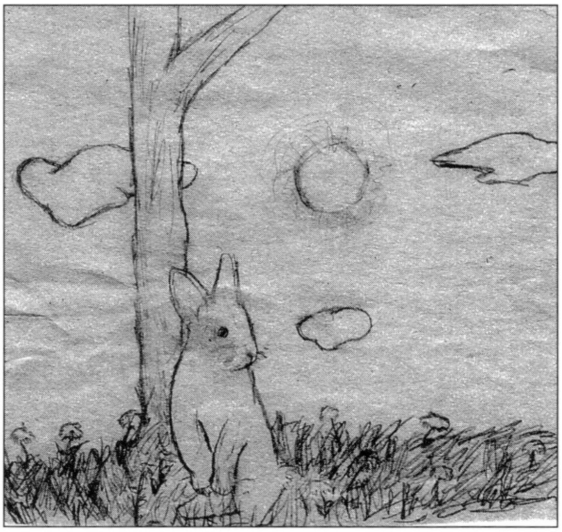

pencil sketch, Noni Brynjolson, age 10, Luxton School

Fig. 14.3. A small preliminary sketch is done to plan the collage and painting. Students can begin to think about what textures and materials they will need to collect. The sketch is also a plan for the shapes the students will need to cut out.

Method

Students may begin by drawing their main subjects in their sketchbook (see chapter 3). Remind them to pay attention to how the elements of the picture fit together (fig. 14.3). They can do this by:

- adding detail to fill in huge empty spaces
- making sure the sky and ground meet at the horizon line; the sky isn't just a narrow strip at the top of the page
- looking at the relative sizes of objects in their drawings (see page 92)

Some students may want to work "backwards." Very young students may skip the preliminary drawing exercise. Instead, they may begin with handling materials and experimenting by cutting and gluing. They will use the textures, patterns, shapes, and colors to suggest the images to them as they work.

Look at *Window*, *Alexander and the Wind-up Mouse*, *The Snowy Day*, and *Snowballs* with your students. Ask students to name some of the many materials that were used to make the illustrations. Encourage them to look at how the artists achieved a variety of colors, patterns, and textures by using these materials. Suggest that these elements make the illustrations interesting to look at. Have students touch some of the miscellaneous materials they are going to be using for their collage and describe some of the textures (rough, smooth, soft, and so on). Ask them which textures, colors, and patterns will be right for their subjects and parts of their backgrounds. Now they can begin to select the materials they will be using (fig. 14.4).

Look at *Who Is the Beast?* with your students. Notice how only part of the tiger is showing at a time. Some elements of the picture overlap (are in front of or behind) others.

Show your students how to use scrap materials to fill in the background area, so that the scraps cover all of the cardboard backing. After they have filled in their backgrounds (figs. 14.5 and 14.6), use miscellaneous items to cut out shapes for the main subject. It will be easier to cut out each part of the subject separately. For example, for a cat, cut out the body, head, legs, ears, and tail as separate pieces instead of in one piece. To encourage students to overlap pieces and to think about how they are going to place the pieces, hand out glue only after students have most of their pieces cut out and arranged on the background. Students may wish to make a border design of repeated objects, or ribbon, to frame their collage.

Encourage students to use cut-out pieces instead of markers or pencils. To maintain students' interest in and patience with the project, you may want to suggest they work on their collage in two or three short sessions rather than in one long session.

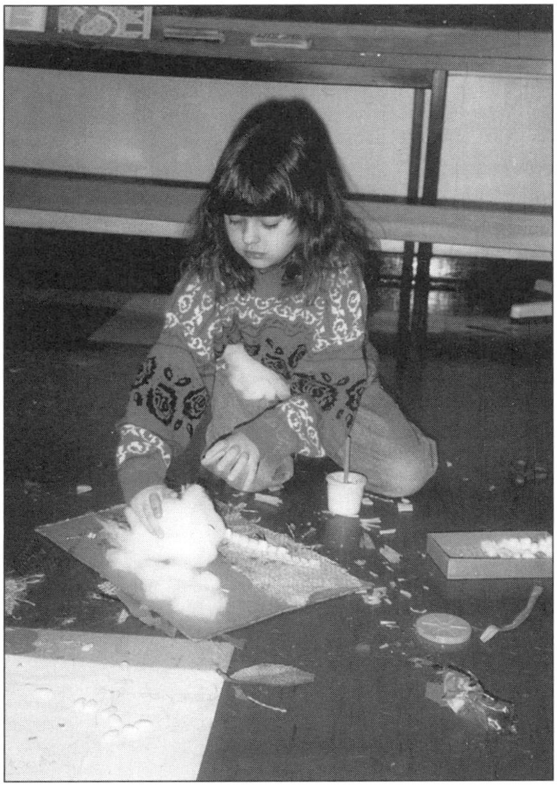

grade 3 student, Luxton School

Fig. 14.4. Make sure students have access to objects with a wide variety of textures, patterns, and colors. This student selected her materials, then began to construct her image.

Tip: Demonstrate how to use white glue without having the glue drip. Use a hot-glue gun with caution (avoid burning fingers or gluing table tops).

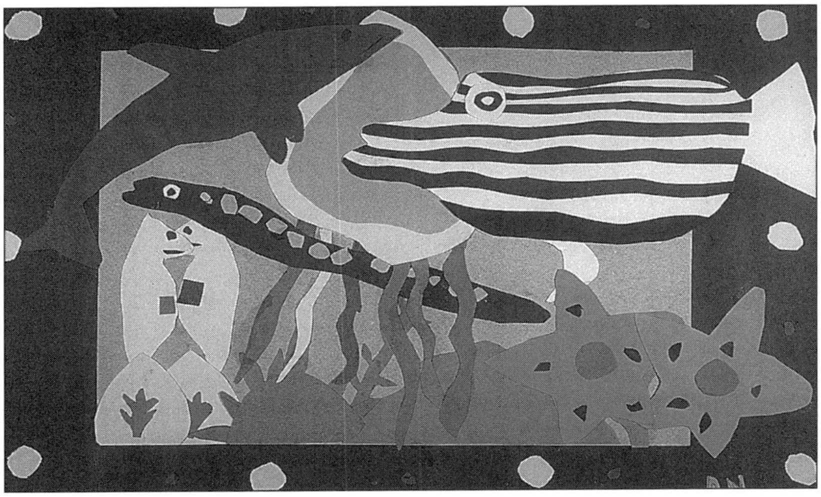

Tropical Fish, cut-paper collage, Dong Nguyen, grade 3, Wellington School

Fig. 14.5. Simple, colored paper can be used to create images with a variety of shapes and patterns. **See color plate.**

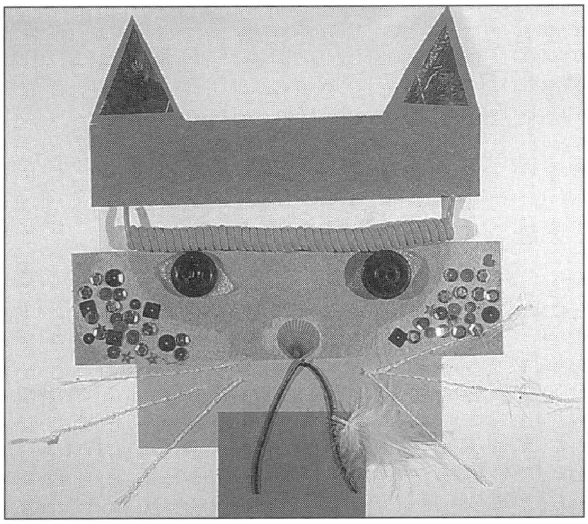

Cat, mixed-media collage, Noni Brynjolson, age 11

Fig. 14.6. Noni constructed this cat out of paper, shoelaces, buttons, sequins, foil, yarn, a feather, and a seashell.

Materials *for painting*

- acrylic or liquid tempera paint
- material for additional texture (sand, confetti, Red River Cereal, and so on. For young students, pre-mix these materials with the paint.)
- palettes (Styrofoam egg cartons are ideal)
- stiff brushes (well-used brushes are fine, $1/2$" to 1" size, or 1 to 2 cm size, flat-head)
- water containers and water
- newspaper or plastic (to cover tables)
- paper towels
- painting smocks (paint may stain clothing)
- pail of soapy water (for washing brushes after painting)

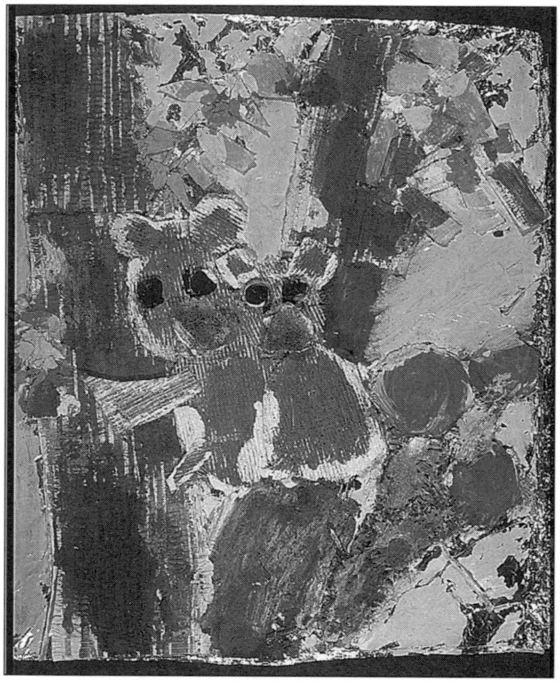

Kaola Bears, mixed media, Channa Tach, grade 2, Wellington School

Fig. 14.7. Channa used a variety of textured wallpapers, buttons, tinfoil, and paint to construct her picture. Her collage would make a good book cover. **See color plate.**

Tip: Introduce painting with a simple color-mixing exercise on scrap paper (or newspaper). Pick a common background color (for example, green or blue) and challenge students to mix as many variations of that color as possible (they can mix small amounts of color onto their palettes and paint small dabs of color on their scrap paper). Try: tinting the color by adding white paint; shading the color with a small amount of black; adding small amounts of other colors such as yellow, blue, red, purple, or brown.

Paint and Texture

Painting on collage is an exercise in mixing paint and texture to create interesting surface and color.

Method for Surface Textures

This is an optional activity to combine with collage. In this case, a collage is constructed with regard to shape and texture—color is ignored and painted in after the initial image is constructed.

Look at *The Dragon's Pearl* and ask students what they notice about the pictures. The illustrator went to China while researching this book and brought back earth, straw, and other materials to mix in with his paint. Fabric, found objects, and a pearl were glued onto the canvas he painted. This approach gives the painting a surface texture that is interesting to look at.

Have students close their eyes and feel their work. Ask them if each part of their collage has an interesting texture to touch. The collages are ready for paint once the glue has dried.

Look again at *Who Is the Beast?* with your students. Notice that there are many colors, not just one kind of green, in the leaves (see chapter 8). Some leaves are odd colors and have interesting patterns.

After your students have mixed several colors, they can now begin to paint their collages. Encourage them to paint over the entire collage—care should be taken to paint up to the outside edges of the pictures. Use large brushes except for very minute detail.

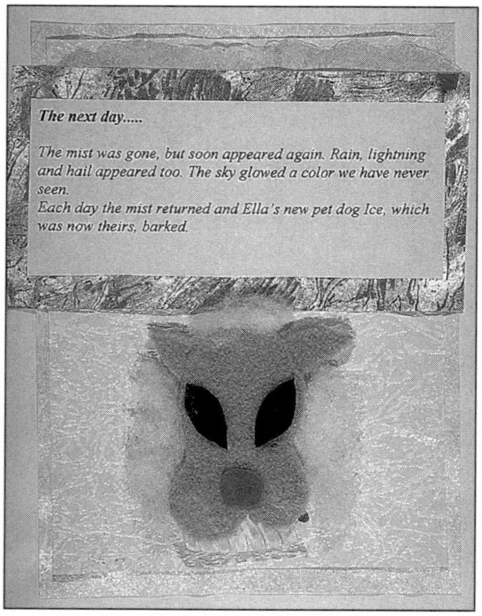

from ***A World Beyond,*** mixed-media collage, Shera M. Starr, age 11, Ecole Prince Charles

Fig. 14.8. For this illustration, Shera used textured wallpaper samples, cotton wool, felt, and a seashell (for the wolf's teeth).

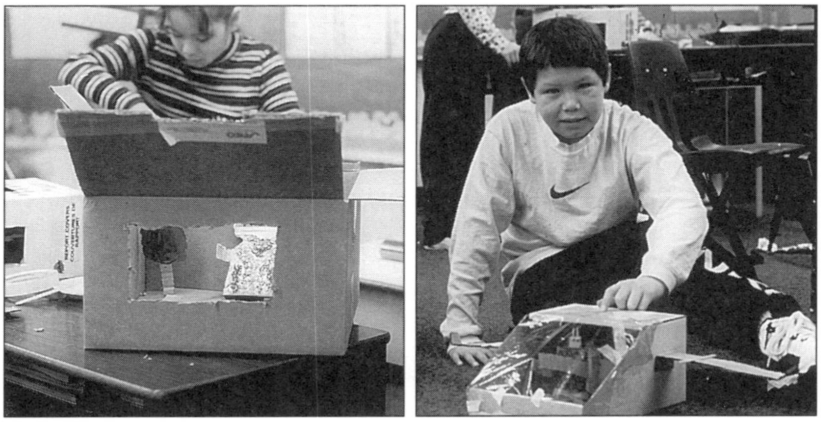

mixed-media sculpture, grade 4 class, Wanipigow School

Fig. 14.9. (left) This student is building a "peek box." (right) This boy's "peek box" evolved into a space ship.

Enrichment

- Use miscellaneous materials to build three-dimensionally.
- Make a "peek box" (fig. 14.9). Cut a viewing hole (1" or 2.5 cm size) at one end of a shoebox. Cut a larger rectangle out of one end of the box's lid and cover with colored cellophane (to let in colored light). Students can make a collage of a scene from a story they have written. Remind them about perspective and depth and about how, inside the box, some things should be placed closer to the eye than others.
- For illustrations for a story, work on small pieces of cardboard—it will be less work to produce a series—or have a group of students work together on one story, producing one illustration each. If collages are very thick or fragile, it may be better to use photographs of them when compiling into a book format. Cover a collage with clear plastic to use as a book cover.
- Make a collage using only one type of material; for example, fabric scraps or a variety of patterned papers.
- For an example of subtle color combined with minimal drawing, look at *The Paper Crane* with your students. Acquire some paint sample papers. Make a collage using only the samples and a pencil drawing.
- For an example of brighter color, with an emphasis on pattern and shape, look at *How the Animals Got Their Colors*. Have students make a collage of brightly colored paper scraps, with interesting edges and patterns.

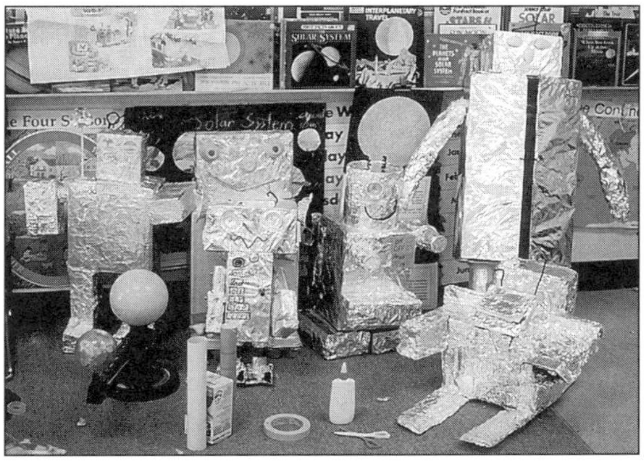

Space Robots, mixed-media sculpture, grade 2, Wellington School

Fig. 14.10. A unit on space turned into a building project. The students in this classroom constructed robots from cardboard boxes, glue, and tape. They then collaged materials onto the surface.

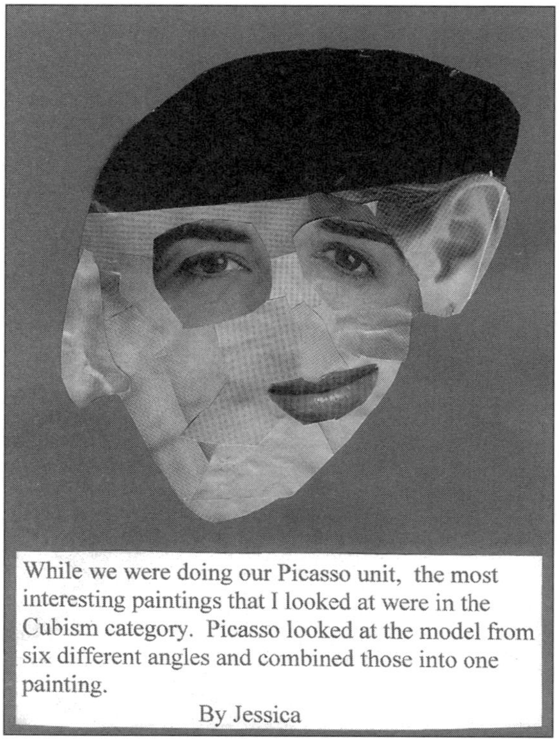

magazine photo collage, Jessica Howison, grade 6, Luxton School

Fig. 14.11. In this magazine collage, Jessica cut out pieces of faces to illustrate her research project on Picasso.

- Look at *Weaving of a Dream* with your students. Have them make a richly colored and patterned collage using candy wrappers, origami paper, or quality, patterned wrapping paper.
- Make a collage in which the subjects and backgrounds are painted separately and glued together when dry. This will make the main subjects "stand out" from the background.
- Add a coat of PVA or acrylic gloss to painted collages to give them a shine. Dab on PVA with a paintbrush. Be careful not to overbrush; it will cause paint to smear. Wash brushes thoroughly after use.
- Have students paint textured paint directly onto plain cardboard. Just sketch a simple image onto the cardboard first with pencil or black pencil crayon. Mix sand or other fine material with acrylic or liquid tempera paint.
- Make a magazine photo collage (fig. 14.11). Students can cut out pieces of magazine photos to build an image (see *8 O'Cluck*). This is a time-consuming process—students will flip through magazines endlessly—but it can result in humorous and convincing images (containing pieces of photographic images).
- Students may combine drawing, text, and collage into one image or illustration. See *Button* for unusual examples that use scribble-drawing, cut-out words from magazines, and cut-out paper samples.
- See *Smoky Night* for examples of using collage for border designs that relate to the subject-matter of the story.

Vocabulary (see appendixes for definitions)

collage	*pattern*	*texture*
horizon line	*shade*	*tint*
overlap	*shape*	

15
Masks

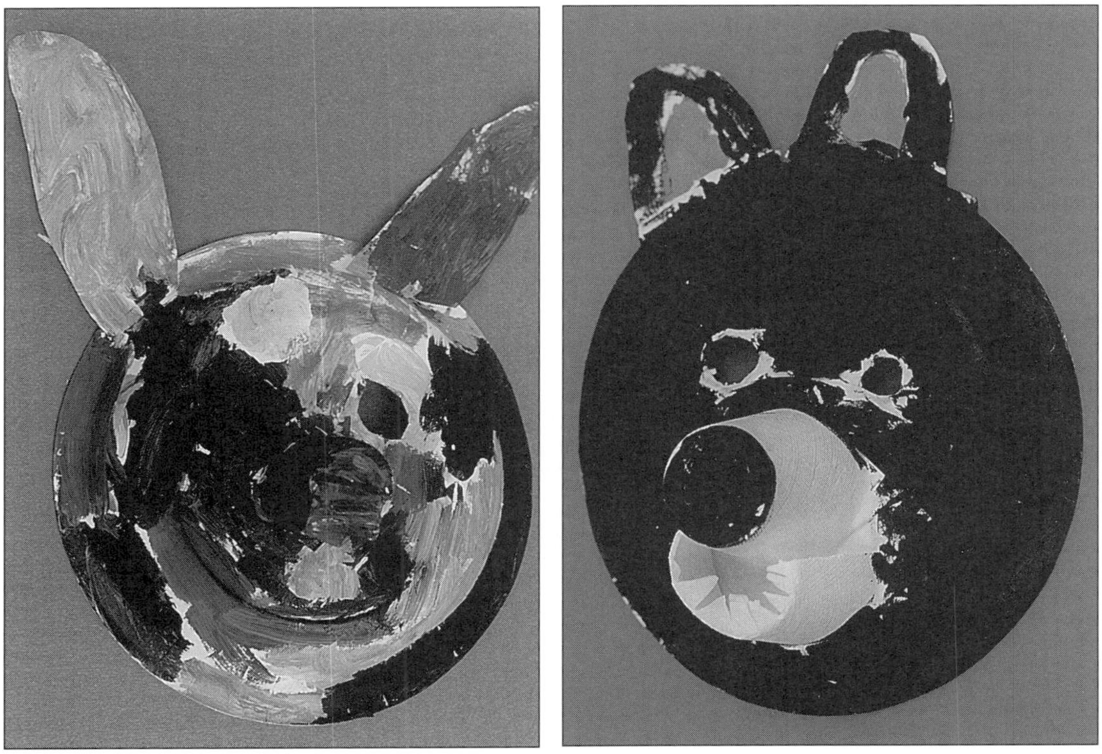

nursery to grade 3, San Antonio School

Fig. 15.1. Playful masks can be constructed from very basic materials.

Introduction

This chapter introduces you to the basic techniques of making masks out of paper, papier-mâché, and plaster. It also shows you how to paint and decorate masks.

Masks can be used as disguises or for inventing characters. They may be combined with drama—acting out plays, legends, or skits—or simply displayed. The fascination of masks is in taking the familiar form of a face and transforming it with animal, magical, eccentric, or expressive properties.

Mask-making may be a good companion exercise to drawing or painting animals, portraiture, or composite creatures (see chapter 5). In mask construction, students gain experience in making cylinders, spheres, cones, boxes, and other basic sculptural forms.

Appropriate Subjects

Have students research a particular subject (for example, undersea creatures, Greek myths, African animals). Having good visual references (calendar photos, postcard pictures, books, magazine photos, and so on) available to students will provide a strong end product.

Preparation

Have students do preliminary sketches in their sketchbooks. Choose which technique you are going to use—paper, papier-mâché, or plaster—using and collect all the necessary materials. Try the exercises (or parts of them) first, to see how to adapt them for your students.

Paper Masks

Materials *for paper masks*

- sketchbooks
- pencils
- erasers
- Manila tag, used file folders, or lightweight cardboard scrap (cereal or chip boxes)
- scissors
- white glue
- masking tape
- staples and stapler
- paper hole punch
- large elastic bands or elasticized string (for wearing masks)
- optional: paper cups, paper plates

Tip: The eyeholes do not necessarily have to correspond to the eyes in the creature's face.

Paper masks are ideal for young students, or as a means to introduce students to mask-making or sculpture.

Preparation

Set out materials. Spread newspapers on table tops in case of glue spills.

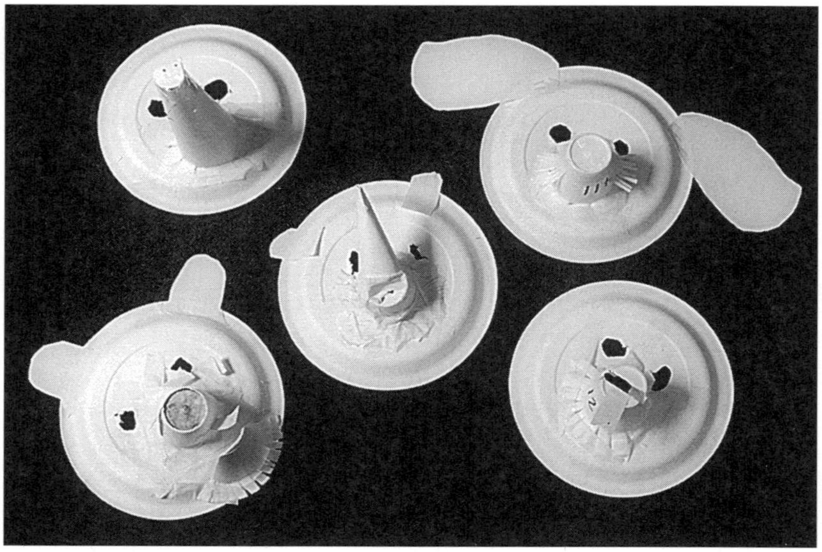

N–3, San Antonio School

Fig. 15.2. Students used cylinders (paper cups and Styrofoam cups), cones, and flat pieces of Manila tag to build ears, snouts, horns, tongues, and whiskers on their animal masks. Cylinders and cones were attached by cutting slits around the rim of the cup, then folding out the edges around the rim, and securing them with glue and masking tape.

Method

Sizing the Mask

Distribute Manila tag or a paper plate to each student. To find out how wide their mask should be, have the students place the Manila tag or paper plate over their face and measure (approximately) from ear to ear. Feel for the placement of the eyes and *carefully* make a pencil mark over each eye. Students can determine how large they want their mask to be by the type of mask and the kind of creature they are designing. Some masks cover only the top half of the face, others come down over the neck. The tag or paper plate can be cut to size, or cut pieces can be added on with staples, tape, or glue. Remember to cut a hole for the nose to protrude, so that masks can be worn up against the face.

Constructing the Mask

After students have done a practice drawing of their creature in their sketchbook, they can use the drawing as a guide to sketch the outline and main features of the creature onto Manila tag or a paper plate. Have them cut carefully around the outline and cut two small holes for the eyes (young students may need assistance with the eyes). If masks are to be worn, punch two holes at ear-level for elasticized string to be attached, then reinforce the holes with masking tape on the back surface of the mask.

Students can use paper-sculpting techniques to build projecting pieces for the masks. To "sculpt" paper, roll paper cones or cylinders, fold boxes or angles, or cut strips for paper curls. Make tabs that can be folded and attached with glue or masking tape to the surface of the mask (fig. 15.2). These volumes can be used to build three-dimensional parts on students' masks—cones for horns, cylinders and cubes for snouts, curls for hair or a mane, and so on. (Paper cups and small, lightweight cardboard boxes provide a helpful shortcut for very young students.) The masks are ready to be painted and decorated.

Papier-Mâché Masks

Materials *for papier-mâché*

- sketchbooks
- pencils
- erasers
- newspapers (lots)
- scissors
- flour (or wallpaper paste)
- several pails (one-gallon size, for mixing paste and for washing-up)
- water
- masking tape (one roll per three or four students)
- whisk, hand-mixer, or blender (for mixing paste)
- optional: petroleum jelly (a thin coating of petroleum jelly on hands and wrists prior to handling paste will make hand washing easier later; dry paste will not stick to the hair on your arms)
- a base for beginning masks (one of: plastic wrap to cover newspaper, paper plates; head-sized balloons; or cheap plastic Halloween mask)
- pieces of cardboard (cereal or potato chip boxes)
- optional: white tissue paper

Books to Have Handy

Teacher Reference
Papiér-Mâché Today

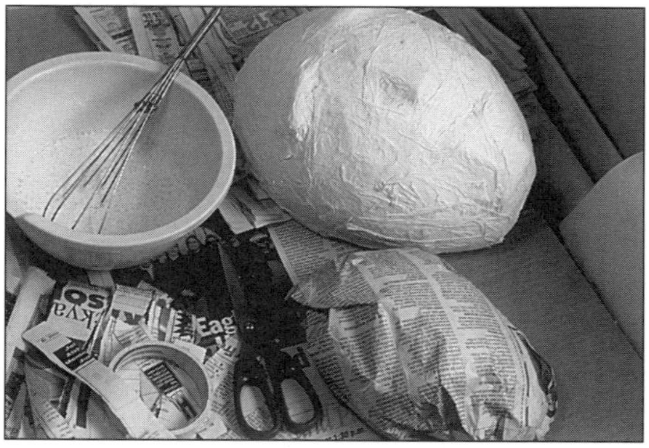

Fig. 15.3. The base at the top has been built around a large balloon. After the papier-mâché dries, the balloon is popped and the back is cut off to form a mask with a very round front. At the bottom, a wad of newspaper, roughly head-sized, has been taped underneath. It will form the base for a leopard mask.

Papier-mâché masks require more time to make than paper masks do. The advantage to papier-mâché masks is a more durable, more versatile, medium.

Preparation

You will need two to three ninety-minute sessions to make papier-mâché masks and another session to paint and decorate them. You will also need a room with lots of table space and no carpet, and additional adults to help young students add protruding features to their masks. Shelf space is required for drying masks. If you are in a damp room or basement room, you will need to turn on a fan or a heater to prevent mold from forming on the drying masks.

Make glue solution ahead of time: add enough flour or wallpaper paste to lukewarm water to make it the consistency of heavy cream. Note that the glue solution will not keep well—a new batch is needed for each session. Use a whisk or beater to eliminate lumps. Cover tables and drying areas with newspapers.

Method

Session One

1. Have students sketch their subjects (faces or heads only) in their sketchbooks to study the shapes they will need to build in order to construct their masks.
2. Choose one of the following for the base:
   - *Newspaper base*: Take several large sheets of newspaper and fold the edges under, leaving a smooth, rounded surface on top (fig. 15.3). Tape the back, and cover with plastic wrap so the mask may be removed later.
   - *Balloon base:* Blow up a balloon to about head-size. Cover with two or three full layers of papier-mâché, and allow to dry. Remove balloon (pop it, if necessary) and cut around the edge. The resulting half-sphere should fit, roughly, over the face (fig. 15.3). If the balloon is totally covered with papier-mâché, it can be cut in half, for two bases.
   - *Paper plates:* Paper plates are easy to use, but provide a flat, uncomfortable mask. Simply build up protruding forms (nose, ears, forehead, chin, horns, and so on) on top of the paper plate.

- *Plastic masks:* You can apply papier-mâché directly onto the plastic mask (it will stay permanently attached). Alternatively, you can cover the plastic mask with petroleum jelly or plastic wrap first to make it easier to separate the mask from the papier-mâché afterwards. You can find inexpensive plastic masks at craft stores or, during Halloween season, at other stores.

3. When the base for the mask has been chosen, the papier-mâché can be applied. Tear newspapers into 1" (2.5 cm) wide strips, making some short and some longer. Dip the newspaper strip into the glue, slide extra glue off with fingers, and place the strip over the base. Smooth each piece on with fingers. Build up at least three layers of criss-crossing strips—the mask will be weak if all pieces go in the same direction. Allow to dry.
4. Leave holes for eyes; or let papier-mâché dry and cut holes with scissors before the next session. Balloon-based masks may be cut open (in half) before the next session.

Session Two (and Three)

This stage may be spread over a couple of classes. Note that if papier-mâché is applied in very thick layers, it may dry very slowly. Also, students with very challenging designs might need to build up the form in several stages. A small horn, for example, is easier to attach than a long one; the small one, when dry, can be lengthened.

Have students look at their sketches or photographs of their creatures, then decide where the surface needs to be built up. Use crumpled newspaper or cut-out cardboard shapes, and masking tape to attach features such as horns, chins, and ears (fig. 15.4a).

Now cover these additions with two, criss-crossing layers of papier-mâché—make sure these additions are securely attached. Other materials—such as sticks and wires—can be attached to the mask with strips of papier-mâché (fig. 15.4b). At this point, pay attention to the surface.

- For a wrinkled surface, dip a partial sheet of newspaper into the glue and scrunch it up slightly when applying.
- For a smooth topcoat, use small pieces (or layers) of white tissue paper.
- For a rough surface, make papier-mâché pulp: mix small squares of newspaper, a small amount of glue, and lots of water (to prevent blender burn-out) together in the blender. Take a handful of pulp, squeeze out extra glue and water, and apply to surface; it can be molded like dough. It may also be sanded smooth when dry.

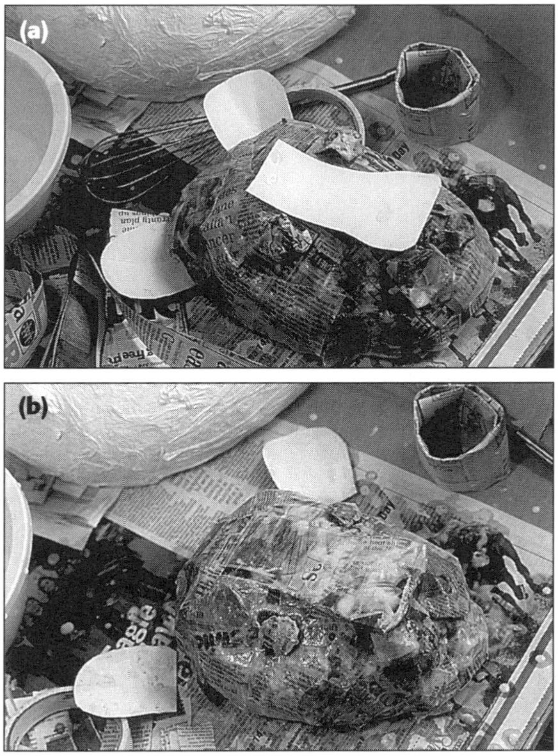

Fig. 15.4. (a) Cardboard cutouts form the ears and nose of the leopard. Balled up newspaper, dipped in the flour and water glue, gives form to the eyes, nose, and cheeks. **(b)** The cardboard and newspaper additions have been smoothed over with a layer of newspaper strips that have been dipped in glue.

Materials *for plaster masks*

- sketchbooks
- pencils
- erasers
- petroleum jelly and hair band or shower cap (to cover students' faces and hair)
- one 5 lb. roll of plaster-embedded gauze wrap per 12 students (may be available at art or medical supply outlets)
- pails or basins (half full of lukewarm water)
- plastic garbage bags
- Kleenex
- scissors
- newspaper
- pieces of cardboard (cereal boxes)
- optional: a camera (making plaster masks is an interesting process to document)

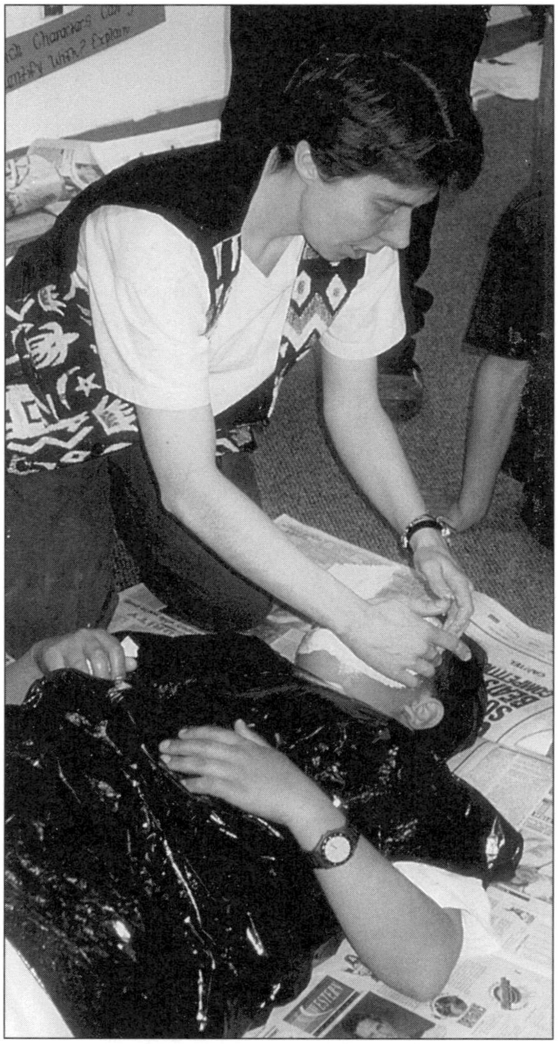

grade 8 class, Wanipigow School

Fig. 15.5. The author covers the face of a trusting student with strips of plaster wrap.

Plaster Masks

Making plaster masks is an interesting experience for students—masks are modeled directly on the students' faces! The materials for plaster masks are quite expensive. The plaster-embedded gauze wrap is very easy to manipulate and build with. When dry, the material is hard and quite durable. It dries very quickly (overnight). This exercise is for students in grades three and up, although it has been done with students in a combined grade one to four class.

Preparation

You will need a couple of ninety-minute sessions to make plaster masks and another session to paint them. You will also need a room with lots of table space and no carpet, and additional adults to help young students. Shelf space is required for drying masks. Cover tables and drying areas with newspapers. Try the project on an acquaintance before you try it with a classroom full of students.

Method

Session One

Explain to your students that you are going to make a plaster mask. Ask for a volunteer to model the technique.

Spread newspaper on an area of the floor. Lay out materials. Have the student who volunteered tie back his or her hair, if necessary, and then coat his or her entire face with petroleum jelly. Pay special attention to any facial hair, such as eyebrows and the base of the hairline (any uncoated skin or hair may stick to the dry plaster and make removal more difficult). Ask the student to lie down face up. Make sure the head is on newspapers, then cover the neck and upper body with a garbage bag to protect clothing. Give the student some Kleenex. This can be used to catch any uncomfortable drips of water.

Cut strips of varying sizes of the plaster wrap. Dip each strip into the water, then slide it between two fingers to remove extra water. Place the strips on the student's face, eventually building up two layers deep everywhere. Avoid the eyes, nostrils, and hair (really brave—and older—students can put petroleum jelly in their eyelashes and straws in their nostrils). Make an "X" of plastic wrap over the bridge of the nose for strength, and reinforce the outside edges of the face with extra strips of plaster. Smooth down each piece gently as it is applied (fig. 15.5).

When you are finished, the student may sit up and walk around or look in a mirror (but should avoid smiling or yawning). The plaster takes about ten minutes to dry. Explain that while the mask is drying, it is going through a chemical reaction that may make the mask feel slightly warm. When it is firm enough, the student can work his or her fingers around the edges of the mask to remove it. The mask will be fragile at this point, so place it on a ball of crumpled newspaper for support, with the student's name underneath. It will take about twenty-four hours to harden. Students may now team up and work on each other's faces. This is an exercise in trust!

Session Two

The masks from session one will become the bases for building interesting creature or character masks.

Have the students look at their sketches, or photographs, of their character or creature, and decide where the surface of their mask needs to be built up to more resemble the original. Cut and/or fold pieces of cardboard and attach to the mask with strips of wet plaster wrap. You can also use pieces of plaster wrap to build up areas and add small bumps, warts, and folds. Dry plaster can be cut with scissors. To enlarge or reshape a mouth or other part of the face, other materials such as sticks, twine, or shells can be incorporated and attached with plaster strips. Set aside and allow to dry (fig. 15.6).

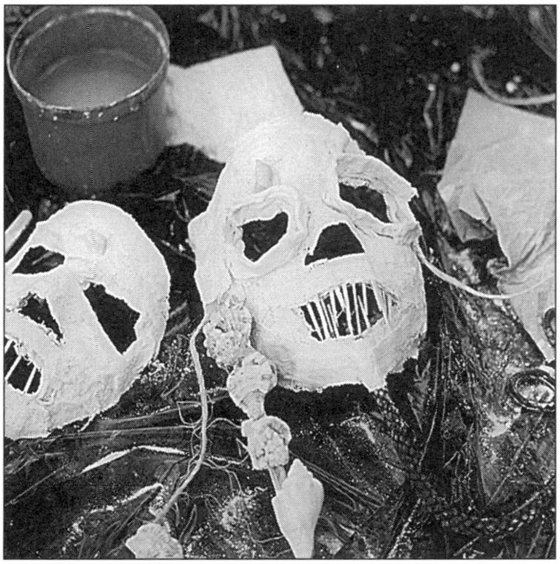

grade 4 students, San Antonio School

Fig. 15.6. Plaster gauze is an easy medium to work with. Students can add features to their mask with dry plaster and strips or lumps of plaster. Other materials, such as cardboard pieces, twine, wire, wooden doweling, and shells, can be attached with plaster strips or with a hot-glue gun after the plaster has hardened (in about 24 hours).

Painting and Decorating (All Masks)

Preparation

Have your students take another look at their visual references. They should look carefully at the particular colors and patterns on their subjects. They may also want to practice mixing some of the colors, or drawing features or patterns on scrap paper or in their sketchbooks.

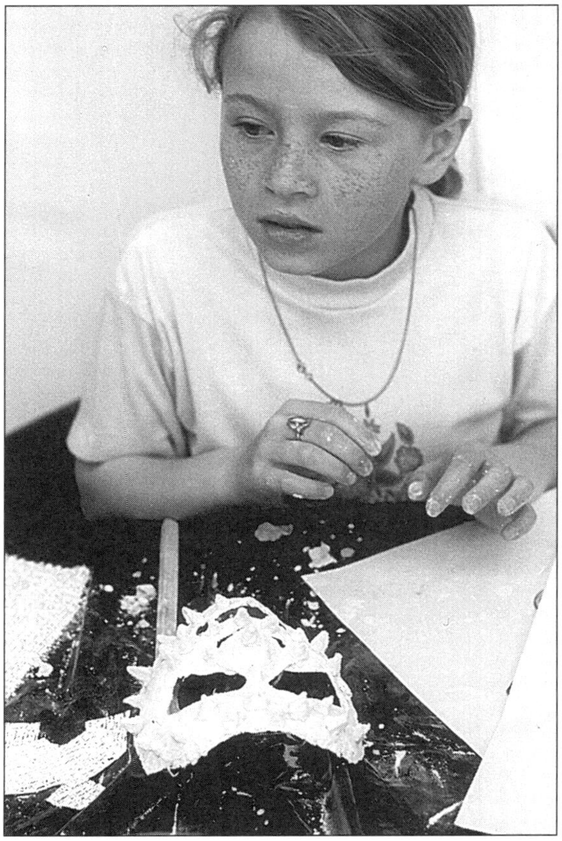

plaster mask, Laura McPherson, age 9, San Antonio School

Fig. 15.7. Laura has nearly completed her plaster mask.

Materials *for painting and decorating masks*

- thick tempera paint, liquid tempera or blocks (acrylic paint may be substituted)
- paintbrushes
- water containers
- newspapers
- miscellaneous (sequins, feathers, fake fur, fabric scraps, colored paper scraps, buttons, shredded paper, glitter, yarn, toothpicks, shells, and so on)
- scissors
- white glue
- hot-glue gun and glue refills
- optional: PVA or acrylic gloss medium (will make the surface shiny and prevent paint from rubbing off)
- pail of warm, soapy water (for washing brushes)

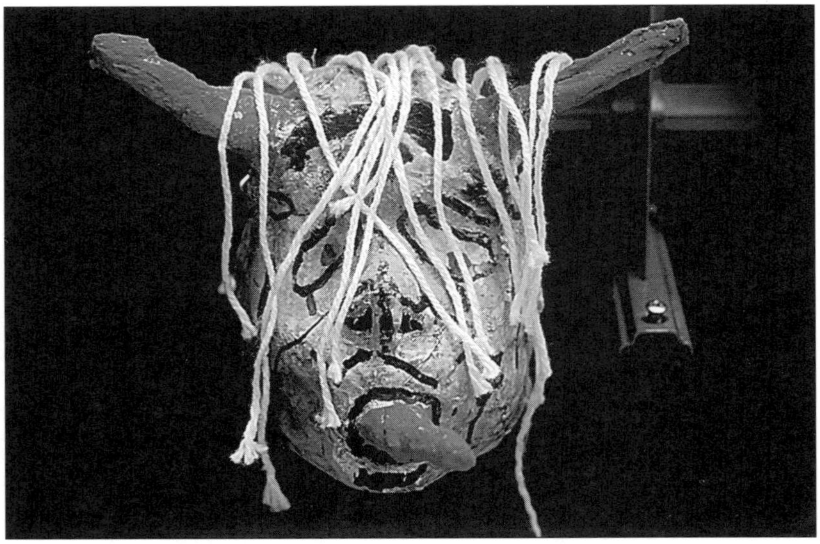

grade 6 student, Sun Valley School

Fig. 15.8. This mask was painted with tempera paint and then coated with PVA to give the surface a gloss. Black lines were added with permanent marker and yarn was used for hair. **See color plate.**

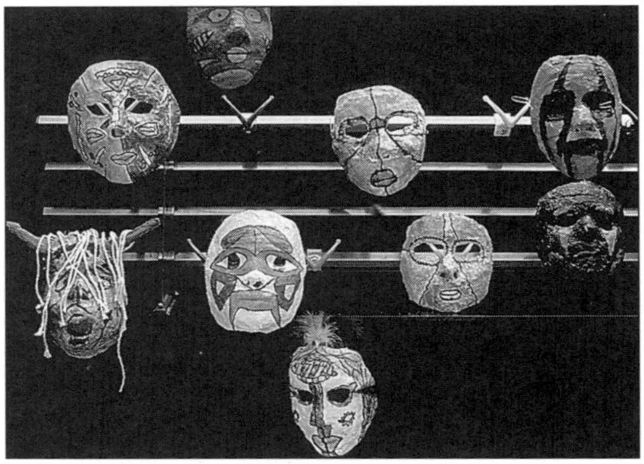

grade 6 students, Sun Valley School

Fig. 15.9. These finished masks were on display in the school's trophy case.

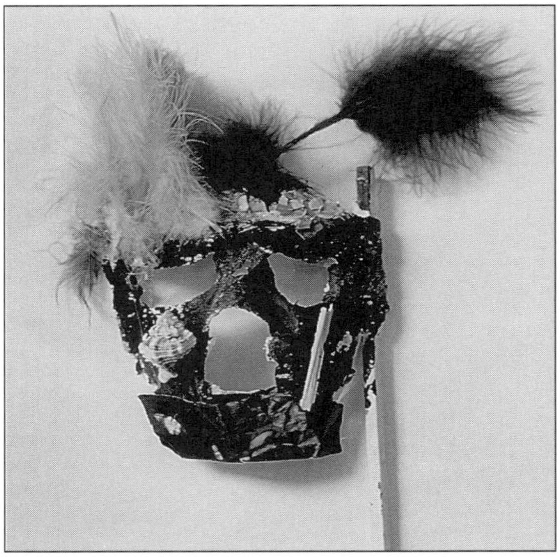

Robyn Kacperski, age 5, San Antonio School

Fig. 15.10. Finished masks can be painted and "decorated" with feathers or shiny materials.

Method

Use thick tempera paint for bright color. Apply white and other light colors first; use dark colors and black last. (See chapter 8 for suggestions about mixing colors and color schemes). Advanced students may do a small color drawing with pencil crayons in their sketchbooks to test colors. Brush paint thoroughly into any rough areas on papier-mâché or plaster masks to ensure the whole surface is covered with paint.

When painting a pattern, paint the background color first, let the paint dry, then paint the spots, stripes, fish scales, and so forth on top. Tempera paint may be coated with PVA or acrylic gloss to give it a shine (fig. 15.8). Just dab the PVA on with a brush. Avoid over-brushing or the paint may smear. Miscellaneous objects may be glued onto the masks when the paint is dry. Use a hot-glue gun to add tufts of hair, fake fur, buttons and feathers; use white glue to add sequins or glitter (figs. 15.9 and 15.10).

Enrichment

- Have students use their masks to play-act in small groups. Start with a story, or students may write a story or screenplay first, using the masks to represent characters in their story. When acting out the play, consider how the characters would move, what noises they would make, and how their voices would sound (fig. 15.11). What setting would the characters live in? What problems might they encounter?

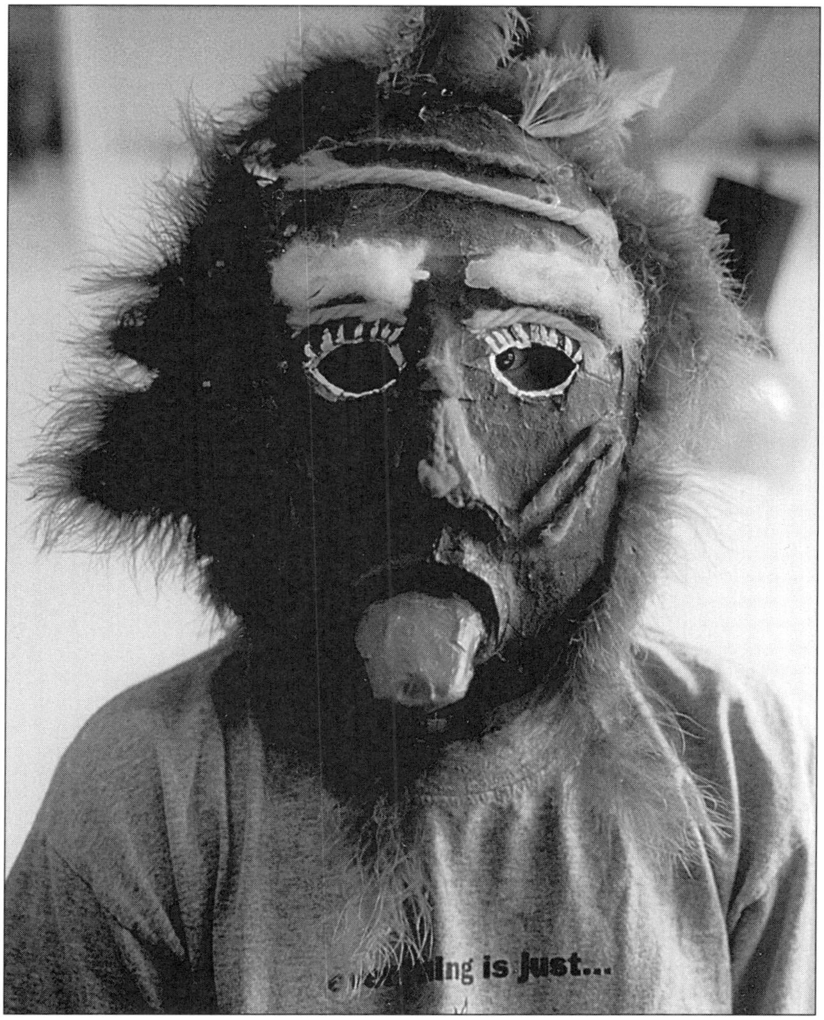

age 12–15 student, Studio Programs, Winnipeg Art Gallery

Fig. 15.11. This mask has a fabric "hood" glued to the back of it for a comfortable fit. Encourage students to act out skits or write plays, using their masks as characters.

- Photograph the masks to use as illustrations or book covers.
- Use papier-mâché to build three-dimensional work (fig. 15.12). Use cardboard, crumpled paper, and tape to build the armature (structure), then cover with papier-mâché.

Vocabulary (see appendixes for definitions)

characters	*play*	*shade*
geometric forms	*relief*	*surface*
papier-mâché	*sculpture*	
pattern	*secondary colors*	

Tip: Use caution when handling a hot-glue gun. Avoid contact with skin. Use over cardboard so that glue doesn't drip onto table tops. If acrylic paint or PVA (gloss medium) is used, ask students to place their brushes into a pail of warm, soapy water. The brushes can be washed at the end of the class. PVA and acrylic paint are hard on brushes!

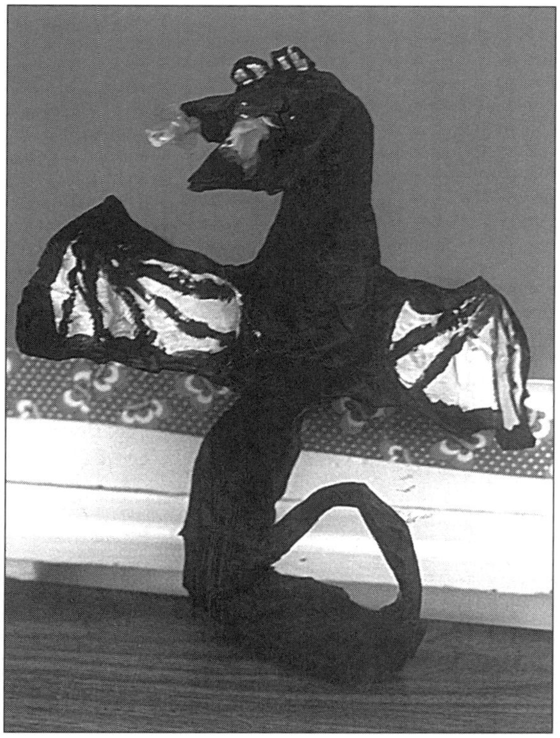

papier-mâché, Jonathan Carandang and Justin March, grade 4–6 class, Luxton School.

Fig. 15.12. This dragon's wings were built from cardboard and papier-mâché.

Afterword
Visual Literacy: Looking at Art

This chapter integrates approaches to looking at, and talking about, visual images—whether those images occur in art masterpieces, picture books, children's art, advertising, or a view through a window. These are all kinds of visual experiences.

We often look at children's artwork and comment with a bland, "that's nice," "I like that," or "good job." Such responses are fairly positive and might be all that time allows for in the middle of a busy class. But they don't really say anything or teach students how to improve their work. Students need more specific feedback. That way, they can begin to evaluate their work and make conscious choices in their artwork.

Students also need to be in an art-friendly environment. Have children's picture books, calendars, art postcards, and other artists' images available to your students. Together, you and your students can look at the artwork and foster an awareness and appreciation of visual art. Encourage them to look at other sources of visual information—advertisements, photographs, natural items, and so on. Visit museums and art galleries. You will find you can open discussion on any work of art (classical, contemporary, or children's) by asking questions and making comments about the media, elements and principles of design, subject, and the impact of the image. Your questions and comments should be thought-provoking and encourage positive responses.

Media

What is it made out of? This question includes the surface that the image is drawn on (for example, paper, wood, canvas) and the media used (for example, paint, pencil, collage). The choice of materials will affect how the picture looks.

Compare the media used for the illustrations in *Have You Seen Birds?* (Plasticine), *The Paper Crane* (cut paper and drawing), *The Dragon's Pearl* (paint mixed with grass and earth on canvas), *Zoom Away* (pencil on paper), and *Would They Love a Lion?* (watercolor and ink on paper). The artwork in each of these books looks very different because of what the illustrations in each are made out of.

If a variety of materials are available to students, you may comment on the choice of materials in a student's work—especially if the materials are used in inventive combinations, or enhance or detract from the student's work. You might say: "I notice that you chose to glue fabric on for the girl's jacket and that you used yarn for her hair" or "The paint made the marker run in this part of the picture. Would you do anything differently next time?"

Design

Visual art may also be analyzed by looking at the elements of design*: shape, line, texture and pattern, value, color, and space.

- Are there obvious shapes contained in the piece? These may be geometric shapes (squares, circles, triangles, for example), organic shapes (blobs, spirals, leaves), or repeated shapes (a recurring "motif" or pattern). Compare the small, intricate, geometric patterns in *Daisy*, the large, simple geometric shapes in *Strega Nona*, and the large, wavy-edged shapes in the landscapes of *The Cremation of Sam McGee*.

  What shape is the entire picture? Look at *The Magic Fan*, *Nanabosho Dances,* and *Animalia* for pictures that are fan-shaped, round, or contain several images on one page.

  Consider the size and shape of the paper that a student has chosen. Are there obvious shapes contained within the piece? "I notice that the house in your picture has a square window and a triangle roof."
- Can you see lines in the piece? Describe them as thick, thin, wobbly, straight, curved, dotted, and so on. Compare the lines in *Would They Love a Lion?* (broken, loose, scribbly), *The Third-Story Cat* (soft edges, blurred edges), *The Cremation of Sam McGee* (colored lines), and *Alexander and the Terrible, Horrible, No Good, Very Bad Day* (even, crosshatched, repeated, and dotted lines).

  Are there variations in the kinds of lines the student has used? "You used a thick, painted line for the trunk of the tree and thin, crooked lines for the branches. I notice wavy, blue lines in the water."
- Do the marks that have been made describe a surface texture? In *The Dragon's Pearl*, the artist mixed grass and earth with the paint to produce a rough surface. In *Alexander and the Terrible, Horrible, No Good, Very Bad Day*, the artist used different pen marks (dotted, short repeated lines, crosshatching, and so on) to suggest different textures. Has the student represented the surface texture of her subject? You might say: "The road at the bottom of your painting where you mixed sand with your paint feels rough" or "I notice that you made short marks with your pencil to show that the bear has fur."

---

* See chapter 6 for principles of design that may be useful when discussing artwork with older or more advanced students.

- Are there strong values in the piece? A strong contrast between light and dark colors, or between areas of reflected light and shadow, can make for a dramatic picture. *Jumanji, Owl Moon,* and *The Magic Paintbrush* have examples of strong light and dark values. Using light and dark values to represent light and shadow is a sophisticated problem for young artists, but some of their work will contain light and dark areas of color. You may comment: "I notice that the whole sky is painted dark blue and gray. It is very dark in your picture. There is a bright yellow light in the window of your house."

- Color can also have an important effect on an image. Colors may be very subdued ("reduced" or gray), as in *Simon and the Snowflakes*, or very bright ("intense" or pure colors) as in *Daisy* or *The Fish Skin*. Some colors may be tinted (have white added to them) or shaded (with black or another dark color added). *The Cremation of Sam McGee* contains many tints and shades.

  Some colors, like those used in *Would They Love a Lion?*, are very transparent; we can see through them to the color underneath. Some colors are opaque (solid, often with light colors applied on top of dark ones), as in *The Pied Piper of Hamelin*.

  The reason a specific color appears in a young student's work, however, may be very simple. Was the paint used straight from the paint pot, or was it mixed together with other colors to make a new color? When students have only been supplied with primary colors (red, yellow, blue), notice where they have mixed secondary colors (orange, green, violet) and brown. You might say: "You discovered how to make green by mixing yellow and blue. Which two colors did you mix to make the orange sun?"

- Some pictures seem to contain very shallow space. The viewer's eye travels across, rather than "into," the picture. *Strega Nona* and *How the Animals Got Their Colors* have examples of illustrations with flat or shallow space, with overall patterns of shapes that are spread across the picture plane. Other pictures create an illusion of depth. The illustrations in *If You're Not From the Prairie* and *Zoom Upstream* use horizon lines, overlapping shapes, perspective, proportion, areas of light and shadow, and foreground detail to make the pictures seem more three-dimensional. The development of space in students' work happens gradually. It begins with simple spatial organization (placing the dot representing a nose between the eyes in a painting of a face). It progresses to the trademark strip of blue across the top of the page and the strip of green at the bottom (the sky is "above," the ground is "below"), and then to more sophisticated overlapping of shapes (only the girl's head is showing, because she is behind the door). You should comment on each small step that students make, even if seems to be accidental: "I like the way the boy's head is overlapping the edge of the house. That shows me that he is in front of the house."

Subject

Tip: For more ideas and specific exercises for looking at art with children, see ***Becoming Human Through Art*** by Edmund Feldman.

What is the artwork about? The subject of a piece of art may be important. A modern re-invention of a fairytale, *The True Story of the Three Little Pigs*, is bound to be illustrated in a style different from the Chinese folk tale, *The Weaving of a Dream*. A funny story, like *Green Eggs and Ham*, will have fun illustrations while a spooky story, like *The Night Rebecca Stayed Too Late*, will have long shadows and dark colors.

In some children's work, the subject may follow very common themes—house, strip of ground, strip of sky, and sun. Any variation may be worthy of comment: "I notice that there are two houses in your picture. I wonder who lives in them?" Some young artists will create expressive pieces: "I can tell by the tears on the girl's face that she is sad. I wonder what happened?"

Impact of the Image

Works of art may have some impact on us as viewers. The drawings of war and peace by children of Sarajevo in *I Dream of Peace* are going to have a strong impact, regardless of many of their design aspects. In other art, the subject may become secondary—in *How the Animals Got Their Colors*, the color and pattern, rather than the simplified forms of the animals, hold our attention.

The most instructive way to respond to your students' artwork is to describe what you see in their work—their choice of media, elements of design, and subject. Students may still seek your reaction to or approval of their work. "But, teacher, do you like it?" Your reaction may be very important to the student. "Yes, Harry, that big yellow sun reminds me of summer. It makes me feel happy and warm." Now Harry may not draw anything but big, yellow suns for the rest of the year! On the other hand, he may have discovered that his work can communicate feelings or ideas that have an effect on other people.

* * *

All of these aspects—media, design, subject, and impact of the image—are part of analyzing and understanding visual information, and of becoming visually literate. When you use them in the classroom, they will help your students to observe, think critically, and value visual communication. Your students will begin to apply observation and evaluation skills to their own work.

Appendixes

Appendix A
Books to Have Handy

Children's Picture Books

Alexander and the Wind-up Mouse by Leo Lionni
A Promise Is a Promise by Robert Munsch and Michael Kusugak
Alexander and the Terrible, Horrible, No Good, Very Bad Day by Judith Viorst
Alexander, Who Used to be Rich Last Tuesday by Judith Viorst
Amazing Grace by Mary Hoffman
Animalia by Graham Base
"Batman," in *The Encyclopedia of Comic Book Heroes* by Michael Fleisher, et. al.
Best Friends by Steven Kellogg
Black and White by David Macauley
Button by Sara Fanelli
Calvin and Hobbes by Bill Waterson
Changes by Anthony Browne
Chicken Little by Steven Kellogg
Daisy by Brian Wildsmith
Dragon by Wayne Anderson
Dragons, Dragons and Other Creatures That Never Were by Eric Carle
Dragon Feathers by Andrej Dugin
Effie by Beverly Allinson
8 O'Cluck by Jill Creighton
Frog, Where Are You? by Mercer Mayer
Green Eggs and Ham by Dr. Seuss
Have You Seen Birds? by Joanne Oppenheim
How the Animals Got Their Colors by Michael Rosen
I Dream of Peace: Images of War by Children of Former Yugoslavia by UNICEF
If You're Not From the Prairie by David Bouchard
It Looked Like Spilt Milk by Charles Green Shaw
Josepha by Jim McGugan
Jumanji by Chris Van Allsburg
Nanabosho Dances by Joe McLellan
Owl Moon by Jane Yolen
Rumpelstiltskin retold by Marie-Louise Gay
Simon and the Snowflakes by Gilles Tibo
Saint Francis by Brian Wildsmith
Smoky Night by Eve Bunting
Snowballs by Lois Ehlert
Strega Nona: An Old Tale by Tomie dePaola
Stringbean's Trip to the Shining Sea by Vera B. Williams

The Baby Who Wouldn't Go to Bed by Helen Cooper
The Cremation of Sam McGee by Robert Service
The Dragon's Pearl by Julie Lawson
The Enchanted Caribou by Elizabeth Cleaver
The Fish Skin by Jamie Oliviero
The House at Pooh Corner by A.A. Milne
The Lazy Bear by Brian Wildsmith
The Little Mouse Trapped in a Book by Monique Felix
The Loon's Necklace by William Toye
The Magic Fan by Keith Baker
The Magic Paintbrush by Robin Muller
The Mitten: A Ukranian Folktale (adapted) by Jan Brett
The Mixed-Up Chameleon by Eric Carle
The Mysteries of Harris Burdick by Chris Van Allsburg
The New Baby Calf by Edith Chase
The Night Rebecca Stayed Too Late by Peter Eyvindson
The Paper Crane by Molly Bang
The Party by Barbara Reid
The Pied Piper of Hamelin by Michele Lemieux
The Rebellious Alphabet by Jorge Diaz
The Shadow Puppet Book by Janet Lynch-Watson
The Snowy Day by Ezra Jack Keats
The Third-Story Cat by Leslie Baker
The True Story of the Three Little Pigs by John Scieszca
The Yesterday Stone by Peter Eyvindson
Tuesday by David Wiesner
Way Home by Libby Hathorn
Weaving of a Dream: A Chinese Folktale by Marilee Heyer
Where the Wild Things Are by Maurice Sendak
Who Is the Beast? by Keith Baker
Window by Jeannie Baker
Would They Love a Lion? by Kady MacDonald Denton
Zoom Away by Tim Wynne-Jones
Zoom Upstream by Tim Wynne-Jones

Teacher References

Becoming Human Through Art by Edmund Feldman
Drawing on the Right Side of the Brain by Betty Edwards
Draw! by Kim Solga
Eyewitness Books (series)
How to Draw Comics the Marvel Way by Stan Lee and John Buscena
Literacy Through the Book Arts by Paul Johnson
Paint! by Kim Solga
Papier-Mâché Today by Sheila McGraw
Painting: A Young Artist's Guide by Elizabeth Waters and Annie Harris
Suddenly! by Colin McNaughton
The Anti-Coloring Book (series) by Susan Striker and Edward Kimmel
The Shadow Puppet Book by Janet Lynch-Watson
Working with Plasticine by Barbara Reid

Appendix B
Tips for Hassle-Free Painting

Painting is a messy activity. Water spills—and it is often the teacher who spills it. Paint ends up on the floor. Tables need washing. Students get paint on their hands and whatever they're wearing. There are reasons why artists have studios and wear dark clothing!

Painting activities do not have to destroy your classroom, however. With some planning, painting can be a calm, everyday activity for you and your students.

- *Collect newspapers for covering table tops and/or desks.* You will then have to wipe up only a few spots at the end of the lesson.
- *Use a large garbage can.* Small wastebaskets won't hold large scraps of paint-splattered, rolled-up newspapers.
- *If you don't have a sink in your classroom, keep pails of soapy water and a roll of paper towels on some newspaper in a corner of the classroom.* Use one pail for collecting paintbrushes at the end of the session—this will prevent the paint from hardening on the brushes. Use another pail for hand washing. Keep a third pail for washing tables and wiping paint spills. Make sure paper towels and rags or sponges are handy.
- *Use paint smocks.* If the students can't bring in old shirts, you can buy shirts inexpensively at second-hand stores. Most paints do not wash easily out of clothing, and in some families buying new school clothes may be a hardship. Students should be able to focus on painting without worrying about ruining their clothing, or of the consequences they may face if they do.
- *Use block tempera paints.* They are easy to clean up. Just wipe them and stack the trays. (Don't stack the blocks together when they're wet. When they dry, you will need a crowbar to pry them apart.) Liquid tempera paint may be set out in Styrofoam egg cartons—just close the lids and store them for up to two weeks. Powdered tempera is more difficult to use—put powder paint in a plastic jar with a tight-fitting lid and shake. Pre-mix lots of colors so that you don't have to mix more in the middle of a painting class.

- *If you have desks in your classroom, establish regular groupings and times for desks to be pushed together* to form groups of four or five. This makes it easier for students to share materials. Delegate one student from each group to get the painting supplies required for the group.
- *Find a place to put the wet paintings.* It is best to lay them flat—hanging the paintings may cause wet paint to drip. Workable solutions include putting down a couple of plastic tablecloths in the hallway, setting up a drying rack, or spreading newspapers along the edges of the classroom.
- *Set up a "painting center"* in one corner of the classroom—on a tiled portion of the floor and near a sink if possible. Four or five students can paint while the rest of the students carry on with other activities. If you have very young students, try to find an assistant, parent volunteer, or older student to help with clean up.
- *Be prepared for "exploration" behavior* when you first introduce paint. Students who are unfamiliar with painting, regardless of age, will be tempted to touch paint and make marks with their fingers. They may take a very long time to complete a painting; they are too busy learning how to mix colors and handle a paintbrush. They may become quite excited and not want to stop at the prescribed time, or they may be quite hesitant to make a mark on paper. You'll need extra patience at this stage—until your students settle in and think of painting as a normal school activity.
- *Plan your first painting sessions to end ten minutes before recess or break time.* You can insist that the students' area (or the entire classroom) is cleaned up before the students leave the classroom.
- *Give students specific clean-up tasks.* It is not enough to say, "Everyone clean up." Chaos will ensue. Put students in charge of specific jobs and the clean up will go quickly and smoothly. Even young students (after some practice) can collect brushes and paints, wash brushes, wipe paint trays, remove newspapers from desks, wipe desks, wash hands, and spot-wipe the floor.

* * *

As your students become experienced with paint and the clean-up routine, painting sessions become much easier. My daughter says her teacher has established a simple solution: "When we need paint we just take it out of the art cupboard. Then we clean up our own mess."

Appendix C
Art Terms

analagous colors: colors next to each other on the color wheel (for example, blue and green; green and yellow)

anatomy: a study of the structures of the body. Artists study the structure of the skeleton, muscles, and tendons in order to accurately represent them.

atmosphere: the mood in a story or illustration, influenced by weather, lighting, color, shadow, setting, details, and so on

background: the area behind the subject; the farthest-away elements in the picture

balance: each element in an image carries "visual weight" that can be offset or balanced by other elements

blind contour: a line-drawing exercise done by looking carefully at the subject while not looking at the drawing surface

block printing: another term for "relief" printing, where a slightly raised or carved surface is rolled with paint or ink to produce a print

blueprint: a method used by architects for copying building plans

caricature: an exaggerated, often humorous, drawing

cartoon: see caricature

characters: the people, animals, or magical beings in a story

collage: cut and paste; a picture constructed from pieces cut out and glued on

collograph: a variety of fairly flat objects glued onto stiff cardboard (in a pattern or randomly) to make a printing plate

color spectrum: the band of colors resulting when white light is passed through a prism

color wheel: a circular arrangement of colors, based on how paint pigments mix to produce the color spectrum

complementary colors: colors opposite each other on the color wheel (for example, red-blue, blue-orange, violet-yellow)

composite: composed, or made up of, several pieces from a variety of sources

composition: the grouping, or placement, of design components on the page

contour: the edges of an object; a line that describes the edges of an object

contrast: a marked difference in color or other component of design; a variety of elements in an image will provide visual interest

cool color: color that is associated with ice and snow (blue, blue-violet, blue-green)

crosshatching: repeated, parallel lines overlaid at an angle to other parallel lines

cut and paste: a technique for building an image out of many small pieces. It may also be called collage. With cut and paste, the pieces of an image are easy to move, allowing choice in placement.

depth: an imaginary measurement from the surface of the page inward; an illusion of three-dimensions, or distance, drawn on a flat surface

detail: attention to particular or minute elements of the image

disguise (costume): a mask or costume that hides one's identity or creates a new identity (for example, superhero, spy, animal character)

dry-brush: a technique for applying paint, using less water, a drier brush, and more opaque paint. Usually used to produce interesting and irregular brush marks.

emphasis: the focal point, or outstanding element, in the image

expression: displaying emotion

expressionism: a school of painting that uses active brush marks to create a more abstract image with shallow space

field of vision: the entire area that you can see

figure drawing: drawing human form

font: how the letters are designed

foreground: what appears to be "in front of" the other elements of the picture; the area that appears to be nearest to the viewer

foreshorten: how an object appears to change as it is tilted toward you (for example, a foreshortened cylinder will appear to be a circle; the front end will appear to be larger than the back)

form: a shape that has been drawn to look three-dimensional as a solid or volume

gesture: movement or expressive action or pose

glazing: layers of transparent color are painted over a base color to produce new colors

geometric form: solids or volumes such as cubes, spheres, and pyramids

graphics: see graphic art

graphic art: drawn or painted images; working with images including advertising art and drawing

gray scale: see value chart

hatching: repeated, parallel lines used to create texture and value

highlights: areas of reflected light; the lightest colors on a subject or in a drawing

horizon line: the edge where the sky meets the ground

horizontal: parallel to the horizon

hue: pure color

illustration: a visual image that (usually) accompanies a written text; a visual image, or series of images, that tell a story

image: a reproduction or representation of a subject (photograph, drawing, painting, and so on)

impress painting: objects with an interesting surface texture or shape are laid on wet paint. The objects are removed when the paint has dried, leaving an imprint behind.

impressionism: a school of painting that focuses on light and color as a subject in painting. Uses looser brush marks, thick paint applied with a palette knife, or small dots of paint. Close-up, the image tends to "dissolve" into individual marks.

intense color: pure color; color that appears brighter from being placed next to its complement

landscape: a drawing or painting of sky and land or water. Usually conveys a sense of space or distance.

life-drawing: see figure drawing

line: a mark made by pulling a pencil across paper; representing the edges or contours of a subject on paper; drawn lines may have different qualities (thick, thin, wobbly, straight, dotted, and so on)

line qualities: lines may be thick or thin, straight or wobbly, scratchy, zigzag, dark or light, broken, smooth and so on. Variations in line add interest to a drawing.

linocut: a relief print made from carving an image into a lino block (a linoleum-like material), and rolling it with printmaking ink or acrylic paint. The image is then transferred onto paper.

look-drawing: looking carefully at a subject while drawing; allowing for a detailed representation of the subject; drawing what you can see, rather than what you assume a subject looks like

manuscript: a written, unpublished text

mixed media: made of more than one art material

modeling: making a form by building up (additive sculpture) or carving away (reductive sculpture)

monochromatic: of one color only

monoprint: a printing process in which a single, unique image is produced

motif: the commonality or repetition of elements in an image

movement: an appearance of action in a drawing, accomplished by including extreme gestures, tilted figures, blurred or multiple outlines, an irregular composition, and so on

mural: a large painting

negative space: the area between and around parts of the subject

opacity: the opposite quality to transparency; an opaque object is one that cannot be seen through

overlap: shapes are placed partially on top ("in front of") or under ("behind") other pieces

paint chemistry: the chemical composition of paint that binds the pigments (the minerals that color paint) together

palette: a tray for holding and mixing colors of paint; also the range of colors used in an image

pattern: repeated shapes or colors arranged in a sequence

perspective: drawing accurately from a particular vantage point to give the appearance of three-dimensions

pictorial space: the illusion of depth in an image; pictorial space may be described as flat, shallow, or deep

perspective: to give the appearance of three-dimensions; placement of objects on the picture plane

picture plane: the (imaginary) front surface of an image

pigments: the ground-up "stuff" that paints are made out of (ochre, cobalt, and so on). Some paints and inks are made of dyes rather than of pigments. Pigments tend to sit on top of a surface; dye colors soak in.

play: a story, usually with dialogue, that is performed by actors

pointillism: small dots of color used to paint an image (like pixels on a computer screen)

portrait: image of a face

pose: the position or stance of a figure

primary colors: red, blue, yellow

printing plate: a surface used to transfer paint or ink onto paper

profile: a side view

proportion: the size and placement of one part of a subject as compared to another

props: objects used by the characters in the story or play

reduced color: color mixed with its complement, brown, or gray

relief: raised area or indent on a more or less flat surface

relief print: a print made from a plate with slightly raised or lowered (carved-out) areas

resolution: the clarity of an image

rhythm: elements placed at intervals throughout an image

rubbings: the "proper" art term is *frottage*; paper is placed over a hard, textured surface and rubbed with a drawing tool (such as crayon or pencil) to produce a pattern

scale: relative sizes of objects; "to scale" means that objects have been drawn to give the appearance of proper size

scene: a selected part of a story or play

scribble-drawing: a loose, relaxed drawing with multiple outlines and wandering pencil marks

sculpture (sculptural): an image or form built into three-dimensions

secondary colors: green, violet (purple), orange

self-portrait: a drawing of one's self

setting: the place where the story happens; the elements in the background of an image that indicate place or atmosphere (trees, moon, water, and so on)

shade: black (or another dark color) added to a color

shading: drawing pencil marks to fill in an area

shadow: an area of darkness. May have the defined shape of an object, if that object is obstructing the light.

shape: a defined area; shapes may be organic (such as teardrop, ovoid) or geometric (for example, square, rectangle, triangle)

shape drawing: simplifying a subject into basic geometric shapes to serve as a guideline for a drawing

sketch: a quick drawing

smudge: a mark made when a drawing medium is intentionally or unintentionally touched or brushed

solid: a three-dimensional form, rather than a flat shape

space: area or depth of field in an image

splatter paint: drips and drops of paint from a toothbrush or paintbrush. The image looks as if it has been spray painted.

still life: a collection of objects used as the subject of a drawing

storyboard: a collection of visual references and thumbnail sketches that serve as a plan for illustrations or other projects

surface: the front or top area; the paper or material on which the image is contained

tanagrams: geometric shapes (parallelograms, triangles, and squares) that may be arranged to make patterns or pictures

tertiary colors: colors that result from combining a primary color and a secondary color: yellow-green, blue-violet, red-orange, and so on

text: the words of a story, poem, research project, or other written work

texture: the tactile quality; how something feels when you touch it; marks drawn to represent the surface of an object (for example, rough, bumpy, smooth, furry, soft); representing a surface by adding textured material to paint or collage

thumbnail sketch: a small, quick drawing (closer to the size of your whole thumb) intended to quickly capture an idea or gesture

tint: white added to a color to produce a lighter version of that color

transparency: the opposite quality to opacity; a transparent object is easy to see through (for example, window glass)

unity: the integrity of an image; the design elements or subjects that hold it together

value: areas of light and dark color; areas of reflected light and shadow

value chart: a gradual shift from light to dark values; an exercise to build skill at noticing and reproducing a variety of values in a drawing

vanishing point: receding parallel lines appear to meet at this point

vantage point: the point from which a scene or subject is viewed; where the viewer is in relation to the subject

vertical: straight up and down; at a 90° angle to the horizon

viscosity: the consistency (or thickness) of a liquid material such as paint

visual reference: a subject to look at while you draw (object, photo, person, and so on)

volume: a three-dimensional form (for example, cylinder, sphere, cube, pyramid)

warm color: color most common to fire (for example, red, orange, yellow)

wash drawing: using a paintbrush with more or less water mixed with paint (more or less white paper showing through the paint) to represent the light and dark values in a subject

wash: a watery application of paint (watery enough to allow drawing to show through)

wet-in-wet technique: the paper is wet before applying paint

Appendix D
Art Materials

blueprint paper: Light-sensitive paper, commonly used by architects and available at a reasonable price at graphic supply outlets. Ask for "blueline, fast-developing paper," pre-cut to size. Store in dark, air-tight wrappings; exposure to light will cause the light-sensitive chemical to dissipate. You can substitute blueprint paper with Solargraphics paper. It is more expensive, but doesn't require ammonia to develop.

baren: A small, slightly rounded wooden tool used in printmaking for rubbing paper. You can substitute with the heel of a hand or the back of a wooden spoon.

bench hook: A piece of plywood that has a strip of wood nailed on each end (one on the top, the other on the reverse side on the bottom) to hook over the edge of a table and provide a stable edge to push against for carving.

brayer: A soft rubber roller used in printmaking to apply paint or ink. Brayers should be between 4" and 6" (10 cm and 15 cm) wide. Rollers must be thoroughly cleaned after use or they develop hard lumps and won't produce an even layer of paint. Store carefully to avoid scratching or gouging the rubber.

chalk or "soft" pastels: Pastels have a much more brilliant color than colored chalkboard chalk. Pastels can be expensive and tend to break easily. Use sparingly on colored construction paper or charcoal paper. Soften edges or erase with a piece of tissue. Finished drawings will be fragile (chalk rubs off easily) unless sprayed with fixative, laminated, or placed in a plastic sleeve.

charcoal: Use charcoal on colored construction paper; sturdy, brown butcher paper; or charcoal paper (this paper has a roughness or "tooth" that holds the charcoal on the surface). Finished drawings will be fragile (charcoal rubs off easily) unless sprayed with fixative, laminated, or placed in a plastic sleeve. Charcoal comes in several forms:

- *Compressed charcoal* is short and square, produces very thick, black lines, and is good for covering large surfaces. Wrap half of the stick with tissue to provide a handle.
- *Sketching or vine charcoal* comes in thin sticks that can be easily broken. It is not as black as compressed charcoal and can be used more like a pencil.
- *Charcoal pencils* are the least messy, but won't produce as dark a line and are not suitable for shading in large areas.

clipboards or drawing boards: These may be necessary to provide support if students are working on a carpeted area or outdoors where they can't work on a hard surface.

colored pencils: These are also called pencil crayons. Colored pencils are a versatile drawing tool—good for small areas of color and detail. Keep colored pencils sharp.

coloring sheets and coloring books: These have no place in the classroom. Any artistic, creative, or motor skills teachers are supposed to teach can be better approached through students' own drawings.

construction paper: see paper

Dessin paper: see paper

erasers: Pink Pearl brand are great erasers that won't leave a pink smudge. "Gum" erasers are tan, square, and soft enough to be useful with pencil or charcoal. "Kneaded" erasers are for charcoal and they can be folded over to provide a clean edge. Avoid plastic erasers; they are too hard for removing anything except ink.

fixative: Spray fixative is toxic and dangerous if inhaled. Check your school's health and safety regulations before you use it. Keep in a locked cupboard, and use in a well-ventilated area after students have left for the day. (You may substitute fixitive with some brands of hair-spray in aerosal cans. Test them first to make sure they dry clear, not yellow.)

glue: There are several kinds of glue available. Use the one most suited to your project.

- *White glue* is required for bonding most surfaces. One solution for storing and using glue is to put glue into squeeze bottles and close with plastic hairpins. This solves the problem of stuck glue lids, and saves having to pour glue into dishes for each project.
- *Pritt,* a powder that is mixed with water, is inexpensive, long-lasting, and works for most cut-and-paste jobs.
- *Paper paste* can be homemade from boiled flour, sugar, and water. It is less drippy than liquid glue, and can be applied with a craft stick or rectangle of cardboard.
- Commercially packaged *gluesticks* are adequate for most cut-and-paste projects, but are expensive. Avoid colored varieties of glue.

gouache: Gouache is an opaque,water-based paint. It is another name for tempera paint.

graphite: This is the black material used in pencils

ink: Drawing ink is expensive, messy, and may stain clothing. Substitute black tempera paint or black felt markers wherever possible. Washable India ink may be diluted with dish soap and water for (slightly) easier clean up. Use ink mixed with varying amounts of water and a paint-brush for a "wash" drawing; use a pen holder and drawing nib (for example, a "crowquill" nib) dipped in ink on a smooth-surfaced paper. Try dipping a feather or sharpened twig in ink for a wobbly, drippy line.

linoleum: This is a soft, smooth product that has little in common with modern flooring products. A new, softer version of block printing material is available at art supply stores. Old linoleum may be heated on a hot plate for easier cutting. Older and more advanced students can use linoleum for relief or block prints (see chapter 12).

markers: Washable, nontoxic markers are usually available in the classrooms. They produce vivid colors. Keep extra lids on hand to replace lost ones. Try brushing water over marker lines to make the colors run in interesting ways. The disadvantage of markers is that color mixing and shading are difficult, and varying the pressure on the marker won't vary the "weight" of the line. Also, they are expensive and tend to dry out if not cared for.

Avoid permanent markers unless they are labeled "nontoxic." Fine-tipped, permanent, felt markers are used for "pen and ink" techniques and with watercolor paint.

Mayfair paper: see paper

modeling tools: Modeling tools are the "proper" tools for modeling with clay or Plasticine, and include carved and pointed wooden tools, and handles with loops of wire at the end for carving areas away. Simple substitutions might include plastic knives, toothpicks, and combs.

oil pastels: These are used for drawing. They produce brighter colors and can be "layered" more effectively than crayons. Encourage students to mix colors. Try scratching lines into thick oil pastel with a sharp pencil.

paint: There are several kinds of paint.

- *Acrylic paint* can be used for printmaking, paper-marbling, and some specialty painting (advanced students may use acrylic paint on paper or canvas). It is not recommended for most painting projects because it is expensive, hard on brushes, and difficult for students to use well. Tempera paint is a good substitute for acrylic paint.

- *Tempera paint* is the prefered school paint. The round blocks of tempera paint are easiest to use. They can be placed individualy in tuna cans or set out in different color combinations. Students can mix colors right on the blocks. Wipe clean with a damp paper towel or sponge. New formulas of liquid tempera, produced by Chromacryl and by Prang, have the bright color and thick texture of acrylic paint, but are still washable. Set out small amounts of liquid paint in Styrofoam egg cartons, or, for younger students, in larger paint pots with lids. Powdered tempera is the most difficult to use, and may not be entirely nontoxic. To mix, place powder and water in a jar with tight-fitting lid and shake well. Mix it with extra water for a paint "wash"; for different consistencies, mix with less water and cornstarch, sand, Glide laundry starch, or dish soap. After using tempera paint, coat the illustration with PVA. Wash brushes in soapy water immediately after use. May stain clothing. (See *Paint!* for other ideas.)

- *Watercolor paint* may come in See for Yourself tablets or Pentel brand tubes. They must be used with watercolor or Dessin paper for salt, plastic wrap, and wet-on-wet techniques to be effective. Use small amounts of paint on a palette or Styrofoam tray. Dried paint may be re-used with a wet paintbrush. Use with a large, soft brush. Replace lids on paint tubes carefully. To use a paint "wash" with very young students, pre-mix watercolor with water, or substitute with food coloring and water. Food coloring will produce bright colors and accurate color mixing—use with a paintbrush or an eyedropper.

paintbrushes: Square, or "flat-headed," paintbrushes are preferred for most work because they can be turned to produce either a wide or thin line. Have a range of brush sizes available to students. Younger students will need large brushes (3/4" or 2 cm); older students will need these as well as finer brushes (1/2" to 3" or 1 cm to 8 cm). Watercolor techniques require large, soft brushes that form a point when wet (slightly used school brushes are adequate).

Clean paintbrushes after each use; keep a bucket of soapy water (dish soap is fine) available for students to drop their brushes in, then wash thoroughly. Store brushes bristle-side up after cleaning. Keep old or damaged brushes on hand to use with glue or PVA. Use feathers, twigs, string, sponges, housepainting brushes, and so on instead of brushes to produce different kinds of marks.

palette: A palette is a surface on which paint colors are mixed. Styrofoam egg cartons (with lids) are good for acrylic and liquid tempera paint. Styrofoam trays can be substituted, and can be used with watercolor paint. (Palette also may refer to the range of colors used in a painting.)

paper: The type of paper used will affect the outcome of the art project.

- *Dessin* paper is fairly expensive, but may be cut into small pieces and rationed out to students for watercolor projects or small-scale drawings. It is available in different "weights"; the heavier variety (100 lb.) is required for watercolor. It is about the least expensive paper, unless you have access to an artist's co-op.

- *Arches, Strathmore,* and *Windsor-Newton* are examples of expensive, quality-brand watercolor papers.

- *Mayfair paper* is heavier than any school or bond paper and allows for more erasing. The surface will hold slightly more graphite and ink than regular paper, making it good for pencil and pen drawings.

- *Construction paper* is good for chalk pastel and charcoal drawing, although "charcoal paper" has more "tooth" (texture) and holds more chalk. Construction paper is also commonly used for cut-paper collage. Brightly colored paper and patterned papers provide a different effect, and might be less likely to fade over time.

- *Manila tag and brightly colored file folders* make excellent covers for assembling students' books. Old file folders make good sturdy "pop-up" books.

- *Soft Manila paper* is adequate for use with tempera paint, but is too soft for most drawing projects; students will erase right through it.
- *Photocopy paper* is adequate for most drawing projects. It tends to be sturdier than most "art" paper. It is, however, not good for painting.
- *Light-sensitive paper* is paper that has been treated with a chemical that will fade when exposed to light and turn permanently blue when exposed to ammonia fumes.

papier-mâché: Papier-mâché is newspaper dipped in a flour-and-water glue: Mix flour with enough water to make a cream-like consistency. Wallpaper paste may be substituted for flour. Papier-mâché pulp is commercially available, but torn newspaper, water, and a blender will produce a similar result.

pencils: Regular HB or "primary printer" pencils are well suited to most drawing projects. Drawing fine lines or light gray tones may require a harder pencil (H pencils are hard; the higher the number next to the H, the harder the pencil). To get a very black line, try a B pencil (the higher the number next to the B, the softer the pencil and the blacker the mark). Pencil "lead" is actually graphite.

plaster wrap: Plaster wrap is gauze containing dry plaster. It is the same stuff that is used in hospitals for plaster casts. Although relatively expensive, it is a versatile (and easy) sculpture material. It is available in large (5 lb.) or smaller rolls. To use, cut into pieces, dip in water, gently scrape off excess water, and shape. Plaster wrap bonds to materials such as cardboard, wood, and wire and may be used for masks (see chapter 15).

Plasticine: This is a brand name for modeling clay—most other brands are inferior. Students can use Plasticine as a substitute for clay, which needs to be fired and painted or glazed. Fimo can also be substituted. It is a self-hardening, but slightly translucent, sculpture material. However, it is expensive.

scissors: While safety is an issue with younger children, sturdy, sharp scissors are required for most projects. A few left-handed pairs may be required. Keeping scissors clean (free of glue) will prolong their life.

sketchbooks: Student sketchbooks may be assembled by students or by a coil-binding device. Make sure covers are sturdy, to provide a solid drawing surface. Whatever paper overflows the supply cupboard is adequate for sketchbooks. Newsprint is the least desirable—it is gray, too soft to withstand much erasing, and too slick to hold much graphite.

smocks: Many art materials will stain clothing. Paint smocks—old shirts and T-shirts work well—save good school clothes from damage.

tempera: see paint

watercolor paint: see paint

wax crayons: Crayons are a common and versatile drawing tool. Use them for crayon-resist, "encaustic"; to make a "mock lithograph"; for a "rubbing"; for drawing.

References

Cited References

The following works are cited in *Art & Illustration for the Classroom*.

Arnheim, Rudolf. *Visual Thinking*. Berkeley and Los Angeles: University of California Press, 1969.

Brittain, W. Lambert. *Creativity, Art and the Young Child*. New York: Macmillan, 1979.

Chapman, Laura H. *Approaches to Art in Education*. New York: Harcourt Brace Jovanovich, 1978.

Edwards, Betty. *Drawing on the Right Side of the Brain: A Course in Enhancing Creativity and Artistic Confidence*, rev. ed. Los Angeles: Tarcher, 1989.

Englebaugh, Debi. *Art Through Children's Literature: Creative Art Lessons for Caldecott Books.* Teacher's Ideas Press, 1994.

Eyewitness series. Toronto: Stoddart Publishing Co., 1990.

Feldman, Edmund. *Becoming Human Through Art*. Englewood Cliffs, NJ: Prentice-Hall, 1970.

Gardner, Howard. *Artful Scribbles: The Significance of Children's Drawing*s. New York: Bann Books, 1980.

———. *The Theory of Multiple Intelligence*. New York: HarperCollins, 1983.

Goldstone, Bette P. "Visual Interpretation of Children's Books." *The Reading Teacher* (April 1989): 592–95.

Johnson, Paul. *Pictures and Words Together: Children Illustrating and Writing Their Own Books*. Portsmouth, NH: Heinemann, 1997.

———. *Literacy Through the Book Arts.* Portsmouth, NH: Heinemann, 1993.

Mavrogenes, Nancy A. "A New Look at the Illustrations of Randolph Caldecott." *Reading-Canada 5*, no. 4: 239–44 (lecture), n.d.

Roucher, Nancy, and Jessie Lovano-Kerr. "Can the Arts Maintain Integrity in Interdisciplinary Learning?" *Arts Education Policy Review* 96, no. 4 (March/April 1995): 20–25.

Sinatra, R., and J. Stahl-Gemake. *Using the Right Brain in the Language Arts*. Springfield, IL.: Charles C. Thomas, 1983.

Tucker, Bill. "Minds of Their Own: Visualizers Compose." *English Journal* (December 1995): 27–31.

Wilson, Marjorie, and Brent Wilson. *Teaching Children to Draw, A Guide for Teachers and Parents.* Englewood Cliffs, NJ: Prentice-Hall, 1982.

Teacher Reference Books

The following teacher references are mentioned in *Art & Illustration for the Classroom*. Teachers will find the books useful for art projects.

Edwards, Betty. *Drawing on the Right Side of the Brain: A Course in Enhancing Creativity and Artistic Confidence*, rev. ed. Los Angeles: Tarcher, 1989.

Feldman, Edmund. *Becoming Human Through Art.* Englewood Cliffs, NJ: Prentice-Hall, 1970.

Johnson, Paul. *Literacy Through the Book Arts.* Portsmouth, NH: Heinemann, 1993.

Lee, Stan, and John Buscena. *How to Draw Comics the Marvel Way*. New York: Simon & Schuster, 1977.

McGraw, Sheila. *Papier-Mâché Today*. Willowsdale, ON: Firefly, 1990.

McNaughton, Colin. *Suddenly!* London: Anderson Press, 1994.

Reid, Barbara. *Working with Plasticine.* Toronto: Kids Can Press, 1988.

Solga, Kim. *Paint!* Danbury, CT: Grolier Educational, 1993.

———. *Draw!* Toronto: McGraw-Hill Ryerson, 1991.

Striker, Susan, and Edward Kimmel. The Anti-Coloring Book (series). New York: Owl Book, Henry Holt & Co., 1984.

Waters, Elizabeth, and Annie Harris. *Painting: A Young Artist's Guide.* Vancouver: Raincoast Books; London, Dorling Kindersley, 1993.

Children's Picture Books

The following books are referred to throughout *Art & Illustration for the Classroom*.

Allinson, Beverly (illustrations by Barbara Reid). *Effie.* Toronto: Summerhill Press, 1990.

Anderson, Wayne. *Dragon.* London: Hutchison Children's Books, 1992.

Baker, Jeannie. *Window.* New York: Greenwillow, 1991.

Baker, Keith. *Who Is the Beast?* San Diego: Harcourt Brace Jovanovich, 1990.

————. *The Magic Fan.* San Diego: Harcourt Brace Jovanovich, 1989.

Baker, Leslie. *The Third-Story Cat.* Boston: Little, Brown & Co., 1987.

Bang, Molly. *The Paper Crane.* New York: Greenwillow, 1985.

Base, Graham. *Animalia.* Toronto: Stoddart, 1988.

Bouchard, David (illustrations by Henry Ripplinger). *If You're Not From the Prairie.* Vancouver: Raincoast Books, Summerwild, 1993.

Brett, Jan (adaptor and illustrator). *The Mitten: A Ukranian Folktale.* New York: Putnam, 1989.

Browne, Anthony. *Changes.* London: J. MacRae Books, 1990.

Bunting, Eve (illustrations by David Diaz). *Smoky Night.* New York: Harcourt Brace & Co., 1994.

Carle, Eric. *The Mixed-Up Chameleon.* New York: Crowell, 1975.

Carle, Eric. *Dragons, Dragons and Other Creatures That Never Were* (compiled by Laura Whipple). New York: Philomel, 1991.

Chase, Edith (illustrations by Barbara Reid). *The New Baby Calf.* Toronto: Scholastic Book Services, Four Winds Press, 1984.

Cleaver, Elizabeth. *The Enchanted Caribou.* Toronto: Oxford University Press, 1985.

Cooper, Helen. *The Baby Who Wouldn't Go to Bed.* London: Doubleday, 1996.

Creighton, Jill (illustrations by Pierre-Paul Pariseau). *8 O'Cluck.* Richmond Hill, ON: Scholastics, 1995.

Denton, Kady MacDonald. *Would They Love a Lion?* New York: Kingfisher, 1995.

DePaola, Tomie. *Strega Nona: An Old Tale.* Eaglewood Cliffs, NJ: Prentice Hall, 1975.

Diaz, Jorge. *The Rebellious Alphabet.* New York: H. Holt & Co., 1993.

Dugin, Andrej (illustrations by Olga Dugina). *Dragon Feathers.* Charlottesville, VA: Thomasson-Grant, 1993.

Ehlert, Lois. *Snowballs.* New York: Harcourt Brace & Co., 1995.

Eyvindson, Peter (illustrations by Rhian Brynjolson). *The Night Rebecca Stayed Too Late.* Winnipeg, MB: Pemmican, 1994.

———. (illustrations by Rhian Brynjolson). *The Yesterday Stone.* Winnipeg, MB: Pemmican, 1993.

Fanelli, Sara. *Button.* New York: Little, Brown & Co., 1994.

Felix, Monique. *The Little Mouse Trapped in a Book.* La Jolla, CA: Star and Elephant Books, Green Tiger Press, 1980.

Fleisher, Michael, et. al. "Batman," in *The Encyclopedia of Comic Book Heroes.* New York: Collier Books, 1976.

Gay, Marie-Louise. *Rumpelstiltskin.* Toronto: Douglas & MacIntyre, 1997.

Hathorn, Libby (illustrations by Gregory Rogers). *Way Home.* London: Andersen Press, 1994.

Heyer, Marilee. *Weaving of a Dream: A Chinese Folktale.* New York: Viking Kestrel, 1986.

Hoffman, Mary (illustrations by Caroline Binch). *Amazing Grace.* London: Frances Lincoln, 1991.

Keats, Ezra Jack. *The Snowy Day.* New York: Viking Press, 1962.

Kellogg, Steven. *Best Friends.* New York: Dial Books for Young Readers, 1986.

———. *Chicken Little.* New York: W. Morrow, 1985.

Lawson, Julie (illustrations by Paul Morin). *The Dragon's Pearl.* Toronto: Oxford University Press, 1992.

Lemieux, Michele. *The Pied Piper of Hamelin.* Toronto: Kids Can Press, 1993.

Lionni, Leo. *Alexander and the Wind-up Mouse.* New York: Pantheon, 1969.

Lynch-Watson, Janet. *The Shadow Puppet Book.* New York: Sterling, 1980.

Macauley, David. *Black and White.* Boston: Houghton Mifflin, 1990.

Mayer, Mercer. *Frog, Where Are You?* New York: Dial Press, 1969.

McGugan, Jim (illustrations by Murray Kimber). *Josepha: A Prairie Boy's Story.* Red Deer, AB: Red Deer College Press, 1994.

McLellan, Joe (illustrations by Rhian Brynjolson). *Nanabosho Dances.* Winnipeg, MB: Pemmican, 1991.

Milne, A.A. (illustrations by Ernest Shepard). *The House at Pooh Corner.* Toronto: McClelland & Stewart, 1928.

Muller, Robin. *The Magic Paintbrush.* Toronto: Doubleday, 1989.

Munsch, Robert, and Michael Kusugak (illustrations by Vladyana Krykorka). *A Promise Is a Promise.* Toronto: Annick Press, 1988.

Oliviero, Jamie (illustrations by Brent Morrisseau). *The Fish Skin.* Winnipeg, MB: Hyperion Press, 1993.

Oppenheim, Joanne (illustrations by Barbara Reid). *Have You Seen Birds?* Richmond Hill, ON: North Winds Press, 1986.

Reid, Barbara. *The Party.* Richmond Hill, ON: North Winds Press, 1997.

Rosen, Michael (illustrations by John Clementson). *How the Animals Got Their Colors.* Toronto: Lester, 1992.

Scieszca, John. *The True Story of the Three Little Pigs.* Lane Smith. New York: Viking, 1989.

Sendak, Maurice. *Where the Wild Things Are.* New York: Harper & Row, 1963.

Service, Robert (illustrations by Ted Harrison). *The Cremation of Sam McGee.* Toronto: Kids Can Press, 1986.

Seuss, Dr. *Green Eggs and Ham.* New York: Random House, 1960.

Shaw, Charles Green. *It Looked Like Spilt Milk.* New York: HarperCollins, 1947.

Tibo, Gilles. *Simon and the Snowflakes.* Montreal: Tundra Books, 1988.

Toye, William (illustrations by Elizabeth Cleaver). *The Loon's Necklace.* Toronto: Oxford University Press, 1977.

UNICEF. *I Dream of Peace: Images of War: by Children of Former Yugoslavia.* New York: HarperCollins, 1994.

Van Allsburg, Chris. *The Mysteries of Harris Burdick.* Boston: Houghton Mifflin, 1984.

———. *Jumanji.* Boston: Houghton Mifflin, 1981.

Viorst, Judith (illustrations by Ray Cruz). *Alexander, Who Used to be Rich Last Tuesday.* New York: Caedmon, 1984.

———. (illustrations by Ray Cruz). *Alexander and the Terrible, Horrible, No Good, Very Bad Day.* New York: Atheneum, 1972.

Waterson, Bill. *Calvin and Hobbes.* Kansas City, MO.: Andrews, McMeel & Parker, 1987

Wiesner, David. *Tuesday.* New York: Clarion Books, 1991.

Wildsmith, Brian. *Saint Francis.* Oxford, UK: Oxford University Press, 1995.

———. *Daisy.* Oxford, UK: Oxford University Press, 1984.

———. *The Lazy Bear.* Oxford, UK: Oxford University Press, 1973.

Williams, Vera B. *Stringbean's Trip to the Shining Sea.* New York: Greenwillow, 1988.

Wynne-Jones, Tim (illustrations by Eric Beddows). *Zoom Away.* New York: HarperCollins, 1993.

———. (illustrations by Eric Beddows). *Zoom Upstream.* Toronto: Douglas & McIntyre, 1992.

Yolen, Jane (illustrations by John Schoenherr). *Owl Moon.* New York: Philomel, 1987.

The following are some other children's picture books teachers may find useful.

Anno, Mitsumasa. *In Shadowland.* New York: Orchard Books, 1988.

Carle, Eric. *The Very Hungry Caterpillar.* New York: Philomel, 1987.

Eyvindson, Peter (illustrations by Rhian Brynjolson). *Sir Thomas A. Cat.* Winnipeg, MB: Pemmican, 1998.

———. (illustrations by Rhian Brynjolson). *Red Parka Mary.* Winnipeg, MB: Pemmican, 1996.

Gammell, Stephen. *Is That You, Winter?* New York: Harcourt Brace & Co., 1997.

Goble, Paul. *The Girl Who Loved Wild Horses.* New York: Bradbury Press, 1985.

Hughes, Shirley. *The Big Concrete Lorry.* New York: Lothrop, Lee & Shepard, 1990.

Mayer, Mercer. *A Boy, a Dog, and a Frog.* New York: Dial Press, 1967.

Smucker, Barbara. *Selina and the Bear Paw Quilt.* Toronto: Lester, 1995.

Varvasovszky, Lazlo. *Henry in Shadowland.* Boston: David R. Godine, 1990.

Wildsmith, Brian. *The Circus.* Brookfield, CT: Millbrook Press, 1996.

Williams, Sue (illustrations by Julie Vivas). *I Went Walking.* San Diego: Harcourt Brace Jovanovich, 1989.

Bibliography

Books for Teachers and Parents

The following books about children and art are for teachers and parents (for more titles, please see References).

Clarke, E. C. "An Investigation into the Relation Between the Developmental Stages of Scribbling and the Developmental Stages of the Directive Function of Speech." Master's Thesis, Cornell University, 1974.

Clemens, Sydney, G. "Art in the Classroom: Making Every Day Special." *Young Children* (January 1991): 4–11.

Cole, Elizabeth, and Claire Schaefer. "Can Young Children Be Art Critics?" *Young Children* (January 1990): 33–38.

Considine, David. "Visual Literacy and the Curriculum: More to It Than Meets the Eye." *Language Arts* 64 (October 1987): 634–40.

———. "Visual Literacy and Children's Books: An Integrated Approach." *School Library Journal* 33 (September 1986): 38–42.

Cummings, Pat (compiler and editor). *Talking with Artists, Volume Two.* New York: Simon & Schuster, 1995.

———. *Talking with Artists.* New York: Bradbury Press, 1992.

Dever, Martha Taylor, and Elizabeth J. Jared. "Remember to Include Arts and Crafts in Your Integrated Curriculum." *Young Children* (March 1996): 69–73.

Dighe, Judith, Zoy Calomiris, and Carmen Van Zutphen. "Nurturing the Language of Art in Children." *Young Children* (January 1998): 4–9.

Dyson, Anne Haas. "Symbol Makers, Symbol Wearers: How Children Link Play, Pictures, and Print." *Young Children* (January 1990): 50–57.

Edwards, Betty. *Drawing on the Artist Within.* New York: Simon & Schuster, 1986.

Feldman, Edmund, B. *Varieties of Visual Experience.* New York: Abrams, 1972.

Fucigna, Carolee, Katherine C. Ives, and William Ives. "Art for Toddlers: A Developmental Approach." *Young Children* (March 1982): 45–51.

Galda, Lee, and Barbara Kiefer. "Children's Books: Accent on Art." *The Reading Teacher* 44, no. 6 (February 1991): 406–14.

Gharbo-Linderman, Marlene. *Art in the Elementary School: Drawing, Painting and Creativity for the Classroom.* Dubuque, IA: W. C. Brown, 1974.

Gillespie, Cindy S. "Reading Graphic Displays: What Teachers Should Know." *Journal of Reading* 36:5 (February 1993): 350–54.

Henriques, Marlene E. "Increasing Literacy among Kindergartners through Cross-Age Training." *Young Children* (May 1997): 42–47.

Herberholtz, Donald. *Artworks for Elementary Teachers.* Dubuque, IA: Brown & Benchmark, 1994.

Hodge, Anthony. *Drawing.* New York: Aladdin Books, Gloucester Press, 1991.

———. *Painting.* New York: Aladdin Books, Gloucester Press, 1991.

Horn, George F. *Experiencing Art in the Elementary School.* Worcester, MA: Davis Publications, 1971.

Hoyland, Michael. *Art for Children.* Glasgow: Robert Maclehouse, 1970.

Hubbard, Ruth. "There's More than Black and White in Literacy's Palette: Children's Use of Color." *Language Arts 67* (September 1990).

Hurwitz, Al. *The Joyous Vision: A Sourcebook for Elementary Art Appreciation.* Englewood Cliffs, NJ: Prentice-Hall, 1977.

Johnson, Mia. "Teaching Children to Value Art and Artists." *Phi Delta Kappan* (February 1997): 454–56.

Johnson, Paul. "Page Consciousness: The Development of Writing with Illustration." *Language Arts* (November 1996): 493–505.

Kiefer, Barbara. "Picture Books as Contexts for Literacy." *Language Arts* 65 (March 1988): 260–71.

Klemin, Diana. *The Art of Art for Children's Books.* Greenwich, CT: Murton Press, 1966.

Knobler, Nathan. *The Visual Dialogue.* New York: Holt, Rinehart & Winston, 1971.

Kovacs, Deborah, and James Preller. *Meet the Authors and illustrators: 60 Creators of Favorite Children's Books Talk About Their Work.* Richmond Hill, ON: Scholastic Canada, 1991.

Kubey, Robert. "The Case for Media Education." *Education Week* X, no. 24 (March 1991).

Mattil, Edward L. *Meaning in Children's Art.* Englewood Cliffs, NJ: Prentice-Hall, 1977.

Marantz, Sylvia S. *Picture Books for Looking and Learning: Awakening Visual Perceptions Through the Art of Children's Books.* Phoenix, AZ: Oryx Press, 1992.

Miller, Peggy J. "Peter Rabbit and Mr. McGregor Reconciled, Charlotte Lives: Preschoolers Re-create the Classics." *The Horn Book Magazine* (May/June 1997).

Mitchell, Florence S. "Introducing Art History Through Children's Literature." *Language Arts* 67 (December 1990).

Nicolaïdes, Kimon. *The Natural Way to Draw.* Boston: Houghton Mifflin, 1975.

Nikola-Lisa, W. "Sound and Sense in Children's Picturebooks." *Language Arts* 74 (March 1997): 168–71.

Notar, Ellen. "Children and TV Commercials: Wave After Wave of Exploitation." *Childhood Education* (winter 1989): 66–67.

Ontario Ministry of Education and Training. "The Common Curriculum: Policies and Outcomes, Grades 1–9." (1995).

Palmer, Barbara, C., Nancy A. Frederick, and Lawrence E. Hafner. "Implications of Piagetian Theory for Correlating Art and Reading." *Reading Horizons* 21, no. 4 (summer 1981): 267–71.

Schiller, Marjorie. "An Emergent Art Curriculum That Fosters Understanding." *Young Children* (March 1995): 33–38.

Seefeldt, Carol. "Art—A Serious Work." *Young Children* (March 1995): 39–43.

Shidler-Lattz, Linda, and Nancy Ratcliff. "Colouring in the Lines: A Tale of Two Children." *Young Children* (January 1998): 68–69.

Smagorinsky, Peter. "Multiple Intelligence in the English Class: An Overview." *English Journal* (December 1995): 19–26.

Solga, Kim. *Make Prints!* Cincinnati, OH: North Light Books, 1992.

———. *Make Sculptures!* Cincinnati, OH: North Light Books, 1992.

Striker, Susan. *Please Touch: How to Stimulate Your Child's Creative Development.* New York: Simon & Schuster, 1986.

Sutherland, Zena. *Children and Books.* 9th ed. New York: Addison-Wesley, 1996.

Szekely, George. *From Play to Art.* Portsmouth, NH: Heinemann, 1991.

Wachowiak, Frank. *Emphasis Art.* New York: Thomas Y. Crowell, 1977.

Warner, Sally. *Encouraging the Artist in Your Child (Even if You Can't Draw).* New York: St. Martins Press, 1989.

Wolf, Aline D. "Art Postcards—Another Aspect of Your Aesthetics Program?" *Young Children* (January 1990): 39–43.

Books for Children

The following picture books, about art and artists, are for children.

Anholt, Laurence. *Camille and the Sunflowers: A Story About Vincent Van Gogh.* Hauppauge, NY: Barron's, 1994.

Bianchi, John. *The Artist.* New York: Firefly, 1993.

Browne, Anthony. *Bear Goes to Town.* New York: Doubleday, 1982.

Carle, Eric. *Draw Me a Star.* New York: Philomel, 1992.

Catalanotto, Peter. *The Painter.* New York: Orchard, 1995.

Crockett, Johnson. *Harold and the Purple Crayon.* New York: Harper & Row, 1959.

DePaola, Tomie. *The Art Lesson.* New York: Putnam, 1989.

Kesselman, Wendy, and Barbara Cooney. *Emma.* New York: Doubleday, 1980.

Lionni, Leo. *Matthew's Dream.* New York: Alfred A. Knopf, 1991.

Muller, Robin. *The Magic Paintbrush.* Toronto: Doubleday, 1989.

Ross, Tom, and Rex Barron. *Eggbert the Slightly Cracked Egg.* New York: Putnam & Grosset, 1994.

Rylant, Cynthia (illustrations by Peter Catalanotto). *All I See.* New York: Orchard, 1988.

Say, Allen. *Emma's Rug778.* Boston: Houghton Mifflin, 1996.

Index